BPEL and Java Cookbook

Over 100 recipes to help you enhance your SOA composite applications with Java and BPEL

Jurij Laznik

BIRMINGHAM - MUMBAI

BPEL and Java Cookbook

First published: September 2013

Production Reference: 1100913

Published by Packt Publishing Ltd.
Livery Place
35 Livery Street
Birmingham B3 2PB, UK.

ISBN 978-1-84968-920-5

www.packtpub.com

Cover Image by Abhishek Dhir (abhishekdhirimages@gmail.com)

Credits

Author
Jurij Laznik

Reviewers
Andrea Barisone
Martin Potocnik
Gregor Srdic

Acquisition Editor
Erol Staveley

Lead Technical Editor
Arun Nadar

Commissioning Editor
Shreerang Deshpande

Technical Editors
Ruchita Bhansali
Kapil Hemnani

Project Coordinator
Apeksha Chitnis

Proofreader
Paul Hindle

Indexer
Hemangini Bari

Graphics
Ronak Dhruv
Yuvraj Mannari

Production Coordinator
Aparna Bhagat

Cover Work
Aparna Bhagat

About the Author

Jurij Laznik is an architect and software engineer with over 14 years of experience in BPEL and Java technologies. In the past decade, he has participated in several large SOA projects in the Energetics and Telecommunication sector. He is an accredited Oracle SOA Implementation Champion by the Oracle Partner Network. In the last five years, he has worked in the banking industry on IT projects as both project manager and system design engineer. He is currently employed as an Oracle programmer at Banka Celje d.d. He is also an assigned lecturer for the Educational Center of Energetics Systems (ICES). He received his Master's degree at the University of Maribor. Currently, he is a PhD student at the Faculty of Computer Science and Information Technology at the University of Maribor, Slovenia.

I'd like to thank my patient wife, Romana, and my two very patient children, Ajda and Urban, who put up with me working long night hours in the home office. I would also like to mention Amber, Apeksha, Arun, and Shreerang at Packt for keeping the project on track and giving me the opportunity to write this book.

About the Reviewers

Andrea Barisone works for a leading Italian IT company and has over 13 years of experience in Information Technology working on corporate projects as a developer and using different technologies. He also has experience with ECM Systems and has several J2EE certifications. He has a great ability to learn new technologies and to exploit knowledge acquired working with different environments and technologies. He has also reviewed the book *Agile Web Development with Rails 4* by Pragmatic Bookshelf. He is currently reviewing the book *Learning Three.js: The Javascript 3D Library for WebGL* by Packt Publishing.

I would like to thank my parents, Renzo and Maria Carla, for the gift of life they gave me, my beloved wife Barbara, and my two wonderful little children Gabriele and Aurora for making my everyday life wonderful.

Martin Potocnik is a creative IT enthusiast who is passionate about making a difference and loves technology. He is an expert in Business Process Management, Cloud Computing, the Internet, and Service-Oriented and Event-Driven Architecture. He is currently a PhD student preparing his doctoral dissertation at the University of Ljubljana. He has participated in several research and applicative BPM, SOA, and EDA projects such as integration of large-scale enterprise information systems, consolidation and optimization of services and business processes, and the development of innovative pilots and blueprints for the largest national telecommunication provider and national banks. He has worked as a researcher, teaching assistant, and as a SOA, BPM, and cloud computing consultant. He is an IBM Certified SOA Associate and his professional interests include Java, Oracle, IBM SOA/BPM platforms, Microsoft .NET, Amazon AWS, and Windows Azure. He is also cofounder and CTO of a high-tech company called Nomnio d.o.o. He is working with his fellow researchers to exploit available technology, knowledge, and experience in order to reinvent the way we live.

Gregor Srdic is an IBM Certified SOA associate and a former researcher and PhD student at the University of Ljubljana. He has worked in the fields of business process management, service-oriented architecture, and business activity monitoring. He has gained valuable experience by participating and leading several national research and industry projects. Today, he is cofounder and CIO of a high-tech company called Nomnio d.o.o. He is working with fellow researchers to exploit available technology, knowledge, and experience in order to reinvent the way we live. He is also co-author of the book *WS-BPEL 2.0 for SOA Composite Applications with IBM WebSphere 7*, published by Packt Publishing in 2010.

www.PacktPub.com

Support files, eBooks, discount offers and more

You might want to visit www.PacktPub.com for support files and downloads related to your book.

Did you know that Packt offers eBook versions of every book published, with PDF and ePub files available? You can upgrade to the eBook version at www.PacktPub.com and as a print book customer, you are entitled to a discount on the eBook copy. Get in touch with us at service@packtpub.com for more details.

At www.PacktPub.com, you can also read a collection of free technical articles, sign up for a range of free newsletters and receive exclusive discounts and offers on Packt books and eBooks.

http://PacktLib.PacktPub.com

Do you need instant solutions to your IT questions? PacktLib is Packt's online digital book library. Here, you can access, read and search across Packt's entire library of books.

Why Subscribe?

- Fully searchable across every book published by Packt
- Copy and paste, print and bookmark content
- On demand and accessible via web browser

Free Access for Packt account holders

If you have an account with Packt at www.PacktPub.com, you can use this to access PacktLib today and view nine entirely free books. Simply use your login credentials for immediate access.

Instant Updates on New Packt Books

Get notified! Find out when new books are published by following @PacktEnterprise on Twitter, or the *Packt Enterprise* Facebook page.

Table of Contents

Preface

This book consists of many recipes providing solutions for the problems that the BPEL and Java developers face performing everyday jobs. The book provides step-by-step examples which get more completed throughout each chapter. It provides a lot of information to the developers with different levels of experience. The book consists of examples focusing on the interaction between Java and BPEL, how to enhance SOA composite applications, and how to make your applications more interactive with custom Java functionality. BPEL has become the de-facto standard for orchestrating web services. BPEL and Java are clamped into Service-oriented Architecture (SOA). Development of efficient SOA composites too often requires usage of other technologies or languages such as Java.Readers who choose to read an entire chapter will first be given a detailed overview of the topic covered in the chapter and why it plays an important role in SOA. The recipes following the introduction concentrate on the specific problems related to the topic area and provide at least one solution to it. Many of the recipes also explore further possible solutions to the presented problems.

What this book covers

Chapter 1, Calling BPEL from Java, explains how to call a BPEL process from Java programs. Invoking synchronous and asynchronous BPEL processes from the Java code is also covered.

Chapter 2, Calling Services from BPEL, introduces the development lifecycle of web services and explains how to call web services from a BPEL process.

Chapter 3, Advanced Tracing and Logging, covers the configuration of logging in Oracle SOA Suite and explains the usage of the BPEL processes and composite sensors.

Chapter 4, Custom Logging in the Oracle SOA Suite, explains the advanced techniques of logging and provides an in-depth view of logging in Oracle SOA Suite.

Chapter 5, Transforming and Validating the BPEL Services, covers the transformation of the variables with XSLT in the BPEL processes and introduces the development of the user-defined functions.

Chapter 6, Embedding Third-party Java Libraries, explains the usage of the extensions in JDeveloper, the BPEL processes, and Oracle SOA Suite in general.

Chapter 7, Accessing and Updating the Variables, will help us discover all the aspects of the variable manipulation in the BPEL processes.

Chapter 8, Exposing Java Code as a SOAP Service, introduces the complete lifecycle of web service development with the bottom-up design approach in Oracle SOA Suite.

Chapter 9, Embedding Java Code Snippets, deals with using and executing the Java code from the BPEL processes and introduces the development sandbox for the Java code to be executed in the BPEL processes.

Chapter 10, Using XML Facade for DOM, focuses on all the aspects of XML façade development, which helps us overcome the problems with DOM manipulation in the BPEL processes from the Java code.

Chapter 11, Exposing Java Code as a Web Service, shows how to expose the Java code to become a web service. The whole web service lifecycle is covered in a neutral vendor solution manner using the JAX-WS annotations.

What you need for this book

To use this book efficiently, the required software to be installed is Oracle SOA Suite 11g v11.1.1.6.0. The majority of the recipes also use Oracle JDeveloper 11g v11.1.1.6.0. Some recipes use the Eclipse development environment. Those recipes were developed using Eclipse IDE Juno v4.2 - SR2. For the web services development, we also use Apache Axis2 v1.6.1. For the advanced logging recipes, we use Apache Log4j v1.2.17.

Who this book is for

This book is aimed at the Java developers who need to use BPEL programming to develop web services for SOA development. It is assumed that readers have some prior knowledge of SOA development. Developers should be experienced with Java programming, but knowledge of BPEL is not necessarily required. It does not matter if you are an experienced developer or just starting to learn. There are recipes suitable for every knowledge level. For beginners, we provide introductory explanations with references. More experienced developers will find the recipe description of how they work and discussion on how the topic can be further enhanced very useful.

Conventions

In this book, you will find a number of styles of text that distinguish between different kinds of information. Here are some examples of these styles, and an explanation of their meaning.

Code words in text, database table names, folder names, filenames, file extensions, pathnames, dummy URLs, user input, and Twitter handles are shown as follows: "Let us examine the `ClientProxy.java` class first. We start, by creating the `ServiceClient` client and prepare the `Options` class to configure the `ServiceClient` client."

A block of code is set as follows:

```
<element name = "fault">
<complexType>
<sequence>
<element name = "msg" type = "string"/>
</sequence>
</complexType>
</element>
```

When we wish to draw your attention to a particular part of a code block, the relevant lines or items are set in bold:

```
@Path("RESTWeatherService")
public class WeatherProvider {

  @GET
  @Path("/query")
  @Produces("text/xml")
  public String getWeatherInfo(@QueryParam("name")
    String name, @QueryParam("zip") String zip) {
    return "<weatherRes>Hello " + name + ".
      The weather in " + zip + " city cloudy. \n" +
        "Temperature is 24 degrees Celsius. \n" +
          "Humidity is 74%</weatherRes>";
    }
  }
```

Any command-line input or output is written as follows:

```
Error deploying BPEL suitcase.
error while attempting to deploy the BPEL component file "C:\Programs\
Oracle\Middleware\user_projects\domains\SOA_Dev\servers\AdminServer\dc\
soa_8606ace0-2193-4
719-8cd7-08b2f0d57a04"; the exception reported is: java.lang.
RuntimeException: failed to compile execlets of BPELProcess2_0
```

```
This error contained an exception thrown by the underlying deployment
module.

Verify the exception trace in the log (with logging level set to debug
mode).
```

New terms and **important words** are shown in bold. Words that you see on the screen, in menus or dialog boxes for example, appear in the text like this: "When you double-click on the Java Embedding activity, a new dialog opens where we have to enter the code. We finish configuring the Java Embedding activity by clicking on the OK button."

Warnings or important notes appear in a box like this.
Tips and tricks appear like this.

Reader feedback

Feedback from our readers is always welcome. Let us know what you think about this book—what you liked or may have disliked. Reader feedback is important for us to develop titles that you really get the most out of.

To send us general feedback, simply send an e-mail to `feedback@packtpub.com`, and mention the book title via the subject of your message.

If there is a topic that you have expertise in and you are interested in either writing or contributing to a book, see our author guide on `www.packtpub.com/authors`.

Customer support

Now that you are the proud owner of a Packt book, we have a number of things to help you to get the most from your purchase.

Downloading the example code

You can download the example code files for all Packt books you have purchased from your account at `http://www.packtpub.com`. If you purchased this book elsewhere, you can visit `http://www.packtpub.com/support` and register to have the files e-mailed directly to you.

Errata

Although we have taken every care to ensure the accuracy of our content, mistakes do happen. If you find a mistake in one of our books—maybe a mistake in the text or the code—we would be grateful if you would report this to us. By doing so, you can save other readers from frustration and help us improve subsequent versions of this book. If you find any errata, please report them by visiting `http://www.packtpub.com/submit-errata`, selecting your book, clicking on the errata submission form link, and entering the details of your errata. Once your errata are verified, your submission will be accepted and the errata will be uploaded on our website, or added to any list of existing errata, under the Errata section of that title. Any existing errata can be viewed by selecting your title from `http://www.packtpub.com/support`.

Piracy

Piracy of copyright material on the Internet is an ongoing problem across all media. At Packt, we take the protection of our copyright and licenses very seriously. If you come across any illegal copies of our works, in any form, on the Internet, please provide us with the location address or website name immediately so that we can pursue a remedy.

Please contact us at `copyright@packtpub.com` with a link to the suspected pirated material.

We appreciate your help in protecting our authors, and our ability to bring you valuable content.

Questions

You can contact us at `questions@packtpub.com` if you are having a problem with any aspect of the book, and we will do our best to address it.

1

Calling BPEL from Java

In this chapter we will cover:

- Deploying a BPEL process
- Gathering a BPEL process's in and out parameters
- Calling a synchronous BPEL process from Java
- Calling an asynchronous BPEL process from Java
- Handling business faults from a synchronous BPEL process
- Handling business faults from an asynchronous BPEL process
- Mapping the results of a BPEL process

Introduction

Business processes are an integral part of every company. As new requirements arise in the business processes, companies pursue its alignment with IT as well. Pursuing the need for IT to efficiently support business processes in companies, the **SOA** (**Service Oriented Architecture**) was identified as the most important IT technology for business process implementation. Depending on the business environment, BPEL can also be considered as a suitable technology in **EDA** (**Event Driven Architecture**), since it provides constructs to handle events through event handlers (`onMessage` and `onAlarm`). Within SOA, the most common practice to implement business processes is by using a **WSBPEL** (**Web Services Business Process Execution Language**), or BPEL for short. Of course, SOA itself does not make it compulsory to use BPEL for business process implementation, and you can also use other workflow languages, such as BPMN, YAWL, and jBPM(JPDL) just to name some. BPEL is an XML-based language for the definition and execution of business processes, and has become the de-facto standard for orchestrating web service compositions. The first official version of BPEL specification was named BPEL4WS 1.1, or BPEL 1.1 for short, in 2003. Later on, a new version, WS-BPEL 2.0, with significant enhancements, was released in 2007.

A BPEL process definition has three main parts:

- **A BPEL file in XML form**: This contains the definition of a process (main activities, variables, events, partner links, fault handlers, compensation handlers, and so on).
- **The WSDL files**: These files present web service interfaces, utilized by the BPEL process for orchestration purposes. Similar to BPEL, WSDL also released several versions of specification, which are widely used today. In 2001, WSDL 1.1 (Web Service Definition Language) was released, followed by WSDL 2.0 (Web Service Description Language) in 2007.
- **The XSD schema files**: These files present XML definitions of the BPEL request, response, and fault messages, as well as the BPEL variable definitions.

The three mentioned parts present the source code of the business process definition. The source code is deployed on a BPEL engine, which is responsible for managing, running, and monitoring the execution of business processes.

We can find many BPEL execution engines on the market. They are either open source or proprietary. We will name just a few of them here which are most commonly used by companies and communities:

Vendor	**Product**	**License Type**	**BPEL specification supported**
Oracle	Oracle SOA Suite	Proprietary	1.1 and 2.0
jBoss	jBPM	Open source	1.1 and partly 2.0
Apache	Apache ODE	Open source	1.1 and 2.0
Active Endpoint	ActiveVOS	Proprietary	1.1 and 2.0
IBM	WebSphere Process Server	Proprietary	1.1

All these BPEL engines have the support of a BPEL specification, either Version 1.1 or 2.0. However, vendors do extend the functionality of the BPEL specification with their own extensions, making migration of business processes between various BPEL platforms more difficult. For example, IBM WebSphere Process Servers provides the possibility to declare inline human tasks, while Oracle SOA Suite provides Java Embedding activity and extension functions to monitor process and perform various XPATH operations.

It is evident that BPM applications are emerging, as business environments are becoming ever more dynamic and the need for agile IT is increasing. BPEL, as an orchestration technology, is able to compose business processes from various services. We can monitor business processes in real time with **BAM** (**business activity monitoring**) solutions, and extend their flexibility with the use of **BRMS** (**business rules management system**).

To successfully integrate a BPEL process with other types of applications, we need to know the description of the provided BPEL process operations, the type of the BPEL process (synchronous or asynchronous), and how to handle various faults thrown from the BPEL process.

In this chapter, we will deal with the deployment of a BPEL process. We will then investigate how applications written in Java efficiently utilize the BPEL processes.

Deploying a BPEL process

This recipe describes how a BPEL process can be deployed in Oracle SOA Suite. We will show the deployment of the BPEL process from a GUI tool as well as from the command line.

Getting ready

We have to set up a BPEL engine and a proper development environment. For the BPEL engine, we use the BPEL Process Manager from Oracle SOA Suite 11*g*. We also use JDeveloper as the development environment.

The installation notes and packages can easily be accessed from the Oracle web page at `http://www.oracle.com/technetwork/middleware/soasuite/downloads/index.html`. An Oracle web account is required in order to access downloads.

We will start with the HelloWorld example from the Oracle SOA Suite examples and will add additional functionality in the later recipes. For this recipe, we will unzip the HelloWorld example to our hard drive.

For this recipe, we use the example from the `https://java.net/projects/oraclesoasuite11g/pages/BPEL` address.

How to do it...

In the following steps, we will cover the actions we need to perform in order to deploy a BPEL process to the Oracle SOA Suite server:

1. To deploy the BPEL process, we first open JDeveloper and select **Default Role**. Depending on the role we choose, JDeveloper enables technologies available inside IDE. We choose the default role, which has the BPEL support enabled. We click on **Open Application...**, select the folder with the HelloWorld sample, and point to the `bpel-101-HelloWorld.jws` file. The project structure in JDeveloper is as shown in the following screenshot:

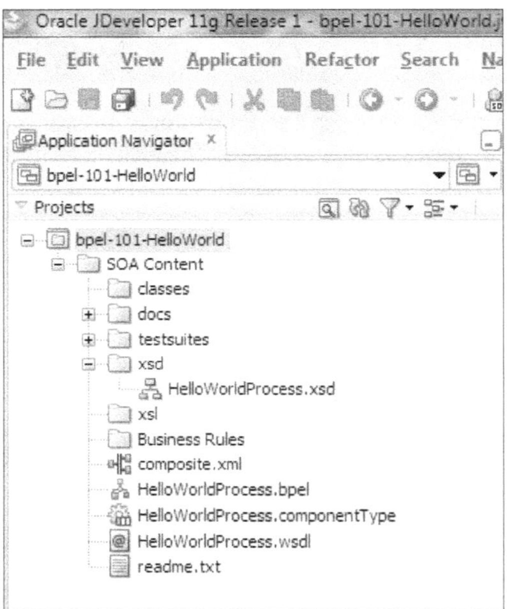

2. We see the `HelloWorldProcess.xsd` file, which contains the XML data type and the XML element structures for the input and output messages that are utilized by the BPEL process. At the top level of the project, we see the `HelloWorldProcess.bpel` file, which contains the BPEL process definition, and `HelloWorldProcess.wsdl` that contains the definition of the BPEL process partner links.

3. To deploy the BPEL process, we right-click on the top-level project in the **Application Navigator**, click on **Deploy**, and select the BPEL process. We select **Deploy to Application Server** and click on **Next**.

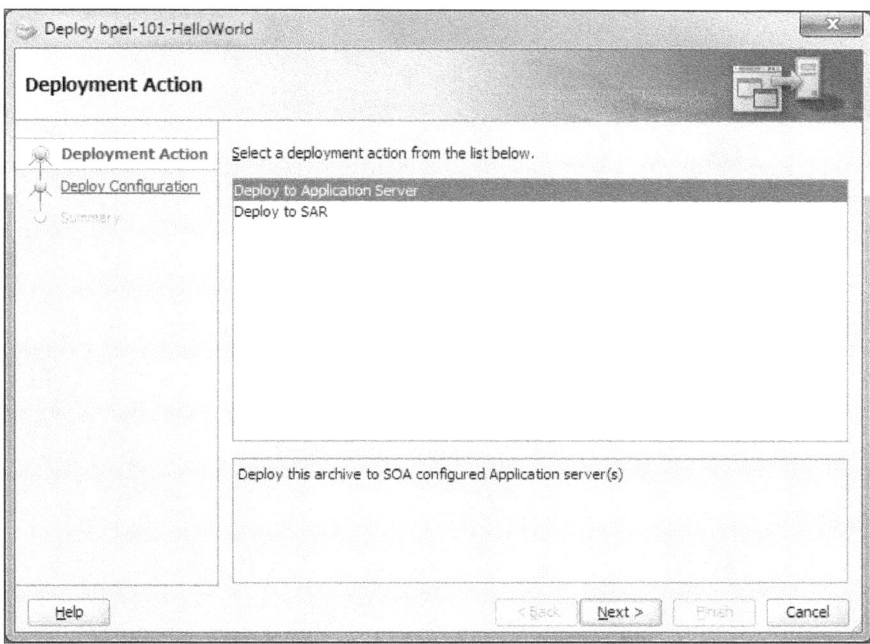

4. For the deployment configuration, we don't change anything; just click on **Next**. At this point, we have to select the application server on which we want to deploy the BPEL process. We click on the plus (**+**) sign and enter the name of the connection in the **Connection Name** field. Then, we click on **Next** and enter the username and password for the application server.

When we follow the default installation notes from Oracle, the default username is `weblogic` and password is `welcome1`.

5. Next, we need to configure the `connection` parameters to the Oracle Weblogic Domain. The name of the Oracle Weblogic Domain can be obtained from the Oracle Weblogic management console.

By default, we can access the Oracle Weblogic management console at the following address: `http://<weblogic_server>:7001/console/`.

6. We leave the other parameters unchanged. We then test the connection to the Oracle Weblogic Domain by clicking on the **Test Connection** button.

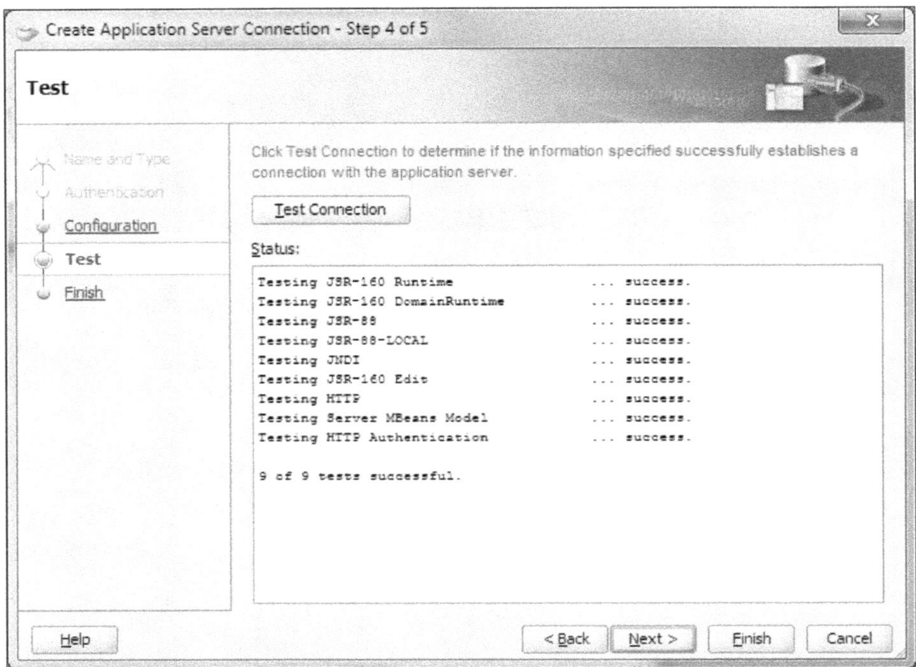

7. Next, we click on **Finish**. Now, we select the newly defined BPEL server and click on **Next**. We can see various information such as the name of the SOA server, the partition to which we want to deploy the BPEL process, the status of the SOA server, and the URL of the server.

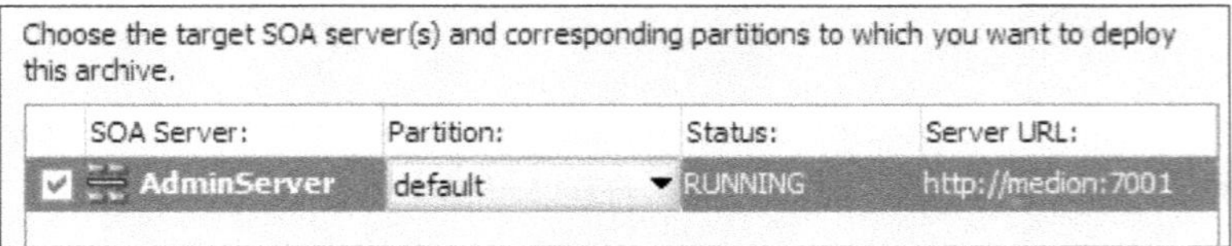

8. We then click on **Next** and **Finish**. The deployment process starts. When the deployment process finishes, we check if the process was successfully registered with the SOA server. We check this via the **Oracle Enterprise Manager** Console.

Also, we check to see if there was no error reported in JDeveloper. If deployment was successful, we will see a message in the JDeveloper deployment log as follows:

```
[10:05:55 PM] Successfully deployed archive sca_bpel-101-
  HelloWorld_rev1.0.jar to partition "default" on server
    AdminServer [http://medion:7001]
```

By default, we access the Oracle Enterprise Manager Console at the following address:

`http://<weblogic_server>:7001/em/`

9. If our `HelloWorld` process appears in the **Oracle Enterprise Manager** Console, we succeeded in deploying the BPEL process; otherwise, we need to examine the error and respond accordingly. In case of an error, we need to first check the JDeveloper messages log, and then the Oracle SOA Suite console log. The Oracle SOA Suite management server logfile can be a useful source of information about the file.

There's more...

After preparing the package for deployment with JDeveloper, we can deploy the BPEL process with the `ant` scripts. The scripts comes handy for continuous integration tasks in staging and production environments, where various testing and deployment tasks are performed automatically. A set of `ant` scripts comes with Oracle SOA Suite in order to compile, build, deploy/undeploy, and test the BPEL processes.

We first open the command prompt and change the directory to the example project home. For the deployment, we execute the `ant` script as shown in the following screenshot:

```
Command Prompt
C:\>cd C:\WorkspaceSOASuite\BPEL_examples\bpel-101-HelloWorld\bpel-101-HelloWorl
d\bpel-101-HelloWorld

C:\WorkspaceSOASuite\BPEL_examples\bpel-101-HelloWorld\bpel-101-HelloWorld\bpel-
101-HelloWorld>ant -f %Middleware_Home%\%SOA_Suite_Home%\bin\ant-sca-deploy.xml
-DserverURL=http://localhost:7001 -DsarLocation=.\deploy\sca_bpel-101-HelloWorld
_rev1.0.jar -Doverwrite=true -DforceDefault=true
Buildfile: C:\Programs\Oracle\Middleware\Oracle_SOA1\bin\ant-sca-deploy.xml
     [echo] oracle.home = C:\Programs\Oracle\Middleware\Oracle_SOA1\bin/..

deploy:
    [input] skipping input as property serverURL has already been set.
    [input] skipping input as property sarLocation has already been set.
    [input] skipping input as property password has already been set.
[deployComposite] Processing sar=.\deploy\sca_bpel-101-HelloWorld_rev1.0.jar
[deployComposite] Adding sar file - C:\WorkspaceSOASuite\BPEL_examples\bpel-101-
HelloWorld\bpel-101-HelloWorld\bpel-101-HelloWorld\.\deploy\sca_bpel-101-HelloWo
rld_rev1.0.jar
[deployComposite] INFO: Creating HTTP connection to host:localhost, port:7001
[deployComposite] Enter username and password for realm 'default' on host localh
ost:7001
[deployComposite] Authentication Scheme: Basic
[deployComposite] Username:
weblogic
[deployComposite] Password:

[deployComposite] INFO: Received HTTP response from the server, response code=20
0
[deployComposite] ---->Deploying composite success.

BUILD SUCCESSFUL
Total time: 21 seconds
C:\WorkspaceSOASuite\BPEL_examples\bpel-101-HelloWorld\bpel-101-HelloWorld\bpel-
101-HelloWorld>_
```

The command with which we started the deployment is as follows:

```
ant -f %Middleware_Home%\%SOA_Suite_Home%\bin\ant-sca-deploy.xml
  -DserverURL=http://localhost:7001
  -DsarLocation=.\deploy\sca_bpel-101-HelloWorld_rev1.0.jar
  -Doverwrite=true
  -DforceDefault=true
```

You can download the example code files for all Packt books you have purchased from your account at `http://www.packtpub.com`. If you purchased this book elsewhere, you can visit `http://www.packtpub.com/support` and register to have the files e-mailed directly to you.

The `ant` script parameters have the following meanings:

- `-f`: It is the location of the deployment script
- `-DserverURL`: It is the base URL of the Oracle SOA Suite server
- `-DsarLocation`: It is the location of the deployment package
- `-Doverwrite`: If the BPEL process with the same version is already deployed, we can overwrite it
- `-DforceDefault`: The force to deploy the package to the default domain

Before the deployment starts, we have to enter the username and password of the BPEL server. Again, we open the **Oracle Enterprise Manager** Console in order to check whether the BPEL process was successfully deployed.

Gathering a BPEL process's in and out parameters

This recipe will explain the ways of getting input and output parameters about a BPEL process. The information gathered is very important if we want to call the BPEL process from Java applications.

How to do it...

We are deploying the BPEL process on the BPEL server. The business process is now ready to be executed; however, we don't have any information about the business process besides the WSDL location of the business process.

1. In the **Oracle Enterprise Manager** Console, we select the BPEL process from the tree, and click on the following icon:

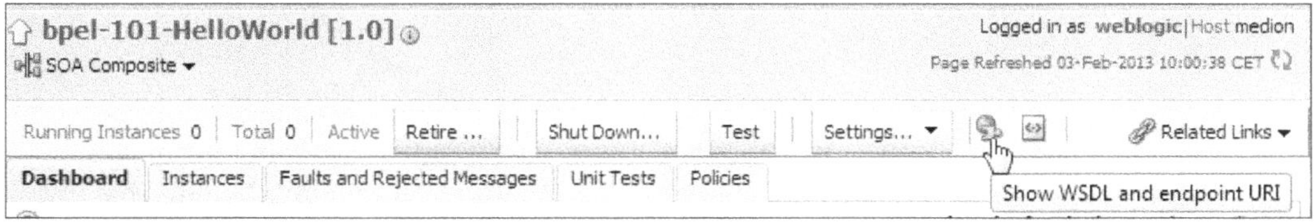

2. We receive information about the business process endpoint URI and a location of the business process WSDL as shown in the following screenshot:

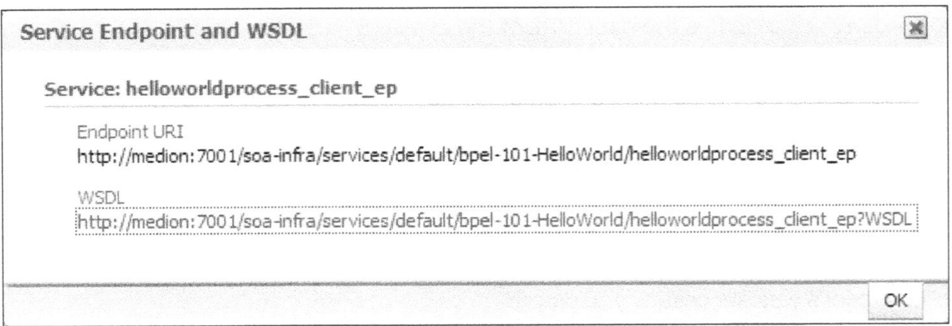

3. By entering the WSDL address into the web browser, we receive a description of the BPEL process interface. In this definition, we check for the input and output messages as follows:

```
<wsdl: message name = "HelloWorldProcessRequestMessage">
  <wsdl: part name = "payload" element = "client:process"/>
</wsdl: message>
<wsdl: message name = "HelloWorldProcessResponseMessage">
  <wsdl: part name = "payload" element =
    "client: processResponse"/>
</wsdl: message>
<wsdl: portType name = "HelloWorldProcess">
  <wsdl: operation name = "process">
<wsdl: input message =
  "client: HelloWorldProcessRequestMessage"/>
<wsdl: output message =
  "client:HelloWorldProcessResponseMessage"/>
  </wsdl:operation>
</wsdl:portType>
```

4. The most interesting part of WSDL is the `<wsdl:operation>` element, which indicates the entry point, the functionality, and the input and output messages of the BPEL process. We see that the input and output parameters both have a defined message in the `client` namespace, which is defined as the XSD schema. We can find its location in WSDL under the `<import>` tag. We search for the `client: process` input parameter in the XSD schema:

```
<element name="process">
  <complexType>
    <sequence>
      <element name="input" type="string"/>
    </sequence>
```

```
    </complexType>
</element>
```

5. As we can see, the input parameter takes the `string` variable with the `name` input. Similarly, we explore the output parameter `client: processResponse` in the XSD schema as follows:

```
<element name="processResponse">
  <complexType>
    <sequence>
      <element name="result" type="string"/>
    </sequence>
  </complexType>
</element>
```

6. The BPEL process will return the `string` variable named `result`.

How it works...

In general, there are two approaches to designing the BPEL processes. The first one is the top-down approach, where we first develop the XSD schema and WSDL files, which is also called the **contract-first approach**. The next one is called the bottom-up approach, where we start from the already-written Java code and generate the XSD schema and WSDL files with tools.

The recommended approach when designing the BPEL processes is to first define the XSD schema, which contains the definition of the input and output parameters. This is also the proper place to put the various complex variables used in the business process.

The schema is later used by WSDL to define the BPEL process interface via the `<wsdl:portType>` element. Both WSDL and the XSD schema are packed into the deployment package and deployed to the BPEL server.

> The definition of the input and output parameters in the XSD schema is not mandatory. We can easily define them in WSDL of the BPEL process. However, we lose some of the readability of the WSDL document. Note that such an approach is bad practice and is not recommended, since it hinders the reusability of the XML data types and elements.

See also

- To learn about the deployment of a BPEL process, refer to the previous recipe, *Deploying a BPEL process*

Calling a synchronous BPEL process from Java

This recipe explains how to call a synchronous BPEL process from Java. When a client calls a synchronous BPEL, it gets blocked until the BPEL process finishes the processing and returns the response. Usually, synchronous BPEL processes are designed for cases where the operation will be completed in a relatively short time. For long-running operations, we instead design asynchronous BPEL processes. This recipe will also cover how to prepare a Java package for integration with Java applications. From the client perspective, a synchronous BPEL process can be invoked in the same way a synchronous web service could. The client is most commonly called `proxy`, and it is used to ease the connection between the two technologies. In our case, we would like to call the BPEL process, which is mainly the XML content, from Java and proxy is helping us to get across the gap between those two technologies.

How to do it...

In order to call a synchronous BPEL process, we will develop a Java client using the JDeveloper wizard. After completing this recipe, we will be able to call a synchronous BPEL process from the Java client application.

1. First, we create another project in JDevelper. On the previously created BPEL sample project, we right-click, and select **New...**. From the **Business Tier** category, we select **Web Services** and then we select **Web Service Proxy** under **Items** as shown in the following screenshot:

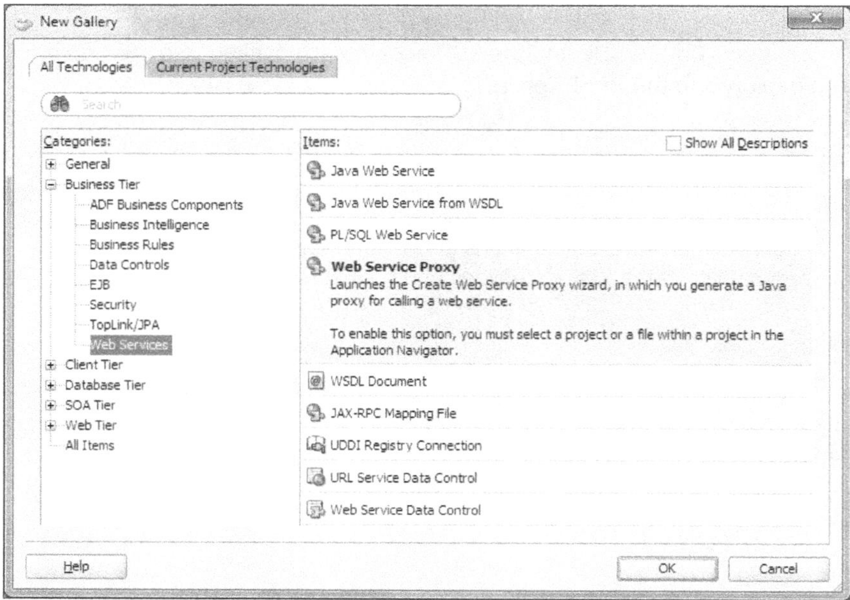

2. Then, we click on **OK**, which shows the welcome screen, and then we click on **Next**. We have to enter the WSDL location of the BPEL process in the next window. We also have the ability to choose whether we want to copy the WSDL file into the project.

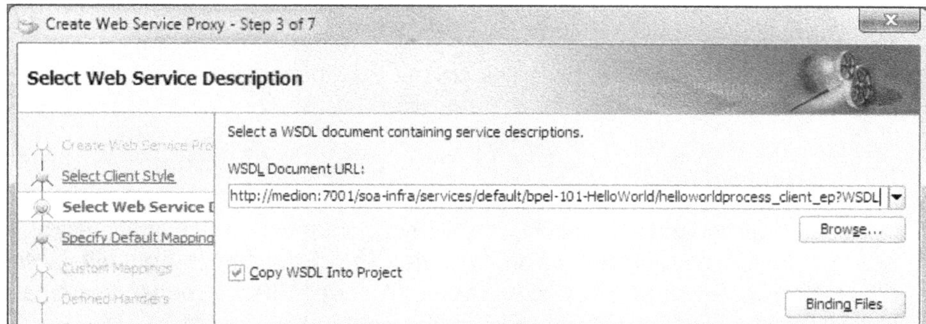

We can either choose the file location from the hard drive or enter the URL for the WSDL location of the BPEL process.

3. In the next window, we have to enter the name of the Java packages. We have to enter the package name of the proxy files (that is, **Root Package for Generated Types**) and **Package Name**, which is where the files for the XML serialization will be placed, as shown in the following screenshot:

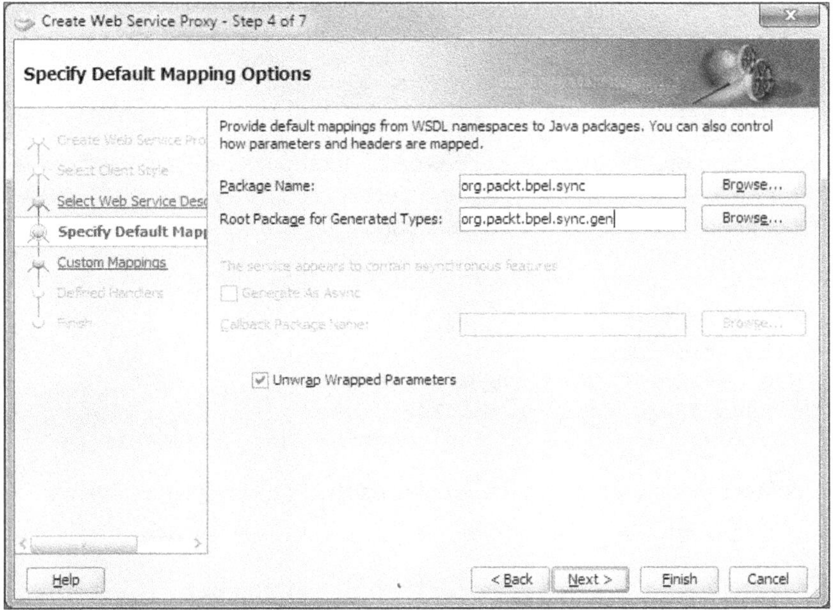

4. We have inserted all the mandatory fields necessary to create the BPEL process proxy, so we conclude the wizard by clicking on **Finish**.
5. In JDeveloper, we see that a number of files were generated in a separate project. The package `org.packt.bpel.sync.gen` contains the files that are used for transformation between XML and Java.
6. Let us check the `Process.java` file. We see that the class contains only one member as follows:

    ```
    @XmlElement(required = true)
    protected String input;
    ```

    The code is annotated with the `@XmlElement` annotation, which indicates the usage of **JAXB** (**Java Architecture for XML Binding**). The JAXB implementation enables conversion from Java to XML and vice-versa. We need this conversion because data in Java is stored in objects, while BPEL holds data in XML format.

This variable presents the input parameter of the BPEL process. The class also contains two helper methods for setting the value and getting the value of the variable. Similarly, we can check the `ProcessResponse.java` class file which contains the output parameter of the BPEL process.

The most interesting generated file is `HelloWorldProcess_ptClient.java`. This file contains skeleton prepared to call the BPEL process.

7. The code starts with the reference to the BPEL process. Since the BPEL process is exposed as a web service, the code is as follows:

    ```
    @WebServiceRef
    private static Helloworldprocess_client_ep
      helloworldprocess_client_ep;
    ```

    We can also note the `@WebServiceRef` annotation, which is used by **JAX-WS** (**Java API for XML Web Services**). The annotation indicates a reference to the web service port, or in our case, the BPEL process port.

8. We need to instantiate the proxy to the BPEL process and get the reference to the endpoint as follows:

    ```
    helloworldprocess_client_ep =
      new Helloworldprocess_client_ep();
    HelloWorldProcess helloWorldProcess =
      helloworldprocess_client_ep.getHelloWorldProcess_pt();
    ```

9. We define the input and output variables as the `String` type as follows:

    ```
    String input = "Jurij";
    String output;
    ```

10. Remember that the BPEL process is taking `string` as an input. As a result, the BPEL process returns a concatenated string starting with `Hello`, followed by the input string, and concluded with three exclamation marks. Finally, we call the BPEL process and write results to the output as follows:

```
output = helloWorldProcess.process(input);
System.out.println
  ("Business process returned:" + output);
```

11. As a result of the BPEL process call, we receive the following output to JDeveloper:

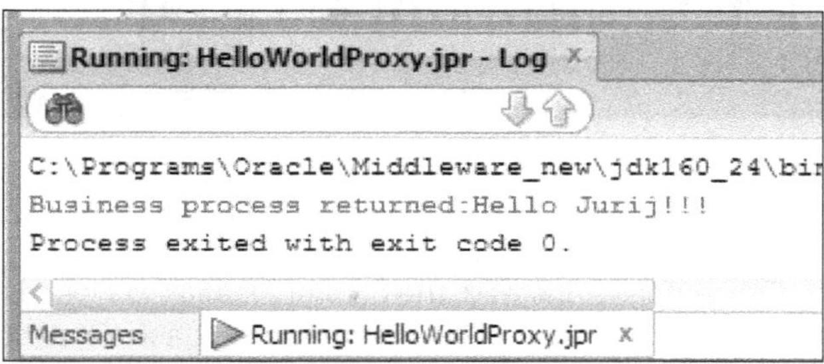

Running: HelloWorldProxy.jpr - Log
C:\Programs\Oracle\Middleware_new\jdk160_24\bi
Business process returned:Hello Jurij!!!
Process exited with exit code 0.
Messages
Running: HelloWorldProxy.jpr

12. We can see that the BPEL process was executed in the **Oracle Enterprise Manager** Console as shown in the following screenshot:

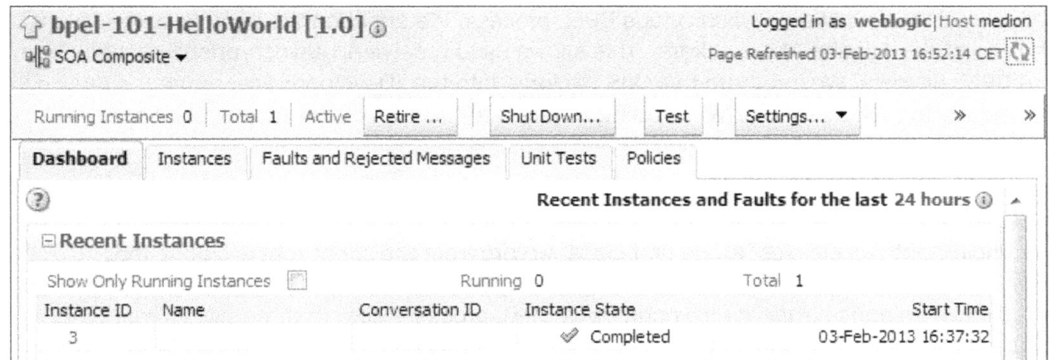

13. We can now see that the BPEL process completed successfully.

How it works...

With the wizard in JDeveloper, we prepare the Java proxy for calling the BPEL process using the wizards in JDeveloper. When the client is executed, it converts the parameters from Java types to XML types via JAX-WS. Then, the call to the BPEL process is performed, and after the BPEL process finishes, the client receives the result in XML. The XML types are then converted back to Java types.

There's more...

We can define different options when creating the BPEL process proxy as follows:

- By creating asynchronous methods
- By defining the security policies for the BPEL process
- By defining the handlers which deal with the web service messages

Calling an asynchronous BPEL process from Java

This recipe explains how to call an asynchronous BPEL process from Java-based applications. Asynchronous communication is broadly used for long-running business processes. When a client invokes a long-running business process, it usually cannot wait long periods (days, weeks, and so on) for the response. Instead, the communication is closed, and a response from the business process is captured by listening for the callback. This recipe also uses the Apache AXIS package.

Getting ready

In this recipe, we call an asynchronous BPEL process. We enriched the sample scenario with the use of the Apache AXIS package. This allows us to receive an asynchronous callback from the BPEL process. We integrate the AXIS package into the JDeveloper environment simply by unpacking the AXIS package, and adding its jars into the JDeveloper project classpath.

How to do it...

We implement two classes. In the first class, we program the client that is calling the asynchronous BPEL process. In the second class, we prepare a callback class that is used to handle the response from the asynchronous BPEL process. Note that the asynchronous BPEL process is not sending a response to the client via a reply activity. Instead, the BPEL process is using the `callback` method, which contacts the client, of course, if one is listening.

1. Let us examine the `ClientProxy.java` class first. We start by creating the `ServiceClient` client and preparing the `Options` class to configure the `ServiceClient` client as follows:

   ```
   ServiceClient client = new ServiceClient();
   Options opts = new Options();
   ```

2. To configure the `ServiceClient` client, we set the parameters as follows:

```
opts.setTo(new EndpointReference("http://medion:7001/soa-
  infra/services/default/HelloWordlAsync
    /helloworldasyncprocess_client_ep"));
opts.setAction("process");
opts.setUseSeparateListener(true);
```

   We instruct AXIS where the BPEL endpoint is, which actions we want to call, and the type of the listener (callback) we want to use. With the `setUseSeparateListener` call, we instruct AXIS to send a SOAP message over two separate channels, thus enabling the asynchronous communication.

3. We engage the `addressing` module of the AXIS package as follows:

```
client.engageModule("addressing");
```

   With this line of code, we actually enable the WS-Addressing module inside the AXIS package. The WS-Addressing module provides transport-neutral mechanisms to address web services and messages. In AXIS, this package is a prerequisite for the asynchronous communication.

4. Finally, we set the options to the service client and fire a non-blocking request to the asynchronous BPEL process as follows:

```
client.setOptions(opts);
client.sendReceiveNonBlocking(createPayLoad(),
  new BPELCallback());
```

   The non-blocking request enables the client to continue its processing without actually waiting for the BPEL process to finish. The `createPayLoad()` method is a helper method used to create a request message for the BPEL process. The helper method is generating XML content out of the Java class through JAXB. We build the request with the help of the XML document builder.

5. The code which simulates further processing of the client is as follows:

```
System.out.println("send the message");
while (!isFeedback) {
  Thread.sleep(5000);
  System.out.println("waiting ....");
  }
System.exit(0);
```

   The main thread is sleeping for five seconds, and after that period is over, it checks if the response was already received from the BPEL process. In the meantime, the client can process other requests. When the client receives the response from the BPEL process, it exits.

6. We created a code for handling the BPEL process response in the `BPELCallback.java` class. We implemented the `onMessage` and `onComplete` methods. When the reply arrives from the BPEL process, we print out the complete SOAP message as follows:

```
public void onMessage(MessageContext messageContext) {
  SOAPBody msg = messageContext.getEnvelope().getBody();
  System.out.println(msg);
  }
```

7. When the transmission is complete, the method `onComplete` is invoked, and we signal the program from which we received the reply from the asynchronous BPEL process as follows:

```
public void onComplete() {
  System.out.println("Transmission finished.");
  ClientProxy.isFeedback = true;
  }
```

8. After running the example, we check the client console output. As we can see, the message is sent to the BPEL process and the client program continues its work. When the response is retrieved from the BPEL process, we see that the message is retrieved within the callback handler, and that means the program exits.

```
send the message
waiting ....
waiting ....
waiting ....
waiting ....
<env:Body xmlns:env =
  "http://schemas.xmlsoap.org/soap/envelope/">
    <processResponse xmlns =
      "http://xmlns.oracle.com/HelloWorldAsync
        /HelloWordlAsync/HelloWorldAsyncProcess">
   <result>Hello </result>
</processResponse></env:Body>
Transmission finished.
waiting ....
[SimpleHTTPServer] Stop called
Process exited with exit code 0
```

9. We also check the **Audit Trail** of the BPEL process. We see that the BPEL process received the message, executed the flow of activities, and at the end, contacted the client and sent a response to it as shown in the following screenshot:

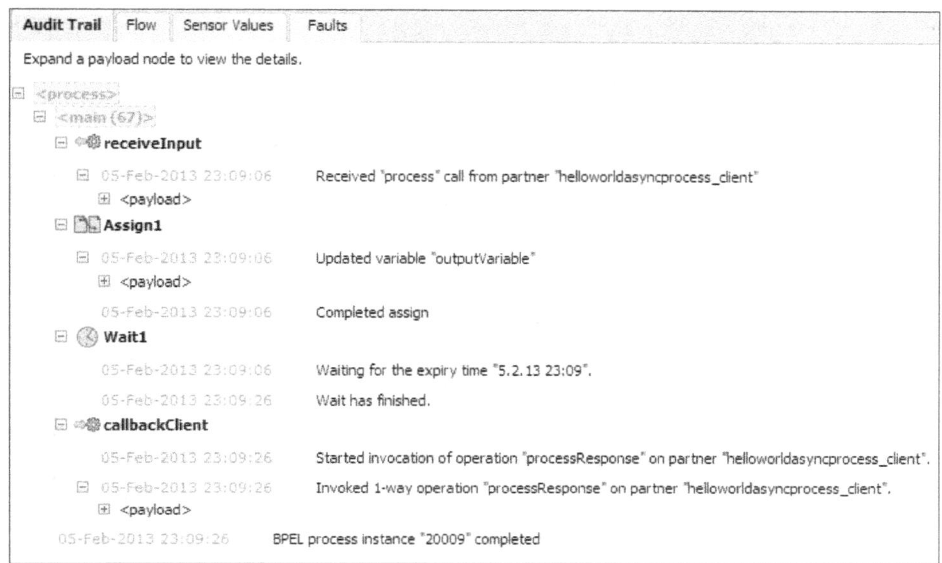
Audit Trail
Flow
Sensor Values
Faults
Expand a payload node to view the details.
<process>
<main (67)>
receiveInput
05-Feb-2013 23:09:06
Received "process" call from partner "helloworldasyncprocess_client"
<payload>
Assign1
05-Feb-2013 23:09:06
Updated variable "outputVariable"
<payload>
05-Feb-2013 23:09:06
Completed assign
Wait1
05-Feb-2013 23:09:06
Waiting for the expiry time "5.2.13 23:09".
05-Feb-2013 23:09:26
Wait has finished.
callbackClient
05-Feb-2013 23:09:26
Started invocation of operation "processResponse" on partner "helloworldasyncprocess_client".
05-Feb-2013 23:09:26
Invoked 1-way operation "processResponse" on partner "helloworldasyncprocess_client".
<payload>
05-Feb-2013 23:09:26
BPEL process instance "20009" completed

How it works...

Asynchronous communication between the BPEL server and client is different than in synchronous communication. In synchronous communication, the BPEL process is invoked, the process flow is executed, and the result is returned to the client. The whole time the BPEL process is executed, the client is blocked. In asynchronous communication, the BPEL process is invoked and the communication is closed. We describe such a call as **one-way invocation**. When the BPEL process execution is finished, the BPEL engine initiates communication with the client and sends back the response via callback. An asynchronous BPEL process does not block the client. This means that as soon as the client initiates the asynchronous BPEL process, it can continue with other tasks. We can see that the asynchronous BPEL processes are used for long-running transactions where we cannot predict when they will finish. Such transactions can be found using human interaction through human tasks.

In order to enable asynchronous communication between the BPEL process and client, we use the WS-Addressing mechanisms. WS-Addressing provides transport-neutral mechanisms to address web services and messages. In the BPEL engine, the correlation mechanism is used in order to track multiple, long-running executions of the BPEL processes. Correlations help with tracking the route to the corresponding BPEL process instance. The correlation sets present a compound version of correlation, as they are composed of more individual correlations. In our example, the correlation information is hidden behind the scenes as WS-Addressing is automatically set to appropriate properties in communication between the BPEL process and client.

Latest specifications of the WS-Addressing specification can be found at the following URL: `http://www.w3.org/TR/ws-addr-core/`.

Usually, both the BPEL servers as well as the client implementations already provide the libraries that support the WS-Addressing specification. The information about addresses resides in the SOAP Header class. When we initiate the BPEL process, the following attributes are set by the client:

- `wsa:To`: This identifies the asynchronous BPEL process which we want to start.
- `wsa:ReplyTo`: This identifies the address of the client to which the asynchronous BPEL process should return the response.
- `wsa:MessageID`: This identifies the uniquely defined number of a sent message. With this message ID, we match the sent request with the received response.
- `wsa:Action`: This identifies the action which should be executed on the asynchronous BPEL process.

Similarly, when the asynchronous BPEL process has finished its execution, the response is sent to the client. In the response SOAP Header class, the following attributes are set:

- `wsa:To`: This identifies the address of the client.
- `wsa:Action`: This identifies the response action name.
- `wsa:MessageID`: This identifies the uniquely defined number of a sent message. With this message ID, we establish a correlation between the request with the received response.
- `wsa:RelatesTo`: This identifies the message ID of the request. `MessageID` of the request and `RelatesTo` of the response are used by the applications to match the requests against their respective responses.
- `wsa:ReplyTo`: This contains information about where the response should be sent. For the response message from the asynchronous BPEL process, the element is empty.
- `wsa:FaultTo`: This contains information about the faults, if they exist.

Handling business faults from a synchronous BPEL process

This recipe explains how to handle the faults thrown from a synchronous BPEL process. A BPEL process uses the `<throw>` activity in case of exceptional situations. It gives the client feedback on what went wrong with the BPEL process processing. In a scenario where the client is expecting the response message and does not capture the faults thrown from the BPEL process, we can define the inline fault in the BPEL process reply activity.

Getting ready

We modified the synchronous BPEL process to throw an exception when the input parameter says `FAULT`. With the `check_fault` condition, we check if the input parameter contains the word `FAULT`. The modified BPEL process is shown in the following screenshot:

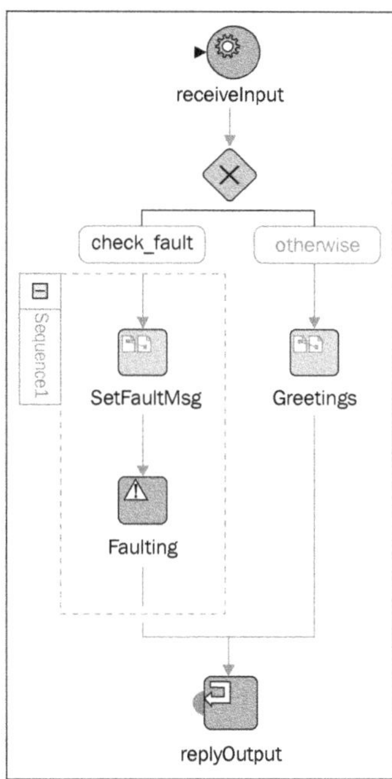

We also need to define the fault structure in the XSD schema (`HelloWorldProcess.xsd`) as shown in the following code:

```
<element name = "fault">
<complexType>
<sequence>
<element name = "msg" type = "string"/>
</sequence>
</complexType>
</element>
```

We define the element `fault`, which contains the element `msg` of the type `string`. We then define the fault message in the WSDL document as follows:

```
<wsdl:message name = "ProcessFaultMessage">
  <wsdl:part name = "message" element = "client:fault"/>
</wsdl:message>
```

We also specify the fault in the `<portType>` and `<binding>` elements of the WSDL document (`HelloWorldProcess.wsdl`). In the following code, we omit the `<binding>` element definition:

```
<wsdl:portType name = "HelloWorldProcess">
  <wsdl:operation name = "process">
  <wsdl:input message = "client:HelloWorldProcessRequestMessage"/>
  <wsdl:output message =
    "client:HelloWorldProcessResponseMessage"/>
  <wsdl:fault name = "fault"
    message = "client:ProcessFaultMessage"/>
  </wsdl:operation>
</wsdl:portType>
```

How to do it...

We create the client proxy the same way we created it in the *Calling a synchronous BPEL process from Java* recipe. We now see the additional class `ProcessFaultMessage.java`. We use this class when the fault occurs in the BPEL process. The class is annotated with the `@WebFault` annotation, which indicates the service specific exception class as follows:

```
@WebFault(faultBean = "org.packt.bpel.sync.gen.Fault",
  targetNamespace = "http://xmlns.oracle.com/
    bpel_101_HelloWorld_jws/bpel_101_HelloWorld/
      HelloWorldProcess", name = "fault")
public class ProcessFaultMessage
extends Exception
```

The `faultBean` attribute defines the Java class that will transform the fault from XML to Java. Additionally, the namespace of the BPEL process is also defined.

We also need to modify the client proxy main class `HelloWorldProcess_ptClient.java`. Since it is possible that the BPEL process throws a fault, we must prepare our client code in advance for such a situation.

1. First, we create the input and output variables as follows:

   ```
   String input = "FAULT";
   String output = "";
   ```

> We changed the code for calling the BPEL process because it requests to be in the `try/catch` block.

```
try {
  output = helloWorldProcess.process(input);
  }
catch (ProcessFaultMessage e) {
  System.out.println( e.getFaultInfo().getMsg());
  }
System.out.println("Business process returned:" + output);
```

2. We run the client and observer BPEL process execution in the **Oracle Enterprise Manager** Console as shown in the following screenshot:

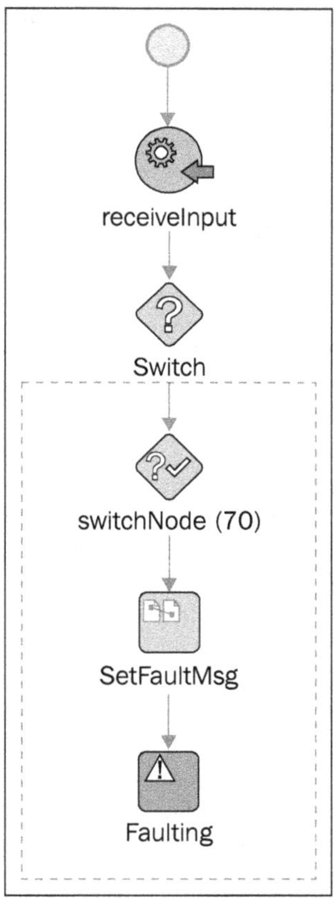

3. The output of the console in JDeveloper contains the following messages:

```
Error while processing input parameter
Business process returned:
Process exited with exit code 0
```

How it works...

The business faults, as opposed to the runtime faults, are thrown by the applications when a problem with processing information occurs. Various situations can cause the BPEL process to throw a fault. The BPEL process might interact with web services and web service itself may throw a fault. Consequently, the BPEL process must react on the fault thrown by web service. When an exceptional situation occurs in the BPEL process, the fault is propagated to the client. As we can see, the newly created class `ProcessFaultMessage.java` extends the `Exception` class. We see that the BPEL faults correspond to the `Exception` class in Java with extensions. The BPEL process also provides the ability to define the compensation handlers. With the compensation handlers, it is possible to undo the actions that were executed during the BPEL process execution. We can consider the compensation handler as a block of code containing the activities performing the compensation tasks.

There's more...

The BPEL specification defines two types of faults. In this, we meet the BPEL process fault; however, there also exists a set of standard faults.

A list of standard faults can be accessed at the following URL: `http://docs.oasis-open.org/wsbpel/2.0/wsbpel-v2.0.pdf` (see *Appendix A, Standard Faults*).

The BPEL standard faults are thrown if the BPEL server encounters some conditions in the runtime environment that do not correspond to the specifications. This category also includes situations where the variables might not be initialized if transformation does not find the XSLT file or if some problems occur on the network.

When we want to add additional information to the already existing fault in the BPEL process, we define new fault message with additional information in the WSDL document of the BPEL process. We then model the fault handling within the fault handler (the `catch` or `catchall` activity). We specify the fault condition that will be caught by the fault handler. Inside the fault handler, we use the `rethrow` activity that throws the fault, which will give the client a better insight into the problem that occurred in the BPEL process.

Handling business faults from an asynchronous BPEL process

The faults that occur either in a synchronous or asynchronous BPEL process are treated the same way inside the BPEL process. The difference, however, exists in the way the client is notified about the fault in the BPEL process. We said earlier that the client is not blocked when calling an asynchronous BPEL process. Since the communication is closed between the BPEL process and client after initiation of BPEL, we need to find a way to notify the client that something went wrong in the BPEL process. This recipe will show you how to handle the faults from the asynchronous BPEL processes.

Getting ready

We modified the asynchronous BPEL process from the *Calling an asynchronous BPEL process* recipe. We added the `If` activity, which checks the content of the input parameter of the BPEL process. If the input parameter contains `FAULT` text, then the BPEL process finishes immediately; otherwise, the BPEL process waits for some time and sends `success` to the client. The modified asynchronous BPEL process is shown in the following screenshot:

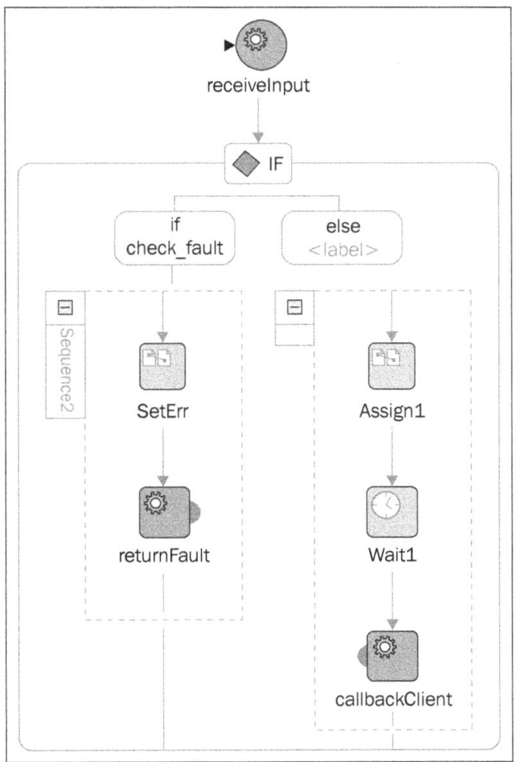

We notify the two reply activities. The `callbackClient` invoke activity is used in case the asynchronous BPEL process finishes successfully. We add the new invoke activity named `returnFault` for cases when we need to report the fault back to the client. We model the asynchronous BPEL process with the additional callback operation because the communication between the BPEL process and client is closed immediately after the client initiates the BPEL process, and there is no way the BPEL process can notify the client about the faults. We start by defining the fault message structure in the `HelloWorldAsyncProcess.xsd` schema as follows:

```
<element name="fault">
  <complexType>
    <sequence>
      <element name="msg" type="string"/>
    </sequence>
  </complexType>
</element>
```

We define the fault message structure the same way as we did with the synchronous BPEL process. We also modify the WSDL description of the asynchronous BPEL process (`HelloWorldAsyncProcess.wsdl`). Initially, we define the message for the fault as follows:

```
<wsdl:message name = "ProcessFaultMessage">
  <wsdl:part name = "message" element = "client:fault"/>
</wsdl:message>
```

We define a SOAP message containing the fault message later inside the `<wsdl:operation>` element of `<wsdl:binding element>` as follows:

```
<wsdl:binding name = "HelloWorldAsyncProcessCallbackBinding"
  type = "client:HelloWorldAsyncProcessCallback">
  <soap:binding transport =
    "http://schemas.xmlsoap.org/soap/http"/>
  <wsdl:operation name = "processFault">
    <soap:operation style = "document" soapAction =
      "processFault"/>
    <wsdl:input>
      <soap:body use = "literal" namespace =
        "http://xmlns.oracle.com/HelloWorldAsync
          /HelloWordlAsync/HelloWorldAsyncProcess"/>
    </wsdl:input>
  </wsdl:operation>
</wsdl:binding>
```

In the synchronous BPEL process scenario, we added the `<wsdl:fault>` information in the `reply` operation. For the asynchronous BPEL process scenario, we model the fault callback as a new `operation` in the callback `portType` as follows:

```
<wsdl:portType name = "HelloWorldAsyncProcessCallback">
  <wsdl:operation name = "processFault">
    <wsdl:input message = "client:ProcessFaultMessage"/>
  </wsdl:operation>
</wsdl:portType>
```

Information about the fault is then sent via the new callback `operation` to the client.

How to do it...

The asynchronous BPEL process does not return a fault in the same way as the synchronous BPEL process. For that purpose, we need to check the response SOAP message to see whether it contains the fault as follows:

```
Iterator<?> it = msg.getChildrenWithLocalName("fault");
if (it.hasNext()) {
  System.out.println("Fault occurred: " + msg.getFirstElement().
    getFirstElement().getText());
  return;
  }
```

If the fault exists, we execute the actions for solving the problems.

How it works...

We know from the previous recipes that calling an asynchronous BPEL process does not block the client. So, in order to retrieve information about the fault, we need to take a different approach as and when we call the synchronous BPEL process. We already mentioned that we defined another operation in reply to `portType`.

We now have a problem, when we send the response information back to the client. Namely, the client does not care, if the message is a success or failure. In any case, the `onMessage` method in the `AxisCallback` class is executed. Here is the reason why we needed to implement the additional code inside the `onMessage` method to check whether we received the fault from the asynchronous BPEL process.

There's more...

Another way of testing whether we received the fault as the response from the asynchronous BPEL process is to take advantage of the WS-Addressing fields in the SOAP Header class of the SOAP message. If we know the operation with which the asynchronous BPEL process is returning the faults to the client, we can check the `<wsa:Action>` element in SOAP Header as follows:

```
<wsa:Action xmlns:wsa = "http://www.w3.org/2005/08/addressing">
  processFault
</wsa:Action>
```

This element identifies the operation that was executed when the asynchronous BPEL process returned the response to the client.

See also

- For more information about asynchronous communication, check out the *Calling an asynchronous BPEL process* recipe

Mapping the results of a BPEL process

The applications that integrate with BPEL processes are most interested in the results. As we saw in the asynchronous scenario recipes, as a result, we receive SOAP Header and SOAP body within SOAP message. The XML presentation is not very useful for Java applications. The better solution would be to instead have Java applications consume the Java Bean classes. For that purpose, different tools exist that enable efficient XML to Java mapping.

In this recipe, we will examine how to map the results of a BPEL process to Java-based clients.

Getting ready

We will need to extend the client proxy from the *Calling an asynchronous BPEL process* recipe, so we need to have the asynchronous BPEL process deployed and the client proxy ready.

First, we will update the response of the asynchronous BPEL process to include more XSD schema elements as follows:

```
<element name = "processResponse">
  <complexType>
    <sequence>
      <element name = "result" type = "string"/>
      <element name = "postalcode" type = "int"/>
      <element name = "temperature" type = "double"/>
      <element name = "person">
        <complexType>
          <sequence>
            <element name = "name" type = "string"/>
            <element name = "lastname" type = "string"/>
          </sequence>
        </complexType>
      </element>
    </sequence>
  </complexType>
</element>
```

If we now call an asynchronous BPEL process, we will receive more information. Also, the information is nested in the response.

How to do it...

1. We will start this recipe by generating the Java Bean class that corresponds to the body of the SOAP response message. We use the `wsimport` command as follows:

   ```
   C:\>wsimport -keep -p org.packt.async.generated -Xnocompile
     -d
   C:\Temp\gen\ http://medion:7001/soa-
     infra/services/default/HelloWordlAsync
       /helloworldasyncprocess
   _client_ep?WSDL
   parsing WSDL...
   generating code...
   C:\>
   ```

In the directory `C:\temp\gen`, the skeleton classes of the corresponding WSDL document are now generated. If we check the content of the directory, we see that there are many more files in it. There are also request classes as well as a client proxy to initiate the BPEL process. For our recipe, we only need the `ProcessResponse.java` file, so we move only this file into our JDeveloper project. In JDeveloper, we create another Java package as shown in the following screenshot:

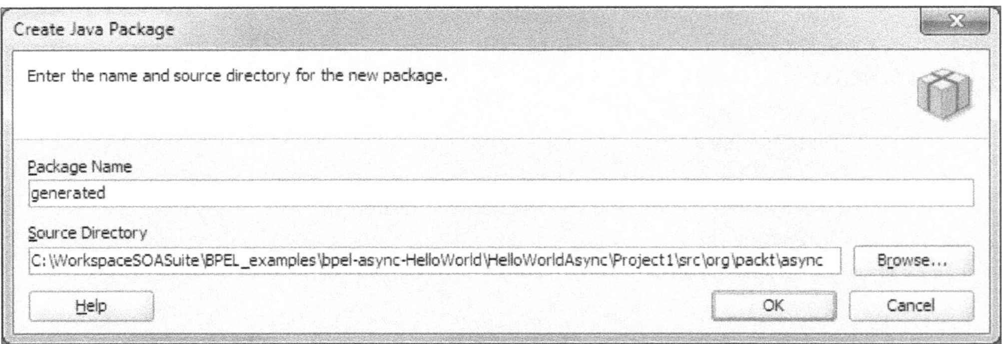

2. We then copy the `ProcessResponse.java` file into the project. Now, our project layout consists of the following classes:

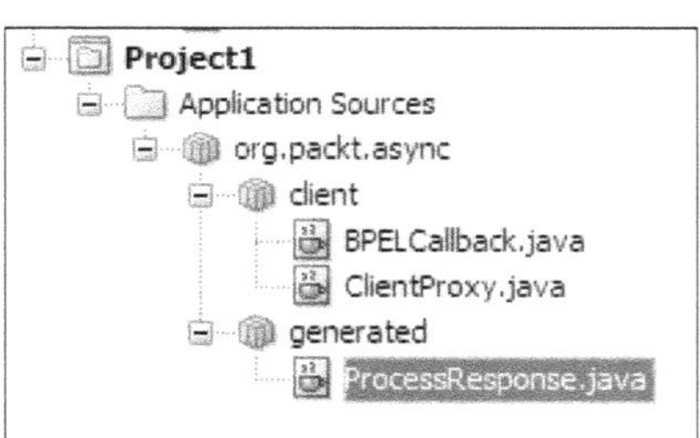

3. We now have to adapt the `ClientProxy` class in order to support the mapping of the result to our Java client. In the AXIS package, there is a utility class, `BeanUtil`, which is used for the deserialization of the XML content into Java classes. We start by preparing the variable of the result as follows:

```
ProcessResponse responseBean;
```

4. We then deserialize the XML content of SOAP message body element through the `BeanUtil` utility class as follows:

```
try {
  responseBean = (ProcessResponse)BeanUtil.deserialize
    (ProcessResponse.class, msg.getFirstElement(),
      new DefaultObjectSupplier(), null);
  }
```

```
catch (AxisFault e) {
  onError(e);
  }
```

5. The XML content of the response from the asynchronous BPEL process is now accessible through the Java Bean as follows:

```
<processResponse Process">
  <result>Hello Jurij</result>
  <postalcode>1430</postalcode>
  <temperature>37.5</temperature>
  <person>
    <name>Jurij</name>
    <lastname>Laznik</lastname>
  </person>
</processResponse>
```

How it works...

The response from the BPEL process presents an XML document wrapped with the SOAP message. The XML format is not very friendly for programming in Java. That is why few implementations arise with the intent to simplify the transformation of XML to Java.

Implementation	Description
JAXB	Java Architecture for XML Binding. The essential tools of JAXB are as follows: ▸ **xjc**: This is used to convert XSD schema types to their corresponding class representation ▸ **schemagen**: This is used to convert the class representations to their respective XSD schema types
JAX-WS	Java API for XML Web Services. The important tools of JAX-WS are as follows: ▸ **wsimport**: This supports the top-down approach of developing JAX-WS web services ▸ **wsgen**: This supports the bottom-up approach of developing JAX-WS web services
JAX-RPC	Obsolete: replaced by JAX-WS

All the implementations mentioned here work with the same basic concept of serialization, deserialization, marshalling, and unmarshalling. In general, serialization and deserialization presents a way of transforming the data structures in a way that we can store them or transfer them between applications or over a network. The synonym for serialization, when we transform Java objects, is marshalling. Consequently, the synonym for the opposite operation, that is deserialization, is called unmarshalling.

The following mapping is used when we convert from XSD schema types to corresponding Java data types:

XML Schema Type	Java Data Type
`xsd:string`	`java.lang.String`
`xsd:integer`	`java.math.BigInteger`
`xsd:int`	`int`
`xsd.long`	`long`
`xsd:short`	`short`
`xsd:decimal`	`java.math.BigDecimal`
`xsd:float`	`float`
`xsd:double`	`double`
`xsd:boolean`	`boolean`
`xsd:byte`	`byte`
`xsd:QName`	`javax.xml.namespace.QName`
`xsd:dateTime`	`javax.xml.datatype.XMLGregorianCalendar`
`xsd:base64Binary`	`byte[]`
`xsd:hexBinary`	`byte[]`
`xsd:unsignedInt`	`long`
`xsd:unsignedShort`	`int`
`xsd:unsignedByte`	`short`
`xsd:time`	`javax.xml.datatype.XMLGregorianCalendar`
`xsd:date`	`javax.xml.datatype.XMLGregorianCalendar`
`xsd:anySimpleType`	`java.lang.Object`
`xsd:duration`	`javax.xml.datatype.Duration`
`xsd:NOTATION`	`javax.xml.namespace.QName`

While the preceding table shows the default mapping between XML data types and Java data types, it is also possible to customize the mapping, usually through the configuration mapping file.

There's more...

Applications written in Java usually do not operate with XML documents. If we want to call a BPEL process, we must also create a request. Until now, we used to build the request with the help of the XML document builder as follows:

```
OMFactory fac = OMAbstractFactory.getOMFactory();
OMNamespace omNs = fac.createOMNamespace
  ("http://xmlns.oracle.com/HelloWorldAsync/HelloWordlAsync
    /HelloWorldAsyncProcess", "");
OMElement method = fac.createOMElement("process", omNs);
OMElement value = fac.createOMElement("input", omNs);
method.addChild(value);
//value.setText("Jurij");
value.setText("FAULT");
```

In the request, we have to know all the information, such as namespace, names of the XML tags, and, of course, the data itself.

To simplify the creation of a request, we can utilize the JAXB tools. First, we will take the `Process.java` class that we created with the `wsimport` tool. We include the class into the JDeveloper project. We need to add namespace info to the annotations in the class file as follows:

```
@XmlRootElement(name = "process", namespace =
  "http://xmlns.oracle.com/HelloWorldAsync/HelloWordlAsync
    /HelloWorldAsyncProcess")
@XmlElement(required = true, namespace =
  "http://xmlns.oracle.com/HelloWorldAsync/HelloWordlAsync
    /HelloWorldAsyncProcess")
```

We can now also change the `createPayLoad()` method in the `ClientProxy.java` class. We create an XML document from the `DocumentBuilderFactory` class as follows:

```
DocumentBuilderFactory dbf = DocumentBuilderFactory.newInstance();
dbf.setNamespaceAware(true);
Document doc = dbf.newDocumentBuilder().newDocument();
```

Then, we create a JAXB context with the following:

```
JAXBContext jc = JAXBContext.newInstance(Process.class);
```

Finally, we create `marshaller` and serialize the request class as follows:

```
Marshaller marshaller = jc.createMarshaller();
marshaller.setProperty(Marshaller.JAXB_FORMATTED_OUTPUT, false);
marshaller.marshal(req, doc);
```

The difference between the previous version of `createPayLoad()` and the newer version is that the previous version lacks transparency and clarity in the code. We can now fill the request data in the following way:

```
Process req = new Process();
req.setInput("JURIJ");
```

And call it as follows:

```
createPayLoad(req)
```

See also

- To learn more about the web services request and the response message structure, refer to the *Introduction* section of *Chapter 2, Calling Services from BPEL* of this book. More information about the tools we used in this recipe is also available in that chapter.
- Refer to `http://docs.oracle.com/javase/7/docs/technotes/tools/share/wsimport.html` for more information about the `wsimport` tool.
- Also, refer to `https://jaxb.java.net/` for more information about the JAXB reference implementation documentation.

2
Calling Services from BPEL

This chapter contains the following recipes:

- Implementing web services with Axis2
- Implementing web services with JAX-WS
- Invoking RESTful web services
- Invoking synchronous web services
- Invoking asynchronous web services
- Dynamic selection of a web service endpoint
- Invoking web services in a sequence
- Invoking web services in parallel
- Handling the faults thrown from web services
- Throwing the faults from BPEL

Introduction

Web services have evolved into a matured technology over the past few years. A web service, as the W3C consortium defines it, is a software system designed to support interoperable machine-to-machine interaction over a network. Large enterprises are seeking ways to make IT more agile to support their business processes. On the one hand, they are trying to make the best out of the existing applications, and on the other hand, they are attempting to minimize the costs of developing new solutions.

The **Service-Oriented Architecture** (**SOA**) presents an architecture that enables agile IT technology for the business process management. With the appearance of web services, the foundation of modular applications was set in SOA. Since web services are technology-neutral, they enable high interoperability. While exposing small-scale application pieces or business services, web services enable integration and reusability. Both facts result in saving time and money.

Web services can be seen as application components or as building blocks of larger applications. The communication between these building blocks is enabled through the open standards, most commonly through HTTP. HTTP is a widely accepted communication protocol between two parties. The traffic can be taken through the proxies and firewalls, which present no obstacle to HTTP communication. Web services consist of two parts. The first part presents the implementation of the web service itself. Web services can be implemented in various programming languages, such as Java, C#, Perl, JRuby, and so on. When the implementation is ready, the second part comes into play, which is the service description or service interface defined through the WSDL document. The service description is universally based on the XML language. The XML language presents a simple, open, and self-describing format. With XML, we can describe many common data types, and we can also define custom data types, if needed.

Web service exposes its implementation or functionality through the web service interface. The web service interface is defined as the **Web Service Description Language** (**WSDL**) document. Remember, WSDL is released in several versions of specifications, which are widely used today. In 2001, **WSDL 1.1** (**Web Service Definition Language**) was released, followed by **WSDL 2.0** (**Web Service Description Language**) in 2007. However, the basic concepts of WSDL did not change. WSDL is based on the XML language. WSDL can be seen as a web service description, consisting of the abstract and concrete part. We first describe the abstract part, which consists of data for exchanging information and operations.

The fundamental part of the WSDL description is the definition of operations. The operations present the distinct functionality that a requestor would request when calling a web service. The requestor would also need information about the input and output parameters of the operations. For that purpose, we defined a part of WSDL that is called **messages**. There are three different types of messages. They can be further defined as input messages, output messages, and fault messages. The messages can be further broken down into parts, which present the building blocks of the messages. Note that for several reasons, it is not recommended to have more than one part in the message. When we define the document/literal binding style, we have problems in cases of more than one part in the message definition. The solution for scenarios where we have more parts defined in the message definition is with the usage of message wrapping, where we end up with one part per message definition. With wrapping, we achieve compliance with **WS-I** (**Web Service Interoperability organization**), and also the document/literal binding style requirements are fulfilled.

Further more describing the concrete part of the WSDL document, the operations are grouped into port type, as shown in the following figure:

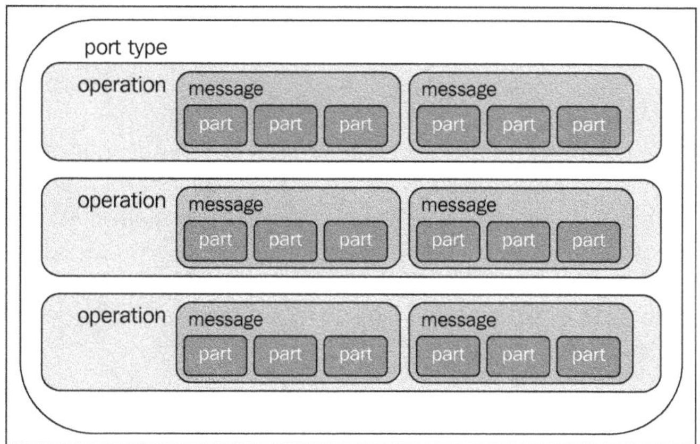

Now we have the service interface described; however, we still need to describe a method of how web services can be called by a client. This is achieved through the `binding` element of the WSDL document. With `binding`, we choose the wire protocol that will be used for calling the web service. To call a web service via HTTP we use the following binding: `http://schemas.xmlsoap.org/soap/http`.

We can also call web service via other protocols, such as SMTP, FTP, MQ, IIOP, and so on. With `binding` (the `soap:body` part) we also define how message parts appear in the SOAP body. The available attribute values are as follows:

- `literal`: This means the message part references a concrete schema definition and will appear directly under the `SOAP:Body` element
- `encoded`: This means that the message part references the abstract schema, which is used to produce the concrete message part, by following the encoding style rules

The sample binding of a web service is shown in the following code:

```
<wsdl:binding name = "HelloWorldProcessBinding"
  type = "client:HelloWorldProcess">
  <soap:binding transport = "http://schemas.xmlsoap.org
    /soap/http"/>
  <wsdl:operation name = "process">
  <soap:operation style = "document" soapAction = "process"/>
    <wsdl:input>
      <soap:body use = "literal"/>
    </wsdl:input>
    <wsdl:output>
      <soap:body use="literal"/>
```

```
      </wsdl:output>
      <wsdl:fault name="fault">
        <soap:fault name="fault" use="literal"/>
      </wsdl:fault>
    </wsdl:operation>
  </wsdl:binding>
```

We can define multiple bindings for different port types. When we define bindings along with the port type, we get the `port` definition. Inside the `port` definition, there is an `address` element, which presents the endpoint (physical location) of web service. The `port` definition now presents a concrete definition of a web service that the client can call. At the top level of the WSDL definition document is the element `service`, which consists of all the ports defined by web service as follows:

```
<wsdl:service name = "helloworldprocess_client_ep">
  <wsdl:port name = "HelloWorldProcess_pt"
    binding = "client:HelloWorldProcessBinding">
  <soap:address location = "http://medion:7001
    /soa-infra/services/default
      /bpel-101-HelloWorld/helloworldprocess_client_ep"/>
  </wsdl:port>
</wsdl:service>
```

When we execute a web service, we need to exchange the messages via some uniform way. We achieve this by using the SOAP protocol. From the architectural point of view, the SOAP protocol defines the SOAP message in the following way:

- SOAP Envelope: This presents the wrap of information to be transferred between the web service and its client.
- SOAP Header: This is an optional part of the SOAP Envelope. Inside the SOAP Header, various information about the transactions in progress are presented.
- SOAP Body: This is a mandatory part of the SOAP Envelope. It contains information that is transferred from web service to its client or vice versa.

One alternative for exchanging the messages is the **REST** (**Representational State Transfer**) style, which we will cover in the *Invoking the RESTful web services* recipe. In this chapter, we will examine different ways of building web services as well as consuming them through BPEL. We will show how to invoke the asynchronous and synchronous types of web services. Also, we will show how to execute web services from BPEL in sequence and in parallel. The last recipes will show you how to handle the faults thrown from web services and how to model the faults in the BPEL processes.

Implementing web services with Axis2

This recipe describes how to implement web services in Apache Axis2. We will show you how to implement the Axis2 annotated web service, and deploy it to the Axis2 server. We will explore the typical lifecycle of a web service.

Getting ready

We use the Eclipse IDE (Eclipse IDE for Java EE Developers Version) for the development of web services. We also need the Apache AXIS2 package for the web service deployment.

Oracle also provides the Oracle Enterprise Pack for Eclipse for those who prefer the Eclipse IDE over the JDeveloper IDE. The package can be found at `http://www.oracle.com/technetwork/developer-tools/eclipse/overview/index.html?ssSourceSiteId=ocomen`.

How to do it...

The following steps present the creation, packaging, and deployment on the Axis2 server, and the testing procedures in the lifecycle of a web service:

1. We will start by creating the project in Eclipse. In the **New Java Project** wizard, we just enter the project name, and then click on **Finish**, since we do not need anything special in the project.
2. We add the POJO class into our project. For our example, we want to prepare a web service that will return the list of hotels that still have available rooms at the given period. We simply create a class with the following code:

```
import java.util.Calendar;

public class BookHotel {
  public String[] availableHotels(Calendar from, Calendar to)
  {
    String[] result = {"Ramada Plaza", "Plaza", "Hilton"};
    return result;
    }
  }
```

We simplified the business code of web service so that no database queries are performed.

We need to position the class at the default package, because in this case the classes with the packages are not supported by Axis2. If we want to place the classes into the packages, we need to define the `services.xml` configuration file.

3. Now we need to decorate the code for our **POJO** (**Plain Old Java Object**) to become a web service. We annotate the class, name web service, and define the target namespace using JAX-WS as follows:

   ```
   @WebService(targetNamespace =
     "http://www.packt.org/book/hotel", name = "HotelBooking")
   ```

4. We also need to annotate the class method as follows:

   ```
   @WebMethod(action = "urn:availableHotels",
     operationName = "availableHotels")
   public @WebResult(partName = "hotels") String[]
     availableHotels(@WebParam(partName = "fromDate")
       Calendar from, @WebParam(partName = "toDate")
         Calendar to)
   ```

The preceding definition contains two parameters, which is not recommended; however, we cannot always avoid it. In our case, if possible, we rather define one parameter enveloping two dates.

We define the action and operations parameters via the `@WebMethod` annotation. We annotate the returning variable with the `@WebResult` annotation. Finally, we annotate the parameters of the method with the `@WebParam` annotation.

We are now ready to deploy our web service to the Axis2 module in the Oracle SOA Suite.

5. For deployment purposes, we create an ant build file. We utilize the ant copy task for copying our web service class file to the server as follows:

   ```
   <copy file = "./bin/BookHotel.class"
     todir = "<Axis2Server> /repository/pojo"/>
   ```

We can check the deployment status in the Axis2 management console. We see that our web service was successfully deployed as shown in the following screenshot:

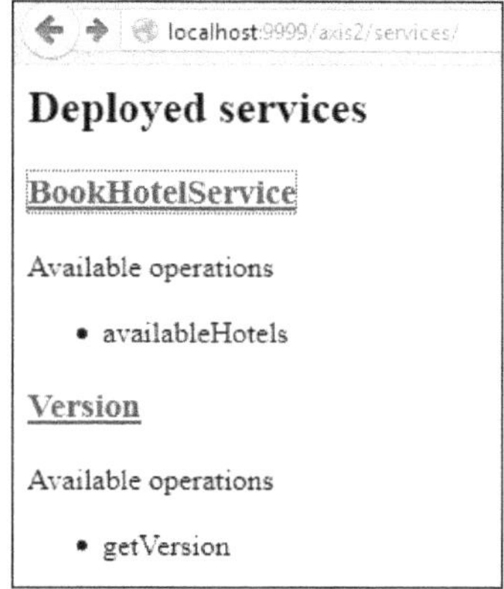

6. We test web service from Eclipse. We use **Web Services Explorer**. First, we select the **WSDL** pane, enter the WSDL location of the web service, and click on **Go**.

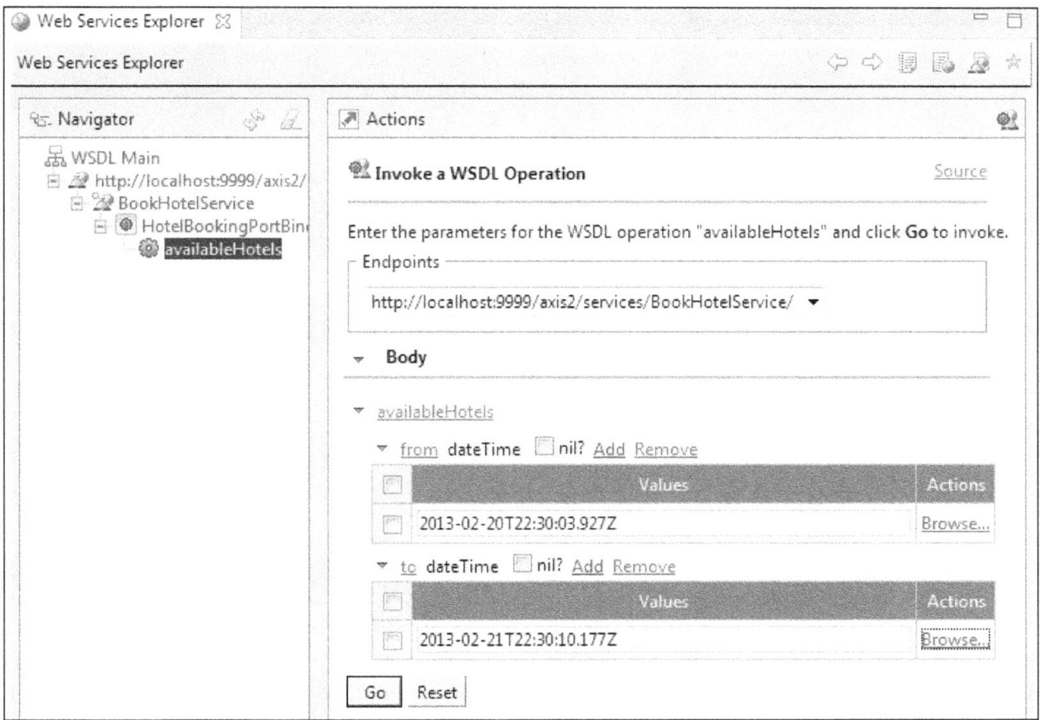

As a result of the web service execution, we see the complete SOAP envelope, with the response in the SOAP Body as follows:

```
<soapenv:Envelope xmlns:soapenv =
  "http://schemas.xmlsoap.org/soap/envelope/">
  <soapenv:Body>
    <dlwmin:availableHotelsResponse xmlns:dlwmin =
      "http://www.packt.org/book/hotel" xmlns:xsi =
        "http://www.w3.org/2001/XMLSchema-instance">
    <hotels xmlns:xs = "http://www.w3.org/2001/XMLSchema"
      xsi:type = "xs:string">Ramada Plaza</hotels>
    <hotels xmlns:xs = "http://www.w3.org/2001/XMLSchema"
      xsi:type = "xs:string">Plaza</hotels>
    <hotels xmlns:xs = "http://www.w3.org/2001/XMLSchema"
      xsi:type = "xs:string">Hilton</hotels>
    </dlwmin:availableHotelsResponse>
  </soapenv:Body>
</soapenv:Envelope>
```

We get three hotels that have available rooms in the specified time frame.

How it works...

Axis2 concentrates on developing web services based on POJO. That way the developer implements the business logic into a Java class, which is later annotated, and becomes a web service.

The Axis2 implementation supports SR 181 annotation specification out of the box.

With annotations it is possible to fully describe the web service class. There is absolutely no need to add any additional description files. Axis2 also enables the deployment of the exploded web service package; that is web services that are not packed into the JAR file. We simply drag-and-drop the class file to the Axis2 server, which is also called the **hot-deployable** method.

There's more...

The development of web service in this recipe had the requirement that the class had to be in the default package. That way we can build the class hierarchies at the default package level only, but we cannot organize the classes into the packages. But usually, we want to have our classes packed into the package. For that purpose, Axis2 requires that we provide the web service description file, named `services.xml`. The file contains the configuration describing the web service, such as the name of the web service, its operations, message receivers, target namespace, and so on.

We will now create another web service that will enable the hotels to trade the price of the room relative to the stocks traded on the stock exchange.

1. We will create the data class for the room price. We will be able to check the bid, ask, and mid-price of the room as follows:

   ```
   package org.packt.ws.axis;

   public class RoomPrice {
     private int ask = 0;
     private int bid = 0;
     private int mid = 0;
     }
   ```

2. Now, we will define the web service class that will retrieve the prices of the room as follows:

   ```
   package org.packt.ws.axis;

   public class RoomPriceService {
     private RoomPrice price;

     public RoomPrice getPrice() {
       return price;
       }

     public void setPrice(RoomPrice price) {
       this.price = price;
       }
     }
   ```

3. Now, we must describe the web service before deploying it. For that purpose, we create `services.xml`, and put it into the `WEB-INF` directory of the project as follows:

   ```
   <service name = "RoomPriceService" scope = "application">
     <description>
       Prices of trading for room
     </description>
       <messageReceivers>
         <messageReceiver mep = "http://www.w3.org/2004/08
           /wsdl/in-out" class =
             "org.apache.axis2.rpc.receivers.RPCMessageReceiver"/>
       </messageReceivers>
     <parameter name="ServiceClass">
       org.packt.ws.axis.RoomPriceService
     </parameter>
   </service>
   ```

We see that `services.xml` define the name of the web service. We also define how the interface interacts with the client via the `messageReceiver` element. We have defined the `IN-OUT` type of communication, since the client will call the web service and also receive information from the web service.

4. Prior to deploying the web service, we have to pack it in the AAR library (the name comes from Axis Archive). We will do this by modifying our `build.xml` file; add lines for packing our files into AAR, and move it to the final server location as follows:

```
<target name = "pack">
  <echo message = "creating jar"/>

  <jar destfile = "build/RoomPriceService.aar">
  <fileset dir = "classes"/>
  <fileset dir = "jar"/> <!-- contains META-INF dir -->
  </jar>
</target>
```

We see the next project outlook in Eclipse as shown in the following screenshot:

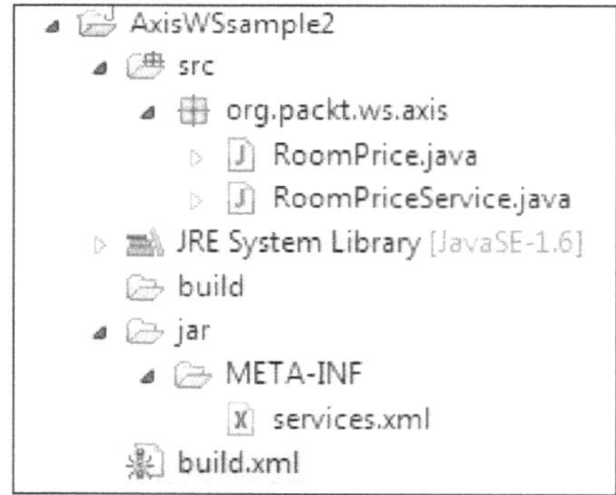

See also

- Axis2 also supports the development of web services based on the JAX-WS specification. We will explain the JAX-WS web services development in our next recipe, *Implementing web services with JAX-WS*.

Implementing web services with JAX-WS

This recipe will explore the implementation of web services with JAX-WS. For web service construction, we will use the top-down approach.

Getting ready

In the recipe *Implementing web services with Axis2*, we started web service implementation with the POJO class. The approach is called the bottom-up design. We will start the development of web services in JAX-WS from the WSDL definition; that is, we will use the top-down approach.

Initially, we create a new Java project in Eclipse. In the wizard, we change the output directory from `bin` to `classes`. When the project is created, we amend it with the following actions:

1. Create the `wsdl` directory. We put it in the WSDL file that is our starting point of creating a web service.
2. Create the build directory. The directory presents the placeholder, where the deployment package will be created.
3. Create an empty `build.xml` file at the top-level project directory.

The WSDL file for our example web service is as follows:

```
<?xml version = "1.0" encoding = "UTF-8" ?>
<wsdl:definitions targetNamespace =
  "http://org.packt.ws.jaxws.async/reservation"
    xmlns:msgel = "http://org.packt.ws.jaxws.async/elts"
      xmlns:res = "http://org.packt.ws.jaxws.async/reservation"
        xmlns:wsdl = "http://schemas.xmlsoap.org/wsdl/"
          xmlns:soap = "http://schemas.xmlsoap.org/wsdl/soap/"
            xmlns:wsaw = "http://www.w3.org/2006/05/addressing
              /wsdl" xmlns:jaxws =
                "http://java.sun.com/xml/ns/jaxws">
  <wsdl:types>
    <xsd:schema targetNamespace =
      "http://org.packt.ws.jaxws.async/elts"
        xmlns:xsd = "http://www.w3.org/2001/XMLSchema"
          elementFormDefault = "qualified">
    <xsd:element name = "ReservationEl"
      type = "msgel:ReservationType"/>
    <xsd:complexType name = "ReservationType">
    <xsd:sequence>
      <xsd:element name = "hotelName" type = "xsd:string"/>
      <xsd:element name = "name" type = "xsd:string"/>
      <xsd:element name = "lastname" type = "xsd:string"/>
      <xsd:element name = "price" type = "xsd:int"/>
      <xsd:element name = "noOfNights" type = "xsd:int"/>
    </xsd:sequence>
    </xsd:complexType>
    <xsd:element name = "ReservationConfirmationEl"
      type = "msgel:ReservationConfirmationType"/>
    <xsd:complexType name = "ReservationConfirmationType">
```

```
    <xsd:sequence>
    <xsd:element name = "confirmationId" type = "xsd:string"/>
    </xsd:sequence>
    </xsd:complexType>
    </xsd:schema>
  </wsdl:types>
  <wsdl:message name = "Reservation">
    <wsdl:part name = "payload" element = "msgel:ReservationEl"/>
  </wsdl:message>
  <wsdl:message name = "Confirmation">
    <wsdl:part name = "payload"
      element = "msgel:ReservationConfirmationEl"/>
  </wsdl:message>
  <wsdl:portType name = "DoReservationAsync">
  <wsdl:operation name = "reserve">
  <jaxws:bindings>
    <jaxws:enableAsyncMapping>true</jaxws:enableAsyncMapping>
  </jaxws:bindings>
  <wsdl:input message = "res:Reservation"
    wsaw:Action =
      "http://org.packt.ws.jaxws.async/reservation/reserve"/>
  <wsdl:output message = "res:Confirmation"
    wsaw:Action =
      "http://org.packt.ws.jaxws.async/reservation/confirm"/>
  </wsdl:operation>
  </wsdl:portType>
  <wsdl:binding name = "DoReservationBind"
    type = "res:DoReservationAsync">
  <wsaw:UsingAddressing required = "true"/>
  <soap:binding style = "document"
    transport = "http://schemas.xmlsoap.org/soap/http"/>
  <wsdl:operation name = "reserve">
  <!-- soap:operation style = "document"
    soapAction =
      "http://org.packt.ws.jaxws.async/reservation/confirm"/-->
  <wsdl:input>
    <soap:body use = "literal" parts = "payload"/>
  </wsdl:input>
  <wsdl:output>
    <soap:body use = "literal" parts = "payload"/>
  </wsdl:output>
  </wsdl:operation>
  </wsdl:binding>
  <wsdl:service name = "ReservationService">
  <wsdl:port name = "DoReservationAsyncPort"
```

```
      binding="res:DoReservationBind">
    <soap:address location = "http://localhost/reservation"/>
    </wsdl:port>
    </wsdl:service>
  </wsdl:definitions>
```

Now, we are ready to start with web service creation.

How to do it...

The following steps will describe the actions needed to be performed during the implementation of the JAX-WS web service:

1. For the purpose of creating a web service from the WSDL document, we use the `wsimport` command that comes with Java SE 6. We prepare the `wsimport` command, and place it in our ant `build.xml` file as follows:

```
<target name = "buildws">
  <echo message =
    "building the web service java classes from wsdl"/>
    <exec executable = "${java.home}/../bin/wsimport">
    <arg line = "-keep -verbose -Xdebug -d classes -p
      org.packt.ws.jaxws.async -s src wsdl
        /ReservationService.wsdl"/>
  </exec>
</target>
```

2. Since the `wsimport` utility prepared the interfaces for the web service, we need to provide its implementation. We create a new implementation class `DoReservationAsyncImpl.java` as follows:

```
@WebService(name = "DoReservationAsync", targetNamespace =
  "http://org.packt.ws.jaxws.async/reservation")
@SOAPBinding(style = javax.jws.soap.SOAPBinding.Style.RPC)
public class DoReservationAsyncImpl {
```

The implementation class does not extend the service interface class. Also, the asynchronous methods are not implemented.

3. Now we have to pack our web service, so we put the following ant task into the `build.xml` file as follows:

```
<target name = "pack">
  <echo message = "creating jar"/>
  <jar destfile = "build/ReservationService.jar"
    basedir = "/classes"/>
</target>
```

4. The last step of the recipe presents the deployment of the packed jar to the Axis2 server. To automate the deployment, we put the following line into the `build.xml` file:

```
<target name = "main" depends = "pack">
  <echo message = "deploying sample web service to
    Axis2 servicejars"/>
  <copy file = "build/ReservationService.jar"
    todir = "<Axis_home>/repository/servicejars"/>
</target>
```

We can check the deployment status in the Axis2 Management Console.

How it works...

There are two complementary approaches to building web services. The first one is bottom-up, where we start by coding web services in Java classes. Furthermore, we annotate the code with the web service annotations and at the end we deploy the web service. At the same time, the WSDL document is generated based on the annotated Java classes and their methods.

The second approach presents the top-down approach. In this case, we receive the WSDL document of the web service. With the utility, we create Java classes for the data model and service interface classes. The real implementation of the web service has to be provided by us. After packing the web service artifacts along with the implementation, we are ready to deploy and use our web service. It is worth mentioning that the top-down approach is the recommended one, and whenever possible we should use this approach. The benefits of starting with the top-down approach are numerous. We can start the design with the WSDL document, which is also WS-I compliant.. Furthermore, the development team that will use the web service can start coding the clients right away. This approach is sometimes also called the **WS contract-first** approach.

The Java API for XML Web Service 2.0 (JSR 224) or **JAX-WS** provides the ability for developers to expose Java code as a web service. The tools provided to support the JAX-WS web service development fully supports the top-down and bottom-up approach.

In this recipe, we started from the WSDL document, then generated the portable artifacts, and prepared the implementation. If we look at the web service artifact, we see that three methods were created. For the synchronous web service call we have the following code:

```
@WebMethod
@WebResult(name = "ReservationConfirmationEl", targetNamespace =
  "http://org.packt.ws.jaxws.async/elts", partName = "payload")
public ReservationConfirmationType reserve(@WebParam(name =
  "ReservationEl", targetNamespace =
    "http://org.packt.ws.jaxws.async/elts", partName = "payload")
      ReservationType payload);
```

There are two additional methods created for the asynchronous web service call. Remember, we use the asynchronous web service call when designing the BPEL process, supporting the long-running business process as follows:

1. The first generated method utilize the callback invocation model. With this type of invocation, we first issue the request, and then we check in intervals, to see if the server responds.

   ```
   @WebMethod(operationName = "reserve")
     public Future<?> reserveAsync(@WebParam(name =
       "ReservationEl", targetNamespace =
         "http://org.packt.ws.jaxws.async/elts",
           partName = "payload") ReservationType payload,
             @WebParam(name = "reserveResponse",
               targetNamespace = "", partName =
                 "asyncHandler") AsyncHandler
                   <ReservationConfirmationType>
                     asyncHandler);
   ```

2. The second method is generated when we decide to use the polling invocation model. In this invocation model, we issue the request, and then poll the response from the server to identify if the web service has finished its processing yet. When the execution of the web service operation is done, we receive the actual `Response` object as the result.

   ```
   @WebMethod(operationName = "reserve")
     public Response<ReservationConfirmationType>
       reserveAsync(@WebParam(name = "ReservationEl",
         targetNamespace =
           "http://org.packt.ws.jaxws.async/elts",
             partName = "payload") ReservationType payload);
   ```

After packing up the web service into a jar, we were able to deploy it, and consume it. The final outlook of the Eclipse project is as shown in the following screenshot:

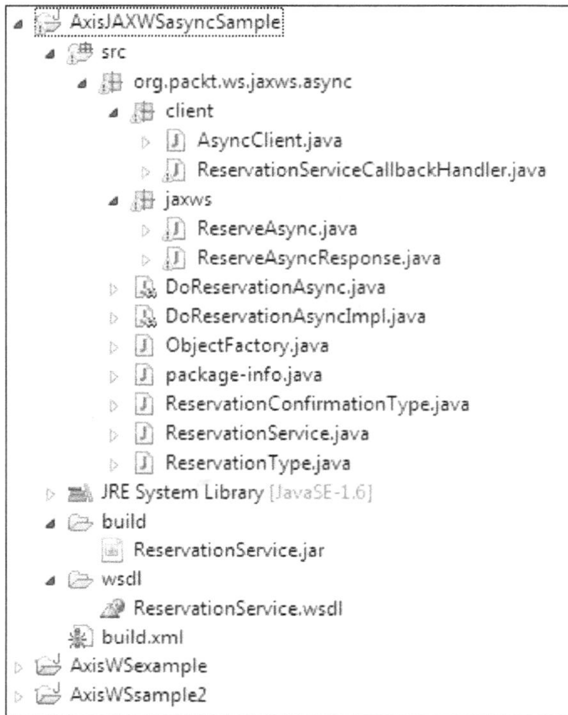

The project contains the portable artifacts and implementation of the web services we provide. Also, in the `wsdl` directory resides the WSDL document from which we generated the portable artifacts. In the build directory, we have a package ready to be deployed.

There's more...

We decided to use the callback invocation model with this recipe. To test the web service, we also prepared the client that calls the asynchronous web service.

1. First, we define the variables. We need to define the asynchronous callback handler and an input variable.

```
ReservationServiceCallbackHandler aHandler = new
  ReservationServiceCallbackHandler();
ReservationType input = new
  ObjectFactory().createReservationType();
```

2. We invoke the web service method.

```
Future<?> resp =
  svc.getDoReservationAsyncPort().reserveAsync
    (input, aHandler);
```

3. The next step depends on how we want to handle the response. Either we wait for the response in our client, or we give the waiting task to some external application that then collects the responses and acts accordingly. We created the loop in our test client.

```
while (!resp.isDone()) {
  Thread.sleep(5000);
  System.out.println("sleeping");
  }
```

4. We handle the response when it becomes available.

```
ReservationConfirmationType response =
  aHandler.getOutput();
if (response ! = null) {
  String responseStr = response.getConfirmationId();
  System.out.println
    (">> Confirmation id is: " + responseStr);
  }
```

5. We receive the following output, when we run the client code:

```
>> Sending the following input
  Name: Jurij
  Lastname: Laznik
  Hotel name: Plaza
  Number of nights: 2
  Price: 100
sleeping
sleeping
>> Confirmation id is: dbf93989-c8fd-47f7-9e7c-25b155aedf27
```

See also

- For a bottom-up approach of web service development, see the *Implementing a web service with Axis2* recipe

Invoking the RESTful web services

The REST web services are becoming more and more popular, because of their simplicity over the SOAP and WSDL-based web services. This recipe will explore how to call the RESTful web services from the BPEL process.

Getting ready

We have prepared a RESTful web service that returns the weather conditions based on the city criteria. The web service is developed in JDeveloper and deployed to the Oracle SOA Suite server. We developed the RESTful web services with Jersey, which supports the JAX-RS (the Java API for the RESTful web services) specification covered by Java Specification Request 311.

We created the sample RESTful weather service with the following code:

```
@Path("RESTWeatherService")
public class WeatherProvider {

  @GET
  @Path("/query")
  @Produces("text/xml")
  public String getWeatherInfo(@QueryParam("name")
    String name,@QueryParam("zip") String zip) {
    return "<weatherRes>Hello " + name + ".
      The weather in " + zip + " city cloudy. \n" +
        "Temperature is 24 degrees Celsius. \n" +
          "Humidity is 74%</weatherRes>";
    }
  }
```

The highlighted text marks the JAX-RS annotations. With the `@Path` annotation, we identify the path where the RESTful services will reside. With the `@GET` annotation, we identify the type of the communication we will use with the service. The `@Path` annotation on the method identifies the subpath of the service. The `@Produces` annotation defines the type of the response we will receive as a result of the service call, in our case, text/xml. The `@QueryParam` annotation identifies the parameter of the web service. The source file is then packed into the WAR file and deployed into Oracle SOA Server.

> The BPEL server in the Oracle SOA Suite does not support the invocation of the RESTful web services out-of-the box and nor does any other BPEL server. The reason is that the BPEL engines follow the BPEL specification closely, which does not cover invocation of the RESTful web services.

There exists many ways to call the RESTful web services from the BPEL process.

How to do it...

We will learn how to call the RESTful web service from the BPEL process by modifying the WSDL document. Instead of defining the web service in the `<wsdl:binding>` element of WSDL, we will use the `<http:binding>` element.

1. We will start the recipe by creating the WSDL document of the weather web service. We create the WSDL document manually. As an input parameter, we take the name of a person and zip code of a city. We return a message about the current temperature, humidity, and weather as the result.

   ```
   As an input and output messages, we define the following
   structure:
   <types>
   <xsd:schema elementFormDefault = "qualified"
     targetNamespace = "http://org.packt.rest/Weather">
     <xsd:element name = "weatherRes" type = "xsd:string"/>
     <xsd:element name = "weatherReq">
     <xsd:complexType>
       <xsd:sequence>
         <xsd:element name = "name" type = "xsd:string"/>
         <xsd:element name = "zip" type = "xsd:int"/>
       </xsd:sequence>
     </xsd:complexType>
     </xsd:element>
   </xsd:schema>
   </types>
   <message name = "GetWeather">
     <part name = "payload" element = "tns:weatherReq"/>
   </message>
   <message name="GetWeatherResponse">
     <part name = "payload" element = "tns:weatherRes"/>
   </message>
   ```

2. The port type definition of the web service is defined as follows:

   ```
   <portType name = "WeatherPT">
     <operation name = "QueryWeather">
       <input message = "tns:GetWeather"/>
       <output message = "tns:GetWeatherResponse"/>
     </operation>
   </portType>
   ```

3. The most important part is the definition of the web service binding. Note that instead of using the `<wsdl: binding>` element we use the `<http:binding>` element. Also the input and output message elements have the HTTP namespaces as follows:

```
<binding name = "WeatherBind" type = "tns:WeatherPT">
  <http:binding verb = "GET"/>
    <operation name = "QueryWeather">
      <http:operation location = "/weather"/>
        <input>
          <http:urlEncoded/>
        </input>
        <output>
          <mime:mimeXml part="payload"/>
        </output>
    </operation>
</binding>
```

4. Finally, we define the service endpoint configuration as follows:

```
<service name = "WeatherService">
  <port name = "Weather" binding = "tns:WeatherBind">
    <http:address location =
      "http://medion:7001/weatherservice/jersey
        /RESTWeatherService/query"/>
  </port>
</service>
```

5. With WSDL we have access to the RESTful web services. Now, we create the BPEL process. We have to enter our name and zip code as the input parameters for the BPEL process. The actions in the BPEL process are as follows:.

    - We assign the zip code parameter from the BPEL process request to the web service input variable:

```
<assign name = "AssignParams">
  <copy>
    <from>$inputVariable.payload/client:MyName</from>
    <to>$CallWeather_QueryWeather_InputVariable.payload
      /ns2:name</to>
  </copy>
  <copy>
    <from>$inputVariable.payload/client:MyZip</from>
    <to>$CallWeather_QueryWeather_InputVariable.payload
      /ns2:zip</to>
  </copy>
</assign>
```

- We perform the web service call:

```
    <invoke name = "CallWeather" partnerLink =
"WeatherSvcs"
      portType = "ns2:WeatherPT" operation = "QueryWeather"
        inputVariable =
          "CallWeather_QueryWeather_InputVariable"
            bpelx:invokeAsDetail = "no"
              outputVariable =
                "CallWeather_QueryWeather_OutputVariable"/>
```

- At the end we pick up the result of the web service call and form the reply to the client as follows:

```
<assign name = "AssignResult">
  <copy>
    <from>$CallWeather_QueryWeather_OutputVariable.
payload
      </from>
    <to>$outputVariable.payload/client:result</to>
  </copy>
</assign>
```

6. In the next step, we deploy the web service to the Oracle SOA Suite server.
7. For testing purposes we use the Oracle Enterprise Manager Console, where we run the BPEL process. In the request window, we enter the following data:

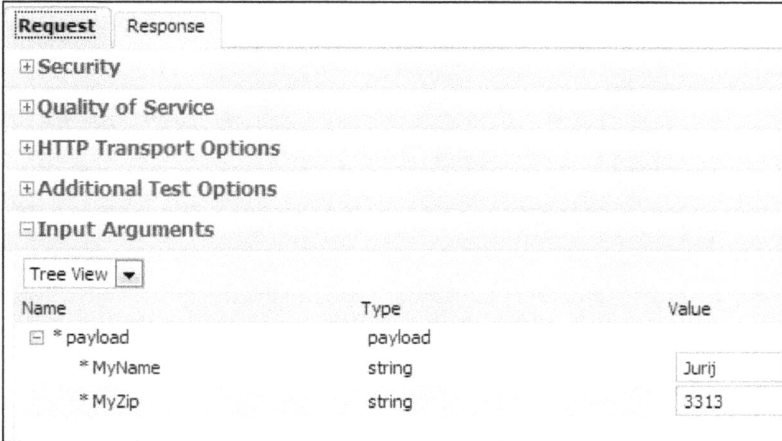

8. In the response window, we receive the following information:

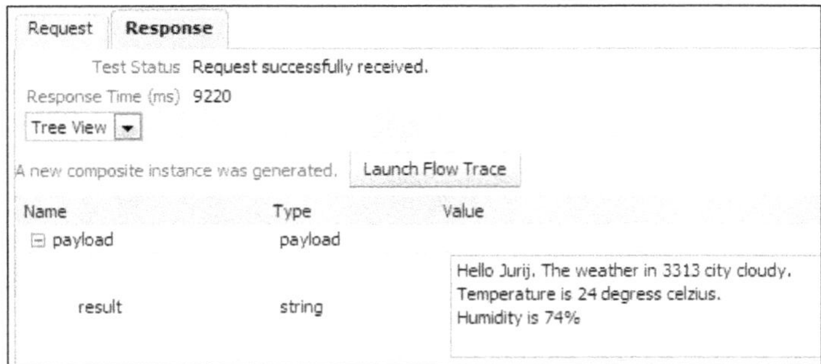

9. In the audit trail of the BPEL process, we check the request and response of the web service as shown in the following screenshot:

How it works...

The Oracle BPEL server does not support a call to the RESTful web services out-of-the-box. Instead, we need to use a trick. By providing the WSDL description of the RESTful web services, we enable a call from the BPEL process to the RESTful web services. The crucial change in the WSDL document is done inside the `<wsdl:binding>` tag.

In this recipe, we provide one way of calling the RESTful web services from the BPEL process. Oracle SOA Suite also provides the mediator functionality, which can be utilised to invoke the RESTful web services.

The binding type

The WSDL document supports the following two types of bindings:

- `<soap:binding>`: This attribute is described with the style and transport types. Its most common usage is the document for style and HTTP as a transport.
- `<http:binding>`: This is what we used to call the RESTful web services. We define it to use the `GET` method over HTTP to communicate with the web service.

The operation attribute

With the operation attribute, we define the operations that `portType` exposes. Inside the operation attribute, we usually define the `SOAPAction` parameter as follows:

```
<soap:operation soapAction = "<URI>"/>
```

Instead of `<soap:operation>`, we use `<http:operation>`. We define on which path the web service is found as follows:

```
<http:operation location = "/weather"/>
```

The binding element in the WSDL document of the weather service now reads as follows:

```
<binding name = "WeatherBind" type = "tns:WeatherPT">
  <http:binding verb = "GET"/>
    <operation name = "QueryWeather">
      <http:operation location = "/weather"/>
        <input>
          <http:urlEncoded/>
        </input>
        <output>
          <mime:mimeXml part="payload"/>
        </output>
    </operation>
</binding>
```

Invoking the synchronous web service

The BPEL process acts as an orchestration component of SOA. One of its fundamental abilities is to invoke web services. This recipe describes how to invoke the synchronous web service.

Getting ready

Before we start with the recipe, we need access to the synchronous web service. We will use the weather service from the *Invoking the RESTful web services* recipe.

How to do it...

The following steps describe the actions necessary in order to design the BPEL process for invoking the synchronous web service:

1. We start the recipe by modeling the SOA composite. We add the web service to the SOA composite, and it should look like the following screenshot:

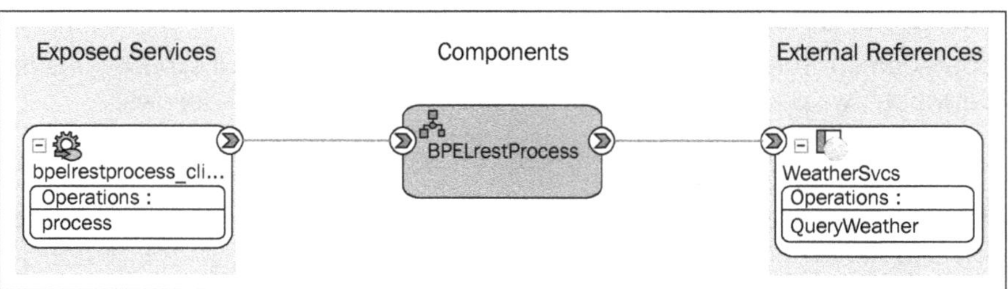

2. In the BPEL process, we first assign the parameters for the web service. Next, we invoke the web service with the `<invoke>` activity as follows:

```
<invoke name = "CallWeather" partnerLink = "WeatherSvcs"
  portType = "ns2:WeatherPT" operation = "QueryWeather"
    inputVariable =
      "CallWeather_QueryWeather_InputVariable"
        bpelx:invokeAsDetail="no"
            outputVariable =
              "CallWeather_QueryWeather_OutputVariable"/>
```

3. We finish modeling by assigning the web service results to the BPEL process output variable. Now, we are ready to deploy the BPEL process and test it inside the Oracle Enterprise Management Console. In the excerpt of **Audit Trail**, we see that the web service was invoked in a synchronous way as shown in the following screenshot:

CallWeather

25-Feb-2013 20:06:20 Started invocation of operation "QueryWeather" on partner "WeatherSvcs".

25-Feb-2013 20:06:20 Invoked 2-way operation "QueryWeather" on partner "WeatherSvcs".

<payload>

How it works...

We know that the SOAP over HTTP web service is exposed via the WSDL document. The synchronous and asynchronous web services are distinguished by the port type definition. Usually, we can distinguish the asynchronous web service from the synchronous web service in a way that the asynchronous web service has only the input message defined in the port type definition. Also the asynchronous web service has a callback port type defined. For our weather service, the port type definition is as follows:

```
<portType name = "WeatherPT">
  <operation name = "QueryWeather">
    <input message = "tns:GetWeather"/>
    <output message = "tns:GetWeatherResponse"/>
  </operation>
</portType>
```

We can see that for the `QueryWeather` operation, the input and output variables are defined. For the synchronous web service, we use the request-response type of operations in the communication between the client and web service. This means that the client is operating in the blocking mode. The client invokes the web service and provides the input message and waits until the web service finishes and provides the output message. Note, the synchronous web service invocation is not a recommended approach to use in the long-running business processes. We introduce a web service in the BPEL process via `partnerLink`. When `partnerLink` is defined, we can call the web services with the `<invoke>` activity. The most common format of the `<invoke>` activity is as follows:

```
<invoke partnerLink = "NCName"
  portType = "QName"?
  operation = "NCName"
  inputVariable = "BPELVariableName"?
  outputVariable = "BPELVariableName"?>
</invoke>
```

We have to define the `partnerLink` name, `portType`, and `operation`. If the web service also expects the parameters or the return values, we also need to declare the input and output variables.

There's more...

We can also declare the fault in the synchronous web service port type. The faults are used when the web service cannot complete its operation successfully. The port type definition then states as follows:

```
<portType name = "WeatherPT">
  <operation name = "QueryWeather">
    <input message = "tns:GetWeather"/>
    <output message = "tns:GetWeatherResponse"/>
    <fault message = "tns:weatherStationUnreachable"/>
  </operation>
</portType>
```

The fault in the BPEL process can then be caught inline in the BPEL process `<invoke>` activity, or by the `<catch>` activity by the fault handler as follows:

```
<invoke partnerLink = "NCName"
  portType = "QName"?
  operation = "NCName"
  inputVariable = "BPELVariableName"?
  outputVariable = "BPELVariableName"?>
  <catchfaultName = "FaultVariable"></catch>
</invoke>
```

See also

- For calling the asynchronous web services, see the *Invoking the asynchronous web service* recipe
- In cases when the fault handling needs to be implemented, see the *Handling the faults thrown from web service* recipe

Invoking the asynchronous web service

The asynchronous web service is opposite to the synchronous request-response mechanism, as the asynchronous web services use a one-way mechanism. This type of invocation is recommended for long-running web services. The asynchronous web service invocation is especially handy in scenarios where we cannot expect the response in a reasonable time constraint such as the integration of payment systems between banks where confirmations are sent according to the contracts and can take from a few seconds to a few days. In this recipe, we will explore how to invoke the asynchronous web service from the BPEL process.

Getting ready

Before we start with the recipe, we need access to the asynchronous web service. Since the BPEL processes also have the possibility to be exposed as the web services endpoints, we will use the asynchronous BPEL process for this recipe. That way we will also show how to call one BPEL process from another BPEL process.

How to do it...

The following steps show how to invoke the asynchronous web service from the BPEL process:

1. We start the recipe by modeling the SOA composite. We add the web service, in our case, the asynchronous BPEL process to the SOA composite, and it should look as follows:

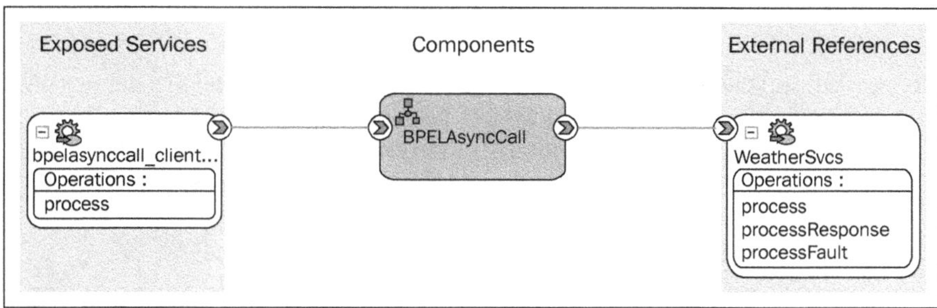

2. In the BPEL process, we first assign the parameters for the web service. Next, we invoke web service with the `<invoke>` activity as follows:

```
<invoke name = "InvokeAsyncWS" inputVariable =
  "InvokeAsyncWS_process_InputVariable" partnerLink =
    "AsyncWS" portType = "ns1:HelloWorldAsyncProcess"
      operation = "process" bpelx:invokeAsDetail = "no"/>
```

3. In order to receive the response from the called web service, we need to use the `<receive>` activity, which presents an entry point for the web service callback method as follows:

```
<receive name = "ReceiveAsyncWS" createInstance = "no"
  variable = "ReceiveAsyncWS_processResponse_InputVariable"
    partnerLink = "AsyncWS" portType =
      "ns1:HelloWorldAsyncProcessCallback"
        operation = "processResponse"/>
```

4. Now, we are ready to deploy the BPEL process and test it inside the Oracle Enterprise Management Console. In the excerpt of **Audit Trail**, we observe that the web service was invoked in an asynchronous way as follows:

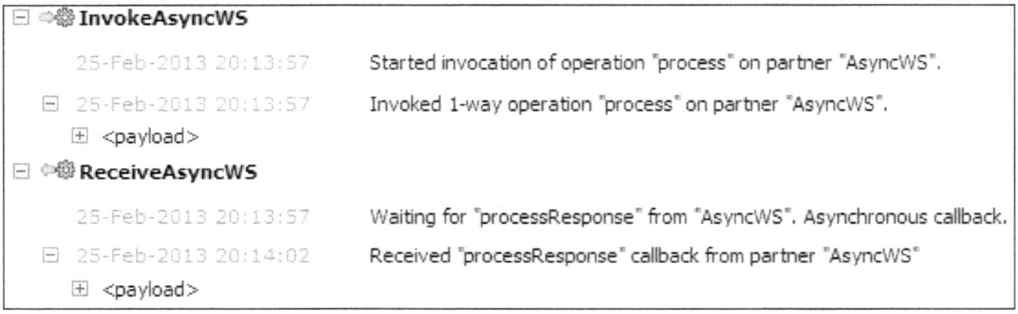

InvokeAsyncWS

25-Feb-2013 20:13:57	Started invocation of operation "process" on partner "AsyncWS".
25-Feb-2013 20:13:57	Invoked 1-way operation "process" on partner "AsyncWS".
<payload>	

ReceiveAsyncWS

25-Feb-2013 20:13:57	Waiting for "processResponse" from "AsyncWS". Asynchronous callback.
25-Feb-2013 20:14:02	Received "processResponse" callback from partner "AsyncWS"
<payload>	

How it works...

As with the synchronous web services, the asynchronous web services are also defined by the WSDL documents. If we check the port type, we spot the difference. Opposite to the synchronous web service, the asynchronous web service defines two port types as follows:

```
<wsdl:portType name = "HelloWorldAsyncProcess">
  <wsdl:operation name = "process">
    <wsdl:input message =
      "client:HelloWorldAsyncProcessRequestMessage"/>
  </wsdl:operation>
</wsdl:portType>
<wsdl:portType name = "HelloWorldAsyncProcessCallback">
  <wsdl:operation name = "processResponse">
    <wsdl:input message =
      "client:HelloWorldAsyncProcessResponseMessage"/>
  </wsdl:operation>
</wsdl:portType>
```

The port type definition comes out of the asynchronous nature of the web service. The two port types define the two one-way operations.

We call the asynchronous web service from BPEL with the `<invoke>` activity as follows:

```
<invoke name = "InvokeAsyncWS" inputVariable =
  "InvokeAsyncWS_process_InputVariable" partnerLink =
    "AsyncWS" portType = "ns1:HelloWorldAsyncProcess"
      operation = "process"/>
```

Due to the one-way mechanism, only the input variable is specified and no output variable.

To receive the reply from the web service call, we use the `<receive>` activity as follows:

```
<receive name = "ReceiveAsyncWS" createInstance = "no"
  variable = "ReceiveAsyncWS_processResponse_InputVariable"
    partnerLink = "AsyncWS" portType =
      "ns1:HelloWorldAsyncProcessCallback"
        operation = "processResponse"/>
```

The `<receive>` activity is different from the `<invoke>` activity. Based on the WS-Addressing (address and conversation ID) mechanism, the `<receive>` activity picks up the correct message from the web service. Although we are using the `<receive>` activity, the BPEL process will wait until it receives the response. We need to define the name of the `variable`, `partnerLink`, `portType`, and `operation`.

There's more...

We can also declare the fault in the asynchronous web service port type. Due to the one-way operation of the web service, we can only define the faults in the callback port type. Again, the faults are used when the web service cannot complete its operation successfully. The port type definition then states as follows:

```
<wsdl:portType name = "HelloWorldAsyncProcessCallback">
  <wsdl:operation name = "processResponse">
    <wsdl:input message =
      "client:HelloWorldAsyncProcessResponseMessage"/>
  </wsdl:operation>
  <wsdl:operation name = "processFault">
    <wsdl:input message = "client:ProcessFaultMessage"/>
  </wsdl:operation>
</wsdl:portType>
```

We see that the fault is modeled as an additional operation. The faults in the BPEL process are then modeled via the `<pick>` activity as follows:

```
<pick name = "PickMsg">
  <onMessage variable = "OnMessage_processResponse_InputVariable"
    partnerLink = "AsyncWS" portType =
      "ns1:HelloWorldAsyncProcessCallback" operation =
        "processResponse">
    <assign name = "AssignOK">
      <copy>
        <from expression = "string('OK')"/>
        <to variable = "outputVariable" part = "payload"
          query = "/client:processResponse/client:result"/>
      </copy>
    </assign>
  </onMessage>
  <onMessage variable = "OnMessage_processFault_InputVariable"
    partnerLink = "AsyncWS" portType =
      "ns1:HelloWorldAsyncProcessCallback" operation =
        "processFault">
    <assign name = "AssignFault">
      <copy>
        <from expression = "string('FAULT')"/>
        <to variable = "outputVariable" part = "payload"
          query = "/client:processResponse/client:result"/>
      </copy>
    </assign>
  </onMessage>
</pick>
```

The graphical presentation of the BPEL process is as follows:

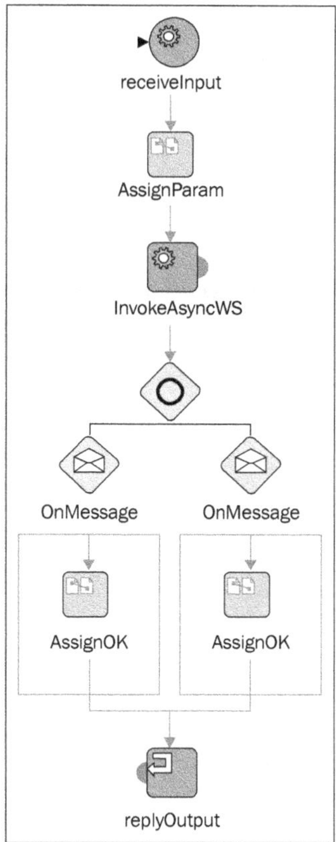

Based on the type of the message returned from the asynchronous web service, we can decide on how to proceed with the BPEL process execution.

Another approach of modeling the asynchronous web service call from the BPEL process is usage of the event handlers to react on occurring of the message or alarm event.

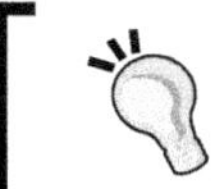

More information on the event handlers can be found in the official Oracle documentation available at `http://docs.oracle.com/cd/E19182-01/821-0539/ggbyb/index.html`.

See also

- For calling the synchronous web services, see the previous recipe *Invoking the synchronous web service*
- In cases when the fault handling needs to be implemented, see the *Handling the faults thrown from the web service* recipe
- We have covered the asynchronous transport in *Chapter 1, Calling the asynchronous BPEL process from Java*

The dynamic selection of the web service's endpoint

In this recipe, we will explore how to dynamically call web services from the BPEL process. Such an approach can be useful in an early stage of the SOA adoption or when we don't have the middleware infrastructure set up yet and we have, for example, a set of redundant web services. In such a scenario, we need to provide ourselves with the functionality for the BPEL process to dynamically select the web service's endpoint.

Getting ready

We start this recipe by deploying the same web service to multiple instances of the servers. We decided to use the hotel reservation service from the *Implementing web services with Axis2* recipe. We deployed the web service to the three instances of the server. The interface of web service remains the same; however, the address on which the web services reside do change as follows:

```
Server 1: <soap:address location =
  "http://192.168.1.101:7777/axis2/services/BookHotelService/"/>
Server 2: <soap:address location =
  "http://192.168.1.101:8888/axis2/services/BookHotelService/"/>
Server 3: <soap:address location =
"http://192.168.1.101:9999/axis2/services/BookHotelService/"/>
```

How to do it...

In the following steps, we will describe the actions to be performed in order to configure the BPEL process to dynamically select the web services endpoint:

1. First we create the BPEL process. The BPEL process can either be synchronous or asynchronous. As an input parameter we take two dates, presenting the `from` and `to` reservation dates as follows:

   ```
   <element name = "process">
     <complexType>
   ```

```
    <sequence>
      <element minOccurs = "0" name = "from" nillable =
        "true" type = "dateTime"/>
      <element minOccurs = "0" name = "to" nillable =
        "true" type = "dateTime"/>
    </sequence>
  </complexType>
</element>
```

We introduce the decision element. The criteria we took is the year of the `from` parameter as shown in the following figure:

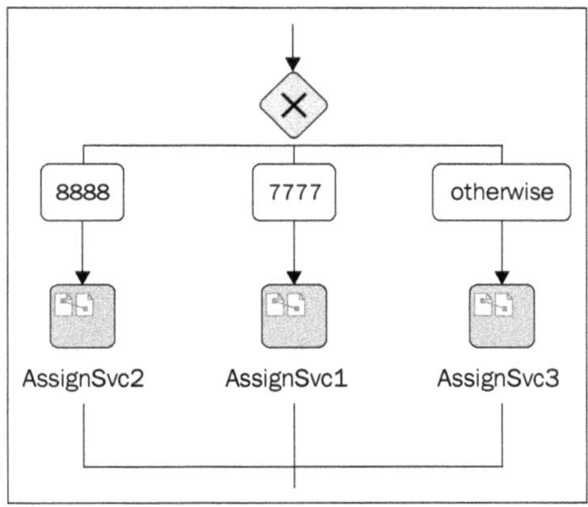

2. Based on the decision criteria, we set the endpoint parameters for the web service. We created the `EndpointReference` variable and initialize it with the following literal:

```
    <copy>
      <from><EndpointReference xmlns =
        "http://schemas.xmlsoap.org/ws/2003/03/addressing">
  <Address/>
</EndpointReference></from>
      <to variable = "EndpointReference"/>
    </copy>
```

3. Based on the decision criteria, we set the web service endpoint address as follows:

```
<bpelx:append>
  <bpelx:from variable = "address"/>
  <bpelx:to variable = "EndpointReference"
    query = "/ns2:EndpointReference/ns2:Address"/>
</bpelx:append>
```

4. Finally, we copy the endpoint reference variable to the `partnerLink` element as follows:

```
    <copy>
      <from variable = "EndpointReference"/>
      <to partnerLink = "BookHotelSvc"/>
    </copy>
  </assign>
```

5. We model the BPEL process so that the parameters are set to the web service variable, the web service is invoked, and after the web service invocation the results are picked up as shown in the following screenshot:

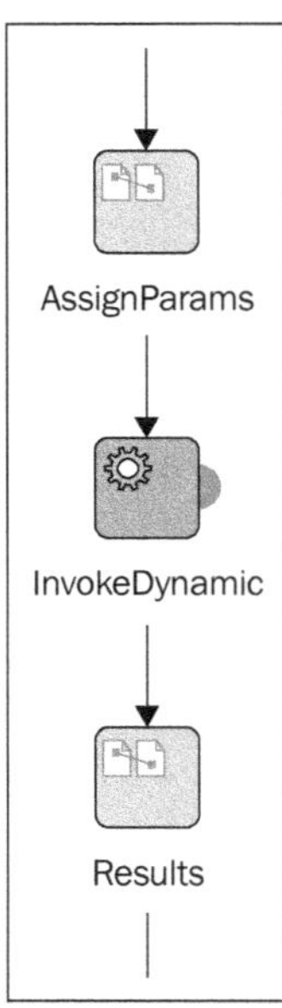

How it works...

One of the advantages of the BPEL processes is that it is possible to invoke a web service with the dynamic partner links. If we have redundant web services, it is the easiest way of using the dynamic partner links. That way we simply change the address of the web service endpoint, and we can immediately consume the web service.

> The dynamic partner links, as shown in this recipe, are supported only for the BPEL 1.1 specification BPEL processes.

The dynamic partner links take advantage of the WSA mechanism. In WSA, the various data about the web service endpoint can be found. The only two parameters that can be changed are as follows:

- `<wsa:Adress>`: This defines the location of the web service endpoint
- `<wsa:ServiceName>`: This defines the name of the service and the port used

> The recipe will work only in the web service, which will use the dynamic partner links that will have the same web service interface (`messages`, `portType`, and `binding`).

There's more...

It is also possible to extend our BPEL process to include the partner links of all three web services. Then, we model the BPEL process same way as we have in this recipe. The only difference is in the assign activity, where we now set the endpoint address data. Instead of dynamically assigning data to the invoke activity, we could use three separate invoke activities and set one partner link to each of them.

Actually , the dynamic selection of the web service is highly dependent on the infrastructure we have at our disposal. This recipe explained the dynamic selection of web services with no external help of other technologies. We could, however, use the service registry for web service discovery along with late binding through a mediator.

See also

- For the web service implementation and deployment, see the *Implementing web services with Axis2* recipe

Invoking web services in a sequence

In this recipe, we will identify how to call web services in a sequence from the BPEL process. The sequential web service invocation presents one of the basic workflow concepts. We use this approach when we have several web services in our business process and each of them needs to wait for the previous one to finish.

Getting ready

We need to set up an environment where we can access multiple web services. Since the BPEL processes are also exposed as web services, we can also call another BPEL process in a sequence.

How to do it...

The following steps explain how to call a web service in a sequence from the BPEL process:

1. We will start with the creation of an empty BPEL process. We can choose the synchronous or asynchronous BPEL process. We start by adding the web services references to the SOA composite. We add the following two web service references:
   - `BookHotelSvc`: This web reference helps to gather the hotel names that have available rooms in a selected period
   - `RoomPriceSvc`: This web reference queries the room price in the hotel

   The SOA composite or **SCA** (**Service Composition Architecture**) outlook is as shown in the following screenshot:

   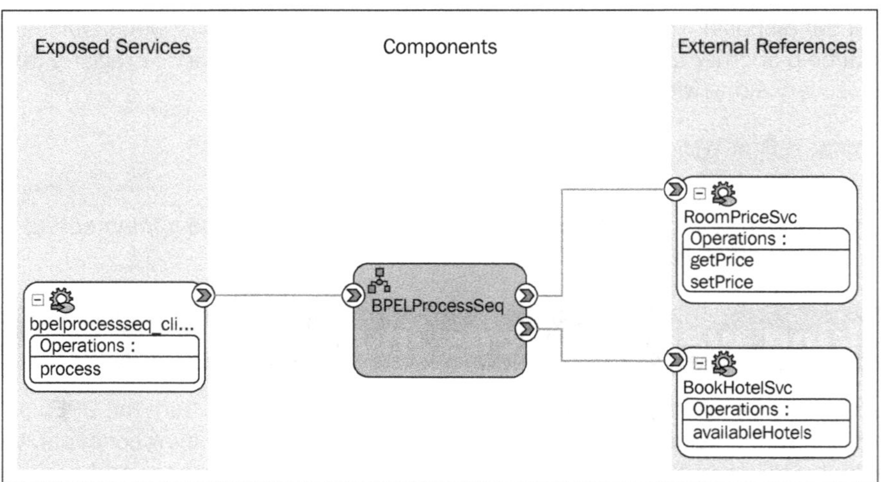

   In the SCA we can see the interconnection between the BPEL processes, how the BPEL process is exposed as web service, and which web services the BPEL process is referencing. We describe here the SCA from the BPEL process point of view; however, other components, such as human tasks, mediator components, business rules, and various adapters fit in.

2. We will continue by modeling the BPEL process. We add the sequence activity and continue with the assign and invoke activity combination for both web services we want to call as follows:

```
<sequence name = "Hotels_And_Prices">
  <assign name = "AssignAvailHotels">
    <copy>
      <from>xp20:current-dateTime()</from>
      <to>$AvailableHotels_availableHotels_InputVariable.
        parameters/ns1:from</to>
    </copy>
    <copy>
      <from>xp20:current-dateTime()</from>
      <to>$AvailableHotels_availableHotels_InputVariable.
        parameters/ns1:to</to>
    </copy>
  </assign>
<invoke name = "AvailableHotels" bpelx:invokeAsDetail =
  "no" partnerLink = "BookHotelSvc" portType =
    "ns1:HotelBooking" operation = "availableHotels"
      inputVariable =
        "AvailableHotels_availableHotels_InputVariable"
          outputVariable =
            "AvailableHotels_availableHotels_OutputVariable"/>
  <assign name = "AssignRoomPrice">
    <copy>
      <from>$inputVariable.payload/client:input</from>
      <to>$GetRoomPrice_getPrice_InputVariable.parameters
        </to>
    </copy>
  </assign>
<invoke name = "GetRoomPrice" bpelx:invokeAsDetail = "no"
  partnerLink = "RoomPriceSvc" portType =
    "ns2:RoomPriceServicePortType" operation = "getPrice"
      inputVariable = "GetRoomPrice_getPrice_InputVariable"
        outputVariable =
          "GetRoomPrice_getPrice_OutputVariable"/>
</sequence>
```

3. We deploy the BPEL process to the server and run it from the Oracle Enterprise Manager Console. We check **Audit Trail** of the BPEL process instance. We can observe that the web services we run are in a sequence, one after another, as shown in the following screenshot:

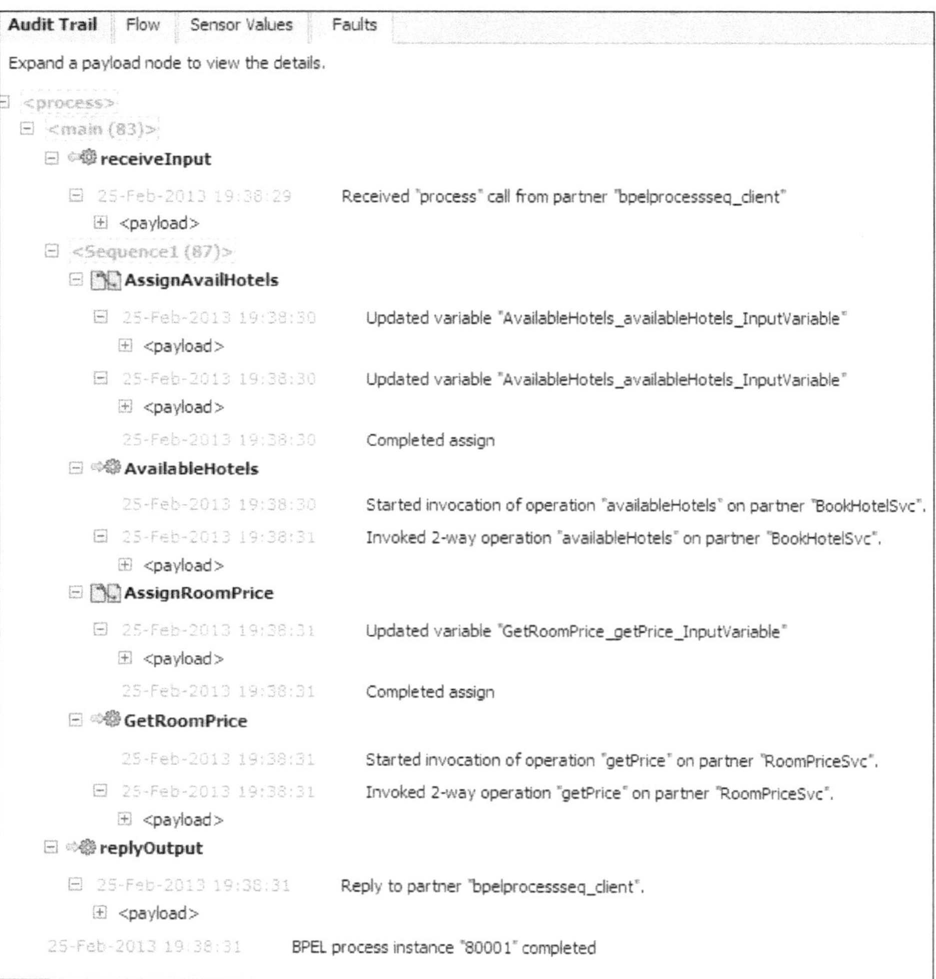

How it works...

In cases when the calls to multiple web services are dependent, we use the sequential execution of web services. Such a case can, for example, be a loan approval. Suppose we have a web service for the loan approval and a web service for the money transfer. It is obvious that money cannot be transferred before the loan is approved.

The sequence execution of web services in the BPEL process is achieved through the sequence activity. We used the sequence activity in this recipe in order to ensure that we get the price of the hotel room, only if the room is available.

See also

- To develop and deploy web services, see the *Implementing web services with Axis2* and *Implementing web services with JAX-WS* recipes

Invoking web services in parallel

In cases where the invocation of web services is not interdependent, we can invoke web services in parallel. The parallel invocation shortens the BPEL process execution time. In this recipe, we will show you how to invoke web services in parallel.

Getting ready

For this recipe we will consume two web services. We will check for the hotel room and car availability in parallel. The availability data will give us information on hotels, where the rooms are available, and a car that is available for the date range. In order to complete the recipe, we need to deploy `BookHotelService` and `BookCarService`. The procedure for deploying web services can be taken from the *Implementing web services with Axis2* recipe.

How to do it...

The following steps will cover the necessary activities to design the BPEL process for the parallel web service invocation:

1. We start by creating the SOA composite. We add two web service references and wire them to the BPEL process as shown in the following screenshot:

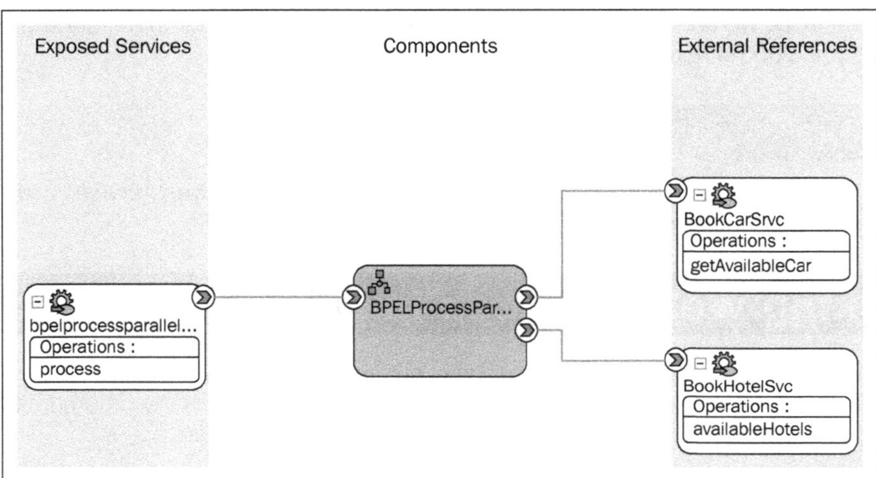

2. We start modeling the BPEL process by assigning the parameters for the web service calls. In the assign activity, we map the input parameters to the web service's input parameters as follows:

```
<assign name = "AssignData">
  <copy>
    <from variable = "inputVariable" part="payload"
      query = "/client:process/client:from"/>
    <to variable =
      "InvokeHotelSrvc_availableHotels_InputVariable"
        part = "parameters" query =
          "/ns2:availableHotels/from"/>
  </copy>
  <copy>
    <from variable = "inputVariable" part = "payload"
      query = "/client:process/client:to"/>
    <to variable =
      "InvokeHotelSrvc_availableHotels_InputVariable"
        part = "parameters"
          query = "/ns2:availableHotels/to"/>
  </copy>
```

```
    <copy>
      <from variable = "inputVariable" part = "payload"
        query = "/client:process/client:from"/>
      <to variable =
        "InvokeCarSrvc_getAvailableCar_InputVariable"
          part = "parameters"
            query = "/ns1:getAvailableCar/ns1:from"/>
    </copy>
    <copy>
      <from variable = "inputVariable" part = "payload"
        query = "/client:process/client:to"/>
      <to variable =
        "InvokeCarSrvc_getAvailableCar_InputVariable"
          part = "parameters"
            query = "/ns1:getAvailableCar/ns1:to"/>
    </copy>
  </assign>
```

3. Next, we include the `<flow>` activity that enables the parallel processing. Inside the `<flow>` activity we add two `<invoke>` activities for the web service calls as shown in the following screenshot:

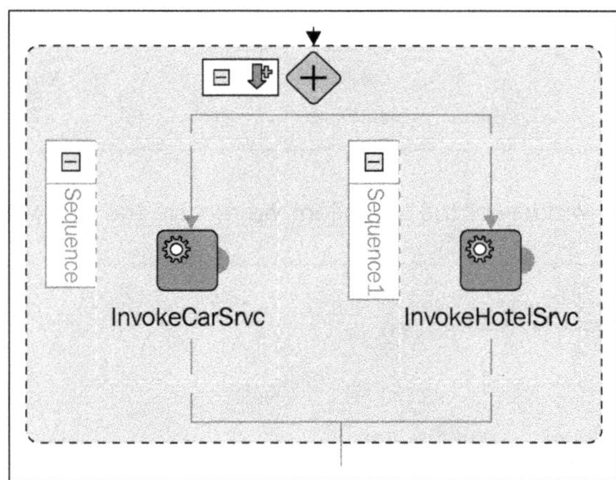

4. We use the `<assign>` activity for mapping the results to the output variable as follows:

```
<assign name = "Result">
  <copy>
    <from expression = "concat(string(bpws:getVariableData
      ('InvokeHotelSrvc_availableHotels_OutputVariable',
        'parameters','/ns2:availableHotelsResponse/
          hotels')), '  ', bpws:getVariableData
            ('InvokeCarSrvc_getAvailableCar_OutputVariable',
```

```
                'parameters',
                 '/ns1:getAvailableCarResponse/ns1:return'))
                   "/>
      <to variable = "outputVariable" part = "payload"
        query = "/client:processResponse/client:result"/>
    </copy>
  </assign>
```

5. We continue the recipe by deploying the BPEL process to the BPEL server and test it via the Oracle Enterprise Management Console. The test request dialog for the BPEL process is shown in the following screenshot:

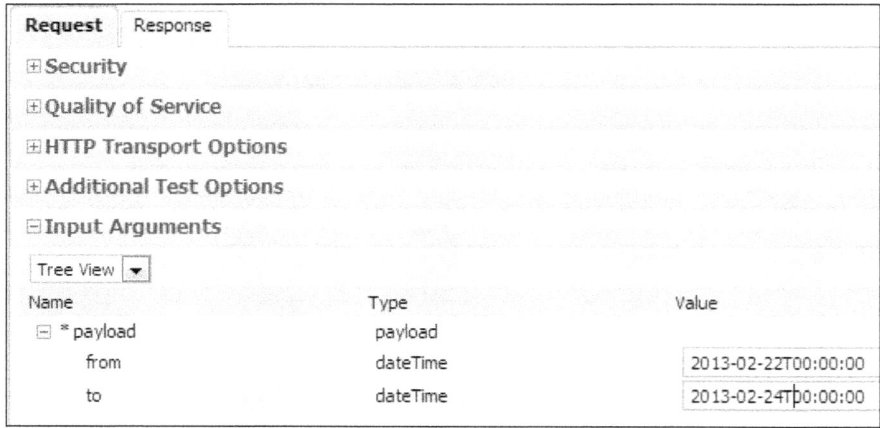

6. In the response window of the test client we receive the following text:

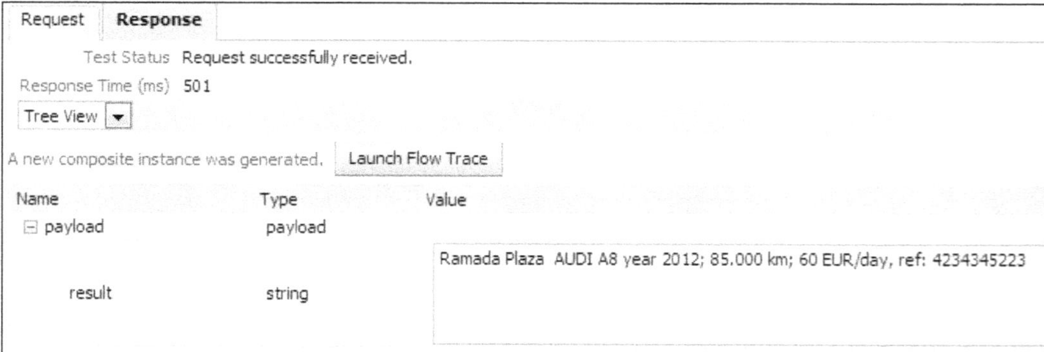

7. In the excerpt of the **Audit Trail** of the BPEL process, we see that two web services were invoked in parallel. They were invoked at the same time, as shown in the following screenshot:

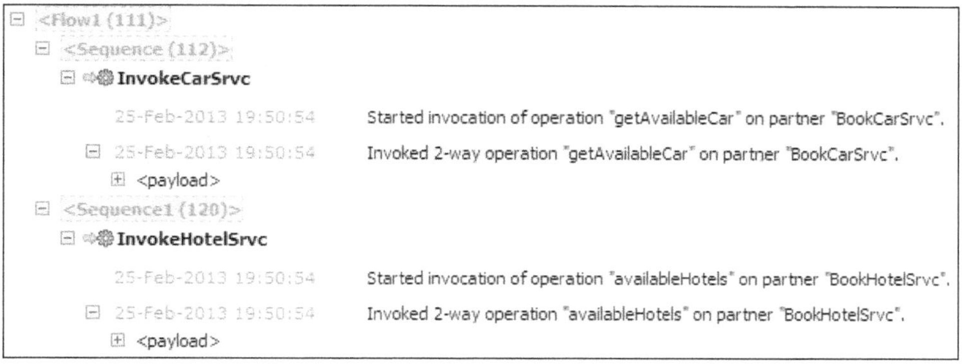

```
<Flow1 (111)>
  <Sequence (112)>
    InvokeCarSrvc
      25-Feb-2013 19:50:54   Started invocation of operation "getAvailableCar" on partner "BookCarSrvc".
      25-Feb-2013 19:50:54   Invoked 2-way operation "getAvailableCar" on partner "BookCarSrvc".
        <payload>
  <Sequence1 (120)>
    InvokeHotelSrvc
      25-Feb-2013 19:50:54   Started invocation of operation "availableHotels" on partner "BookHotelSrvc".
      25-Feb-2013 19:50:54   Invoked 2-way operation "availableHotels" on partner "BookHotelSrvc".
        <payload>
```

How it works...

The BPEL specification provides the `<flow>` activity for the purpose of concurrency and synchronization. If there is a need to invoke web services in parallel, then we should use the `<flow>` activity. The activity also ensures that all web services provide a reply before continuing the BPEL process.

There's more...

It is possible to combine sequence and parallel execution of web services. We can bring the sequential execution into the parallel execution, and vice versa. We will show on the abstract layer how a mix of sequential and parallel processing is achieved.

Let's take our recipe and extend it with a requirement that, when we receive information about the hotel and car, we would like to confirm the reservation. We omit the details from the code and leave only the activities. The BPEL process now reads as follows:

```
<sequence name = "Sequence">
  <flow name = "Flow1">
    <sequence name = "Sequence1">
      <invoke name = "InvokeCarSrvc"/>
    </sequence>
    <sequence name = "Sequence2">
      <invoke name = "InvokeHotelSrvc"/>
    </sequence>
  </flow>
  <invoke name = "InvokeConfirmReservation"/>
</sequence>
```

We see that the `<invoke>` activities are nested into the `<flow>` and `<sequence>` activities.

See also

- To explore the sequential invocation of web services in the BPEL process, see the *Invoking web service in a sequence* recipe

Handling the faults thrown from a web service

The faults are one of the most important aspects of the BPEL process. In this recipe, we will explore how to handle the faults that are thrown from the web service.

Getting ready

This recipe explains how to handle the faults thrown from the synchronous web service.

How to do it...

We will modify the BPEL process we created in the *Invoking web services in parallel* recipe and name it `BPELProcessFault`. If we now run the BPEL process, it will complete with the faults. Now, we have to adapt the BPEL process in order to catch the faults thrown from the web service.

1. We add the `<catch>` activity to the scope, where we invoke the web service. We model the `<catch>` activity with the following parameters:

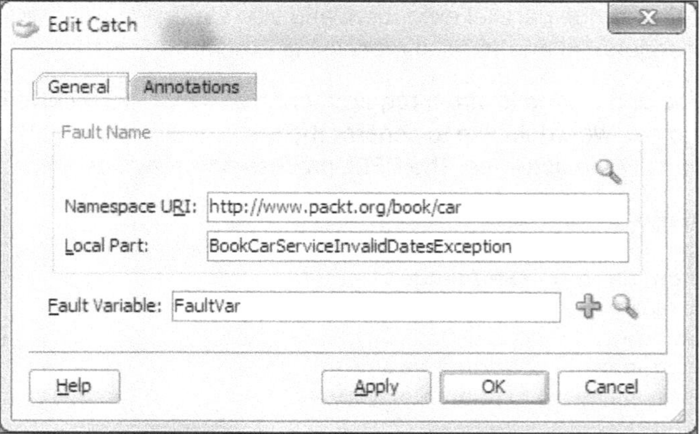

2. Inside the `<catch>` activity we add the `<assign>` activity, where we report that something went wrong to the client calling our process as follows:

```
<faultHandlers>
  <catch faultName =
    "ns1:BookCarServiceInvalidDatesException"
      faultVariable = "FaultVar">
    <assign name = "AssignFault">
      <copy>
        <from expression = "string
          ('Problem with the BPEL process !!!!!')"/>
        <to variable = "outputVariable" part = "payload"
          query = "/client:processResponse/client:result"/>
      </copy>
    </assign>
  </catch>
</faultHandlers>
```

The final outlook of the BPEL process for handling faults is as follows:

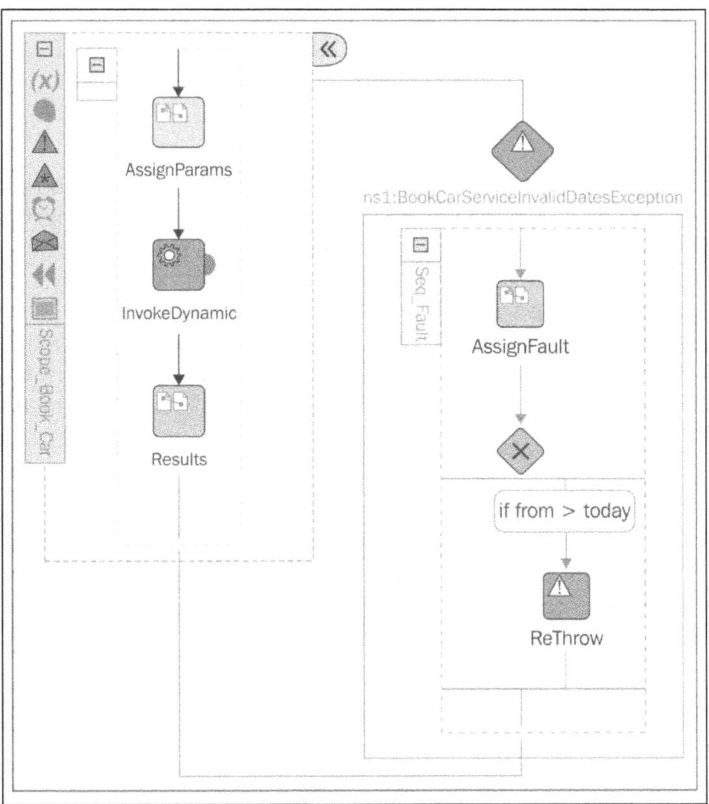

3. Now, if we run the BPEL process that finishes successfully, we get the following response:

Name	Type	Value
⊟ payload	payload	
result	string	AUDI A8 year 2012; 85.000 km; 60 EUR/day, ref: 4234345223

4. In case of the fault, we receive the following response from the BPEL process:

Name	Type	Value
⊟ payload	payload	
result	string	Problem with the BPEL process !!!!!

How it works...

The faults are specified in the port type when we invoke the synchronous web service. The web service itself creates the fault and fills it with information about the fault. This fault message is received by the BPEL process that invokes faulted web service. Based on the criteria about the fault message, the BPEL process catches the fault with the information within. Based on the fault type and information inside the fault, we can decide how to proceed with the BPEL process execution. The fault handler can affect only the scope that encloses it. When the fault occurs in the scope, the BPEL process execution continues after the scope definition. If the fault handler is attached to the outer most scope, then the BPEL process finishes after the fault is handled.

There's more...

There are cases where the fault message is not known. If we cannot define the message or we fail to catch every fault that comes from the web service invocation, we utilize the `<catchAll>` activity. The `<catchAll>` activity does not have any conditions and simply consumes any fault coming into the BPEL process.

We can have multiple <catch> activities per scope in the BPEL process; however, there must exist only one <catchAll> activity per scope. The same functionality can be found in the Java programming language. We can see the BPEL <catch> activity as the Java catch statement with the named exception. Similarly, we can see that the BPEL <catchAll> activity is similar to the Java statement `catch(Exception e)`.

Throwing the faults from BPEL

In this recipe, we will identify the ways of how to throw the faults from BPEL. For this recipe, we will adapt the BPEL process from the previous recipe.

How to do it...

In the previous recipe, we saw that the web service performed the check against the dates. However, we would like to change the BPEL process so that some basic checking on the dates is performed in the BPEL process. We will check if the `from` and `to` dates are the same. If they are the same, we will throw the fault.

1. We start by defining the new schema element for the fault.

```
<element name = "faultResponse">
  <complexType>
    <sequence>
      <element name = "msg" type = "string"/>
    </sequence>
  </complexType>
</element>
```

2. We also define the new message in WSDL that will hold information about the fault.

```
<wsdl:message name = "EqualDatesFault">
  <wsdl:part name = "fault"
    element = "client:faultResponse"/>
</wsdl:message>
```

3. In the next step, we extend the port type of the BPEL process. Notice the fault element that we added.

```
<wsdl:portType name = "BPELProcessFault">
  <wsdl:operation name = "process">
    <wsdl:input message =
      "client:BPELProcessFaultRequestMessage"/>
    <wsdl:output message =
      "client:BPELProcessFaultResponseMessage"/>
```

```
    <wsdl:fault message = "client:EqualDatesFault" name =
      "fault"/>
  </wsdl:operation>
</wsdl:portType>
```

4. In the BPEL process, we take the `<switch>` activity. We set the condition on dates and put the `<throw>` activity inside of the `<switch>` activity. The `<throw>` activity would throw the fault we defined in the previous steps.

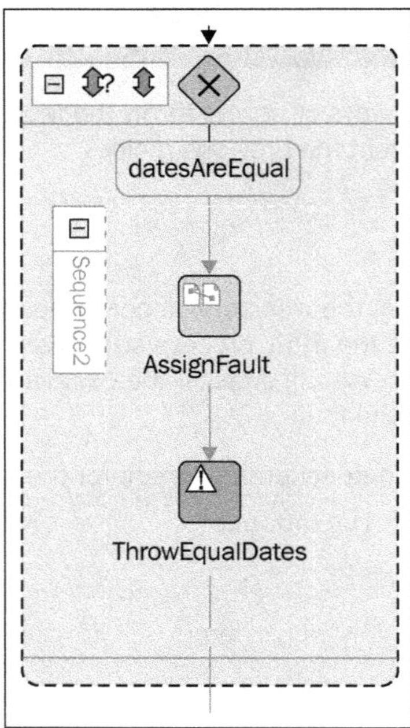

5. Now we run the BPEL process and define the same date in the `from-to` parameters. We can see that the fault was thrown from the BPEL process and that the BPEL process did not finish successfully.

```
ThrowEqualDates
  25-Feb-2013 22:17:09  "{http://xmlns.oracle.com/Seq_and_Parallel_BPEL/ParallelBPEL/BPELProcessFault}fault" has been thrown.
    <payload>
      <bpelFault>
        <faultType>1</faultType>
        <fault>
          <part name="fault">
            <faultResponse>
              <msg>Dates are equal !</msg>
            </faultResponse>
          </part>
        </fault>
      </bpelFault>
```

There's more...

We do a check about the fault in the fault handlers. In cases where the BPEL process cannot recover from the fault, we sometimes want to rethrow the fault to the client, calling the BPEL process.

1. We do this by using the `<throw>` activity. We define the same parameters as we did for the `<catch>` activity as shown in the following screenshot:

2. We set the condition for checking the dates in the `<switch>` activity as follows:

```
bpws:getVariableData('inputVariable','payload',
  '/client:process/client:from') > xp20:current-dateTime()
```

3. The modified fault handler of the BPEL process is as shown in the following screenshot:

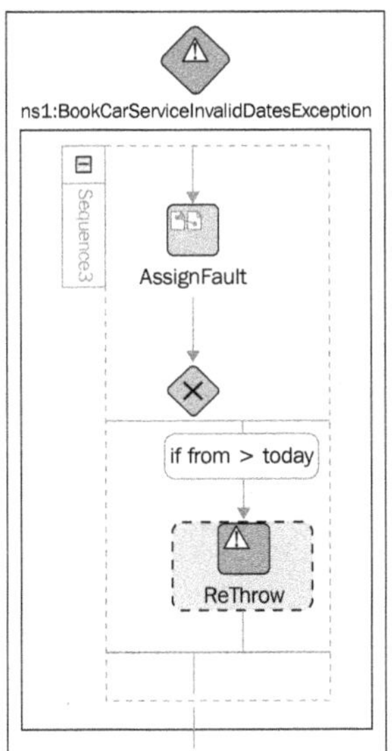

3
Advanced Tracing and Logging

In this chapter, we will cover the following recipes:

- Creating a custom logger in a BPEL process
- Defining composite sensors
- Adding a composite sensor
- Monitoring a composite sensor
- Configuring the logfiles
- Changing the level of tracing
- Editing the logfiles
- Viewing logfiles in the Enterprise Manager Console
- Viewing metrics and statistics

Introduction

In this chapter, we will explore the tracing and logging techniques in the Oracle SOA Suite. Note that the BPEL specification does not define the tracing and logging in a BPEL process. Rather, both functionalities require a BPEL server vendor extension. Tracing as well as logging becomes handy in various situations. If there are problems during BPEL process deployment, we can check the logfiles to see what went wrong if the error is not recognized from the console.

Another example is in situations where we know something is wrong inside a BPEL process; however, we are unable to pinpoint the exact position in the code. In that case, we use the tracing functionality to drill down into the problem to find the root cause of the situation we are investigating. The tracing functionality is also used for tracking a business process execution. Tracing provides insightful information on the steps performed by the business process. Tracing is more focused on the business process execution while logging is more oriented towards what is happening with the system. Of course, we have no problem configuring logging to be enabled only for a particular component. We can distinguish between the tracing and logging functionality from the point of view of the context they cover. While logging covers mainly the technical details of BPEL process execution, it is fair enough to say that tracing is more often used to cover the business aspects of BPEL process execution. Oracle SOA Suite provides two instruments for efficient tracing described as follows:

- **End-to-end instance tracing**: We can trace a business process from start to finish inside the Oracle SOA Suite boundaries. With end-to-end instance tracing, we are able to trace all the data and flow from the beginning to the end of the BPEL process execution, being either response, fault, exit, or termination. For example, we can trace the business process that initiates from the portal. Also, the request from/to **Oracle Service Bus** (**OSB**) can be traced. Further more, we can trace a BPEL process and its external web services interaction and also the human task workflow interaction. In a single trace, we can receive, for example, a call from one BPEL process to an other BPEL process.
- **Sensors**: Sensors are used as a springboard when we need to investigate the facts of a business process. Facts, for example, are presented in variables holding information, either business or process type. If we want to start investigating some problem, we need to gather information about the business process, and here we can utilize the sensors. In the Oracle SOA Suite, we can define two types of sensors:
    - **Composite sensors** are defined at the level of **SCA** (**Service Component Architecture**) composite. Remember we said that SCA involves interconnection between BPEL processes, how a BPEL process is exposed as a web service, and which web services a BPEL process is referencing. The composite sensors provide the ability to implement tractable fields on messages. We use composite sensors to monitor incoming and outgoing messages. The composite sensors are defined for the services and the referenced bindings.
    - **BPEL process sensors** are defined inside a business process. We can define BPEL sensors on variables, faults, and activities.

The sensor values are propagated via different channels. The common channel where data for both types of sensors is published is the database storage. Additional to this, the BPEL process sensor values can be propagated via a JMS queue, JMS topic, Custom Java class, and JMS adapter. We can observe the values of the sensors via the Oracle Enterprise Manager Console. The sensor values are seen in flow trace information of a business process instance. Sensor information has a separated section along with the flow of BPEL process and fault occurred in the business process.

The logging functionality provides very valuable information about what is happening inside the application. With the logging information, we can gather information about problems in the application, identify the flow of the problem, and learn the application's functioning. In the distributed environments where business processes run, the logging functionality is a fundamental requirement for the inter-exchange of information between systems. We can find different logging flavors in the Oracle SOA Suite. The fundamental logging system is the **Java Utilities Logging** (**JUL**) utility. We can also use the LOG4J logging framework. As the native logging support, Oracle SOA Suite uses the **Oracle diagnostic logging** (**ODL**) functionality.

The LOG4J project home page can be accessed at the following URL:
`http://logging.apache.org/log4j/1.2/`

The elements that perform the logging job consist of formatters and handlers. The formatter defines the layout of the information to be logged. We have a plethora of formatters. For example, `XMLFormatter` wraps the logging content into XML and passes the content to the defined handler. As a result, we are able to see the XML formatted logging information. While the formatters define how the logging information will look, we can say that the handlers define where the logging information will be stored. While `ConsoleHandler` defines that logging information is printed to the console, `FileHandler` stores the logging information into a file.

In the following table, we summarize the most common properties of the three mentioned logging facilities:

Logging mechanism	Configuration	Formatters	Handlers

Java Utilities Logging	Properties file / via code	`SimpleFormatter`
		`XMLFormatter`
			`StreamHandler`
			`ConsoleHandler`
			`FileHandler`
			`SocketHandler`
			`MemoryHandler`

LOG4J	Properties file / via code	`EnhancedPatternLayout`
		`HTMLLayout`
		`PatternLayout`
		`SimpleLayout`
		`XMLLayout`
		`SerializedLayout`
		`SyslogLayout`
			`ConsoleAppender`
			`FileAppender`
			`JMSQueueAppender`
			`JMSTopicAppender`
			`OutputStreamAppender`
			`RollingFileAppender`
			`SMTPAppender`
			`SocketAppender`
			`SyslogAppender`

Logging mechanism	Configuration	Formatters	Handlers
ODL	Properties file / via Oracle Enterprise Manager Console	The logs are produced as plain text or XML	Primarily logging to the file

Each of the logging mechanisms also supports different types of log levels. Log levels define the granularity of the logging information. For example, the DEBUG log level shows all the logging information that exists, while the ERROR log level shows only critical business process information such as occurring exceptions. It is important to set a proper log level in order not to not collect too much or too little logging information. If we have too much logging information, it is much more difficult to find errors. The following table shows the mapping of the log levels between different logging mechanisms:

Java Utilities Logging	LOG4J	ODL
SEVERE	ERROR	INCIDENT_ERROR:1
	FATAL	INCIDENT_ERROR:4
		INCIDENT_ERROR:14
		INCIDENT_ERROR:24
		ERROR:1
WARNING	WARN	ERROR:7
		WARNING:1
		WARNING:7
INFO	INFO	NOTIFICATION:1
CONFIG	N/A	NOTIFICATION:16
FINE	DEBUG	TRACE:1
FINER	TRACE	TRACE:16
FINEST	TRACE	TRACE:32

The following recipes will show you how to most effectively utilize the tracing and logging functionality of Oracle SOA Suite.

Creating a custom logger in a BPEL process

In this recipe, we will define a custom logger for a BPEL process. We will define a custom logger as an addition to the already existing loggers available for BPEL processes. The custom loggers are used in a scenario where there is a special requirement that ODL cannot fulfill, for example, if some logging information needs to be sent over the TCP socket, or if we want to provide special formatting types for logging.

Getting ready

Before we start with the recipe, we need to deploy a BPEL process. We will use the BPEL process from the *Calling web services in sequence* recipe defined in *Chapter 2, Calling Services from BPEL*. We defined two web services. The first one gives us the list of available hotels in the predefined date range. With a call to the next web service, we receive the price for the room in the hotel. Finally, we check for the car reservation.

How to do it...

In the following steps, we define the actions that need to be performed in order to define a custom logger in a BPEL process:

1. We start the recipe by defining the Java class for the custom logger. For the purpose of logging, we will use `JUL`. We name the class `LogTheBpel` and put it into the `org.packt.log` package. We retrieve the logger by using name criteria:

   ```
   private static final Logger logger = Logger.getLogger("oracle.soa.
   Logger");
   ```

   > `oracle.soa.Logger` is a standard Oracle logger where we can log the messages and then inspect them among other messages. Loggers are organized in hierarchies, which provide higher flexibility for filtering that we can set in order to reduce or increase the verbosity of loggers. The loggers are organized in a parent-child relationship. The parent of the logger `oracle.soa.Logger` we use in our example is `oracle.soa`. However, our logger might also have its child logger with the name `oracle.soa.Logger.Process`.

2. We prepare the static method that enables us to log the message as shown in the following code:

   ```
   public static final void log(String message) {
     logger.log(Level.WARNING, message);
   }
   ```

The log method can be defined in different ways. We define one method with two parameters; that is, `log_level` and `message`. Then, we call the method using `log(Level.INFO, "TEST")`. Another approach is to prepare a set of methods for each log level and with only one message parameter. In this case, the call might be like `logInfo("TEST")` or `logWarning("TEST")`. We also need to configure the formatter by issuing the static statement:

```
static {
  LogFormatter.configFormatter(logger);
}
```

3. Before including the custom logger into the BPEL process, it should be tested. For that purpose, we use the JUnit test cases. The following is the test method code:

```
@Test
public void testLog() {
  LogTheBpel.log("Test message");
}
```

   If we run the test case, we see that the run is successful.

4. Now we are ready to introduce the custom logger to the BPEL process. At the very beginning of the BPEL process definition, inside the process tag, we add the import statements for the classes as shown in the following code:

```
<import location="java.util.logging.Logger" importType="http://
schemas.oracle.com/bpel/extension/java"/>
<import location="java.util.logging.Level" importType="http://
schemas.oracle.com/bpel/extension/java"/>
<import location="oracle.fabric.logging.LogFormatter"
importType="http://schemas.oracle.com/bpel/extension/java"/>
```

   With this preceding code, we import the classes that need to be loaded that we can use in our custom logger.

5. Next, we use the Java Embedding activity to call the custom logger as shown in the following code:

```
<extensionActivity>
  <bpelx:exec name="Java_Embedding1" language="java">
    <![CDATA[org.packt.log.LogTheBpel.log("Hello from process with
id: " + getInstanceId());]]>
  </bpelx:exec>
</extensionActivity>
```

6. We initiate the BPEL process and then check the results in the Oracle Enterprise Manager Console. On the SOA domain, we right-click and select **Logs** and **View Log Messages**. We can see that the message from the BPEL process appears in the log as shown in the following screenshot:

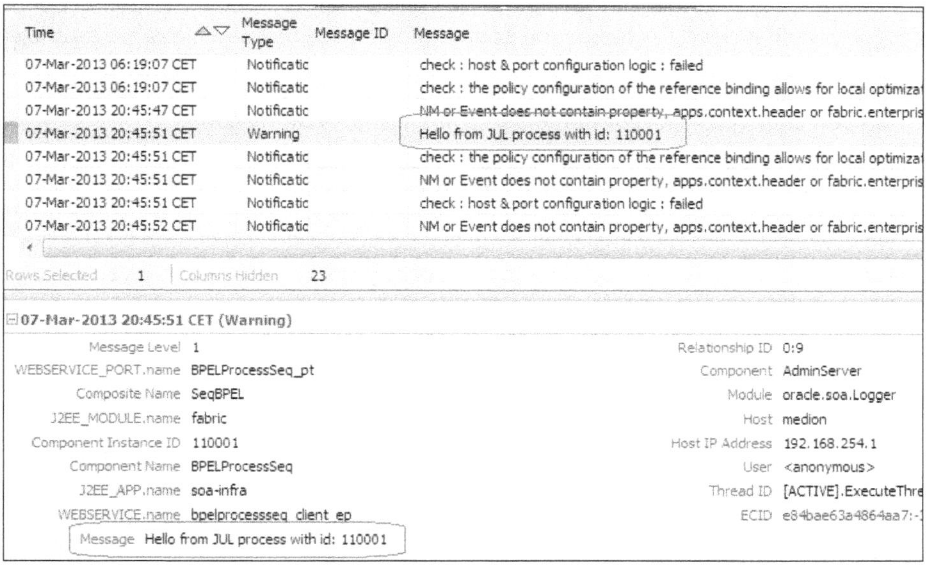

Time	Message Type	Message ID	Message
07-Mar-2013 06:19:07 CET	Notificatic		check : host & port configuration logic : failed
07-Mar-2013 06:19:07 CET	Notificatic		check : the policy configuration of the reference binding allows for local optimiza
07-Mar-2013 20:45:47 CET	Notificatic		NM or Event does not contain property, apps.context.header or fabric.enterpris
07-Mar-2013 20:45:51 CET	Warning		Hello from JUL process with id: 110001
07-Mar-2013 20:45:51 CET	Notificatic		check : the policy configuration of the reference binding allows for local optimiza
07-Mar-2013 20:45:51 CET	Notificatic		NM or Event does not contain property, apps.context.header or fabric.enterpris
07-Mar-2013 20:45:51 CET	Notificatic		check : host & port configuration logic : failed
07-Mar-2013 20:45:52 CET	Notificatic		NM or Event does not contain property, apps.context.header or fabric.enterpris

Rows Selected 1 | Columns Hidden 23

07-Mar-2013 20:45:51 CET (Warning)

Message Level	1	Relationship ID	0:9
WEBSERVICE_PORT.name	BPELProcessSeq_pt	Component	AdminServer
Composite Name	SeqBPEL	Module	oracle.soa.Logger
J2EE_MODULE.name	fabric	Host	medion
Component Instance ID	110001	Host IP Address	192.168.254.1
Component Name	BPELProcessSeq	User	<anonymous>
J2EE_APP.name	soa-infra	Thread ID	[ACTIVE].ExecuteThr
WEBSERVICE.name	bpelprocessseq_client_ep	ECID	e84bae63a4864aa7:-
Message	Hello from JUL process with id: 110001		

How it works...

In this recipe, we utilize the JUL functionality. We use the logger that is standard to the Oracle SOA Suite. Therefore, when we run the BPEL process, we see that our message appears among other log messages.

Note that the recipe is targeted at BPEL 2.0 processes. If we want to use logging in BPEL 1.1 processes, we must follow the following guidelines:

1. Instead of the `<import>` tag in the BPEL definition file, we use the `<bpelx:exec>` tag. This is shown in the following code:

```
<bpelx:exec import="java.util.logging.Logger" />
<bpelx:exec import="java.util.logging.Level" />
<bpelx:exec import="oracle.fabric.logging.LogFormatter" />
```

2. Also, the Java Embedding activity that is used is different for BPEL 1.1 processes as shown in the following code:

```
<bpelx:exec name="Java_Embedding1" language="java" version="1.5">
      <![CDATA[org.packt.log.LogTheBpel.log("Hello from process
with id: " + getInstanceId());]]>
</bpelx:exec>
```

There's more...

In this recipe, we reused the logger from the Oracle SOA Suite. Sometimes, especially in a hurry, such a log presents us with too much information to diagnose. Consequently, we might find ourselves having a trouble identifying the root cause of the problem. To define our own named logger, we first need to change the source of the `LogForBpel` class file as shown in the following steps:

1. We can change the logger name as shown in the following code:

   ```
   private static final Logger logger =
     Logger.getLogger("org.packt.log.Logger");
   ```

2. Now, we register a new logger with the Oracle SOA Suite. We search for the `<domain_home>\config\fmwconfig\servers\AdminServer\logging.xml` file and register our logger:

   ```
   <logger name="org.packt.log" level="WARNING:1">
     <handler name="odl-handler" />
   </logger>
   ```

3. In order to make the changes effective, we need to restart the Oracle SOA Suite server. Next, we redeploy the BPEL process with the changed logger name to the server and run it. We can see that in the Oracle Enterprise Manager Console, the message that was logged under a different logger will appear as shown in the following screenshot:

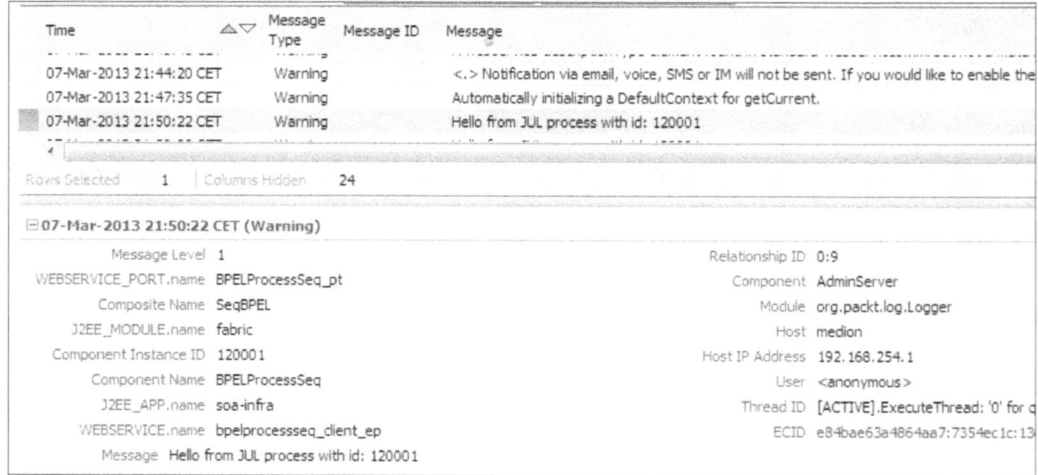

Also, if we want, there is a possibility to filter the messages coming only from our logger, which can be done by a defining proper filter in the Oracle Enterprise Manager Console.

Quick debug logger for the BPEL process

One of the logging methods that the Oracle SOA Suite provides is adding information to the audit trail of the BPEL process. The command is basically a one-liner and is added into the Java Embedding activity:

1. In JDeveloper, we edit the Java Embedding activity and add the `addAuditTrailEntry` command as shown in the following code:

```
<extensionActivity>
  <bpelx:exec name="Java_Log_JUL" language="java">
    <![CDATA[
org.packt.log.LogDynamic.log("Hello from Log4J process with id: "
+ getInstanceId());
addAuditTrailEntry("Info from Java activity. " +
getInstanceId());]]>
  </bpelx:exec>
</extensionActivity>
```

2. In the Audit Trail, we can see that the line message we added in the Java Embedding activity appears as shown in the following screenshot:

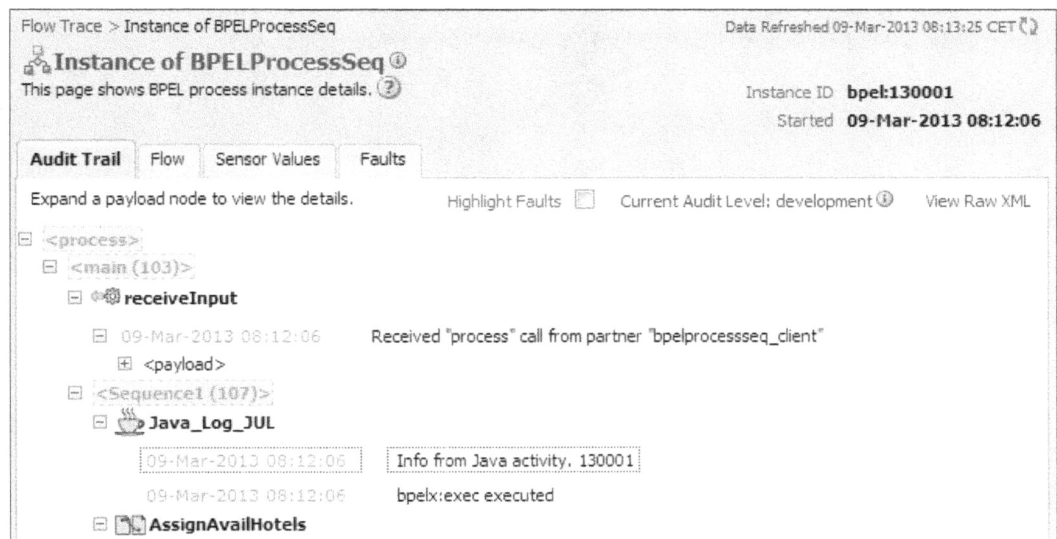

See also

Further discussion of logfiles can be found in the *Configuring the logfiles* recipe of this chapter.

Defining composite sensors

In this recipe, we will examine how to define composite sensors for tracing purposes. Further, we will also show you the ways to define sensors in a BPEL process. We define composite sensors at the level of SCA when we want to monitor input and output messages of a BPEL process. Composite sensors also provide a convenient way of tracking fields on messages.

Getting ready

As a starting point, we need a BPEL process. We can define a new one or reuse an existing one. For this recipe, we will extend the BPEL process that we used in the *Creating a custom logger in a BPEL process* recipe.

How to do it...

In this recipe, we will walk through the steps needed to define a composite sensor in SCA:

1. Initially, open the composite of the BPEL process. In the composite, select the **BookHotelSvc** service. Then, right-click and select **Configure Sensors...** from the toolbar as shown in the following screenshot:

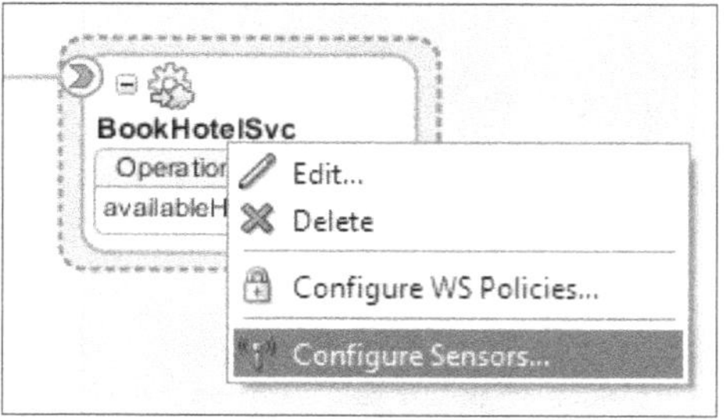

2. We choose to add the sensor to the composite and fill the dialog with the data as shown in the following screenshot:

3. Then, click and get the sensor defined at the composite. Spot the sensor icon at the top right corner of the following screenshot:

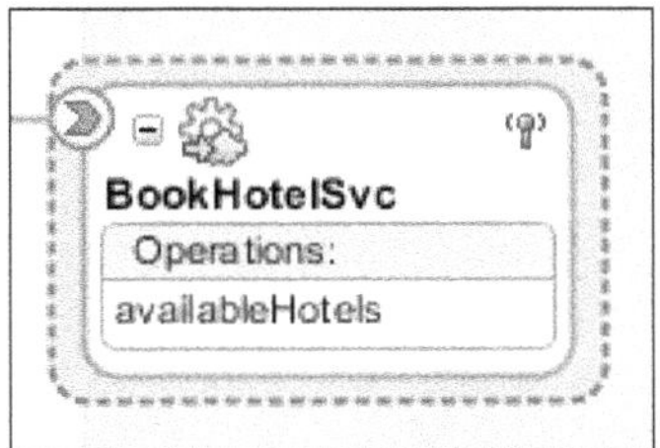

How it works...

The most interesting part of the composite sensor definition is the **Add** dialog. The fields in the dialog have the following meaning:

- **Name**: In this field, we enter the name of the composite sensor. We see the sensor name later in the flow trail of the Oracle SOA Suite Enterprise Manager Console.
- **Operation**: In this field, we specify which operation on a web service that sensor will monitor.
- **Expression**: In this field, we define the expression that sensor will evaluate. The expressions can be as follows:
    - **variables**: The sensor gets the value of the variable we select from the variables dialog
    - **expressions**: The sensor gets the value of the expression we define through the Expression Builder
    - **properties**: The sensor gets the value of the message header property
- **Filter**: In this field, we define when the sensor is triggered. We can define, for example, whether the sensor is triggered when a customer wants approval for a loan of a predefined amount at the bank.
- **Composite Sensor Action**: In this field, we define where the value of the sensor will be reported. For composite sensors, the values can only be reported to the database.

There's more...

The Oracle SOA Suite also provides the ability to define the sensors inside a BPEL process. Three types of sensors can be defined: variable, activity, and fault. We use the BPEL sensors to collect information that is interesting to us during the BPEL process instance lifecycle. Within the business process, we can check the activation and completion of a specific activity or monitor a modification of a variable value inside the BPEL process. The activity sensors are used to monitor the execution of an activity. It is also possible to monitor the variables of an activity. Variables sensors are used to monitor the variable of a BPEL process, for example, input and output messages. Fault sensors are used to monitor BPEL process faults.

Defining a variable sensor in BPEL

In JDeveloper, in the top-right of the BPEL layout window, we click on the **Monitor** button. We are going to define a variable sensor to monitor the room price in the BPEL process:

1. The following window is shown in JDeveloper as part of the process tree structure. We can see the sensors section with three subsections (**Activity**, **Variable**, and **Fault**) in the following screenshot:

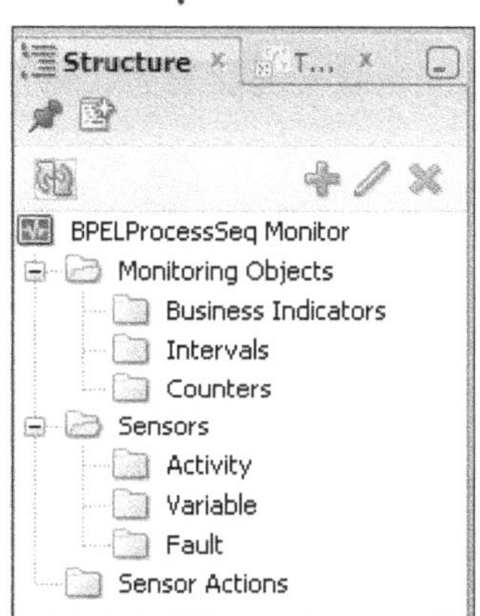

2. Select the **Variable** subsection, right-click, and choose **Create**. The dialog opens, and inside this dialog, we define the following fields:
   - **Name**: In this field, we enter the name of the sensor (`RoomPriceSensor`)
   - **Target**: This field is used to specify the BPEL process variable for the sensor (`$GetRoomPrice_getPrice_InputVariable/parameters/ns2:getPrice`)
   - **Configuration**: In this field, we enter the specification of the sensor variable (see `VariableConfig` tag in next code)
   - **Sensor Action**: This field defines where the information about sensor values will be stored

```
<sensor sensorName="RoomPriceSensor" classname="oracle.
tip.pc.services.reports.dca.agents.BpelVariableSensorAgent"
kind="variable" target="$GetRoomPrice_getPrice_InputVariable/
parameters/ns2:getPrice">
  <variableConfig outputDataType="getPrice"
outputNamespace="http://axis.ws.packt.org"/>
</sensor>
```

3. Finally, when you click on **OK**, the variable sensor is defined in the BPEL process. We can see that we get a new file in the top level project structure named `BPELProcessSeq_sensor.xml`. This file holds the sensor definitions.

Defining an activity sensor in BPEL

Similar to defining a variable sensor, we can define an activity sensor in BPEL as shown in the following steps:

1. In the **Activity** subsection, right-click and choose **Create**. The dialog opens and we fill it with the following data:
   - **Name**: This field is used to specify the name of the sensor (`RoomPriceSensorActivity`).
   - **Activity Name**: This field is used to specify the activity for the sensor (`GetRoomPrice`).
   - **Configuration**: In this field, we enter the specification of the sensor variable (see the variable tag in the next code snippet). We define which variable will be used for the sensor and the time when the evaluation for the sensor will be performed. The evaluation time is defined as shown in the following table:

Evaluation time	Description
Activation	This evaluation is performed just before the activity is executed.
Completion	As opposed to the Activation, this evaluation is performed immediately after the activity is executed.
Fault	The sensor is evaluated in case of fault occurrence during the activity execution.
Compensation	The sensor is evaluated when the associated scope is compensated. When the BPEL process has a compensation handler defined and the fault occurs in the BPEL process, the compensation handler procedure is executed. At the start of the compensation activity, the event is fired to monitor the activity.
Retry	The sensor is evaluated when the activity is retried.
All	The sensor includes all of the above situations.

   - **Sensor Action**: This field defines where the information about sensor values will be stored.

   We define the activity sensor of the `GetRoomPrice` Invoke activity. We will check the sensor value upon the completion of the activity as shown in the following code:

```
<sensor sensorName="RoomPriceSensorActivity" classname="oracle.
tip.pc.services.reports.dca.agents.BpelActivitySensorAgent"
kind="activity" target="GetRoomPrice">
  <activityConfig evalTime="all">
    <variable outputDataType="RoomPrice" outputNamespace="http://
axis.ws.packt.org/xsd" target="$GetRoomPrice_getPrice_
OutputVariable/parameters/ns2:getPriceResponse/ns2:return"/>
  </activityConfig>
</sensor>
```

2. Click on **OK** and you'll get the activity sensor defined in the BPEL process.

Defining a fault sensor in BPEL

Similar to defining a variable and activity sensor, we can define a fault sensor in BPEL as shown in the following steps:

1. In the **Fault** subsection, we right-click and choose **Create**. The dialog opens and we fill it with the following data:
   - **Name**: This field is used to specify the name of the sensor (`CarFaultSensor`)
   - **Fault QName**: This field is used to specify the fault used for the sensor (`sns1:BookCarServiceInvalidDatesException`)
   - **Sensor Action**: This field defines where the information about sensor values will be stored

   ```
   <sensor sensorName="CarFaultSensor" classname="oracle.tip.
   pc.services.reports.dca.agents.BpelFaultSensorAgent" kind="fault"
   target="sns1:BookCarServiceInvalidDatesException"/>
   ```

2. Click on **OK** and you'll get the fault sensor defined in the BPEL process.

The sensor action

The sensors in BPEL have a wider range of sensor actions than the ones in composite. The sensor actions define where the sensor data will be published. Depending on the sensor action we define, the sensor data gets published into the defined endpoint. The sensor actions that can be associated with BPEL sensors are as follows:

- **Database**: This is where the sensor data is stored into the database
- **JMS queue**: This is where the sensor data is published via the JMS queue
- **JMS topic**: This is where the sensor data is published via the JMS topic
- **Custom**: This is where the sensor data is sent to the custom Java class
- **JMS adapter**: This is where the sensor data is published to the JMS queue/topic of various providers

See also

We will cover the addition of a sensor to a composite and a BPEL process in the next recipe. The monitoring of sensors is covered in the *Monitoring a composite sensor* recipe.

Adding a composite sensor

In the previous recipe, we saw how to define composite and BPEL sensors. This recipe will show you how to add different types of sensors to a composite and BPEL process.

Getting ready

For adding a composite sensor, we will use the example from the *Defining composite sensors* recipe. Remember we defined one composite sensor and three BPEL sensors.

How to do it...

In the following recipe, we will add a composite sensor to the SCA. We first add the composite sensor to the `BookHotelSvc` service in the composite structure. We already saw in the previous recipe that an icon appears indicating that the sensor is added to the composite. To add a composite sensor in JDeveloper there are two ways:

1. We can add a composite sensor by clicking on the toolbar icon in the composite design view as shown in the following screenshot:

With this option, you will receive a list of all possible candidates where you can place the composite sensor as shown in the following screenshot:

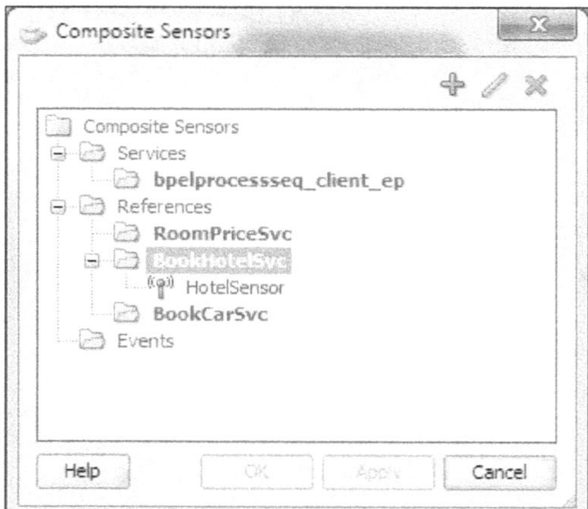

2. Another way to add a composite sensor is to select the web service in the composite and then right-click and select **Configure Sensors...**.

How it works...

When adding composite sensors, the following two files are created in the project structure:

- `sensor.xml`: This file contains the sensor definitions as shown in the following code:

```
<?xml version="1.0" encoding="UTF-8"?>
<sensors xmlns="http://xmlns.oracle.com/bpel/sensor">
  <sensor sensorName="HotelSensor" kind="reference"
target="undefined" filter="" xmlns:ns="http://www.packt.org/book/
hotel">
    <referenceConfig reference="BookHotelSvc"
expression="concat($in.parameters/ns:availableHotels/ns:from, $in.
parameters/ns:availableHotels/ns:to)" operation="availableHotels"
outputDataType="string" outputNamespace="http://www.w3.org/2001/
XMLSchema"/>
  </sensor>
</sensors>
```

- `sensorAction.xml`: This file contains the sensor action definitions as shown in the following code:

```
<?xml version="1.0" encoding="UTF-8"?>
<actions xmlns="http://xmlns.oracle.com/bpel/sensor">
  <action name="JMSSensorAction_HotelSensor" enabled="false"
publishType="JMSQueue" publishTarget="">
    <property name="JMSConnectionFactory"/>
  </action>
  <action name="DBSensorAction" enabled="true"
publishType="BpelReportsSchema" publishName="" filter=""
publishTarget="">
    <sensorName>HotelSensor</sensorName>
  </action>
</actions>
```

Any subsequent addition of new composite sensors is stored into these two files.

There's more...

Occasionally, when we want to monitor a BPEL process in more detail, we should also add BPEL sensors. We achieve this by opening the BPEL process and then clicking on the Monitor icon at the top-right corner of the BPEL process design view:

1. We enter into the monitoring mode where we add sensors for the BPEL process as shown in the following screenshot:

2. It is possible to add BPEL sensors to any activity in the business process by right-clicking on the activity:

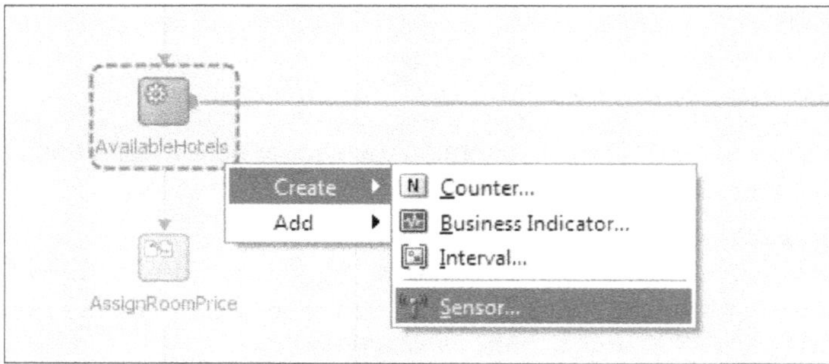

Adding a BPEL sensor for JMS queuing

In this recipe, we will see how to define a BPEL sensor that will report data to the JMS queue. For that purpose, we need to define the JMS queue on the Oracle WebLogic server. This approach represents a loosely coupled solution to monitoring. Also, the solution represents robust architecture from a disaster recovery point of view. For example, if the database crashes, the messages stay in the JMS waiting for the database to come back online. This approach is also recommended if you want to integrate with the third-party business activity monitoring systems.

> Some very useful documentation on JMS queuing is available at the official Oracle WebLogic website: `http://docs.oracle.com/cd/E12840_01/wls/docs103/messaging.html`.

To use a JMS queue in the BPEL sensors, we need two pieces of information. The first one is the **JMS Connection Factory** (holds the information about the connection to the JMS queues and presents the pool of connections) and the second one is **Publish Target** (in our case, this field holds the JNDI name of the JMS queue; otherwise, this field holds various information depending on the publishing type specified).

In JDeveloper, we need to define the sensor action. We do this by right-clicking on the **Sensor Actions** option in the project structure window and then selecting **Create...**. We then fill the dialog with the requested data as shown in the following screenshot:

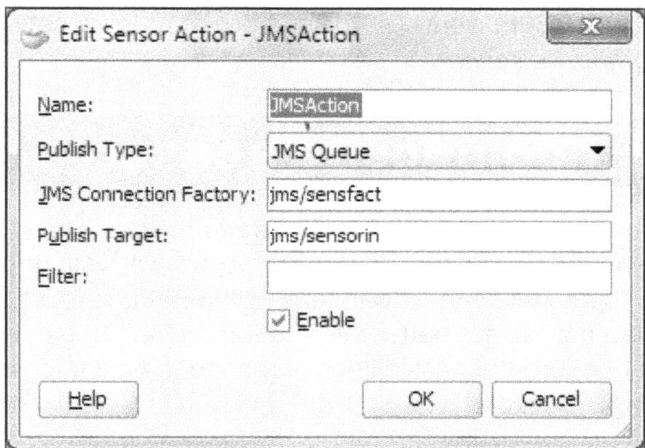

We define the sensor in the BPEL process. Note that instead of a database sensor action, we will use the JMS sensor action.

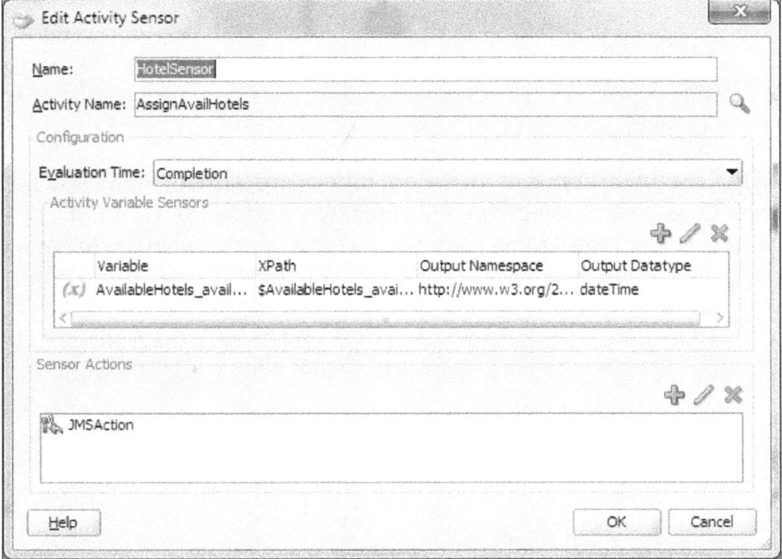

By running the BPEL process, we won't see any JMS sensor information in the Audit Trail or logs of the BPEL process. We can however, check the content of the JMS queue via the Oracle WebLogic Administration Console.

See also

To cover all palette of sensor management in the Oracle SOA Suite, we still need to cover the monitoring of composite and BPEL sensors. To see how we monitor sensors, look at the next recipe, *Monitoring a composite sensor*.

Monitoring a composite sensor

This recipe presents the continuation of the previous two recipes where we first defined and then added composite and BPEL sensors. In this recipe, we will walk through the monitoring of the composite sensors as well as the monitoring of the BPEL sensors. As a result of the composite sensor monitoring, we get better information on the happenings inside the BPEL process. This recipe will explore the possibilities of monitoring a composite sensor from the Oracle Enterprise Manager Console.

Getting ready

For this recipe, we will use the composition defined in the *Defining composite sensors* and *Adding a composite sensor* recipes.

How to do it...

First, you will have to initiate the BPEL process:

1. Check the execution status of the recent running instance in the Oracle Enterprise Manager Console and select the BPEL process instance from the BPEL process dashboard. Under **Flow Trace**, you'll find a screen as shown in the following screenshot:

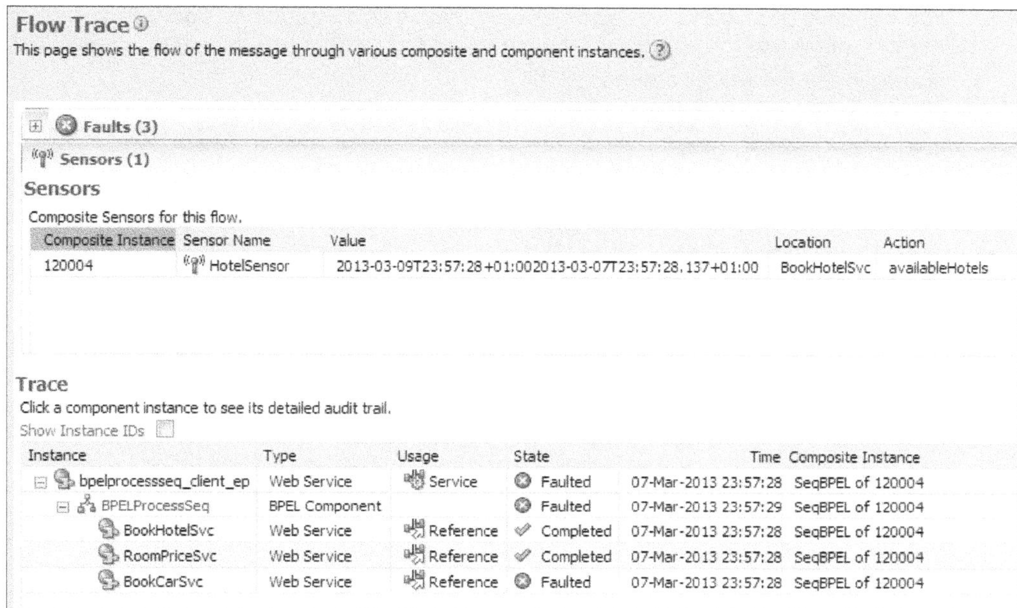

In the preceding screenshot, in **Trace**, you can see that the `BPELProcessSeq` instance finished in the **Faulted** state. The `BookHotelSvc` and `RoomPriceSvc` instances finished successfully. However, you can see that `BookCarSvc` had problems. Without further investigating the trace of the BPEL process, check the composite sensor value. It indicates two dates in a from-to pair. You will immediately spot that the from-date is greater than the to-date. This indicates that there might be some problems with the inserted dates.

2. You will have to further investigate the root cause of the problem. Click on the link of the faulted BPEL component. The details of the BPEL process instance opens as shown in the following screenshot:

By selecting the **Sensor Values** tab, you will notice that the fault sensor was fired. By checking the details of the fault sensor, you can see that, the problem occurred because of the dates. If we also had the Oracle BAM server instance running, you could configure the composite sensors to provide data for BAM. This will enable us to monitor the BPEL process through a BAM solution.

How it works...

The sensors are evaluated as the composite is executed. The value of the sensor depends on the criteria we set as the condition. You can monitor the input or output messages on the composite. Furthermore, you can monitor variables, activities, or faults in the BPEL processes. Depending on what sensor action you define, the evaluated values of sensors can be sent to different locations (please read the *Sensor action* section in the *Defining composite sensors* recipe).

The evaluated values of composite sensors that have the database sensor action defined are stored into the database. The name of the table is `COMPOSITE_SENSOR_VALUE` and it is defined in the `DEV_SOAINFRA` schema. We can query the sensor values by `composite_instance_id` or by the sensor name:

```
select * from DEV_SOAINFRA.COMPOSITE_SENSOR_VALUE where SENSOR_NAME =
'HotelSensor';
```

The preceding code applies only to composite sensors that have the database sensor action defined.

Configuring the logfiles

In this recipe, we will discuss the configuration of the logfiles. The configuration of the logfiles is important because it enables us to fine-tune the information we want to gather from the BPEL process execution.

Getting ready

For this recipe, there is no special preparation needed. However, further discussion will lead us to more specific configuration of the logfiles. For that purpose, we will use the BPEL process that we prepared for this chapter. The BPEL process first checks the hotel availability, receives the room price, and checks for car availability.

How to do it...

By following the next steps, we will configure logfiles through the Oracle Enterprise Manager Console:

1. Log in to the Oracle Enterprise Manager Console.

2. Select **soa-infra** from the tree on the left side. Then, right-click on **soa-infra** and select **Logs** | **Log Configuration**.

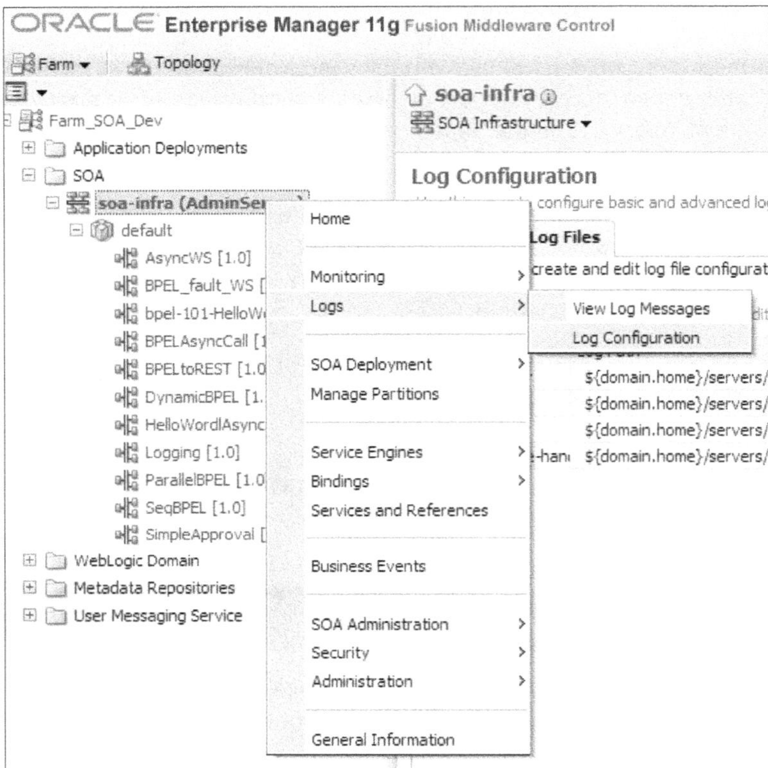

3. The **Log Configuration** opens and you have two tabs to choose. The **Log Levels** tab is used for changing the level of tracing that we use for a particular logger. At the moment, we are more interested in the **Log Files** tab. We will create a new logfile for the logging. Thus, we select **odl-handler** and click on the **Create Like...** button:

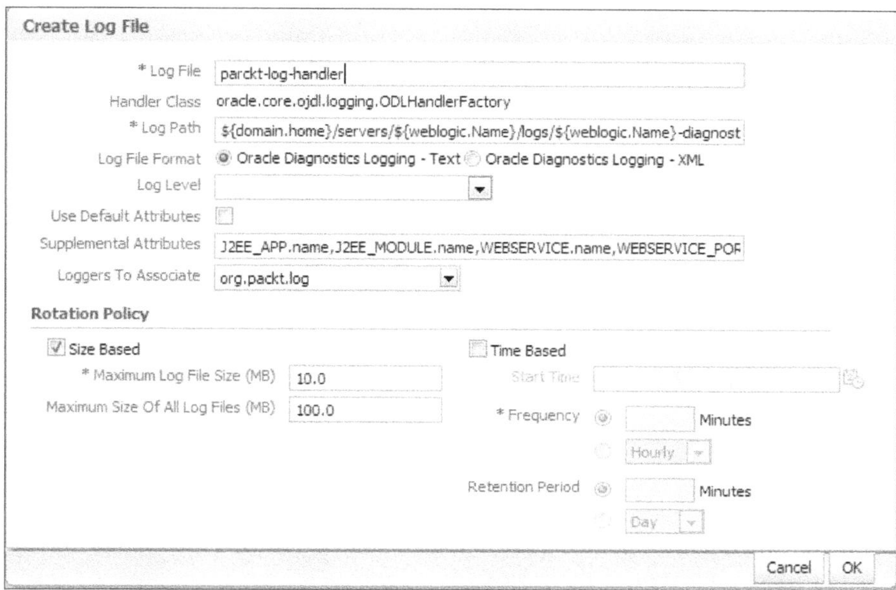

4. In the **Create Log File** window, enter the following fields:
    - **Log file**
    - **Log Path**
    - **Loggers to Associate**

Now we have defined the logger file in order to separate logging for our custom logger defined in the *Creating a custom logger in a BPEL process* recipe.

How it works...

Oracle SOA Suite has its logging configuration managed through the Oracle Enterprise Manager Console. There exist the following four predefined logfiles for the Oracle SOA Suite components:

- `em-log-handler` (logs the enterprise manager data)
- `em-trc-handler` (logs the enterprise manager data)
- `odl-handler` (logs the general diagnostic data)
- `owsm-message-handler` (logs diagnostic data for the Oracle Web Service Manager)

By defining the logfile, there is no logging enabled yet. To enable logging, we must configure that through the loggers in the **Log Levels** tab. We will cover this in our next recipe, *Changing the level of tracing*.

There's more...

In a BPEL process, there is also a possibility to configure the logfiles autonomously from the Oracle SOA Suite. We will utilize the sample BPEL process we prepared in previous recipes with the LOG4J logging utility. Our task is to make every BPEL process instance log into its own logfile. The format of the logfile name is `log_BPEL_<instance_id>.log`:

1. In the JDeveloper project, we add the LOG4J library into the `SCA-INF/lib` directory.
2. Additionally, create the LOG4J properties file. Place the properties file into the SOA domain server root location `<domain_home>`. The content of the LOG4J properties file we defined is as shown in the following code:

```
log4j.rootLogger=debug, stdout, BPEL
log4j.appender.stdout=org.apache.log4j.ConsoleAppender
log4j.appender.stdout.layout=org.apache.log4j.PatternLayout
# Pattern to output the caller's file name and line number.
log4j.appender.stdout.layout.ConversionPattern=%5p [%t] (%F:%L) -
%m%n
log4j.appender.BPEL=org.apache.log4j.RollingFileAppender
log4j.appender.BPEL.File=example.log
log4j.appender.BPEL.MaxFileSize=100KB
log4j.appender.BPEL.MaxBackupIndex=5
log4j.appender.BPEL.layout=org.apache.log4j.PatternLayout
log4j.appender.BPEL.layout.ConversionPattern=%d [%t] %-5p %c %x -
%m%n
```

That's it! We prepared the infrastructure to utilize the custom logfile defined outside of the Oracle SOA Suite framework.

Creating a log for every BPEL instance run

We will now create the `Logger` class which will use the infrastructure we just prepared:

1. In JDeveloper, we define a new class and name it `LogDynamic`. In the static section, we set the properties file for logging and extract `FileAppender` from the logging configuration as shown in the following code:

```
static {
  String sLog4jFile = "C:\\Programs\\Oracle\\Middleware\\user_
projects\\domains\\SOA_Dev\\dyna_log4j.properties";
```

```
    PropertyConfigurator.configure(sLog4jFile);
    Logger rootLogger= Logger.getRootLogger();
    Enumeration appenders = rootLogger.getAllAppenders();
    while(appenders.hasMoreElements()) {
      Appender currAppender = (Appender) appenders.nextElement();
      if(currAppender instanceof FileAppender) {
        fa = (FileAppender) currAppender;
      }
    }
  }
```

2. In the log procedure, first set the filename for the logging if it is not already set as shown in the following code:

```
  if (fa!= null) {
    if(fa.getFile().indexOf(pid) == -1)
    {
      fa.setFile("C:/temp/log_BPEL_" + pid + ".log");
      fa.activateOptions();
    }
  }
```

3. Next, we perform the actual logging:

```
logger.log(Level.INFO, message);
```

4. In the BPEL process, use the Java Embedding activity to call the logging method as shown in the following code:

```
<extensionActivity>
  <bpelx:exec name="Java_Log_JUL_LOG4J" language="java">
    <![CDATA[
      org.packt.log.LogDynamic.log("Hello from Log4J process with
id: " + getInstanceId(), ""+ getInstanceId());
    ]]>
  </bpelx:exec>
</extensionActivity>
```

See also

In the next three recipes, we will discuss *Changing the level of tracing*, *Editing the logfiles*, and *Viewing logfiles in the Enterprise Manager Console*.

Changing the level of tracing

In this recipe, we will discuss how the level of tracing effects the information being collected. The level of tracing is important when we search for the root cause of a problem. When the tracing is too verbose, we might not see the error message. On the contrary, when the tracing is not very verbose, we might spot the problem only after the BPEL process has been terminated by the fault.

How to do it...

We will adjust the log level through the Oracle Enterprise Manager Console. We log in with the administrator account and follow the next steps:

1. Select **soa-infra** from the tree on the left side. Then, right-click on **soa-infra** and select **Logs** | **Log Configuration**.
2. The **Log Configuration** window opens and we have two tabs to choose from as shown in the following screenshot. The **Log Levels** tab is used for changing the level of tracing that we use for a particular logger:

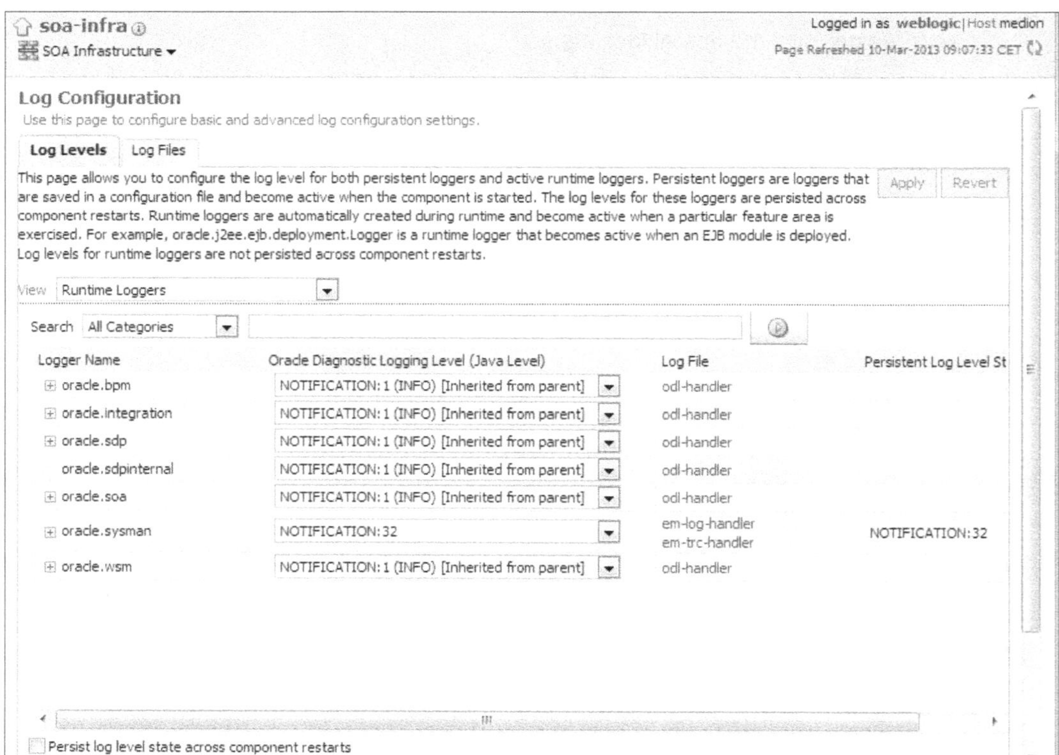

3. Under the **Logger Name** column, select the logger for which you want to adjust the log level.
4. With the help of a drop-down menu, we adjust the level of tracing as shown in the following screenshot:

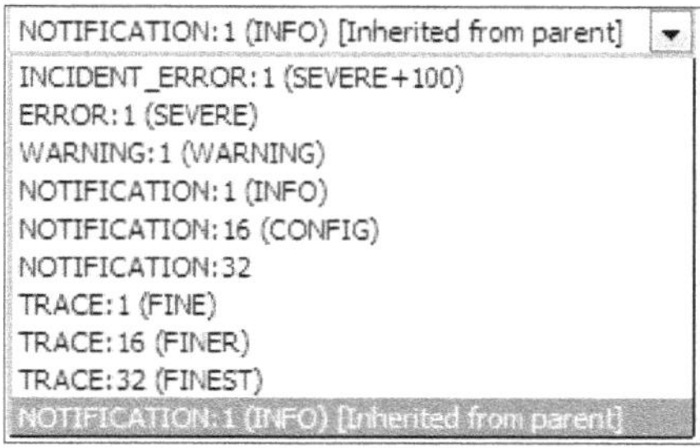

By defining the lowest level of tracing, we get the maximum verbosity of tracing possible. Note that the lower trace levels also enable the tracing from all log levels that are higher.

5. Click on the **Apply** button for the changes to take effect. In case you change your mind, choose the **Revert** button to discard the changes:

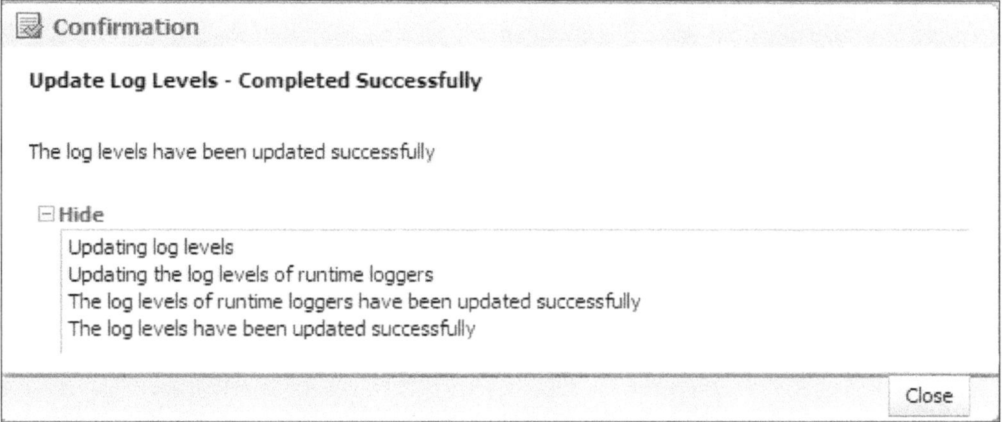

Confirmation
Update Log Levels - Completed Successfully
The log levels have been updated successfully
Hide
Updating log levels
Updating the log levels of runtime loggers
The log levels of runtime loggers have been updated successfully
The log levels have been updated successfully
Close

How it works...

The tracing and logging model in Oracle SOA Suite is based on the **Oracle diagnostic logging** (**ODL**) model and shares similarities with the Java Utilities Logging (JUL) facilities. This is also shown in the Oracle Enterprise Manager Console where the log level option contains its corresponding log level in the JUL.

Loggers are organized in hierarchies, which means loggers that are lower in the hierarchy take settings from parents.

Changes made to loggers are valid as soon as we click on the **Apply** button in the **Log Level** tab. There is no need to restart the server.

There's more...

Remember: in this chapter, we define two custom loggers:

- **Logger**: This logs information through `odl-log-handler` in the Oracle SOA Suite (we implement it in the *Creating a custom logger in a BPEL process* recipe)
- **Dynamic logger**: This uses its own LOG4J infrastructure (we implemented it in the *Configuring the logfiles* recipe)

From the aspect of setting the log level, there is one significant difference between these two approaches.

In the first approach, the logger is completely integrated into the Oracle SOA Suite logging mechanism. Therefore, it is possible to change the level of tracing from within the Oracle Enterprise Manager Console. Also, the changes are applied immediately.

On the other hand, the second approach is less flexible. We have to handle the log configuration changes outside of Oracle SOA Suite. Also, as we develop it, the changes to the log level do not take effect on the already running instances of the business processes. Rather, the changes do take effect only in the newly initiated business processes.

In the recipe *Configuring the logfiles*, we defined a new logfile for our custom logger. Remember we said that although the logfile is created, there are still no log messages in the file. We will configure the log level of our custom logger now.

Configuring the level of the custom loggers

In the following steps, we will show you how to configure the log level of the custom logger through the Oracle Enterprise Manager Console:

1. Go to the **Log Levels** tab in the Oracle Enterprise Manager Console.

2. From the view, select **Loggers with Persistent Log Level State**. A section opens as shown in the following screenshot:

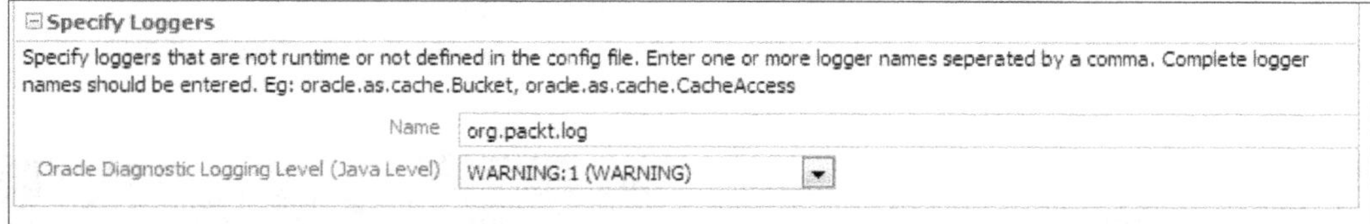

Specify Loggers
Specify loggers that are not runtime or not defined in the config file. Enter one or more logger names seperated by a comma. Complete logger names should be entered. Eg: oracle.as.cache.Bucket, oracle.as.cache.CacheAccess
Name
org.packt.log
Oracle Diagnostic Logging Level (Java Level)
WARNING:1 (WARNING)

3. Enter the logger name and the log level and click on the **Apply** button.
4. Now we have to define to which logfile the logger will send messages. Thus, go to the **Log Files** tab and select **packt-log-handler** and then click on the **Edit Configuration...** button.

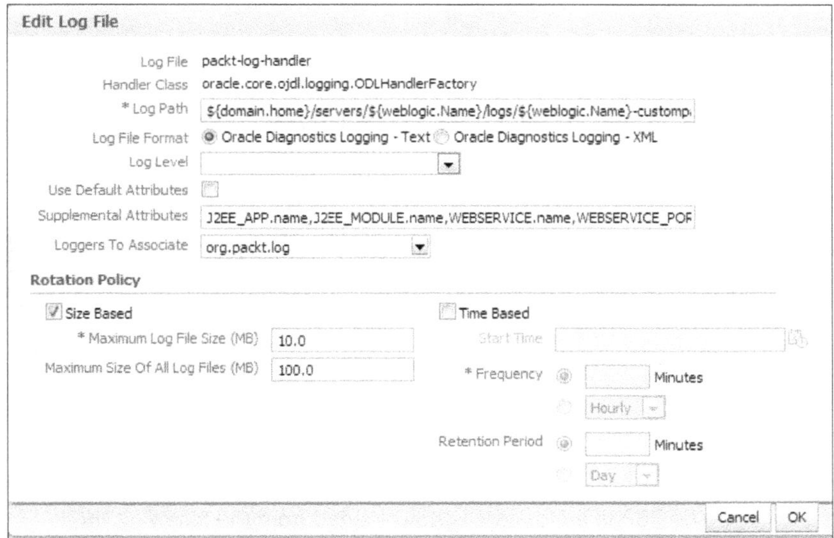

5. Now you have to associate the logger with the logfile. Choose the **org.packt.log** logger from the drop-down menu of the **Loggers To Associate** option. Then, click on **OK**.
6. If you run the BPEL process which uses our custom logger now, you'll see the following line in the logfile:

```
[2013-03-10T16:43:09.994+01:00] [AdminServer] [WARNING] []
[org.packt.log.Logger] [tid: 14] [userId: <anonymous>] [ecid:
e84bae63a4864aa7:-7492ef57:13d54c9a59f:-8000-0000000000000f43,0:2]
[WEBSERVICE_PORT.name: BPELProcessSeq_pt] [APP: soa-infra]
[composite_name: SeqBPEL] [component_name: BPELProcessSeq]
[component_instance_id: 140005] [J2EE_MODULE.name: fabric]
[WEBSERVICE.name: bpelprocessseq_client_ep] [J2EE_APP.name: soa-
infra] Hello from JUL process with id: 140005
```

See also

In the previous two recipes, we configured the logfiles and set the trace level. For more information on editing and viewing the logfiles, refer to the recipes *Editing the logfiles* and *Viewing logfiles in the Enterprise Manager Console*.

Editing the logfiles

When the logfiles are set up and are accepting the messages, the next step is to see what is logged into the logfiles. This recipe will show you how to efficiently edit the logfiles. For example, we need to edit the logfiles in case we diagnose a problem and we need to send an excerpt of the logs to the support center. We also need to edit the logfiles when we search for some particular line of log.

How to do it...

All the logging made in Oracle SOA Suite is somehow file-based, except the console logger:

1. In order to edit a logfile, we first have to identify the location of the logfile.

   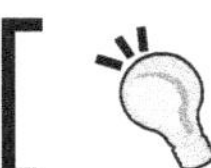

   We can find the location of logfiles in the Oracle Enterprise Manager Console.

2. When we find the location, we can use the Windows native editors such as Notepad and WordPad or some freeware editors such as PSPad and Notepad++.

   ```
   notepad AdminServer-diagnostic.log
   ```

   The PSPad editor can be downloaded from the following URL:

   `http://www.pspad.com/`

   Notepad++ can be downloaded from the following URL:

   `http://notepad-plus-plus.org/`

3. When the logfiles are open, you can browse for the information you are looking for. However, note that editing is meant in a sense of viewing and searching and not changing the content of a logfile.

There's more...

In time, the number of logfiles will grow and can easily exceed several hundred Megabytes. In situations where we deal with big logfiles, we need a different approach in the editing logfiles. One utility worth mentioning is **tail**. For UNIX systems, this is a standard utility.

For Windows systems, there is a port project that you can find at `http://sourceforge.net/projects/tailforwin32/?source=dlp`.

Another utility called Bare Tail can also be used, and it can be found at `http://www.baremetalsoft.com/baretail/`.

To edit the logfile with the tail utility, issue the following command:

```
<tail_install_dir>\Tail.exe -f AdminServer-diagnostic.log
```

We get the window of tail with the logfile edited. New messages are coming in at the bottom of the logfile as shown in the following screenshot:

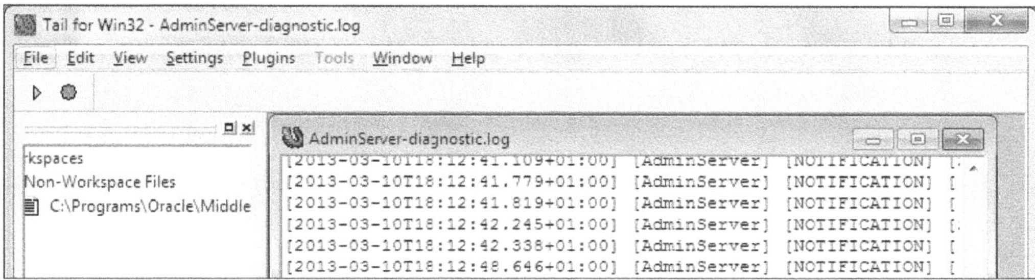

See also

To view the content of the logfiles from the Oracle Enterprise Manager Console, refer to the next recipe, *Viewing logfiles in the Enterprise Manager Console*.

Viewing logfiles in the Enterprise Manager Console

This recipe explains the functionality of viewing the logfiles in Oracle SOA Suite via the Oracle Enterprise Manager Console. This functionality provides a number of possibilities to format and filter for best user experience.

How to do it...

The following steps show the necessary actions required to view logfiles in the Enterprise Manager Console:

1. Log in to the Oracle Enterprise Manager Console.
2. Right-click on the domain name and select **Logs** | **View Log Messages** as shown in the following screenshot:

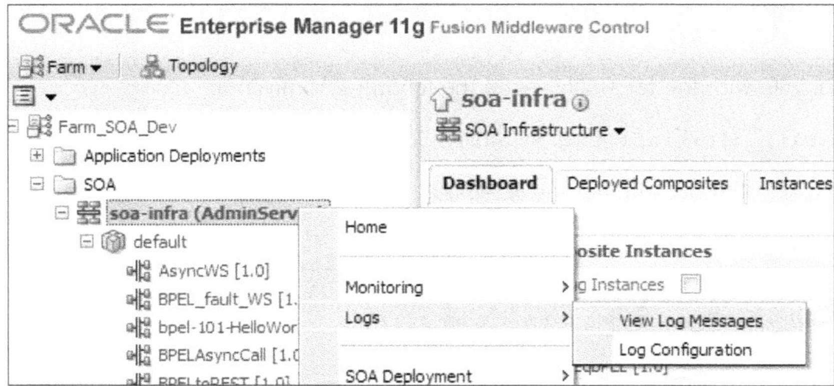

3. You'll get the main window for exploring the logfiles as shown in the following screenshot:

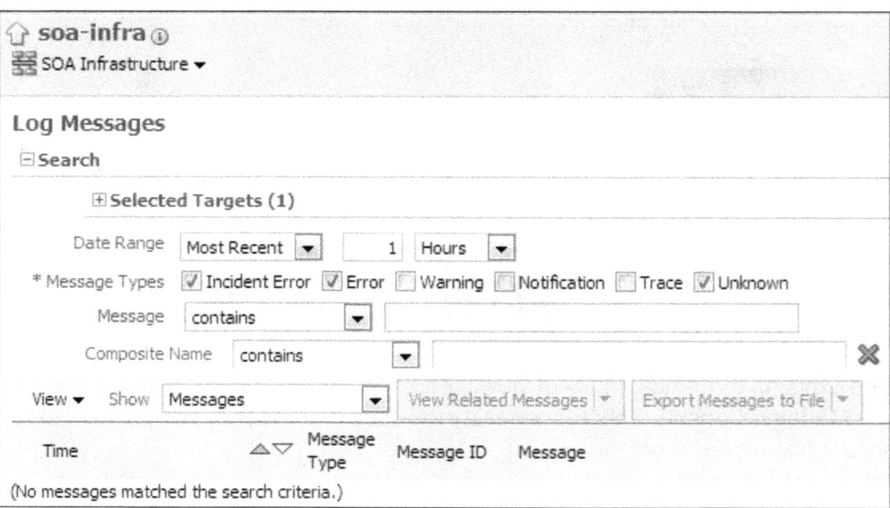

4. Enter the search criteria. Let us search by the Execution Context ID (ECID) number. The ECID number can be found in multiple places such as the flow trace, audit trace, or even the log message in the Oracle SOA Enterprise Manager Console. The ECID number's intention is to link together information over multiple BPEL process instances initiated by a single SOA request. Click on the **Add Fields** button and add the **ECID** field because it is not enabled by default as shown in the following screenshot:

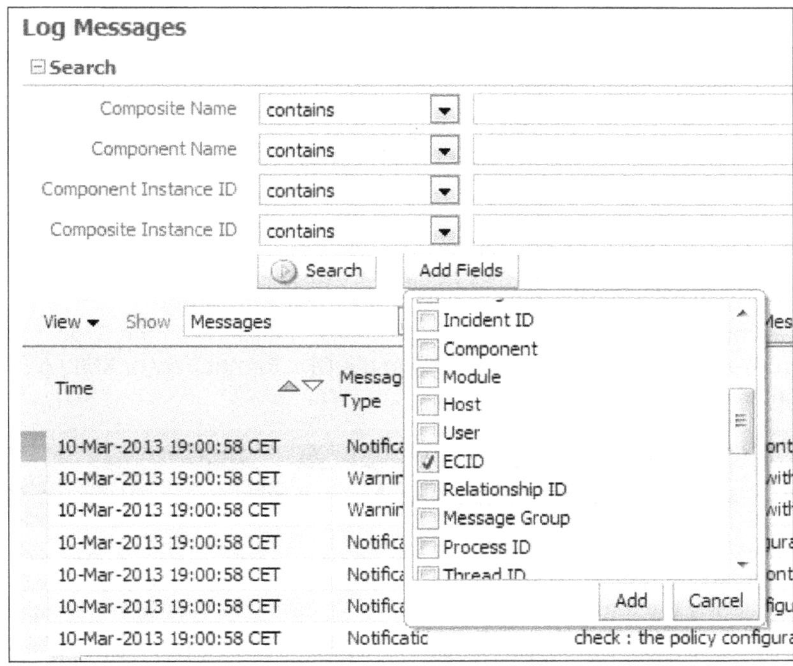

5. Enter the ECID number and click on the **Search** button. You'll receive the messages related to the particular ECID number as shown in the following screenshot:

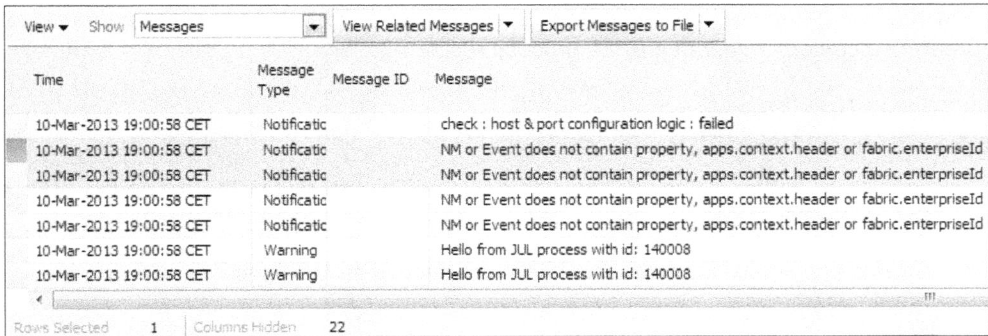

How it works...

The logging mechanism is based on the files, either raw or XML formatted. The initial search range is performed on all the logfiles defined in the Oracle Enterprise Manager Console. However, the scope of the search can also be adjusted.

Based on the search criteria, the result is shown in the view part of the **Log Messages** window. The result view provides functionality to customize the output.

You can customize the output columns by selecting **View** and **View columns**.

Another way to customize the output is by viewing the related messages based on the criteria. You can do this by clicking on **View Related Messages** and then selecting one of the two possibilities:

- **Time**: You'll get the messages related by the time
- **ECID** (**Execution Context ID**): You'll get the messages related by the ECID

We can also export the results as a file. We can do this by clicking on the **Export Messages to File** button. We can export messages either in the ODL format (raw or XML) or as a **comma separated values** (**CSV**) file.

Viewing metrics and statistics

Logging and tracing are the tools for identifying what is going on in the system and with particular business processes. Another important aspect of keeping a system in good condition is gathering the information via metrics and statistics. This way, we can identify the troubles a system might have on an operational level. We are also able to explore a system's overall health condition.

Getting ready

To show you how gathering information works, we will use the BPEL process we prepared for the *Creating a custom logger in a BPEL process* recipe.

How to do it...

The following steps in this recipe will describe how to efficiently review the previously collected metrics and statistics:

1. Start the recipe by logging in to the Oracle Enterprise Manager Console with the admin user.

2. From the left tree, select the **SOA** server, right-click on it, and select **Monitoring** | **Performance Summary** as shown in the following screenshot:

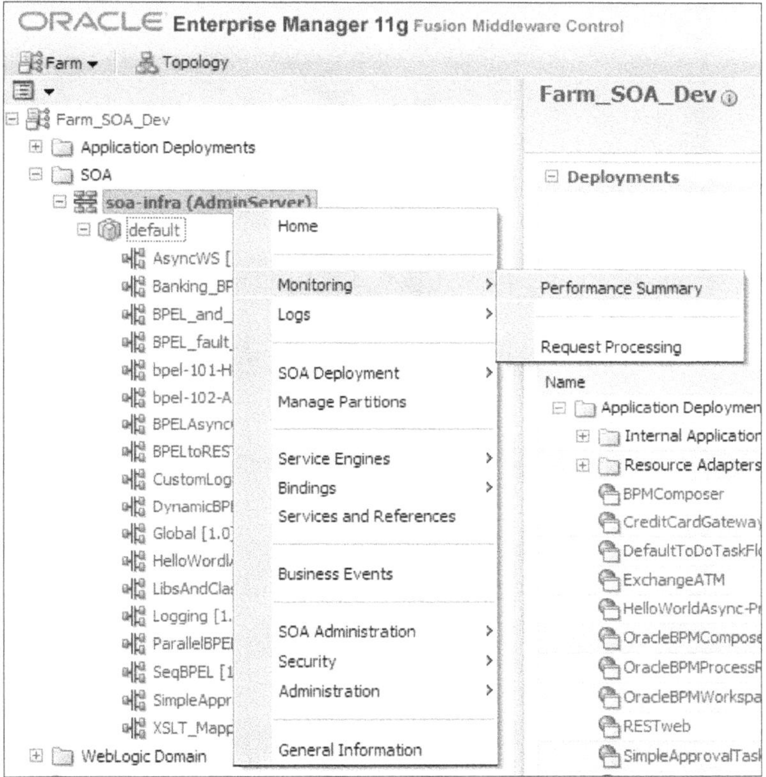

3. We get a window with some basic metric definitions. Click on the **Show Metric Palette** button in the palette search for our BPEL process (it should be under the **Members** | **default** | **Members** section).
4. From the **SOA Composite - Rate Metrics** section, we select the following two metrics:
   - **Synchronous messages throughput in the last 5 minutes**
   - **Total synchronous messages average time**

5. The Performance Summary chart now looks as shown in the following screenshot:

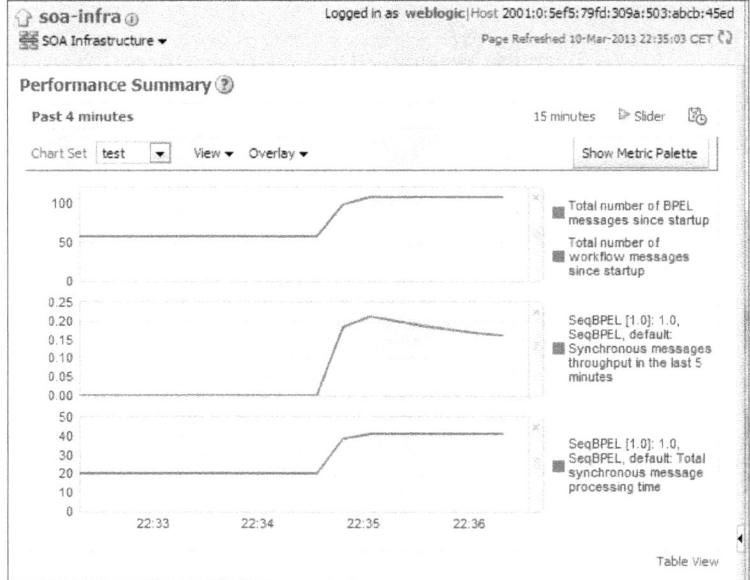

6. Click on the **Table View** link below the charts to see the tabular presentation of the data as shown in the following screenshot:

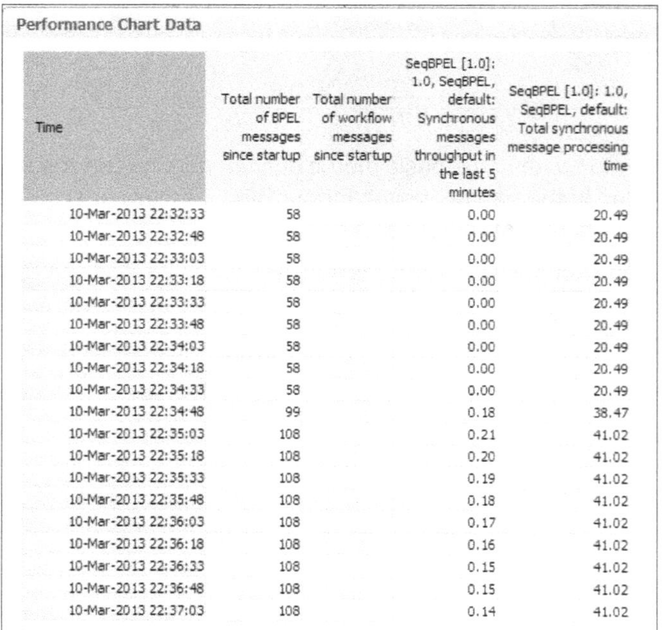

Performance Chart Data

Time	Total number of BPEL messages since startup	Total number of workflow messages since startup	SeqBPEL [1.0]: 1.0, SeqBPEL, default: Synchronous messages throughput in the last 5 minutes	SeqBPEL [1.0]: 1.0, SeqBPEL, default: Total synchronous message processing time
10-Mar-2013 22:32:33	58		0.00	20.49
10-Mar-2013 22:32:48	58		0.00	20.49
10-Mar-2013 22:33:03	58		0.00	20.49
10-Mar-2013 22:33:18	58		0.00	20.49
10-Mar-2013 22:33:33	58		0.00	20.49
10-Mar-2013 22:33:48	58		0.00	20.49
10-Mar-2013 22:34:03	58		0.00	20.49
10-Mar-2013 22:34:18	58		0.00	20.49
10-Mar-2013 22:34:33	58		0.00	20.49
10-Mar-2013 22:34:48	99		0.18	38.47
10-Mar-2013 22:35:03	108		0.21	41.02
10-Mar-2013 22:35:18	108		0.20	41.02
10-Mar-2013 22:35:33	108		0.19	41.02
10-Mar-2013 22:35:48	108		0.18	41.02
10-Mar-2013 22:36:03	108		0.17	41.02
10-Mar-2013 22:36:18	108		0.16	41.02
10-Mar-2013 22:36:33	108		0.15	41.02
10-Mar-2013 22:36:48	108		0.15	41.02
10-Mar-2013 22:37:03	108		0.14	41.02

How it works...

Oracle SOA Suite comes with a predefined set of metrics out of the box. The metrics provide valuable feedback from the system. The metrics are divided into two major groups: the first group contains generic metrics and the second one contains process-oriented metrics. We can also set a different time range for data collection, from a few minutes to weeks or months.

There is one additional concept worth mentioning. When you log in to the Oracle Enterprise Manager Console, you'll see the dashboard. The dashboard will show you the health of the system from a single point of view. It is divided into the following sections:

Recent Composite Instances: In this section, you will see the latest business process instances that were started

Deployed Composites: In this section, you will see all the deployments and their corresponding status

Recent Faults and Rejected Messages: This section will show you whether some extraordinary event is requesting immediate attention

Service Engines: This section will show you the number of deployments and the of the number of faults on the deployed modules

Composite Instances: This section will show you the faults in graphical presentation number of instances created since server startup as well as the number of faults originated from the instance run

There's more...

Since SOA (and BPEL as a part of it) acts as an orchestrating technology, we would also like to know in what condition the system is in at the time of processing requests from outer systems. For that purpose, we can utilize the request processing statistics:

1. Start the recipe by logging in to the Oracle Enterprise Manager Console with the admin user.
2. From the left tree, select the **SOA** server, right-click on it, and select **Monitoring** | **Request Processing**.
3. You'll get a window that contains the following predefined set of statistics:
    - Average sync and async request processing times on each of the servers
    - Average sync and async request processing times at the level of service infrastructure
    - Average processing times for binding components (web services and Java EE Connector Architecture).

4. In the Oracle SOA Suite Mangement Console, you'll get the following window containing information about statistics:

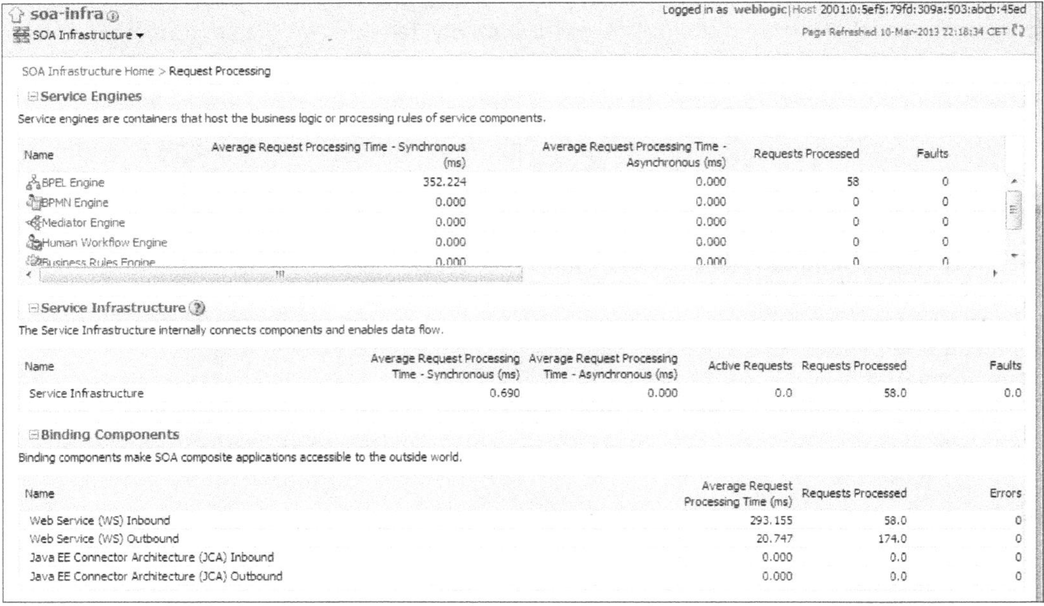

4

Custom Logging in the Oracle SOA Suite

This chapter contains the following recipes:

- Logging to a custom file
- Configuring custom handlers
- Logging exceptions
- Enabling logging on the BPEL server
- Redirecting System.out and System.err files
- Setting up a rotation logfile

Introduction

We have covered advanced tracing and logging techniques in *Chapter 3, Advanced Tracing and Logging*. Occasionally, we may need functionality that is not a part of the vendor product. In such cases, additional workaround and customization techniques are suitable for logging and tracing purposes. One of the most common techniques is to set up a mechanism to decouple the interesting part of logging information into a separate logging file. To fine-tune the logging, we define various logging handlers which help us to capture the wanted information.

Another aspect of logging is presentation of exceptions and faults in the logfiles. The captured information must be taken correctly and with the proper level of severity. In the Oracle SOA Suite, important sources of information can be found in the audit trail. In this chapter, we show how to set different levels of audit trail.

Sometimes, we encounter a situation where some part of the application or the third-party library prints useful information to the standard output and error files. Our job is to pick up such information and redirect it to the logfile.

Depending on the tracing level, the amount of tracing and logging information can grow significantly. For that purpose, it is worth considering the usage of rotation logfiles. Most logging frameworks and the **ODL** (**Oracle Diagnostic Logging**) support time-based and size-based log rotation.

Logging to a custom file

Occasionally, you may want to separate a part of logging to a separate logging file. That way, you can instantly separate the desired logging from the main logging flow, leaving the original logging configuration untouched. In this recipe, we will define a custom logfile so that only the information we want to gather will be collected. The rest of the configuration will remain intact.

Getting ready...

For completing this recipe, you'll need a BPEL process. Any BPEL process is suitable, and of course, we need a running Oracle SOA Suite server.

How to do it...

The following steps will describe how to configure the custom logfile through the Oracle SOA Enterprise Manager Console:

1. Start by logging in to the Oracle Enterprise Manager Console. On the **soa-infra** node, right-click and select **Logs** | **Log Configuration** as shown in the following screenshot:

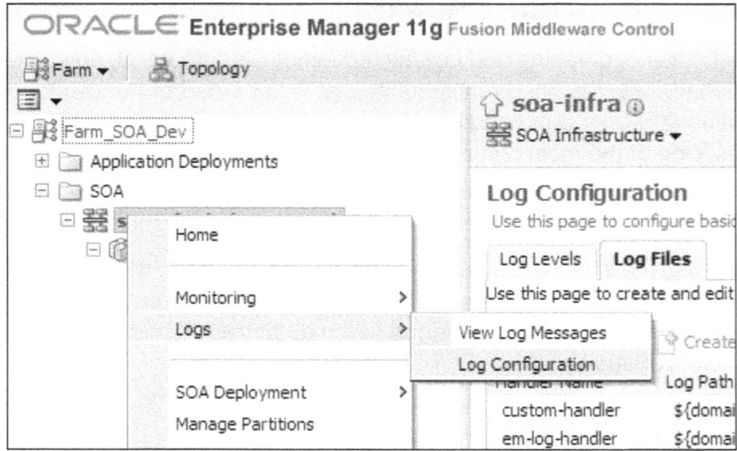

2. Choose the **Log Files** tab and click on the **Create...** button. A pop-up window appears where you configure the custom logging file. You have to supplement the mandatory fields and choose loggers in the **Loggers To Associate** drop-down list as shown in the following screenshot:

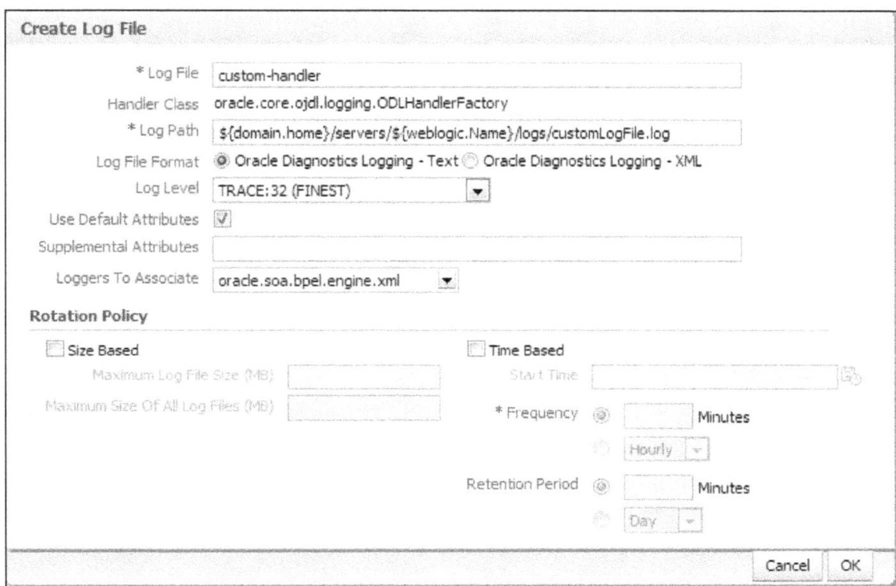

3. After the successful completion of the configuration, you'll receive a confirmation message as shown in the following screenshot:

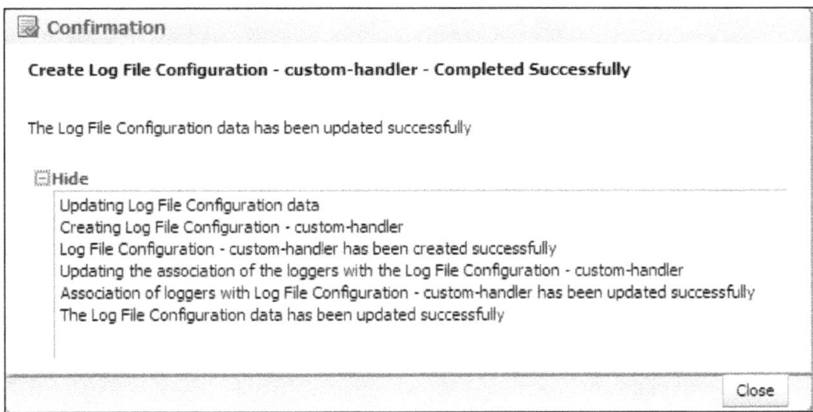

4. `custom-handler` is now listed in the table of logfiles. There is no need to restart the server.

How it works...

The location of the logging configuration for the Oracle SOA Suite is held in the `${domain.home}\config\fmwconfig\servers\AdminServer` directory. More precisely, the file containing the logging information is named `logging.xml`. Let's check the configuration file. The changes we made through the Oracle Enterprise Manager Console appeared in the following files:

- The following are the changes in the configuration of log file:

```
<log_handler name='custom-handler' class='oracle.core.ojdl.
logging.ODLHandlerFactory' level='NOTIFICATION:32'>
  <property name='useDefaultAttributes' value='false'/>
  <property name='format' value='ODL-Text'/>
  <property name='path' value='${domain.home}/servers/${weblogic.
Name}/logs/customLogFile.log'/>
  <property name='useSourceClassAndMethod' value='TRACE:1'/>
</log_handler>
```

In the preceding code, with the `name` attribute of the `<log_handler>` element, we define the name of the log handler. With the `format` property, we define the format of the logging data to be used. We can choose either text or XML format. With the `path` property, we define the location of the logfile. With the `useSourceClassAndMethod` property, we define the logging level to be used for logging information.

- The following are the changes in the configuration of loggers reporting to the newly created logfile:

```
<logger name='oracle.soa.bpel.engine.xml'>
  <handler name='custom-handler'/>
</logger>
```

Logging in the Oracle SOA Suite is based on Java Logging functionality. Although the configuration itself is separated, there is nothing stopping you from using Java Logging elements.

Now that we have logging configured, it is time to start an instance of the BPEL process to check what gets logged. We have set the logging level to `TRACE`, so we should get quite a verbose output in the custom logfile. You can run the BPEL process from *Assigning date or time to the variables* recipe defined in *Chapter 7, Accessing and Updating the Variables*. By examining the logfiles, you will see the following lines of code (the beginning of the lines are truncated for better readability):

```
[SRC_METHOD: evaluate] XPathQuery[xp20:current-time()], XPath Result
is: 13:05:32.429+02:00
[SRC_METHOD: evaluate] XPathQuery[xp20:format-dateTime(bpws:getVar
iableData('FormatDate'), '[D01]/[M01]/[Y0001]')], XPath Result is:
01/05/2013
[SRC_METHOD: evalQuery] evaluate PathQuery[/client:proces sResponse/
client:result] on oracle.xml.parser.v2.XMLElement@64feb8
```

With this output, we are able to identify what evaluations are performed in the BPEL process due to the XML operations.

Configuring custom handlers

This recipe explains how to configure different logging handlers in the Oracle SOA Suite. Although many of the logging handlers already exist, occasionally we may need some special functionality, such as the ability to log into databases or logging via web services. The number of log handler classes in the Oracle SOA Suite is quite limited. Actually, if you check the `logging.xml` file, you'll only find two types: `oracle.core.ojdl.weblogic.DomainLogHandler` and `oracle.core.ojdl.logging.ODLHandlerFactory`. For this recipe, we will define a custom handler and use it in our configuration. The custom handler will enable each instance of the BPEL process to log into its own logfile.

How to do it...

The following steps describe the actions required to create and configure a custom log handler:

1. Start by creating an empty Java project in JDeveloper and name it **LoggingHandler**.
2. In the project, create a Java class (`CustomLogger.java`) in the `logging` package as shown in the following code:

   ```
   package logging;
   public class CustomLogger extends Handler {
   ```

3. This new class extends the Java Logging class, `java.util.logging.Handler`, which presents the default template class to design the new log handlers. `CustomLogger` will create a logfile in the Java `temp` directory and name it with your computer name and append the extension `log` to it.
4. To proceed, we define two output streams. They are used to direct flow of the logs to the output file as shown in the following code:

   ```
   FileOutputStream fileOutputStream;
   PrintWriter printWriter;
   ```

5. Continue with the definition of the constructor. We first concatenate the log filename from the various sources as shown in the following code:

   ```
   InetAddress iAddress = InetAddress.getLocalHost();
   String hostName = iAddress.getHostName();
   String tempDir= System.getProperty("java.io.tmpdir");
   String fileLoc= tempDir + hostName + ".log";
   And finally create concrete output streams:
   fileOutputStream = new FileOutputStream(fileLoc);
   printWriter = new PrintWriter(fileOutputStream);
   ```

6. To create the operable log handler, we have to override three methods. The first one is the `publish` method, which is used to write data to the file as shown in the following code:

```
public void publish(LogRecord record) {
  if (!isLoggable(record))
    return;
    printWriter.println (getFormatter().format(record));
}
```

7. We also override the `flush` method because we need to flush the content to the output stream as shown in the following code:

```
public void flush() {
  printWriter.flush();
}
```

8. We also override the `close` method as shown in the following code:

```
public void close() {
  printWriter.close();
}
```

9. Now that we have the custom logger class written, we prepare the package for deployment. At the project root, right-click and select **Project Properties...**. In the tree, select **Deployment** and then click on the **New...** button as shown in the following screenshot:

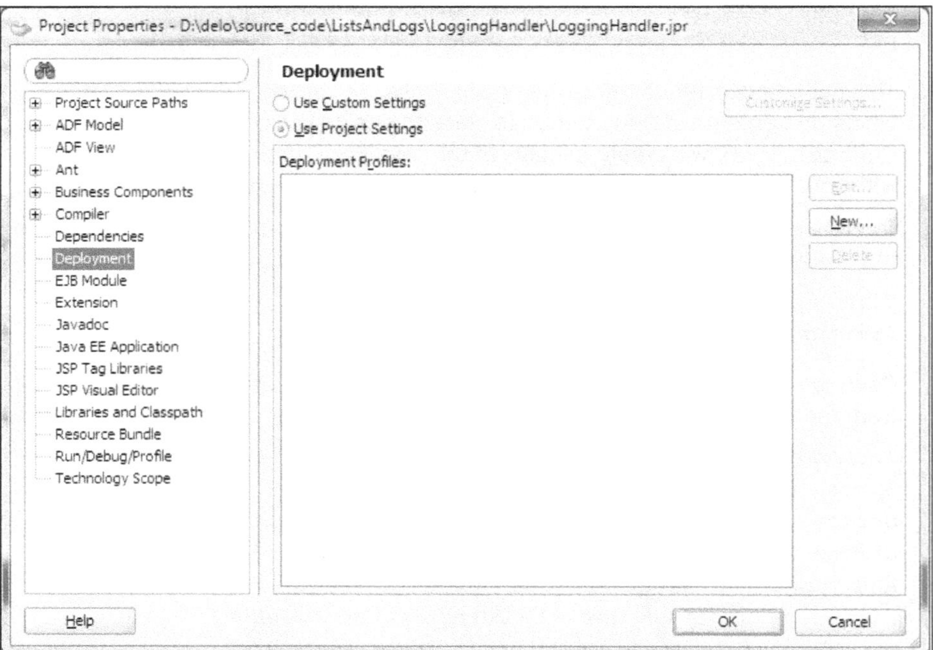

10. The **Create Deployment Profile** dialog shows up where we name our JAR file. Click on the **OK** button as shown in the following screenshot:

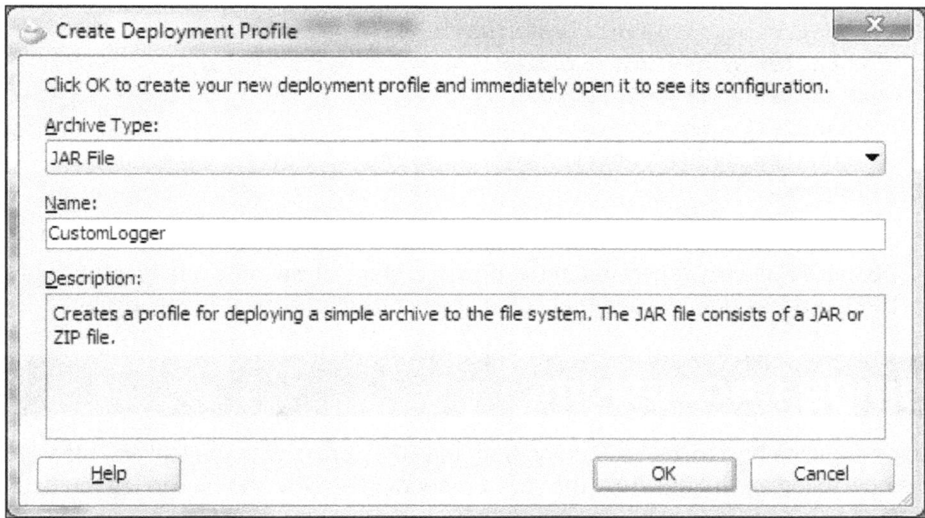

11. We get the **Edit JAR Deployment Profile Properties** dialog and we can simply confirm it by clicking on the **OK** button. Close the **Project Properties...** dialog by clicking on the **OK** button.

12. We'll create a jar file now. On the project root icon, right-click and select **deploy** and then select the deployment profile you just prepared for the JAR creation. The wizard opens but we skip the steps and click on the **Finish** button. The created JAR file is waiting to be picked at the `deploy` directory of the project.

13. Copy the JAR file to the Oracle SOA Suite server shared library location that is located at:

    ```
    ${domain.home}/lib
    ```

14. Now we need to configure the custom handler. Unfortunately, this step needs to be performed manually, because the Oracle Enterprise Manager Console does not show the newly added custom handler. So, let's locate the `logging.xml` file that holds the logging configuration at the following path:

    ```
    ${domain.home}\config\fmwconfig\servers\AdminServer\logging.xml
    ```

15. Open the `logging.xml` file and define a new log handler inside it as shown in the following code:

    ```
    <log_handler name='custom-java-handler' class='logging.
    CustomLogger' level='TRACE:32' formatter='java.util.logging.
    SimpleFormatter'/>
    ```

    We can see that the handler as well as the formatter belongs to the Java Logging utility.

16. Add the log handler to the logger's configuration. Note that the name of the handler must be identical to the one in the `<log_handler>` element as shown in the following code:

    ```
    <logger name='' level='WARNING:1'>
      <handler name='odl-handler'/>
      <handler name='wls-domain'/>
      <handler name='console-handler'/>
      <handler name='custom-java-handler'/>
    </logger>
    ```

17. The last action we need to perform is to restart the Oracle SOA Suite in order to pick up the JAR file we generated in the previous steps. If we initiate the instance of the BPEL process now, we see that some lines of logging appear in the logfile.

Logging exceptions

This recipe explains how to log exceptions from the BPEL process to the logfiles. We will examine how to log exceptions from the Java Embedding activity and how to log faults to the logfiles.

Getting ready...

To complete this recipe, we need to create an empty composite. Also, we need an empty synchronous BPEL 2.0 process.

To log the exceptions, we will extend the logger we defined in the *Creating a custom logger in a BPEL process* recipe of *Chapter 3, Advanced Tracing and Logging*. In this recipe, we will also reuse the logging configuration created in that recipe. We extend the `LogTheBpelExt` class by adding an additional method called `logException` as shown in the following code:

```
public static final void logException(String msg, Exception e) {
  logger.logp(Level.SEVERE, "", "", msg, e);
}
```

This method enables the logging of exceptions on BPEL processes.

How to do it...

To handle exceptions occurring from code execution in a Java Embedding activity, perform the following steps:

1. Open the BPEL process and put the Java Embedding activity (`Java_Math`) inside it

2. The following is the code inside the `Java_Math` activity:

```
try
{
  int a= 7 / 0;
}catch (ArithmeticException ex) {
  org.packt.log.LogTheBpelExt.logException("Java_Math: Error in
calculations", ex);
}
```

3. The execution of the preceding code obviously causes a `divide by 0` exception, so we will be able to see something in the logfile.
4. After deploying the BPEL process and running it, we see the following exception logged into the logfile (the whole stack is not shown because it is not relevant for the recipe):

```
[2013-05-04T09:03:11.143+02:00] [AdminServer] [ERROR] [] [org.
packt.log.Logger] [tid: 14] [userId: <anonymous>] [ecid: e84b
ae63a4864aa7:3c5d9698:13e6e331391:-8000-0000000000000c55,0:2]
[WEBSERVICE_PORT.name: CustomLog_pt] [APP: soa-infra] [composite_
name: CustomLogging] [component_name: CustomLog] [component_
instance_id: 320002] [J2EE_MODULE.name: fabric] [WEBSERVICE.
name: customlog_client_ep] [J2EE_APP.name: soa-infra] Error in
calculations[[
java.lang.ArithmeticException: / by zero
  at orabpel.customlog.ExecLetBxExe0.execute(ExecLetBxExe0.
java:72)
  at com.collaxa.cube.engine.ext.bpel.common.wmp.BPELxExecWMP.__
executeStatements(BPELxExecWMP.java:42)
```

5. We see that the exception itself along with the stack trace is logged into the logfile.

The exception is logged into the logfile; however, the audit trail shows the successful completion of the Java Embedding activity.

There's more...

Another possibility for logging exceptions in BPEL is to log information from the faults that are caught. With this in mind, we will now amend the BPEL process so that it will cause a fault throw:

1. First, we add an `assign` activity where we want to read data from the uninitialized variable as shown in the following code:

```
<assign name="SimulateException">
  <copy>
    <from>$outputVariable.payload/client:result</from>
```

```
      <to>$nulString</to>
    </copy>
  </assign>
```

2. This code will cause the `selectionFailure` system fault. Now we model the `catch` activity as shown in the following code:

```
<catch faultName="bpel:selectionFailure">
  <sequence name="Sequence2">
    <extensionActivity>
      <bpelx:exec name="Java_Report_Exc" language="java">

<![CDATA[org.packt.log.LogTheBpelExt.logException("bpel:selectionF
ailure", null);]]>
      </bpelx:exec>
    </extensionActivity>
  </sequence>
</catch>
```

3. We use the Java Embedding activity (`Java_Report_Exc`) in combination with the `<catch>` activity, and we put the code for the logging exception inside. The `<catch>` activity reacts to the business fault, and the code in `Java_Report_Exc` logs the exception. In the logfile, we can see the following code lines:

```
[2013-05-05T11:41:56.110+02:00] [AdminServer] [ERROR] [] [org.
packt.log.Logger] [tid: 21] [userId: <anonymous>] [ecid: e84b
ae63a4864aa7:40df49d2:13e701bae95:-8000-000000000000680f,0:2]
[WEBSERVICE_PORT.name: CustomLog_pt] [APP: soa-infra] [composite_
name: CustomLogging] [component_name: CustomLog] [component_
instance_id: 330023] [J2EE_MODULE.name: fabric] [WEBSERVICE.
name: customlog_client_ep] [J2EE_APP.name: soa-infra]
bpel:selectionFailure
```

The Oracle SOA Suite does not provide any convenient method to access business fault information from within a Java Embedding activity.

Enabling logging on the BPEL server

This recipe explains several levels of auditing logs in the BPEL server. Here we talk mostly about tracking the execution of a composite and tracking the manipulation of the payload data. We need such information in cases where problem occurs in the BPEL process and we need to track the data flow of the business process or simply to debug the execution of the BPEL process in the early stages of development.

Getting ready...

To complete this recipe, we don't need to do anything special besides running the Oracle SOA Suite server.

How to do it...

The following steps show you how to configure different levels of audit logging on the Oracle SOA Suite server:

1. We will perform the whole recipe through the Oracle Enterprise Manager Console. So, first log in to the console. Right-click on the infrastructure node (**soa-infra**) and select the **SOA Administration** | **Common Properties** option as shown in the following screenshot:

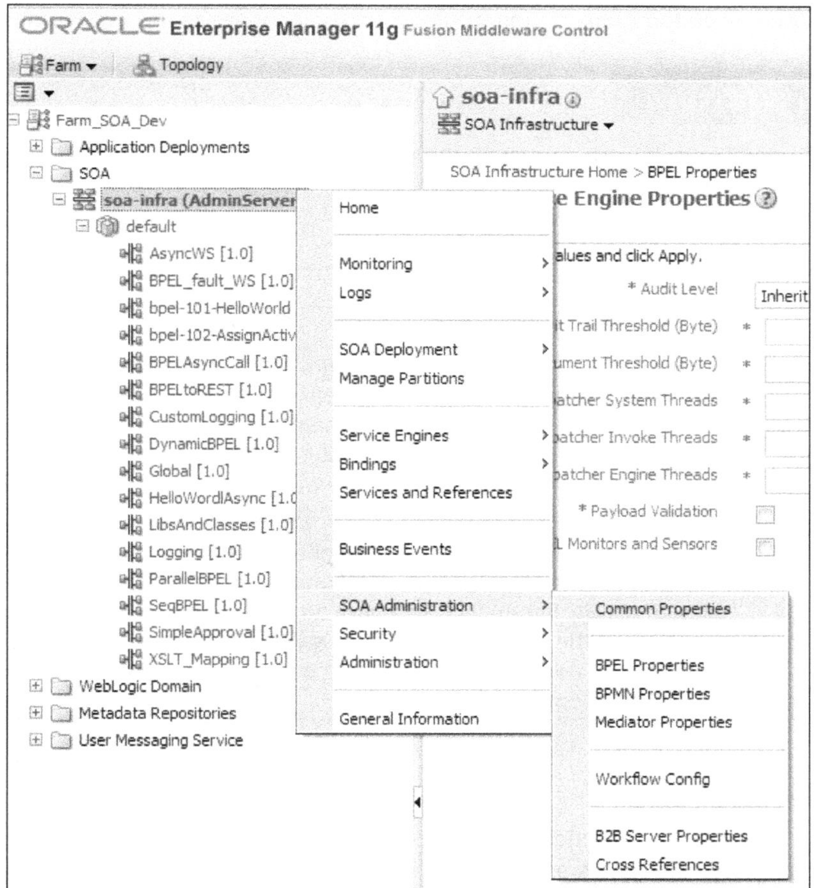

2. The **Common Properties** window opens where we can select the **Audit Level**. Select **Development** as the default audit level as shown in the following screenshot:

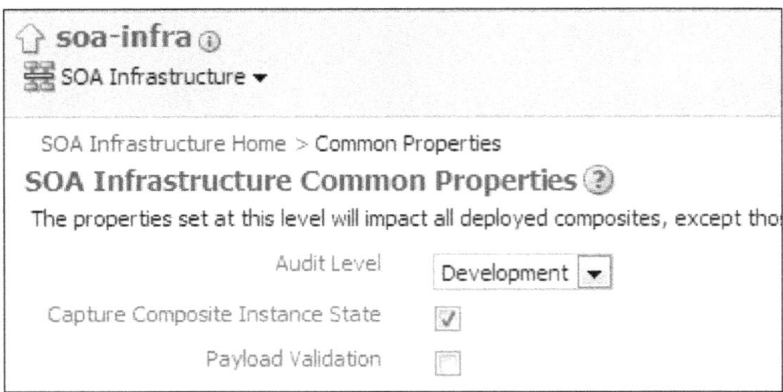

3. By clicking on the **Apply** button, you confirm the changes to the configuration.

How it works...

Changing the audit level has an impact on the amount and verbosity of information collected from the Oracle SOA Suite server. At the level of SOA configuration, there are several possible audit levels as shown in the following table:

Audit level	Description
Off	No logging is performed of any kind.
Production	This audit level provides a minimal amount of information at the level of the SOA infrastructure. The components such as the BPEL engine do not capture the payload traces. Consequently, we are not able to inspect the changes in the payloads from the audit trail. Therefore, the BPEL engine also does not store information about the assign activities. We should choose this setting for the production environment, as the name itself suggests.
Development	This setting is the most appropriate one for development environments. We can inspect the complete set of information in the audit trail along with the assign activity information and payload information. Note that this setting is heavy on the performance of the Oracle SOA Suite. As such, when using this setting, we can experience some performance delays on the Oracle SOA Suite server operations.

There's more...

Up until now, we have only described how to set up the audit level at the level of the SOA infrastructure. Nonetheless, it is also possible to set up the audit level at the level of the BPEL engine. Moreover, we are able to choose from two additional levels of audit trails.

To set up the audit level of the BPEL engine, we repeat step 1 from this recipe. Instead of **Common Properties**, we now select **BPEL Properties** as shown in the following screenshot:

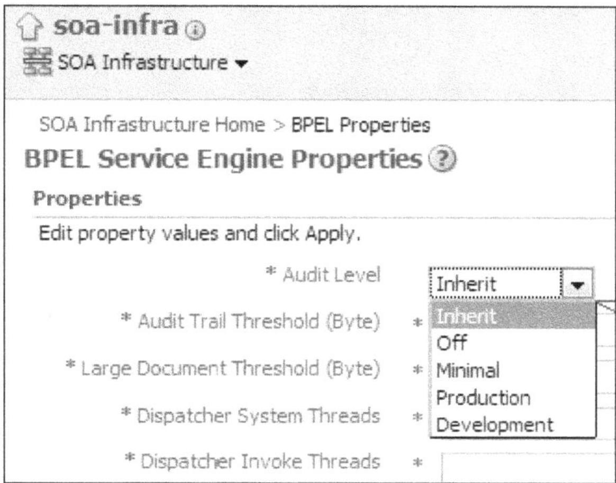

By confirming the configuration, the audit level is used immediately.

In the **BPEL Service Engine Properties** dialog, we see two additional options in the audit level:

Audit level	Description
Inherit	If this option is set, the same level of auditing is used as for the SOA infrastructure. Otherwise, this option precedes the SOA infrastructure setting.
Minimal	As the name suggests, this option provides minimum amount of trail data. The BPEL engine does not capture any audit data. On the other hand all other events get logged.

Redirecting System.out and System.err files

In some cases, we may want to integrate into our BPEL processes other components or applications that print their log information either to standard output, standard error, or both. This recipe will show you how to redirect those outputs to the logfile in order to have logging information in one place.

Getting ready...

To complete the recipe, we will amend the BPEL process from the *Logging exceptions* recipe. Since the main flow of the BPEL process already throws an exception, we will continue explaining this recipe at the fault handler branch of the BPEL process.

How to do it...

In order to redirect the System.out and System.err streams, we create two additional classes in the project:

1. The LogStream class extends the Java PrintStream class. Although there are a number of constructor methods and a number of overridden methods, there is only one method we will describe here, and that is println of type string, as shown in the following code:

   ```
   @Override
   public void println(String x) {
       StackTraceElement caller =
         Thread.currentThread().getStackTrace()[2];
       LogTheBpelExt.log( caller.getClassName() + "  " + caller.
   getMethodName() +
         "  " + caller.getLineNumber() + ": " + x);
   }
   ```

   In the preceding code, we redirect the stream from calling its super method to call of the log method in our custom logger class. Besides that, we also decode the string with useful information about the call stack.

2. We also implement the Redirector singleton class used as a crossover between the redirected and non-redirected logging stream.
3. First, we declare two stream variables that we use as a backup of the original streams as shown in the following code:

   ```
   private static PrintStream origOut;
   private static PrintStream origErr;
   ```

4. The most important methods in the Redirector class are activate() and deactivate(), which are used as the activator and deactivator of the redirection streams respectively.
5. The following is the code for the activate() method:

   ```
   public static void activate() {
     origOut= System.out;
     System.setOut(new LogStream(System.out));
     origErr= System.err;
     System.setErr(new LogStream(System.err));
   }
   ```

6. The following is the code for the deactivate() method:

   ```
   public static void deactivate() {
     System.setOut(origOut);
     System.setErr(origErr);
   }
   ```

7. Now it is time to use the two new classes in the BPEL process. We add the Java Embedding activity into the BPEL process. Insert the following code into the activity:

```
System.out.println("Some output from out - no redirect");
System.err.println("Some output from err - no redirect");
org.packt.redirect.Redirector.getinstance().activate();
System.out.println("Some output from out - redirect");
System.err.println("Some output from err - redirect");
org.packt.redirect.Redirector.getinstance().deactivate();
```

From the preceding code, we can predict that the first two lines will be shown on the console output. Then, we activate the redirection of the output streams. The following two lines should appear in the custom logfile. And finally, we deactivate the redirection. The redirection is taking effect on the BPEL process instance.

Indeed, if we deploy the BPEL process and observe the execution of the instance, we first see the following output in the console:

```
Some output from out - no redirect
Some output from err - no redirect
```

Further, we also see the following two lines in the custom logfile (`AdminServer-custompackt.log`):

```
<6.5.2013 23:26:34 CEST> <Warning> <org.packt.log.Logger> <BEA-000000>
<orabpel.customlog.ExecLetBxExe2  execute  87: Some output from out -
redirect>
<6.5.2013 23:26:34 CEST> <Warning> <org.packt.log.Logger> <BEA-000000>
<orabpel.customlog.ExecLetBxExe2  execute  88: Some output from err -
redirect>
```

We can conclude that the redirection succeeded as we saw in the console and in the custom logfile.

Setting up a rotation logfile

There are few cases where the amount of log information becomes so huge that they are impossible to handle. For that reason, we can configure the logfiles to rotate size-based, time-based, or both.

Getting ready...

This recipe can be considered as a fine-tune addition to the *Logging to a custom file* recipe. We will simply expand on this recipe by adding rotation capabilities to our custom logfile.

How to do it...

We can define the rotation logfile by logging in to the Oracle Enterprise Manager Console and then right-clicking on the **soa-infra** node. Then, select **Logs** and **Log Configuration**. In the **Log Configuration** window, select the logfile definition and click on the **Edit Configuration...** button as shown in the following screenshot:

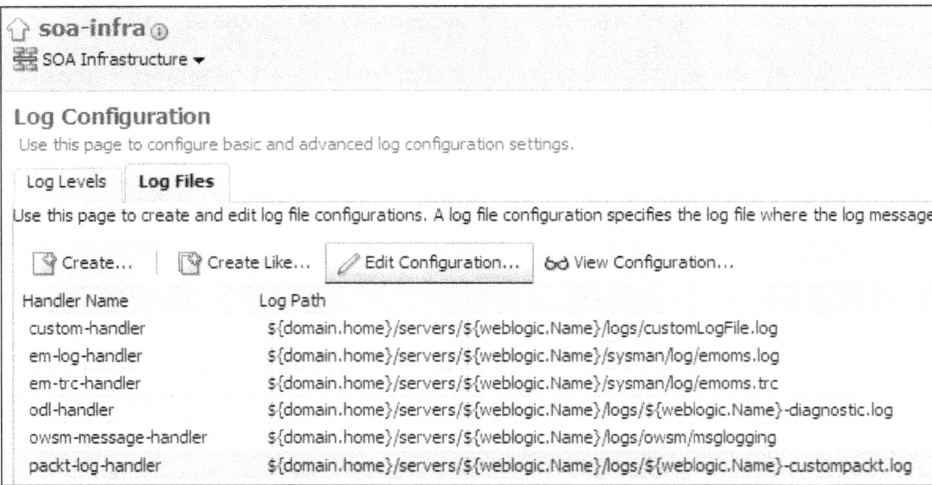

In the **Edit Log File** window, we define the rotation policy for the selected logfile as shown in the following screenshot:

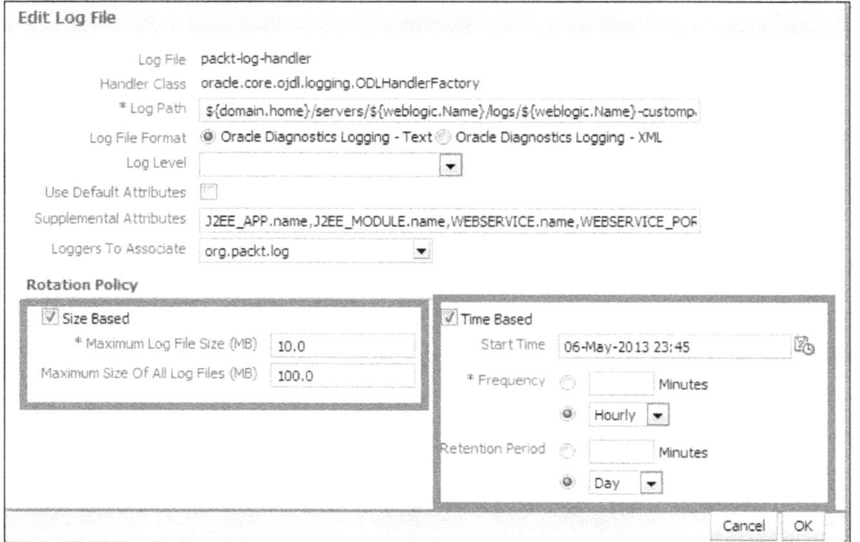

Click on the **OK** button to confirm the changes. There is no need to restart the Oracle SOA Suite server for changes to take effect.

How it works...

We have the following two types of rotation policies, which can also be combined:

- **Size based**: In this rotation policy, we define the maximum size of a single logfile. We can also define the maximum size of all logfiles in the rotation. For example, if we set the maximum size of a single logfile to 10 MB and the maximum size of all the logfiles in the rotation to 100 MB, we will have a maximum of 10 files with the size of 10 MB in rotation. When the logfile size reaches the maximum, the oldest log information gets deleted, thus providing new logging space.
- **Time based**: In this rotation policy, we have two important options. The first one is frequency, where we define at what time periods new logfiles will be created every hour. If we set frequency to **Hourly**, a new logfile will be created. Another option is retention period, where we define how long the logfiles are kept before they are purged. If we set the option to **Day**, one-day-old logfiles will be purged every day.

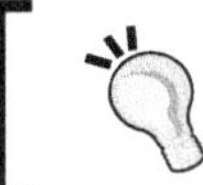

Although both the preceding options can be mixed in configuration, it is advisable to choose only one of them to avoid unexpected logging behavior.

See also

For information on how to set up the custom logfile, refer to the *Logging to a custom file* recipe.

5
Transforming and Validating the BPEL Services

This chapter contains the following recipes:

- Using the XSLT transformation in BPEL
- Generating the XSLT map with the XSLT mapper
- Performing copy between the variables
- Using the functions in the transformation operations
- The chaining functions
- Defining and importing the user-defined functions
- Using the xsl:for-each command
- Defining a parameter
- Defining a variable
- Validating the variables with the <assign> activity

Introduction

In the SOA architecture, BPEL plays the role of the orchestration technology. Its main task is to efficiently coordinate the interaction between web services in the business processes. With the vendor extensions, it is also possible to orchestrate EJB, Java, Spring, REST, and the other compositions.

The design of the BPEL processes requires the orchestration of many web services, each with its own interface and a way of interaction with the outer environment. There will be rare cases when web services along with a business process are in our domain. Web services, in this case, are distinct entities, and so we need to adapt our business process to the interface of the calling web service. In such a scenario, we often encounter the incompatibilities of the web service interfaces. Consequently, the job of BPEL is also the translation of some web service outcome to become the request of another web service. We have already seen that some basic transformations can be done with the assign activity, especially if the `from` and `to` variables are of the same kind.

For a more complex mapping, we use the **XSLT** (**Extensible Stylesheet Language Transformations**) transformation abilities of Oracle SOA Suite since XSLT presents an XML document describing the transformation. The purpose of XSLT is to perform the transformation from XML document to XML document, HTML pages, plain text, and other formats. Oracle SOA Suite also provides a built-in XSLT engine, and therefore it is easy to utilize XSLT with Oracle.

We create the XSLT transformation with the help of JDeveloper which provides a component named the XSLT mapper, which is opened when we double-click on the `Transform` activity. The result of the XSLT transformation activity is the `<assign>` activity in the business process and a transformation file that has the XSLT extension. The XSLT transformation files are stored in the XSLT directory in the JDeveloper project. We can use two views to design the XSLT transformations in JDeveloper. The first one is the visual mapping editor, where we can do most of the job by using drag-and-drop. The other view is the source view, where we change the XSLT code manually.

When we are satisfied with the XSLT transformation file, we can test if the transformation works as expected since JDeveloper also offers the testing facility.

Another important aspect of data manipulation is validation. The business data in a BPEL process is stored in the variables. Data is in the XML format. With validation, we want to ensure that the XML content conforms to the well-defined paradigm and also follows the defined structure of the XML schema. Furthermore, our goal is to catch the invalid XML data as soon as possible. Invalid XML data can cause unpredictable damage to a BPEL process, thus leaving the BPEL process in an unknown state. To repair such a BPEL process, it is often not enough to perform fault handling or compensation, since fault handling and compensation might also use the faulty data to perform its tasks. Rather, manual changes of modifications are needed, which for example include manual SQL insert/update/delete statement execution on the databases.

In this chapter, we will focus on the recipes that provide efficient XSLT transformation as well as validation of the XML data.

Using the XSLT transformation in BPEL

In this recipe, we will show the usage of the `Transform` activity in JDeveloper. The XSLT mapping activity is exposed as the Oracle extension activity in JDeveloper.

Getting ready

Before we start with the recipe, we prepare an empty SOA composite project with the default synchronous BPEL process. We reuse the web service for querying about the available car. The input parameter presents a `from-to` date range, and the output of the web service call returns the available car at the specified date range. We also add the following two `<assign>` activities:

- The first one assigns the request data to the input variable of the web service
- The second one assigns the response from the web service to the response of the BPEL process

How to do it...

In the JDeveloper environment, we pick the `Transform` activity from the **Oracle Extensions** tab in the **Component Palette**. We put the `Transform` activity into the BPEL process as shown in the following screenshot:

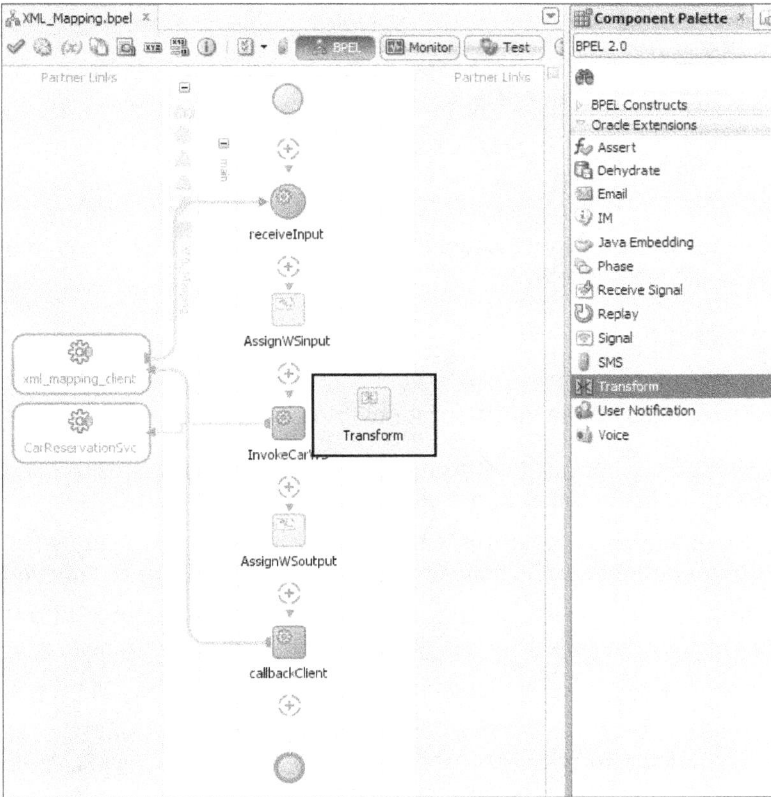

We have just created a transformation activity in the BPEL process.

How it works...

In the BPEL process we created previously, we had two assign activities. With the first one, we assign the values from the request variable of the BPEL process to the input variable of the invoke activity. With the second assign activity, we copy the content of the invoke activity output variable to the response variable of the BPEL process. This approach works perfectly in a relatively straightforward definition of the variable. For example, we can use the assign activity if the variables have the same name but different namespaces. This way, we deliberately violate the well-form of the XML document; however, we can get data without much of an effort.

We can also use the assign activity if the same definition of the request and response messages applies to the BPEL process as well as to the web service that is called from the BPEL process. However, if we have more complex structures of the variables, it is recommended that we use the transform activity. Basically, the transform definition is the same as the assign activity with a slight difference. In the following code, note the `<bpelx:annotation>` element, which gives the activity the transform look in JDeveloper:

```
<assign name = "Transform1" xml:id = "id_29">
  <bpelx:annotation xml:id = "id_30">
      <bpelx:pattern patternName = "bpelx:transformation"
       xml:id = "id_31"/>
   </bpelx:annotation>
</assign>
```

At runtime, when the BPEL engine encounters the `Transform` activity, it runs the built-in XSLT engine in order to execute the activity.

There's more...

Oracle SOA Suite provides several functions for utilizing the XSLT engine as follows:

- `bpel:doXslTransform()`: This function from the BPEL Extensions section is used for an XSLT transformation with multiple sources
- `ora:doXSLTransform()`: This is the same function as `bpel:doXslTransform()` with a slight difference; it is defined in the BPEL XPath Extension functions section
- `ora:doXSLTransformForDoc()`: This function is used for an XSLT transformation where the XSLT template matches the document we want to transform
- `ora:processXSLT()`: This function returns the result of the XSLT transformation
- `xdk:processXSLT()`: This function is same as `ora:processXSLT()`; however, it is used for backward compatibility since it uses the Oracle XDK XSLT processor

See also

- If we try to deploy the BPEL process that we created, there will be errors reported. The reason for the errors is that the `Transform` activity has not been configured. In the next recipe, we will configure the `Transform` activity and make the BPEL process deployable again.

Generating the XSLT map with the XSLT mapper

This recipe will explore how to configure the `Transform` activity. We will create an XSLT transformation file and use it to map the output variable of a web service to the response variable of the BPEL process. In this recipe, we will convert the semicolon delimited result text into an XML-formatted result.

Getting ready

If we now run the BPEL process we created in the previous recipe without the `Transform` activity, we will get a simple string response as shown in the following screenshot:

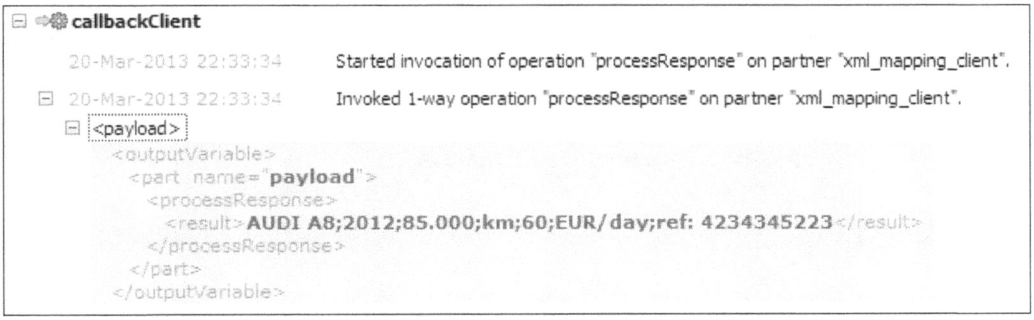

```
callbackClient
   20-Mar-2013 22:33:34   Started invocation of operation "processResponse" on partner "xml_mapping_client".
   20-Mar-2013 22:33:34   Invoked 1-way operation "processResponse" on partner "xml_mapping_client".
   <payload>
     <outputVariable>
       <part name="payload">
         <processResponse>
           <result>AUDI A8;2012;85.000;km;60;EUR/day;ref: 4234345223</result>
         </processResponse>
       </part>
     </outputVariable>
```

The response can be read well from the screen; however, if we need to process the response any further, we need to split the response by the delimiter and process the result. A more applicable solution is to use the XML format, which is easy to process.

We will extend the example from the previous recipe by adding additional elements to the response message. We open the `XML_Mapping.xsd` file and add the following lines to the `processResponse` element as follows:

```
<element name = "processResponse">
  <complexType>
    <sequence>
```

```
        <!--element name = "result" type="string"/-->
        <element name = "carBrand" type="string"/>
        <element name = "year" type="int"/>
        <element name = "milleage" type="int"/>
        <element name = "price" type="int"/>
        <element name = "ref" type="string"/>
      </sequence>
    </complexType>
  </element>
```

We need to comment out the previous content of the response message in order to receive only the XML-formatted output.

How to do it...

The following steps show you how to configure the `Transform` activity in order to transform the semicolon text into XML-formatted content:

1. In JDeveloper, we remove the `AssignWSoutput` activity since it no longer correctly maps the output of the web service to the output of the BPEL process.
2. We replace the assign activity with the transform activity and name it `TransformWSoutput`.
3. We right-click on the `Transform` activity and select **Edit**. We get the following dialog:

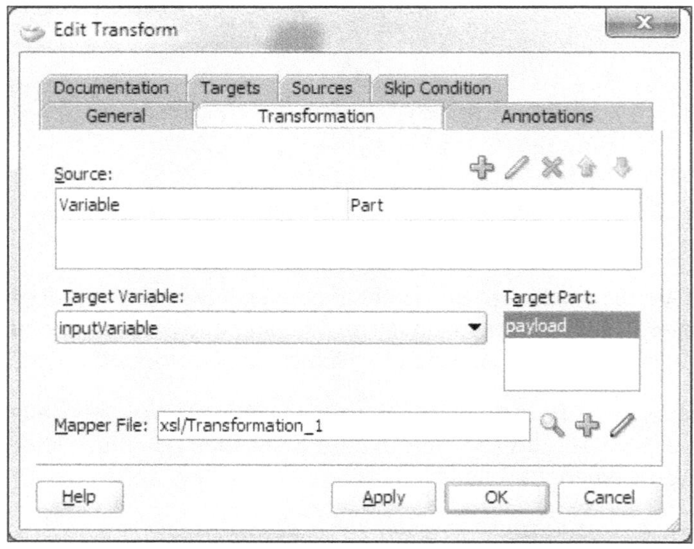

We get a set of tabs; the one that interests us is labeled **Tranformation**.

4. As we will map the output of the web service to the response of the BPEL process, we follow these actions:
    1. Click on the plus sign (**+**) and select `InvokeCarWS_getAvailableCar_OutputVariable` and parameters as a source variable.
    2. From the **Target Variable**, select **outputVariable** and **payload** as **Target Part**.
    3. Name the mapper file as `xsl/TransformCarReservationData` and click on the **OK** button.
5. We get the XML mapper in JDeveloper with the source variable on the left, a space for mapping the functions in the middle, and a target variable on the right as shown in the following screenshot:

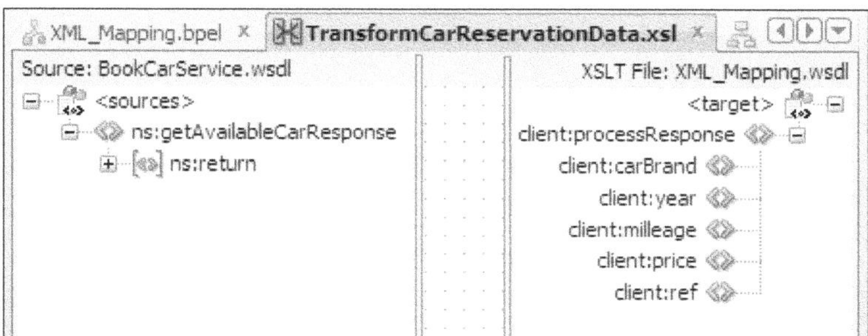

How it works...

The first part of the work is done when we add the `Transform` activity to the BPEL process. We then configure the `Transform` activity with the source and target variables and the XSLT file location definition.

Apart from the `Transform` activity in the BPEL process, we get the new XSLT configuration file in the JDeveloper project.

The transformation operation now presents the assign activity with an annotation and the copy operation. The copy operation takes the input variable and process it through the `ora:doXSLTransformForDoc` function. As a result of the function, we assign the content to the output variable.

If we examine the `TransformCarReservationData.xsl` file, we see that the content is basically empty. What we found is the commented section about mapping the input and output variables and an empty section on the mapping rules.

> Don't change the commented section part of the XSLT file. This may result in problems when JDeveloper tries to visualize the XSLT file in the XSLT mapper.

See also

- In the next recipe, we will perform the operations between the source and target variables. Look at the *Using the functions in the transformation operations* recipe to see how the functions are used in the XSLT transformation file.

Performing copy between the variables

In this recipe, we will show you the various ways of copying between the variables. For that purpose, we will use the XSLT mapper accessed through the transformation activity from JDeveloper.

Getting ready

Before we are able to copy the variables, we need to adapt the BPEL process to contain data suitable for the XSLT mapper. The problem is that the web service in our BPEL process is returning the field separated data; however, we need the XML-formatted data.

1. Our first task is to transform the delimited data format to the XML format. For that purpose, we define a new schema with only one element definition and name it `TempSchema.xsd`.

   ```
   <xsd:element name = "TempElement">
     <xsd:complexType>
       <xsd:sequence>
         <xsd:element name = "pieces" type = "xsd:string"
           minOccurs = "0" maxOccurs = "unbounded"/>
       </xsd:sequence>
     </xsd:complexType>
   </xsd:element>
   ```

2. The element definition basically presents an array of string pieces in `TempElement`. We define the variable (it can either be global or local) in the BPEL process as follows:

   ```
   <variable name = "TempVar" element = "ns3:TempElement"
     xml:id = "id_36"/>
   ```

In general, we use the global variables when we need to reuse the content over the entire BPEL process. If the variable content is used only in a limited scope of the BPEL process, then we define the local variables.

3. Next, we introduce the new assign activity just after the web service call. At this location, we will convert the delimited text to the XML structure as follows:

```
<assign name = "AssignTemp" xml:id = "id_37">
  <extensionAssignOperation xml:id = "id_45">
    <bpelx:copyList xml:id = "id_42">
      <bpelx:from xml:id = "id_43">oraext:
        create-nodeset-from-delimited-string
          ('{http://org.packt.temp}pieces',
            $InvokeCarWS_getAvailableCar_OutputVariable.
              parameters/ns2:return, ';')</bpelx:from>
      <bpelx:to xml:id =
        "id_44">$TempVar/ns3:pieces</bpelx:to>
    </bpelx:copyList>
  </extensionAssignOperation>
</assign>
```

4. We have defined the required elements that we need on the source side of the XSLT mapper. Next, edit the `Transform` activity, and in the sources, replace the previous values with our temporary defined schema.

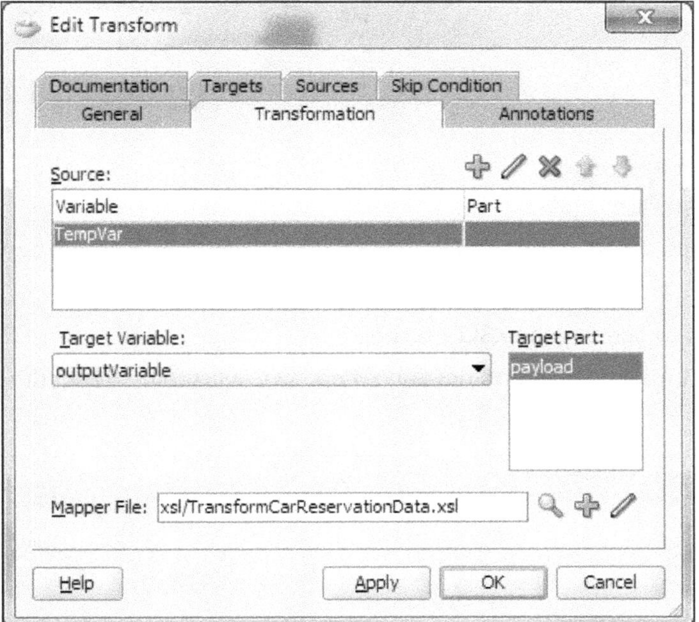

5. Next, edit the XSLT transformation file. Right-click on the sources tree and select **Replace schema**. Select the temporary XSD schema we defined for our transformation, `TempSchema.xsd`, and confirm the change.

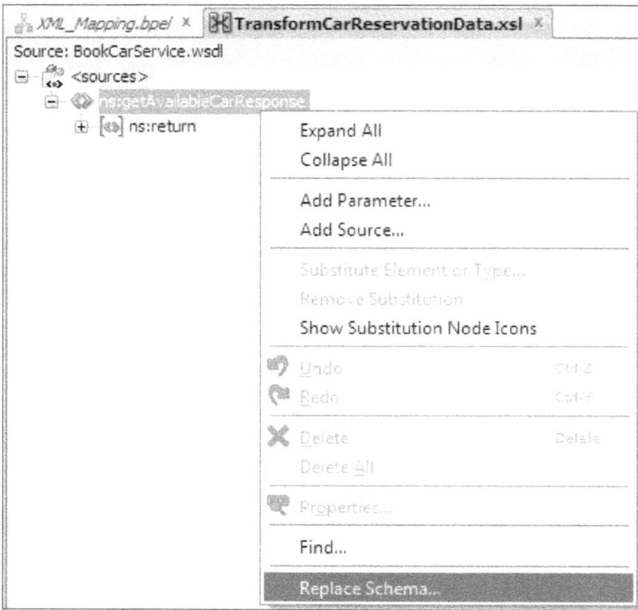

How to do it...

The following steps describe the actions required to transform the content between the BPEL variables:

1. We start by opening the XSLT mapper.
2. The XSLT mapper supports drag-and-drop, so it is just a matter of dragging the sources to the targets.

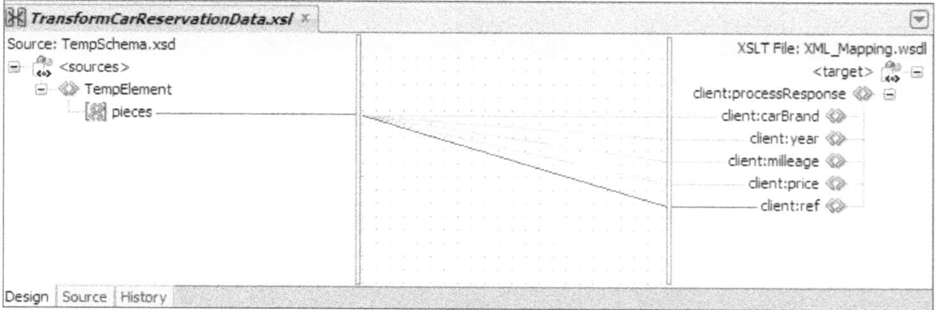

3. Obviously, the result of mapping the array into several distinct fields does not give the results we want. However, with the use of the functions, the desired effect would be achieved. When we are satisfied with the mapping, we save the XSLT mapper file.

How it works...

We see that the XSLT mapper is divided into three sections from left to right. On the left-most side, we see the sources. By defining the sources, we specify where the data should be taken from. On the right-most side, we find the targets. The middle section of the XSLT mapper along with the targets is reserved for the transformation rules and functions for transforming the sources to the targets.

Remember, the underlying presentation of the XSLT mapper presents the physical file with an XSL extension.

There's more...

We will now show you two additional powerful functionalities of the XSLT mapper. One is **Auto Map**, where JDeveloper performs the transformation automatically for us. The next one is **Completion Status**, where we check the completeness of the transformation rules.

Auto Map

A very helpful feature provided by JDeveloper is Auto Map in the XSLT mapper. We configure the Auto Map feature by right-clicking in the middle part of the XSLT mapper and selecting **Auto Map Preferences**. The dialog window appears and we can configure the behavior of the Auto Map feature as shown in the following screenshot:

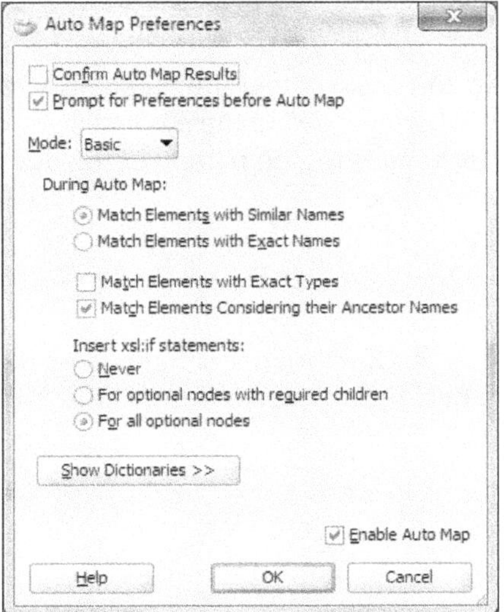

We can select whether Auto Map is enabled or not. Furthermore, we can configure whether we would like to confirm the changes before they actually apply to the XSLT mapper. Last but not least, we define some basic matching criteria that will be applied when performing auto mapping, such as matching by similar names, types, ancestor names, and so on.

In cases, where we define the web service schemas by ourselves, it is recommended to define the XML nodes with similar names. Hence, Auto Map does not have much trouble performing the transformation.

Completion Status

When we work on a large transformation, Completion Status can be a helpful tool. Right-click in the middle part of the XSLT mapper pane and select **Completion Status**, which brings up the dialog with information about the unmapped nodes as shown in the following screenshot:

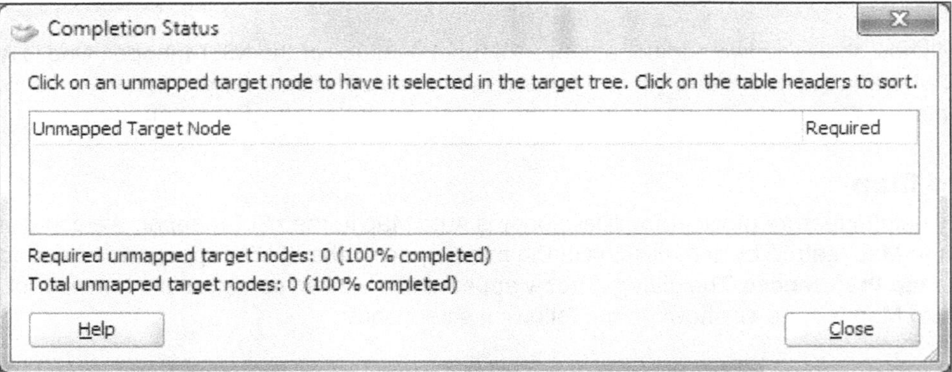

Under the required window, we can see whether the mapping is required on not. This status is taken from the XSD schema where we define the cardinality of the element with the `minOccurs` and `maxOccurs` attributes. At the bottom of the dialog, we see the percentage of how many nodes are still unmapped.

See also

- We explore the usage of the XSLT mapper in the *Using the XSLT transformation in BPEL* recipe. In the next recipe, we will discuss the usage of the functions in XSLT mapper.

Using the functions in the transformation operations

In this recipe, we will examine how the functions are used in the XSLT mapper. The functions provide a convenient way of transforming data in a BPEL process. In this recipe, we will use some of the available functions, such as the multiply operation and the if branch statement.

Getting ready

For this recipe, we will take the example from the *Performing copy between the variables* recipe. We will extend the example by using a function to add a margin to the rent price of the car.

How to do it...

The following steps describe the actions needed to use the functions in the XSLT transformations:

1. Open the XSLT mapper in JDeveloper.
2. We see that all the elements have the transformation links from the source to the target nodes. We delete the link that connects the price by clicking on the link and clicking on the **Delete** button.
3. From the **Component Palette** on the right side, we choose the multiply mathematical function and drop it on the middle section of the XSLT mapper pane.

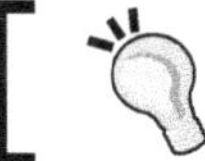

We can find the multiply function under the **Mathematical Functions** section in the **Component Palette**.

We connect the input and output connector of the mathematical function, with the price node from the source and target schema respectively.

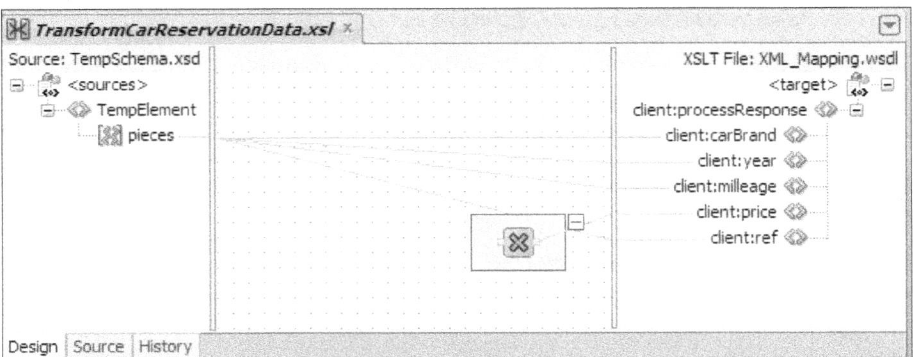

The source part of the variable is not connected to the multiply function. The reason for that is the usage of the source variable, which presents the array of strings. Since we took only one record from the array, JDeveloper deletes the link to the source variable.

4. Finally, we need to set up the formula for the margin. We do this by double-clicking on the multiply function node. The dialog for entering the formula appears, we enter the formula text and confirm it by clicking on the **OK** button.

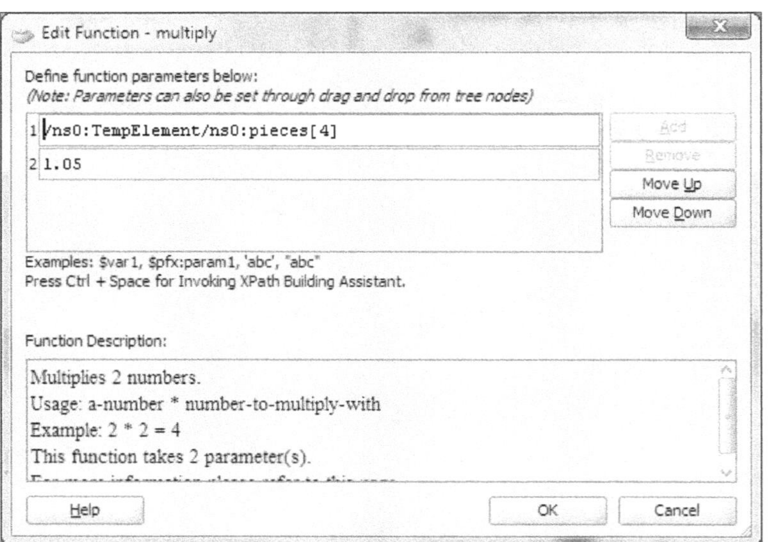

We enter the source node into field 1 (`/ns0:TempElement/ns0:pieces[4]`) and insert the margin into field 2 (`1.05`).

How it works...

The functions we define in the XSLT mapper are stored in the XSL file. JDeveloper provides a convenient way of creating the transformation files. Behind the scenes, JDeveloper is building the XSL file. The XSLT mapper also performs real-time checking of the transformation file. For example, if we put the `if xslt` construct into the mapper pane, it immediately becomes marked with the error icon as shown in the following screenshot:

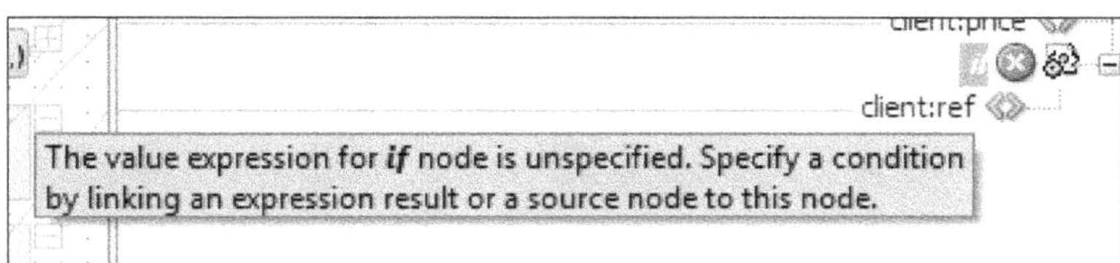

The transformation file is, when finished, interpreted by the built-in XSLT engine when transforming the source variable to the target variable.

Oracle SOA Suite provides a number of functions that we can utilize for transformation purposes as follows:

Function Group	Description
Conversion Functions	Mainly contains the functions to convert the `Boolean` number and the `string` values.
Date Functions	Contains the date manipulation and formatting functions.
Logical Functions	This contains the logical operators such as <, >, =, true, false, or, not, and so on.
Mathematical Functions	Contains the mathematical functions such as abs, ceiling, sum, and so on.
Node-set Functions	This section enables various operations on the variables from the XML point of view. For example, the name function returns the name of the XML node.
String Functions	This section contains a number of string operation functions. Here, we also find the concat, compare, and contains functions.
XSLT Constructs	Contains the most important XSLT constructs. We find here the following constructs: choose, copy-of, for-each, if, otherwise, sort, variable, and when.

See also

- The next recipe explains how to chain the functions.

The chaining functions

When performing the transformations, we sometimes find ourselves in a situation where there is no single operation to perform a transformation the way we want. For example, let's say we would like to first trim two strings and then concatenate them. Since we don't have a single function to perform the task, the XSLT mapper in JDeveloper offers us the functionality of the chaining functions. In this recipe, we will examine how to chain the functions in order to present the complete information from the source to the target content.

Getting ready

We will amend the example from the *Using the functions in the transformation operations* recipe. We will amend the BPEL process so that we now map the correct source content to the target content.

How to do it...

1. We will perform the action of concatenating the `price` element with its money unit. First, we open the XSLT mapper.
2. Then, pick the concat function from the **Component Palette** (**String Functions**). Place it in the box where we calculate the `price` element with the margin.
3. Now, delete the link from the multiply function to the target price node by right-clicking on the line and clicking on **Delete**.
4. Next, drag the connector line from the output of the multiply function to the input of the concat function.
5. Connect the output of the concat function to the `price` element of the target part.
6. We still need to configure the concat function. We right-click on the concat function and select **Properties...**. We leave the field 1 unchanged and into the field 2 we enter `/ns0:TempElement/ns0:pieces[6]`.

7. The properties dialog now shows the following content:

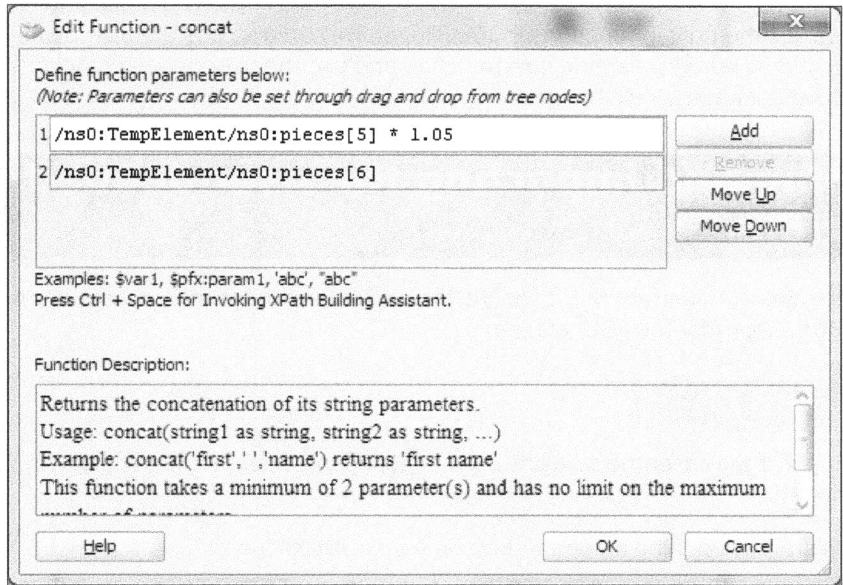

8. We confirm the properties by clicking on **OK** in the dialog.

How it works...

We are able to chain the functions in order to fulfill the needed transformation. JDeveloper, with its XSLT mapper, shows the chain of functions. However, the functions are interpreted as simple operations in the XSL file. Let us check the code from our XSL file, where we used the chaining as follows:

```
<client:price>
  <xsl:value-of select = "concat(/ns0:TempElement/ns0:pieces[5] *
    1.05,/ns0:TempElement/ns0:pieces[6])"/>
</client:price>
```

We can see that there is no multiply function. It is simply a star sign indicating the multiply operation in XSLT. Furthermore, the concat function presents a standard operation for the `string` concatenation in the XSLT specification.

See also

- Besides the built-in functions in JDeveloper, we can also use the user-defined functions. We will examine how to define and use the user-defined functions in JDeveloper in the next recipe.

Defining and importing the user-defined functions

In this recipe, we will illustrate how to define the custom functions in Java and how to import them into JDeveloper for the XSLT mapper.

How to do it...

The following text will cover the steps needed to define the custom functions and import them into JDeveloper:

1. We start by opening an empty Java project in JDeveloper.
2. In the Java project, we create the Java class (`ValueWithUnit.java`) that is used as a placeholder for the function logic. What we do is concatenate the value of the field with its corresponding unit as follows:

```
public class ValueWithUnit {
  public static String formatValueWithUnit
    (String value, String unit) {
    return value + " " + unit;
    }
  }
```

3. Next, we prepare the configuration file. We create a new directory named `xml` in the project and prepare the XML file named `ext-mapper-xpath-functions-config.xml`.

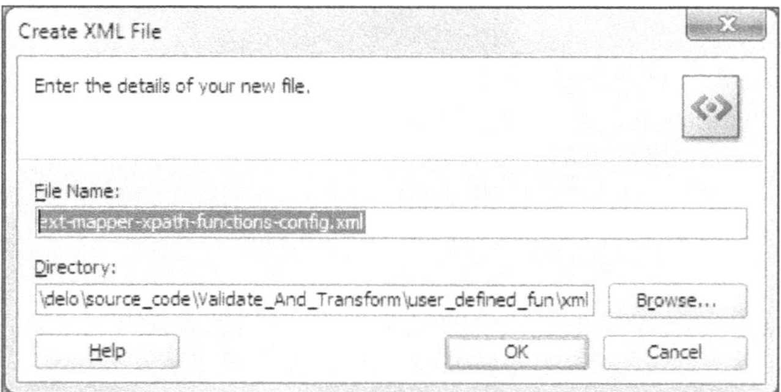

4. In the configuration file, we define the function name, class name, and input and output parameters. We also add the description of the function.

```
<?xml version = "1.0" encoding = "utf-8" ?>
<soa-xpath-functions xmlns =
  "http://xmlns.oracle.com/soa/config/xpath"
    xmlns:ud = "http://www.oracle.com/XSL/Transform/java
      /org.packt.user.defined.ValueWithUnit">
  <function name = "ud:formatValueWithUnit">
  <className>org.packt.user.defined.ValueWithUnit
    </className>
    <return type = "string"/>
    <params>
      <param name = "value" type = "string"/>
      <param name = "unit" type = "string"/>
    </params>
    <desc/>
    <detail>
      <![CDATA[Function concatenates the value and unit.]]>
    </detail>
  </function>
</soa-xpath-functions>
```

5. We are now ready to pack the class file along with the configuration file into the JAR archive for the deployment. For that purpose, we create a new deployment profile for the JAR archive as shown in the following screenshot:

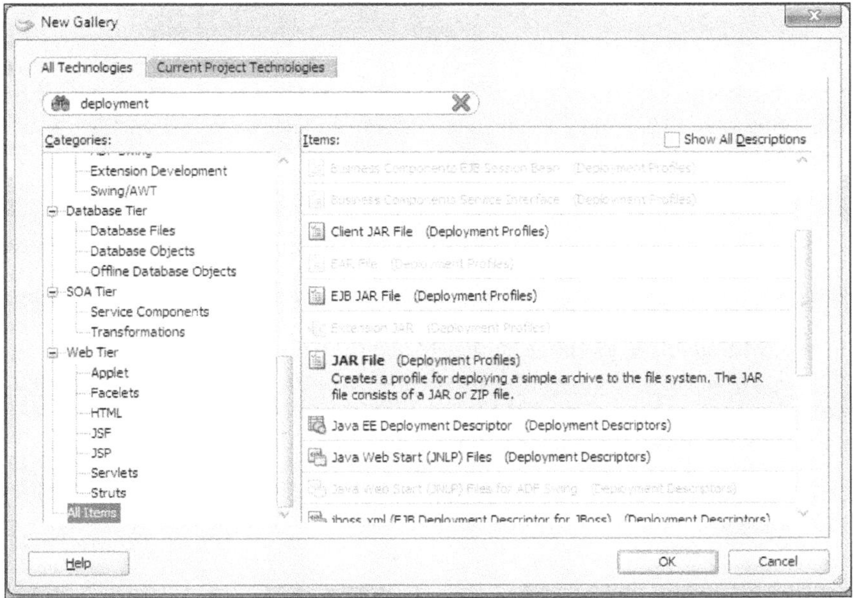

6. In the deployment profile dialog, we enter `UserDefinedFunction` as the name of the deployment profile and click on the **OK** button.
7. We get the dialog to configure the deployment profile. From the tree, we select **Filters** from **Project Output** and deselect the `xml` part from the **Files** tab as shown in the following screenshot:

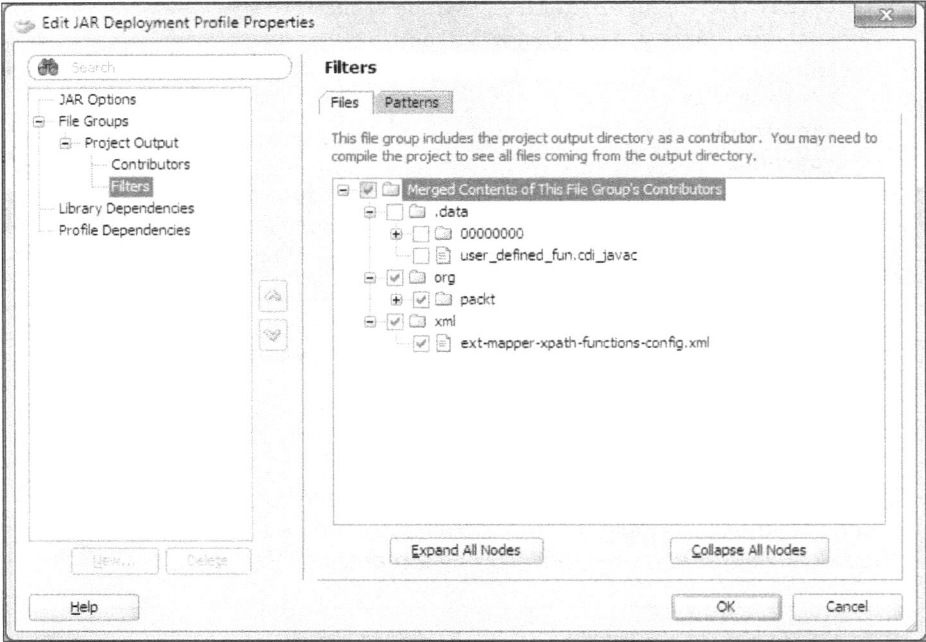

8. In the file group, we create a new group and name it `config`. We define the packaging type of the file group. To configure the file group, we perform the following actions on the following tabs:
   - **config**: In the target directory, we enter `META-INF`
   - **Filters**: In this tab, we deselect everything except for the `xml` directory
9. We confirm the deployment profile configuration by clicking on the **OK** button.

Now we are ready to build the package and deploy it for usage in JDeveloper. At the project root, we right-click and select **Deploy** and **UserDefined Functions...**. The deployment action wizard appears and we confirm the dialog by clicking on **Finish**. We find the created JAR file in the deploy directory of the project.

We install the extension to JDeveloper by selecting the **Tools** menu and then selecting **Preferences**.

Under the **SOA** tab, we select the generated JAR file and click on the **OK** button as shown in the following screenshot:

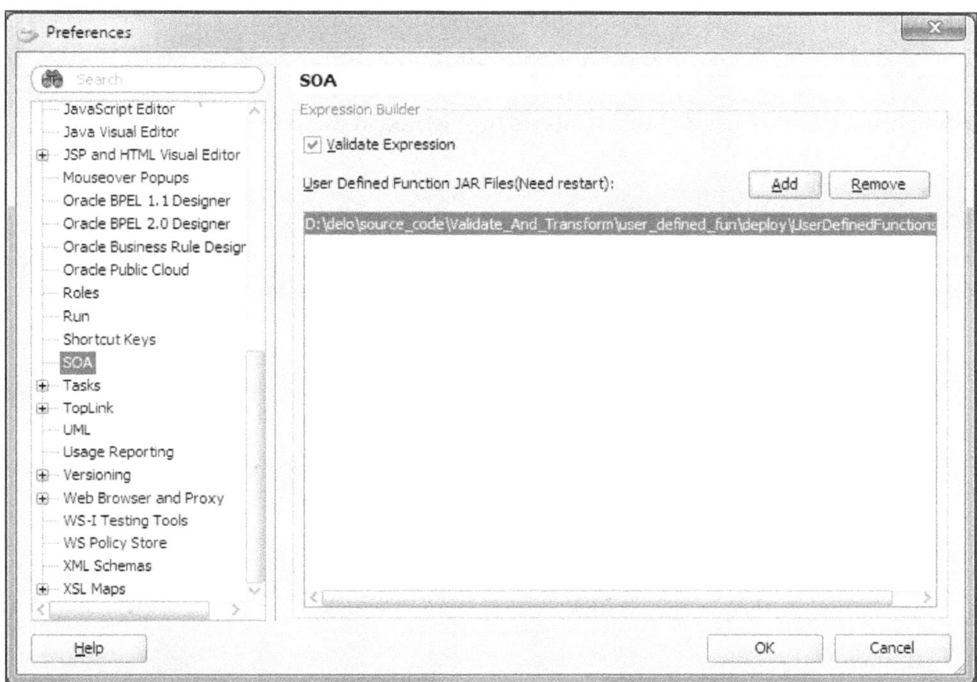

In order to start using the user-defined functions in BPEL processes, we need to restart JDeveloper.

How it works...

The user-defined functions are composed of the Java class and the XML configuration file. The composition packed into the JAR file can be used as an extension function in JDeveloper and Oracle SOA Suite.

Depending on where we want to use the user-defined functions, we define the XML configuration file. The structure of the XML configuration is the same; however, the names differ depending on the area we want to use the functions in as follows:

Purpose of usage	XML configuration file name
Oracle BPEL engine	`ext-bpel-xpath-functions-config.xml`
Oracle Mediator	`ext-mediator-xpath-functions-config.xml`

Purpose of usage	XML configuration file name
XSLT Mapper	`ext-mapper-xpath-functions-config.xml`
Human workflow	`ext-wf-xpath-functions-config.xml`
All of above	`ext-soa-xpath-functions-config.xml`

The configuration file we used in this recipe is highlighted in the preceding table.

There's more...

After the restart, we can see that our user-defined function appears in JDeveloper. It can be picked up from the **Component Palette** and **User Defined Extension Functions** tab.

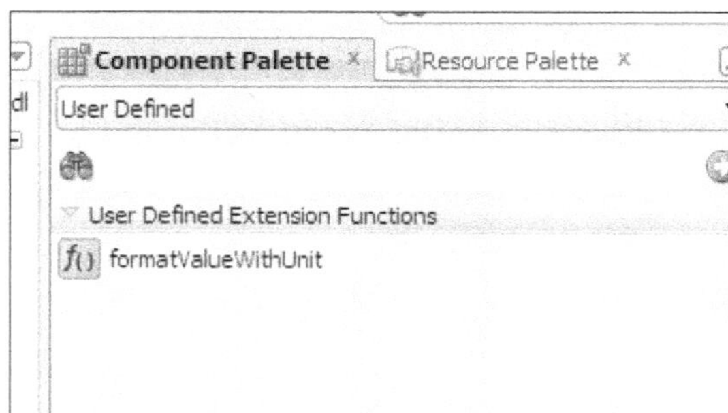

Using the user-defined function

Next, we will show you how to use the user-defined function in JDeveloper:

1. In JDeveloper, we open the XSLT mapper. From the **Component Palette** tab, we pick the user-defined function and put it on the mapper pane.
2. By right-clicking on the new function and selecting **Properties**, we can enter the desired data as shown in the following screenshot:

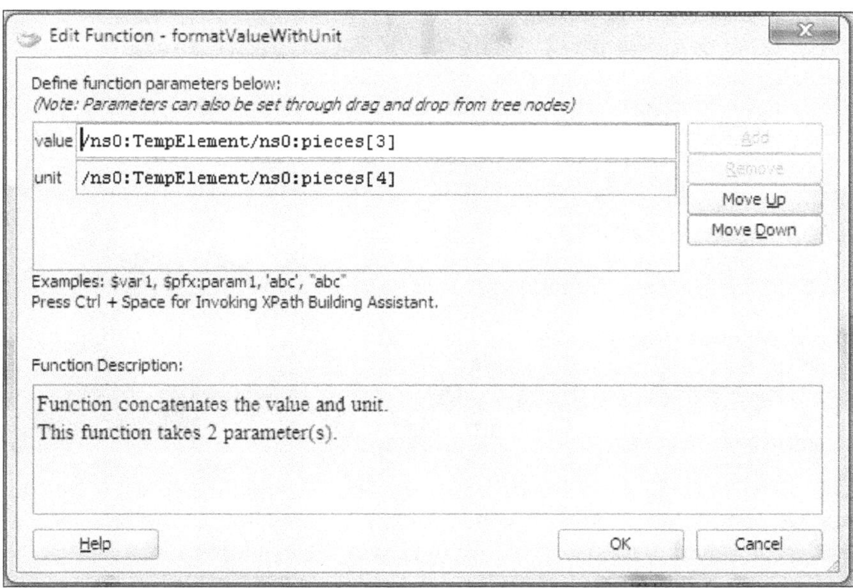

3. An excerpt of the code from the transformation file is as follows:

```
<client:milleage>
  <xsl:value-of select =
    "ud:formatValueWithUnit(/ns0:TempElement/ns0:pieces[3],
      /ns0:TempElement/ns0:pieces[4])"/>
</client:milleage>
```

4. We see that our function will be called with two parameters to be concatenated.

Migrating the user-defined functions to the Oracle SOA server

Oracle SOA Suite provides a placeholder where we put the extensions. We can put the extension in place by executing the following steps:

1. Open the command prompt.
2. Change the directory to `<Oracle_SOA_home>\Oracle_SOA1\soa\modules\oracle.soa.ext_11.1.1\` and copy the extension JAR file into this directory.
3. We execute the ant command to rebuild the extension registry.

```
C:\Programs\Oracle\Middleware\Oracle_SOA1\soa\modules
  \oracle.soa.ext_11.1.1>ant
Buildfile: build.xml
create-manifest-jar: [echo] Creating oracle.soa.ext at
  C:\Programs\Oracle\Middleware\Oracle_SOA1\soa\modules
    \oracle.soa.ext_11.1.1/oracle.soa.ext.jar;
```

```
C:\Programs\Oracle\Middleware\Oracle_SOA1\soa\modules
  \oracle.soa.ext_11.1.1\UserDefinedFunctions.jar;
C:\Programs\Oracle\Middleware\Oracle_SOA1\soa\modules
  \oracle.soa.ext_11.1.1\classes [jar] Updating jar;
C:\Programs\Oracle\Middleware\Oracle_SOA1\soa\modules
  \oracle.soa.ext_11.1.1\oracle.soa.ext.jar
BUILD SUCCESSFUL
Total time: 0 seconds
C:\Programs\Oracle\Middleware\Oracle_SOA1\soa\modules
  \oracle.soa.ext_11.1.1>
```

4. Finally, we start Oracle SOA Suite.

Using the xsl:for-each command

In this recipe, we will examine the usage of the `for-each` command in XSLT. This function is helpful when we need to transform a number of identical elements in the array. We will use the `for-each` command to map (transform) the list of the available cars.

Getting ready

We will modify the example from the *The chaining functions* recipe. For our recipe, we will define a new schema to show how the `for-each` command works. We define a schema that presents a list of the available cars to be rented. The schema is as follows:

```
  <xsd:element name = "WScars">
  <xsd:complexType>
    <xsd:sequence>
      <xsd:element name = "listCars" maxOccurs = "unbounded">
        <xsd:complexType>
          <xsd:sequence>
            <xsd:element name = "carType" type = "xsd:string"/>
            <xsd:element name = "buildYear" type = "xsd:int"/>
            <xsd:element name = "milleage" type = "xsd:int"/>
            <xsd:element name = "pricePerDay" type = "xsd:int"/>
            <xsd:element name = "refNo" type = "xsd:string"/>
          </xsd:sequence>
        </xsd:complexType>
      </xsd:element>
    </xsd:sequence>
  </xsd:complexType>
</xsd:element>
```

We also extend the response element of the BPEL process. We surround it with the element that has the attribute `maxOccurs` set to `unbound` as follows:

```
<element name = "processResponseForEach">
  <complexType>
    <sequence>
      <element name = "availableCars" maxOccurs = "unbounded">
        <complexType>
          <sequence>
            <!-- elements of the car -->
          </sequence>
        </complexType>
      </element>
    </sequence>
  </complexType>
</element>
```

How to do it...

The following steps present the actions required to utilize the `for-each` command in the XSLT transformation to copy the list of the available cars between the two BPEL variables:

1. We define a new transformation XSL file and name it `ForEachUseCase.xsl`.
2. Next, we define the source and target and click on **OK** as shown in the following screenshot:

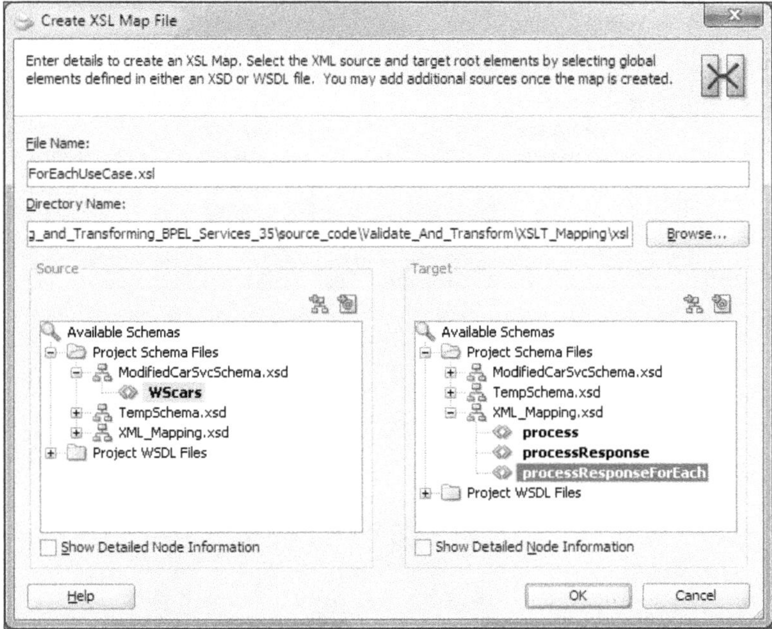

3. From the **Component Palette** tab, we pick the `for-each` function. We find it under the **XSLT Constructs** tab. We drop it into the **availableCars** node on the target side as shown in the following screenshot:

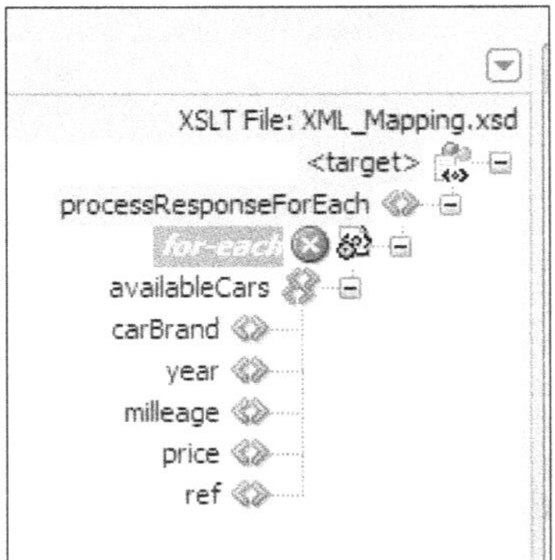

4. We then link **listCars** from the source side to the **for-each** node on the target side.
5. Finally, we link all the **listCars** subnodes from the source side to the **availableCars** subnodes on the target side. The final outlook of the transformation is as shown in the following screenshot:

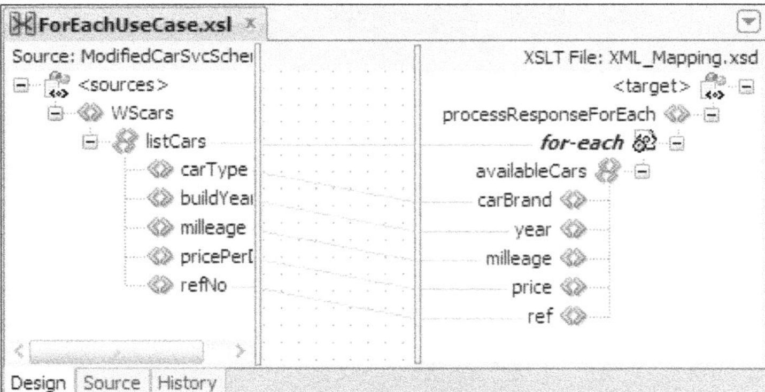

How it works...

In XSLT, the `for-each` element is used for the purpose of repetition. When we operate on the structure of the similar elements, we are able to set the rules for the repetition. Let us check the XSLT code that is generated for the `for-each` function for our recipe as follows:

```
<xsl:for-each select = "/ns0:WScars/ns0:listCars">
  <ns1:availableCars>
    <ns1:carBrand>
      <xsl:value-of select = "ns0:carType"/>
    </ns1:carBrand>
    <ns1:year>
      <xsl:value-of select = "ns0:buildYear"/>
    </ns1:year>
    <ns1:milleage>
      <xsl:value-of select = "ns0:milleage"/>
    </ns1:milleage>
    <ns1:price>
      <xsl:value-of select = "ns0:pricePerDay"/>
    </ns1:price>
    <ns1:ref>
      <xsl:value-of select = "ns0:refNo"/>
    </ns1:ref>
  </ns1:availableCars>
</xsl:for-each>
```

The `for-each` element takes the select attribute, which defines the source nodes that are iterated. Inside the `for-each` element, the target elements are defined along with their corresponding values.

JDeveloper also provides us with the ability to test the transformation file before deployment. We can test the transformation, by right-clicking on the mapper pane and selecting **Test**.

We receive the main pane split into three sections, the input window, output window, and mapping pane, as shown in the following screenshot:

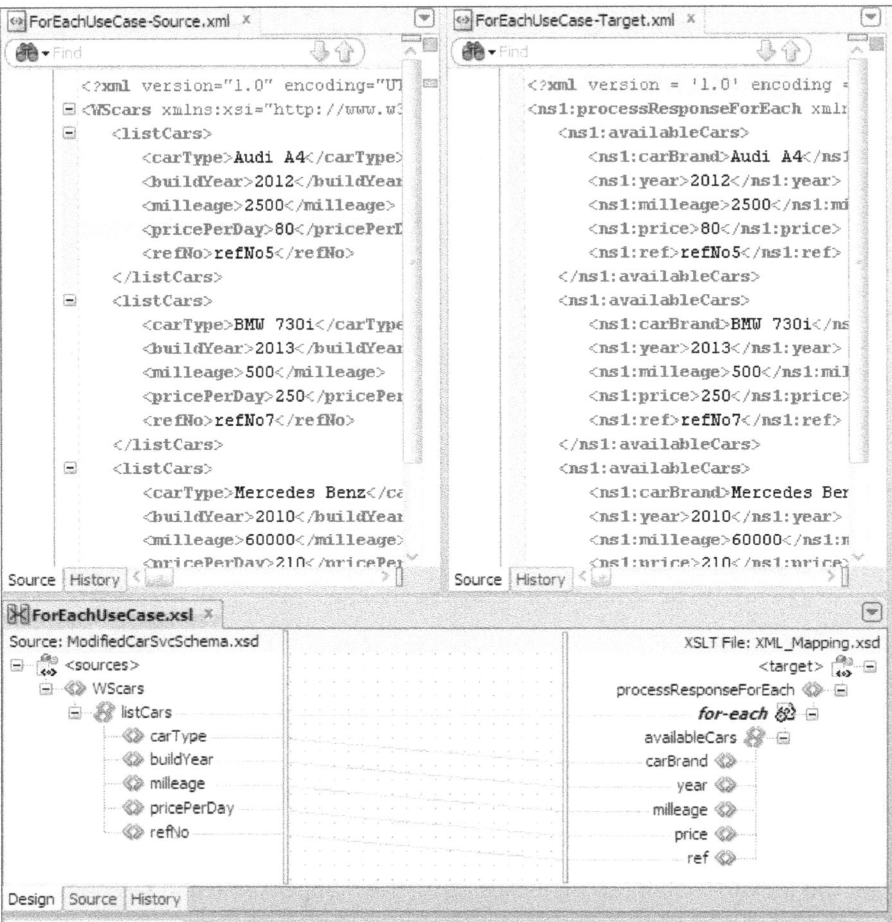

Defining a parameter

This recipe explains how to a the parameter to the mapping file. Parameters are an important aspect of the transformation since they enable us to include some additional content into the transformation. In this recipe, we will show you how to add a parameter that will hold the generated **UUID** (**universally unique identifier**) information.

Getting ready

We will amend the example from the *Using the xsl:for-each command* recipe, by adding a parameter to the source part.

How to do it...

In the following steps, we will create a parameter and configure it to hold the generated UUID information:

1. We right-click on the source side and select **Add Parameter...**.

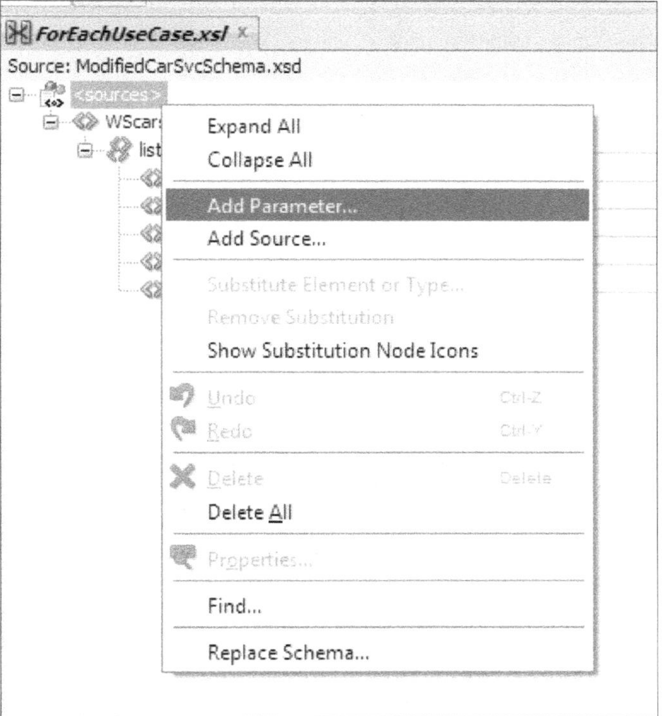

2. We enter the parameter name and check the **Set default value** option in order to initialize the parameter at the beginning of the transformation as shown in the following screenshot:

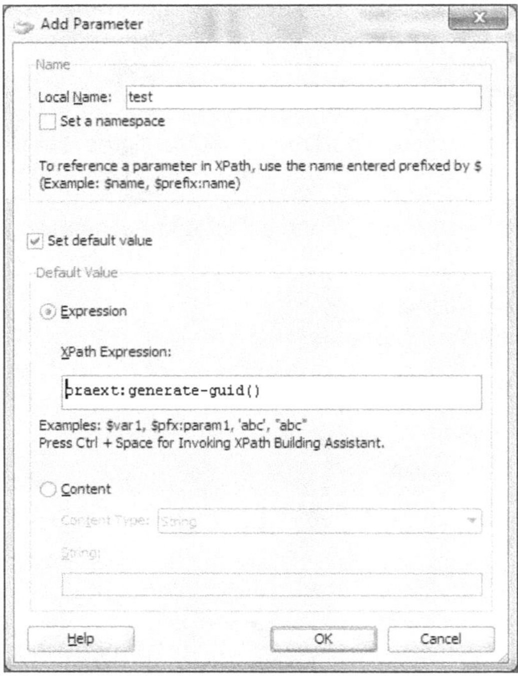

3. After that, we configure the conditions. We will utilize the parameter to set up the reference number in case the source node is empty or missing. We achieve this, by using the not equal XSLT function. The configuration of the function is trivial and consists only of checking, if the car reference number is empty. The final outlook of the mapping is as shown in the following screenshot:

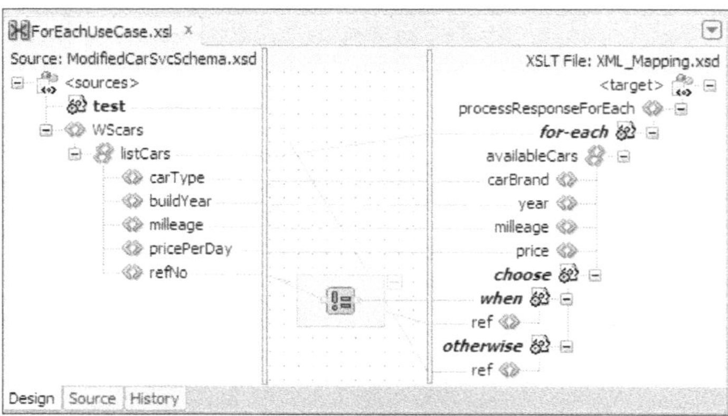

4. Now, if we test the mapping, we see that the parameter is taking into account whether we have a missing or empty reference tag. In source, we have three cars, where the reference tags have the following values:
   - Car 1: `<refNo>refNo5</refNo>`
   - Car 2: `<refNo></refNo>`
   - Car 3: It contains no **refNo** tag
5. The transformation of source presents the following results:
   - Car 1: `<ns1:ref>refNo5</ns1:ref>`
   - Car 2: `<ns1:ref>36333838333930353933313438313534</ns1:ref>`
   - Car 3: `<ns1:ref>36333838333930353933313438313534</ns1:ref>`

How it works...

The parameter in the transformation file is defined as the `xsl:param` tag as follows:

```
<xsl:param name = "test" select = "oraext:generate-guid()"/>
```

The parameter tag consists of the `name` and `select` attributes. We are also able to define the constant value of the parameter. The syntax is similar to the one preceding with a difference that we don't need to set the select part as follows:

```
<xsl:param name = "testConst">Constant value</xsl:param>
```

The function of the parameter is taking the values from the outside and using them inside the transformation file. We can also define the default values of the parameter as we saw in the previous recipe.

See also

- The definition of variables is examined in the next recipe.

Defining a variable

This recipe will examine how to define a variable on the target side. Similar to the previous recipe, we will amend the example from the *Using the xsl:for-each command* recipe by adding a variable to the target part. The variables can be useful when we need a particular piece of information from a BPEL process or when we need to define a constant value which is then used in different places in the transformation. In this recipe, we will create a variable and assign a value to it. The content of the variable presents the rebate on the price of the available cars.

How to do it...

The following steps will describe how to add a variable to the transformation and assign a value to it. On the mapper pane, we right-click on the target side and select **Add Variable...**. A dialog box opens where we define the variable name and optionally its value as shown in the following screenshot:

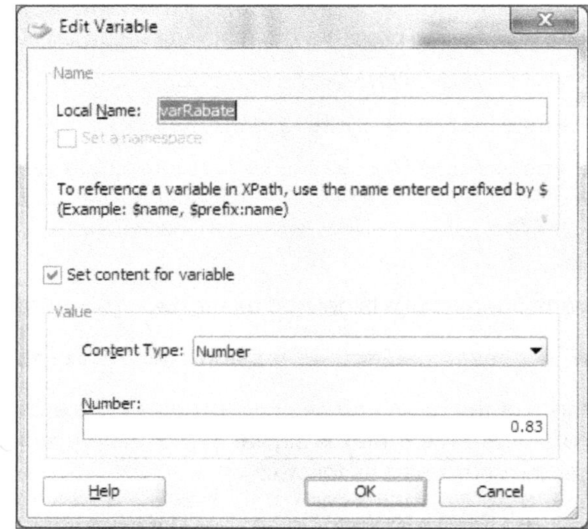

Now that we have defined the variable and set its value, we calculate the rent price of the car and round the result. We define the multiply function in the following way:

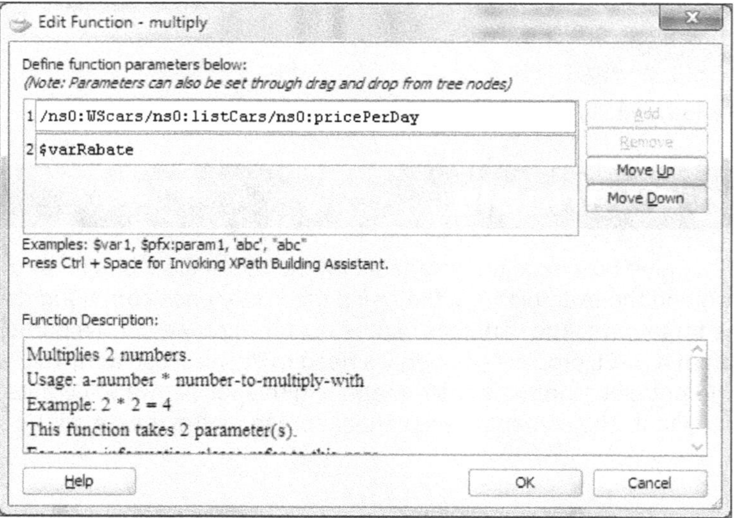

How it works...

As opposed to parameters, it is not possible to set the values of variables from the outside. Rather, our variable is used for internal processing and as the information holder. We can define the following two types of variables:

- **global**: This variable is defined as the child node of the transformation root element
- **local**: The scope of this variable is limited to the scope of the element where the variable is defined

Validating the variables with the <assign> activity

This recipe will examine the validation of the variables through the assign activity in a BPEL process. At first glance, there may be no obvious relation to the transformation; however, providing the qualitative data for the transformation is crucial, otherwise the results of the transformation might be surprising.

Getting ready

We will extend the example from the *Defining the variable* recipe with the validation functionality of the BPEL assign activity.. We will modify the example so that it will fail during validation.

In the `AssignWSinput` activity, we set the wrong XML fragment as follows:

```
<assign name = "AssignWSinput" xml:id = "id_15" validate = "yes">
  <copy xml:id="id_52">
    <from xml:id = "id_53"><literal xml:id =
      "id_54"><getAvailableCar xml:id = "id_62">
    <from xml:id = "id_63">2001-10-26T21:32:52</from>
    <to xml:id = "id_64">2010-05-05T20:00:00</to>
  </getAvailableCar></literal></from>
    <to xml:id = "id_58">
      $InvokeCarWS_getAvailableCar_InputVariable.parameters</to>
  </copy>
</assign>
```

How to do it...

The following steps describe the actions required to validate the variable data before performing other operations including the transformation:

1. In JDeveloper, we open the BPEL process. By double-clicking on the `AssignWSinput` activity, we get the **Edit Assign** dialog.
2. In the dialog box, we select the **General** tab, and check the **Validate** checkbox as shown in the following screenshot:

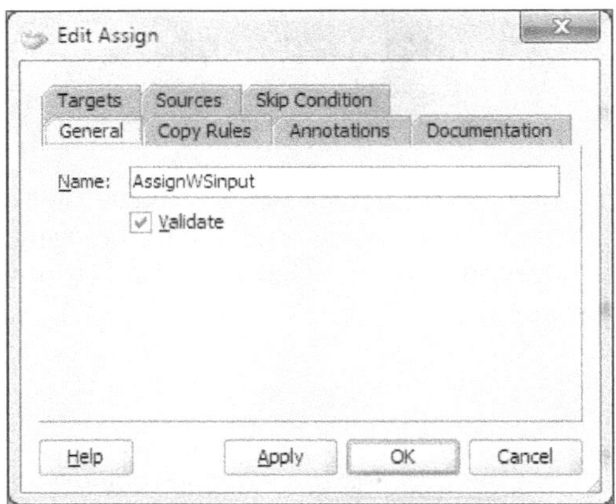

3. We confirm the changes by clicking on the **OK** button.

How it works...

If we deploy the example now, it fails, since the validation of the variable content fails. In the **Oracle SOA Suite Enterprise Manager Console**, we receive the following error:

```
[2013/03/29 00:32:41]
Invalid data: The value for variable "InvokeCarWS_getAvailableCar_InputVariable", part
"parameters" does not match the schema definition for this part Attribute
'http://www.w3.org/XML/1998/namespace:id' not expected.. The invalid xml document is
shown below:
  - <getAvailableCar xml:id="id_62" xmlns="http://www.packt.org/book/car">
      <from xml:id="id_63" xmlns="http://docs.oasis-open.org/wsbpel/2.0/process
      /executable">2001-10-26T21:32:52</from>
      <to xml:id="id_64" xmlns="http://docs.oasis-open.org/wsbpel/2.0/process
      /executable">2010-05-05T20:00:00</to>
    </getAvailableCar>
```

We can see the detailed report in **Flow Trace** about the validation error.

To correct the error, we change the assign activity with the following rule:

```
<copy xml:id = "id_68">
  <from xml:id = "id_69">$inputVariable.payload/client:from</from>
  <to xml:id = "id_70">
    $InvokeCarWS_getAvailableCar_InputVariable.parameters
      /ns2:from</to>
</copy>
<copy xml:id = "id_71">
  <from xml:id = "id_72">$inputVariable.payload/client:to</from>
  <to xml:id = "id_73">
    $InvokeCarWS_getAvailableCar_InputVariable.parameters/ns2:to
      </to>
</copy>
```

We deploy the BPEL process and we observe that the BPEL process completes successfully.

There's more...

Let us check an excerpt of the assign activity as follows:

```
<assign name = "AssignWSinput" validate = "yes">
</assign>
```

We see that the activity itself holds the attribute for the validation.

We can achieve the same behavior with the `Validate` activity. But, before we do that, let us disable the validation in the activity by setting `validate` to `no`.

Now, we put the `Validate` activity right after the assign activity.

We edit the `Validate` activity and add the variables as shown in the following screenshot:

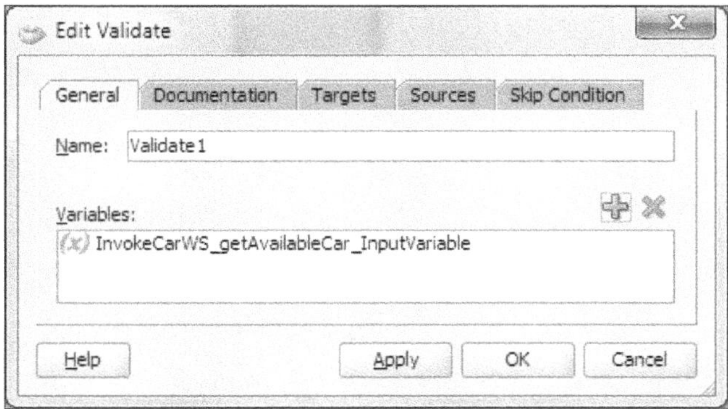

By running the BPEL process, we see that the activity did get executed successfully.

However, if we put the bad variable back, we can observe in **Flow Trace** in the **Oracle SOA Suite Enterprise Management Console** that the `Validate` activity fails as shown in the following screenshot:

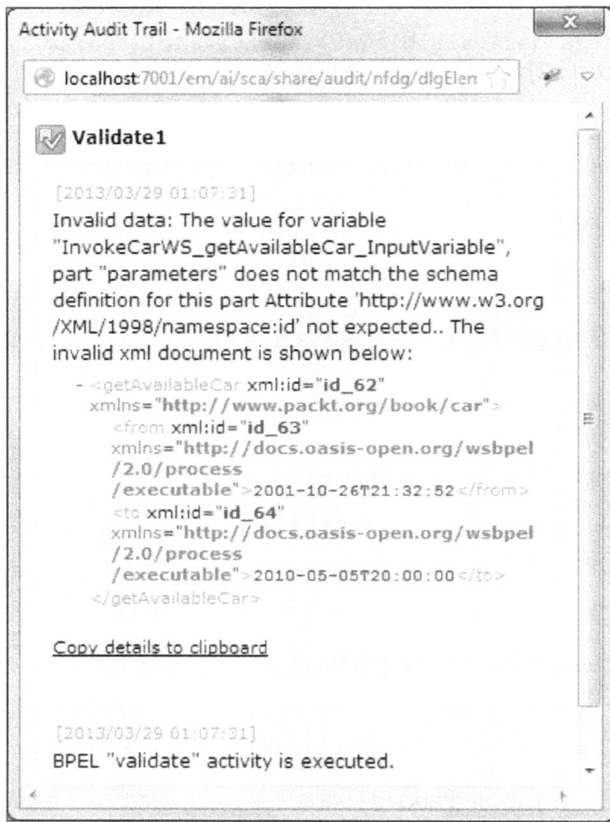

6
Embedding Third-party Java Libraries

This chapter contains the following recipes:

- Adding third-party libraries to the SOA Suite server
- Adding custom classes to the SOA Suite server
- Adding third-party libraries to JDeveloper projects
- Adding custom classes to JDeveloper projects
- Invoking third-party libraries from BPEL 2.0 process
- Invoking third-party libraries from BPEL 1.1 process

Introduction

The Oracle SOA Suite provides you with an SOA platform for the complete management of composite applications. Besides providing out of the box functionality, Oracle SOA Suite also provides abilities to extend its functionality. Since it is based on Java technology, the extensions usually involve Java class files, Java Archives, or both. Along with the configuration, usually in the XML format or properties file, this provides you with extensions of the Oracle SOA Suite suitable for utilization by different clients. Furthermore, the extensions are also exposable to the external environment via web services or by BPEL processes. We can expose various functionalities through extensions, for example, parts of business processes, integrations with payment gateways, logging facilities, support of digital signatures and encryptions, authentication mechanisms, and so on.

Fundamentally, the third-party libraries act in two ways during the development process. When using JDeveloper as the development environment for the Oracle SOA Suite, the third-party libraries need to be placed accordingly. That way, we eliminate much of the issues that can occur in the process of project deployment. We can also develop solutions in Eclipse or NetBeans; however, this is not a topic of this chapter. In this chapter, we will examine recipes for adding custom classes and third-party libraries to the JDeveloper projects and Oracle SOA Suite server. By adding custom classes and third-party libraries to the JDeveloper projects, we are able to deploy different versions of custom classes and third-party libraries with the BPEL processes. Also, by placing custom classes and third-party libraries in the Oracle SOA Suite server extension directory, we are able to use custom classes and third-party libraries globally without packing them into the BPEL process deployment package.

The extension folder for the Oracle SOA Suite is located at the following location:
`%SOA_Home%\soa\modules\oracle.soa.ext_11.1.1`

With extensions in place, the next interesting part involves the usage of extensions. We are focusing on the utilization of extensions in BPEL processes. We will examine how to utilize the embedded extensions in a BPEL process in the **Design** and **Source** view of JDeveloper.

Adding third-party libraries to the SOA Suite server

In this recipe, we will explore how to add third-party libraries to the SOA Suite server. Usually, our intension is to bring some functionality into the BPEL processes. For the practical reason the extensions come packed as the JAR archive, especially in cases where one package contains many classes.

How to do it...

We will add the `Apache Common Codec` library in this recipe. However, this same recipe can also be used for the addition of other third-party libraries. The `Apache Common Codec` library consists of the various encoders for different tasks, such as Base64 encoding/decoding, Digest calculation utilities (MD5 and SHA), and language and network encoders. Follow the given steps to add the library:

1. If the server is running, we need to stop it first. Open the command prompt and issue the following command to stop the server:
   - To stop the server on a Windows OS, issue the following command:

     ```
     C:\>cd %SOA_Home%\bin

     C:\Programs\Oracle\Middleware\user_projects\domains\SOA_
     Dev\bin>.\stopWebLogic.cmd
     ```

- To stop the server on a Unix OS, issue the following command:

```
#> cd $SOA_Home/bin
#> ./stopWebLogic.sh
```

2. After the server has stopped, copy the library (in our case, `commons-codec-1.7.jar`) to the extension folder.
3. After the library is copied, we need to rebuild the extension repository JAR by issuing the `ant` command in the extension directory as shown in the following command line:

```
C:\>cd %Middleware_home%\%SOA_Suite_Home%\soa\modules\oracle.soa.ext_11.1.1

C:\Programs\Oracle\Middleware\Oracle_SOA1\soa\modules\oracle.soa.ext_11.1.1>ant

Buildfile: build.xml

create-manifest-jar:

    [echo] Creating oracle.soa.ext at C:\Programs\Oracle\Middleware\Oracle_SOA1\soa\modules\oracle.soa.ext_11.1.1/oracle.soa.ext.jar :C:\Programs\Oracle\Middle

ware\Oracle_SOA1\soa\modules\oracle.soa.ext_11.1.1\UserDefinedFunctions.jar;C:\Programs\Oracle\Middleware\Oracle_SOA1\soa\modules\oracle.soa.ext_11.1.1\commons-

codec-1.7.jar;C:\Programs\Oracle\Middleware\Oracle_SOA1\soa\modules\oracle.soa.ext_11.1.1\classes

    [jar] Updating jar: C:\Programs\Oracle\Middleware\Oracle_SOA1\soa\modules\oracle.soa.ext_11.1.1\oracle.soa.ext.jar

BUILD SUCCESSFUL

Total time: 0 seconds

C:\Programs\Oracle\Middleware\Oracle_SOA1\soa\modules\oracle.soa.ext_11.1.1>
```

4. Finally, start the Oracle SOA Suite by issuing the following command:

   - To start the Oracle SOA Suite on Windows, issue the following command:

```
C:\>cd %SOA_Home%\bin
C:\Programs\Oracle\Middleware\user_projects\domains\SOA_Dev\bin>.\startWebLogic.cmd
```

   - To start the Oracle SOA Suite on Unix, issue the following command:

```
#> cd $SOA_Home/bin
#> ./startWebLogic.sh
```

How it works...

The Oracle SOA Suite provides the extension directory that is used to hold for the extensions. We drop the extensions in to the `extention` directory for usage in different parts of the Oracle SOA Suite.

One of the important steps in this recipe is rebuilding the repository JAR file which is created by the code procedure and is named `oracle.soa.ext.jar`. If we check the content of its manifest file, we see the following line inside the file:

```
Class-Path: UserDefinedFunctions.jar commons-codec-1.7.jar classes/
```

This content shows us the list of included JARs and classes that reside in the extension directory and are exposed as extensions. This leads us to think that we can organize the extension directory any way we want. We can organize the extension directory in hierarchies and as such make extensions more transparent and manageable. Let's reorganize the extension directory a bit now:

1. Create the directory `apache_ext` in the extension directory.
2. Move the commons codec JAR to the `apache_ext` directory.
3. Issue the `ant` command again and check the manifest file:

   ```
   Class-Path: UserDefinedFunctions.jar apache_ext/commons-codec-
   1.7.jar classes/
   ```

We can see that a new directory structure is taken into account while rebuilding the repository JAR.

When we put an extension with multiple dependency JARs into place, we put the extension JAR into the `extension` directory and the dependency jars into the `%SOA_Home%\lib\` directory. This way, the extension library will find the dependency classes.

There's more...

If we use the extensions in a BPEL process, we need to perform some additional steps of configuration in the Oracle SOA Suite Enterprise Manager Console. These steps are required in case we call the code from the BPEL process Java Embedding activity:

1. Log in to the Oracle SOA Suite Enterprise Manager Console.

2. Right-click on the **soa-infra** node and then navigate to **SOA Administration** | **BPEL Properties** as shown in the following screenshot:

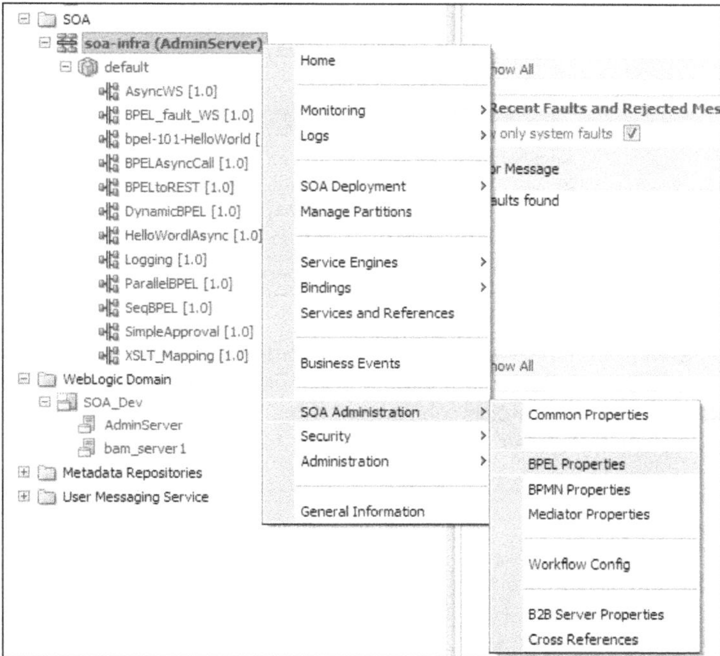

3. The **BPEL Properties** window opens. Select **More BPEL Configuration Properties...** from the window.

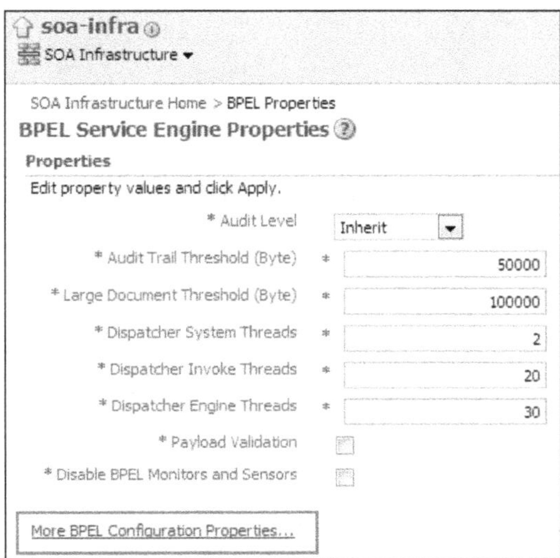

4. In the **System MBean Browser**, select the **BpelcClasspath** property as shown in the following screenshot:

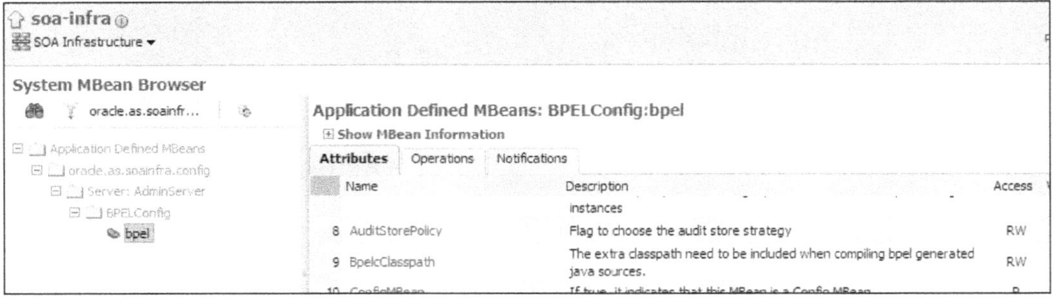

5. The dialog opens; in the **Value** field, enter the newly added JAR. Depending on the platform where we installed the Oracle SOA Suite, we need to use proper separators (on Windows, the separator is – `;`, and on Unix, the separator is the – `:` character) in case we list more JAR files.

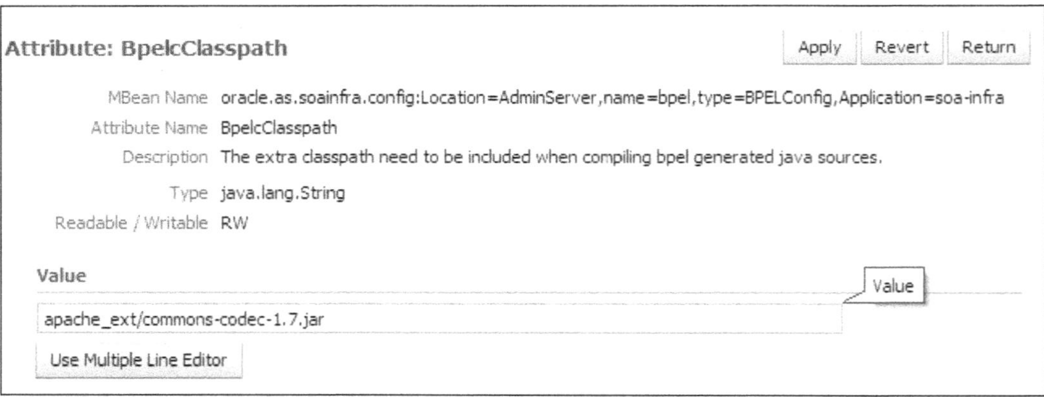

6. Click on the **Apply** button and then on the **Return** button. When you click on the **Apply** button, you'll receive the following notification:

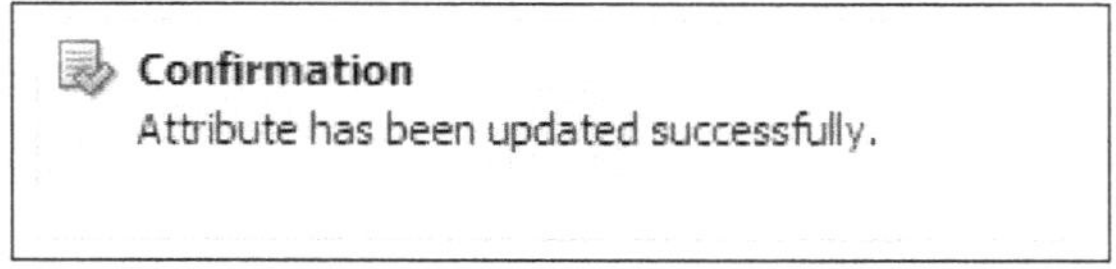

See also

In situations where we write a helper or utility class, it is easier to add it to the Oracle SOA Suite server in class form rather than as a JAR file. That way, we avoid preparing a package for later copy to the Oracle SOA Suite server. To learn how to add a custom class to the Oracle SOA Suite server, refer to the next recipe, *Adding custom classes to the SOA Suite server*.

Adding custom classes to the SOA Suite server

This recipe explains how to add custom classes to the Oracle SOA Suite server. Similar to adding the third-party libraries, the Oracle SOA Suite server provides a convenient placeholder for classes.

How to do it...

We will add classes that take care of loan calculation in this recipe. The same recipe can also be used for the addition of other Java class files:

1. If the server is running, we repeat the step for stopping the Oracle SOA Suite server from the *Adding third-party libraries to the SOA Suite server* recipe.
2. After the server has stopped, copy the class structure (in our case, `LoanInfo.class` and `LoanCalc.class`) to the extension folder.

The extension folder for the Oracle SOA Suite is located at the following location:
`%SOA_Home%\soa\modules\oracle.soa.ext_11.1.1\classes`

The following screenshot shows the tree structure of the `extension` directory after copying the class files:

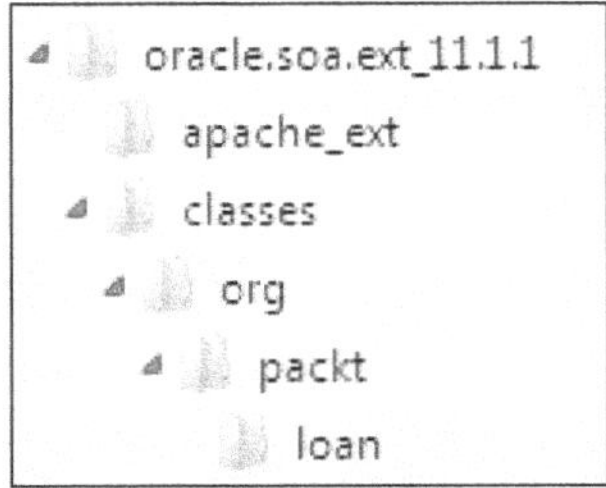

3. Finally, to start the Oracle SOA Suite, repeat the corresponding command from the *Adding third-party libraries to the SOA Suite server* recipe.

How it works...

As we saw in this recipe, the simple classes can be copied directly to the `extension` directory. That way, there is no need to prepare a JAR archive or go through any additional steps. Also, there is no need to copy the complete class structure when one class was changed.

As opposed to adding the JAR files, we can leave out one step. That step is rebuilding the extension repository JAR with `ant`, because the classes directory is included into the manifest file by default. Remember that we have to rebuild the extension repository JAR (`oracle.soa.ext.jar`) in the *Adding third-party libraries to the SOA Suite server* recipe.

When we have custom classes with multiple dependency JARs, we put the custom classes into the `extension` directory and the dependency JARs into the `%SOA_Home%\lib\` directory. This way, the custom classes will find the dependency classes.

Adding third-party libraries to JDeveloper projects

During a project, we usually integrate third-party libraries to perform various tasks, for example, calculating the digest value or connecting to the credit card gateway. This recipe will explain how to add third-party libraries into JDeveloper projects. Since the book scope aims at BPEL and Java, we will be most interested in how to include third-party libraries to be utilized in BPEL processes. When we use third-party libraries only in one BPEL process, then we can deploy a third-party library in the BPEL process deployment package. When multiple BPEL processes are using the same third-party libraries, then we can deploy them as described in the *Adding third-party libraries to the SOA Suite server* recipe to avoid unnecessary redundancy.

Getting ready

We will add the same third-party library to JDeveloper as we did in the *Adding third-party libraries to the SOA Suite server* recipe; that is, `Apache Commons Codec`.

How to do it...

To add third-party libraries to the JDeveloper project, we need to copy the libraries to the `SCA-INF/lib` directory. That way, the libraries are included in the build phase and deployment phase of the project.

How it works...

The SOA projects in JDeveloper have a placeholder (`SCA-INF/lib`) where we put the libraries. This also ensures that libraries are picked by the make process that packs the libraries into the deployment package.

There's more...

The procedure we described in this recipe can be taken into account when we don't have the same set of libraries already deployed in the Oracle SOA Suite server. In cases where the libraries already exist in the Oracle SOA Suite server, we have other options with which to add libraries to the JDeveloper projects. The following two procedures describe the user-defined libraries in JDeveloper and reference the libraries from the JDeveloper project properties. In these scenarios, we reference the third-party libraries and use them inside the BPEL process; however, we don't pack them into the BPEL process deployment package.

Creating a user-defined library and referencing it inside a JDeveloper project

The user libraries in JDeveloper present a group of JARs packed into contextually similar definitions, for example, BPEL Runtime, SOA Runtime, and so on:

1. Right-click on the project and select **Project Properties**. From the tree in the dialog, select **Libraries and Classpat** and then click on the **Add Library...** button as shown in the following screenshot:

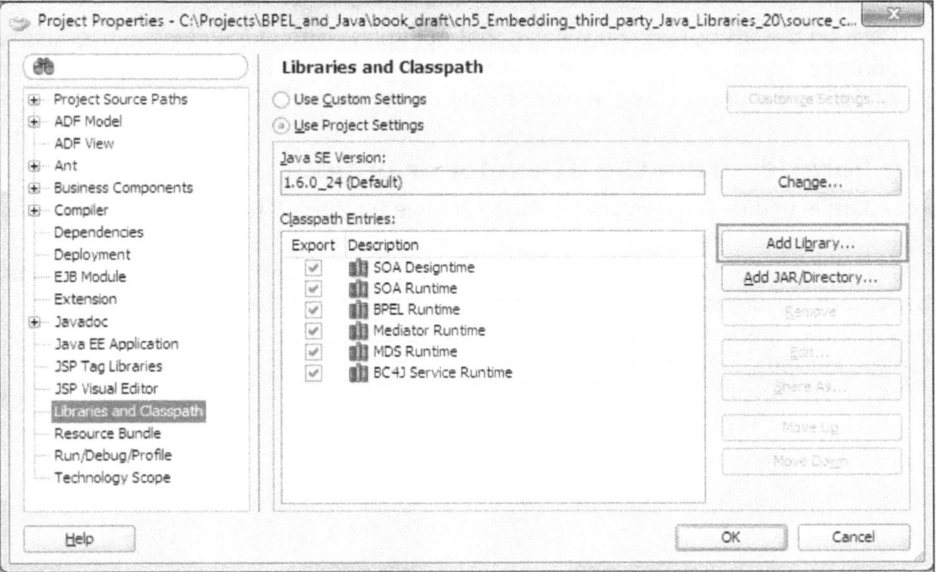

2. In the **Add Library** window, click on the **New...** button.
3. In the **Create Library** dialog, enter the name of the library. The location of the library specifies whether the library is a project or user-oriented. Then click on the **Add Entry...** button on the class, source, or doc path. We have all three JARs, so we add all the relevant libraries as shown in the following screenshot:

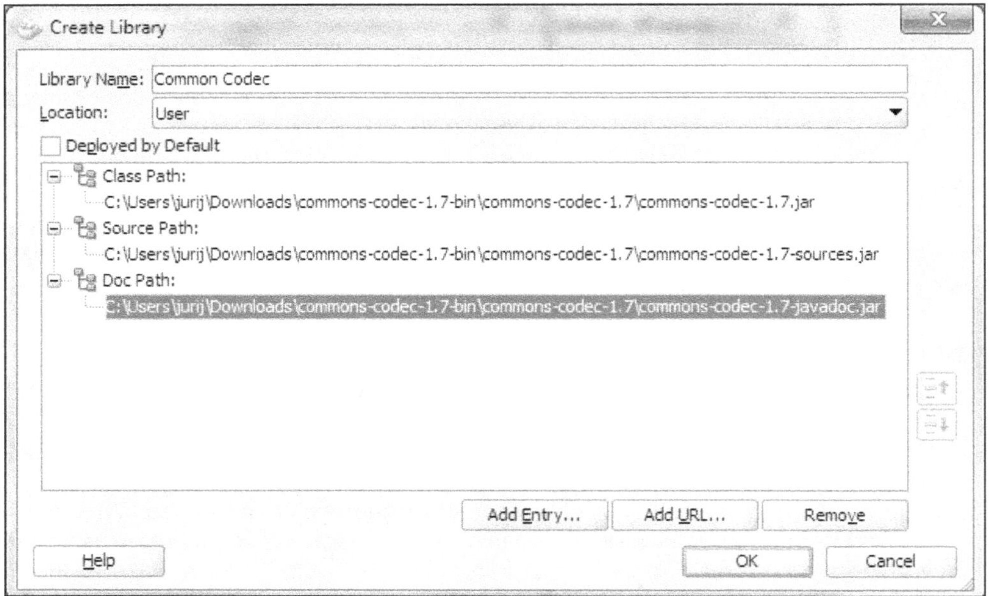

4. Click on the **OK** button. We will see that our library appears under the user-defined libraries. Again, click on the **OK** button. We will see that our library is automatically added to the project libraries. Once again, click on the **OK** button.

Adding libraries from the JDeveloper project properties

This procedure is useful in cases where we don't have multiple JARs to be references and defining a user-defined library presents a work overhead. We are referencing the third-party library directly from the project. Right-click on the project and navigate to **Project Properties**. From the tree in the dialog, select **Libraries and Classpath** and then click on **Add JAR/ Directory...** At the opened dialog, search for the library and click on the **Select** button as shown in the following screenshot:

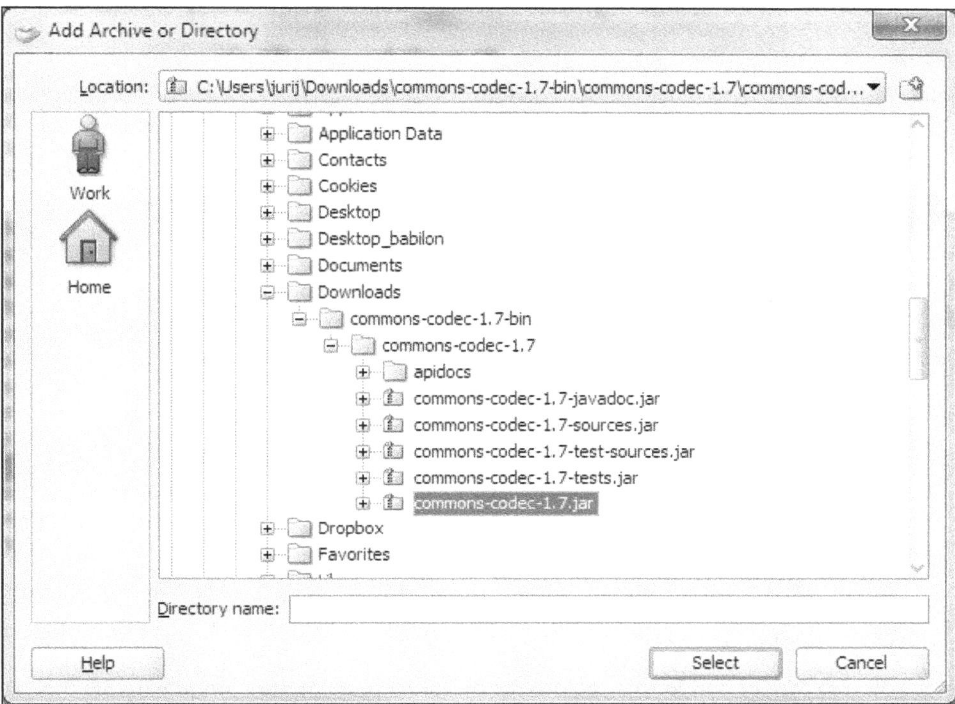

New library now appears under the classpath entries in the project properties dialog.

See also

We will examine how to add classes to JDeveloper projects in the next recipe. We saw the usage of the third-party libraries in the last two recipes.

Adding custom classes to JDeveloper projects

This recipe describes how to add classes to be used inside JDeveloper projects, especially in SOA projects.

Getting ready

We build this recipe on top of the *Adding custom classes to the SOA Suite server* recipe. We will add the SOA composite project where we utilize the classes for calculating loan parameters.

How to do it...

To add custom classes to the JDeveloper project, we need to copy the libraries to the `SCA-INF/classes` directory. That way, the custom classes are included in the build phase and deployment phase of the project.

How it works...

The SOA projects in JDeveloper have a placeholder (`SCA-INF/classes`) where we put the custom classes. This also ensures that libraries are picked by the build process which packs the libraries into the deployment package.

There's more...

The procedure we described in this recipe can be taken into account when we don't have the same set of custom classes already deployed in the Oracle SOA Suite server. In cases where the custom classes already exist in the Oracle SOA Suite server, the following section describes other options with which to add custom classes to the JDeveloper projects:

Adding custom classes from the JDeveloper project properties

Right-click on the project **LibsAndClasses** and select **Project Properties**. From the tree in the dialog, select **Libraries and Classpath** and then click on the **Add JAR/Directory...** button. At the opened dialog, search for the directory that holds the custom classes and click on the **Select** button. We can see how a new custom class directory has appeared under the classpath entries in the project properties dialog:

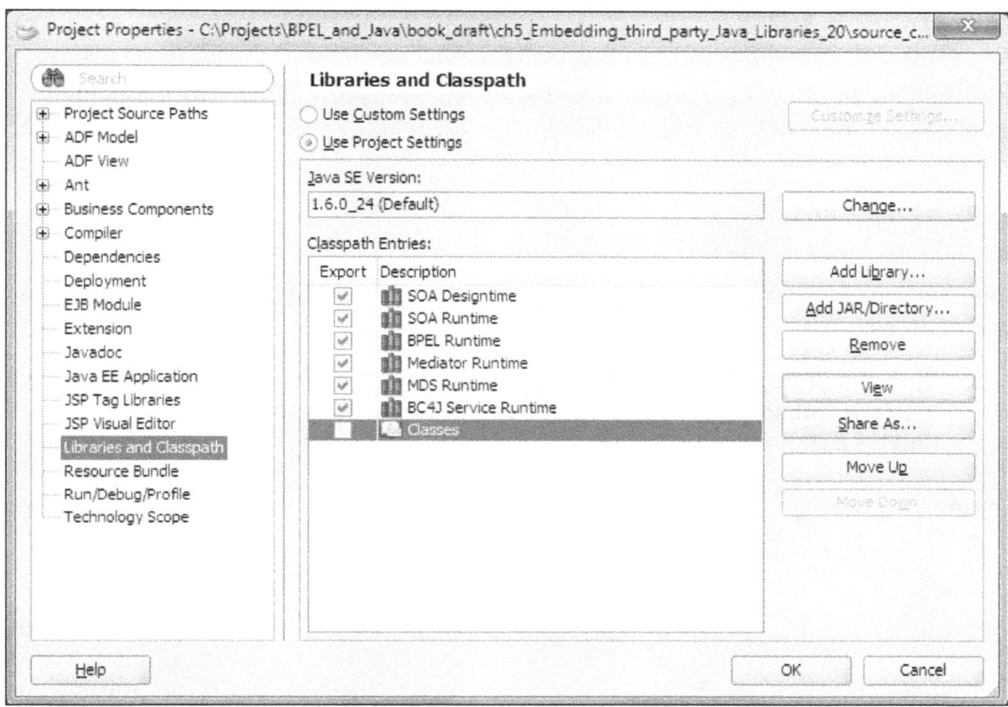

See also

The usage of custom classes in a BPEL process is shown in the *Invoking third-party libraries from BPEL 2.0 process* and *Invoking third-party libraries from BPEL 1.1 process* recipes.

Invoking third-party libraries from BPEL 2.0 process

This recipe explains how to use third-party libraries from a BPEL 2.0 process. We achieve this by using the Java Embedding activity in the BPEL editor. In general, putting a lot of business processing code into the BPEL process does not represent a good practice. Rather, the third-party libraries should be implemented through web services or EJBs. Those web services and EJBs can then be referenced from the BPEL process.

Getting ready

We will amend the JDeveloper project from the *Adding third-party libraries to JDeveloper projects* recipe. We create an empty BPEL 2.0 process and leave the request and response messages unchanged.

How to do it...

To add the code for the third-party library from the Java Embedding activity, we perform the following steps:

1. Open the BPEL process in JDeveloper. To execute the third-party library class, select the **Java Embedding** activity from the **Oracle Extensions** section of **Component Palette** as shown in the following screenshot:

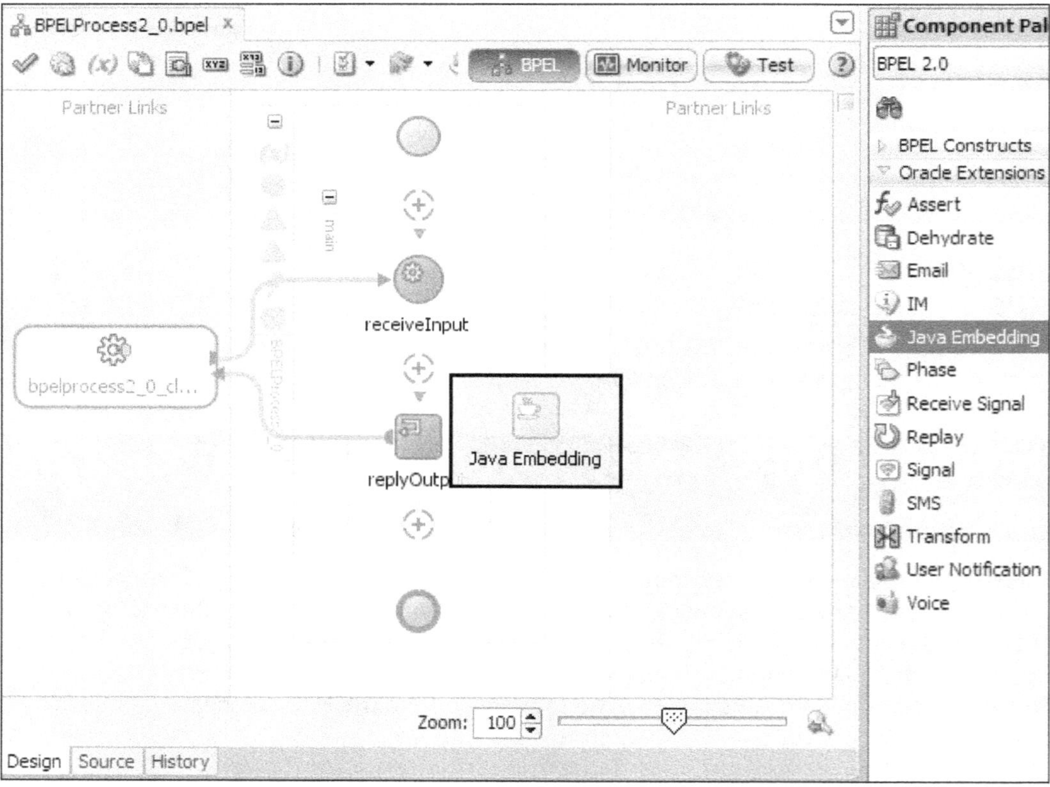

2. When you double-click on the **Java Embedding** activity, a new dialog opens where we have to enter the code. We finish configuring the Java Embedding activity by clicking on the **OK** button as shown in the following screenshot:

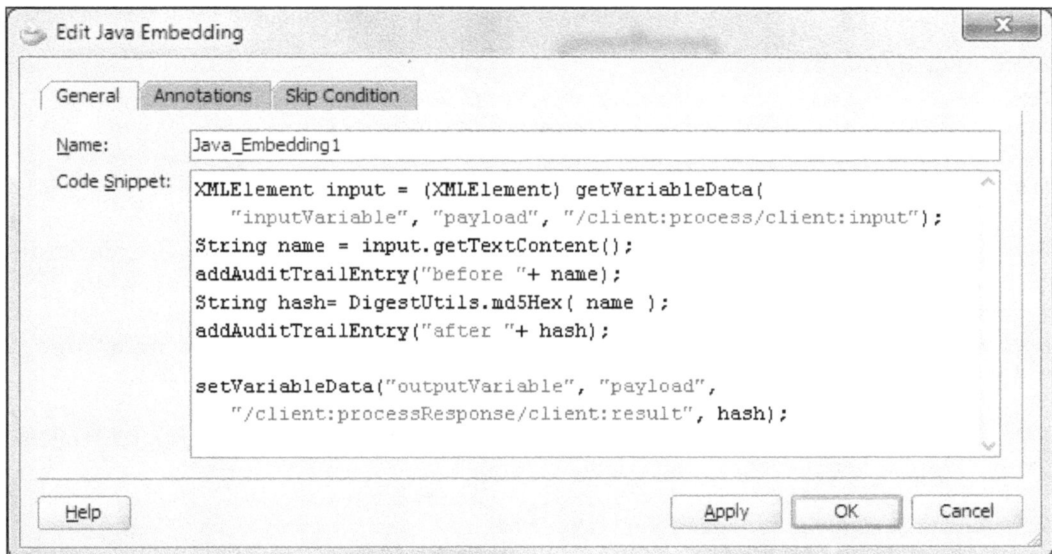

Edit Java Embedding
General
Annotations
Skip Condition
Name:
Java_Embedding1
Code Snippet:
XMLElement input = (XMLElement) getVariableData(
"inputVariable", "payload", "/client:process/client:input");
String name = input.getTextContent();
addAuditTrailEntry("before "+ name);
String hash= DigestUtils.md5Hex(name);
addAuditTrailEntry("after "+ hash);
setVariableData("outputVariable", "payload",
"/client:processResponse/client:result", hash);
Help
Apply
OK
Cancel

3. One additional step we need to perform is to import the `org.apache.commons.codec.digest.DigestUtils` class (contained in the third-party library) in the BPEL process. We do this by switching to the **Source** view. Immediately after the `<process>` tag, add the import statement for the class used in the Java code as follows:

```
  <import location="org.apache.commons.codec.digest.DigestUtils"
importType="http://schemas.oracle.com/bpel/extension/java"/>
  <import location="oracle.xml.parser.v2.XMLElement"
importType="http://schemas.oracle.com/bpel/extension/java"/>
```

How it works...

The Java code is embedded in the XML form of the BPEL process. The same code gets deployed to the Oracle SOA Suite server.

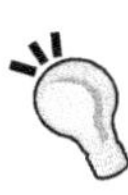

> JDeveloper will not notify us in case there is any error in the code. So, it is advisable to test the deployment of the BPEL process in the integrated SOA server of JDeveloper prior to deploying it to the real Oracle SOA Suite server.

During the preparation of the deployment package, the Java code is packed into a package in a raw format that is not compiled. When the package is deployed onto the Oracle SOA Suite server, all the dependencies (imports) are checked and the code is compiled.

If there is an error in the code, we get an exception in the console similar to the following code:

```
Error deploying BPEL suitcase.
error while attempting to deploy the BPEL component file "C:\Programs\
Oracle\Middleware\user_projects\domains\SOA_Dev\servers\AdminServer\dc\
soa_8606ace0-2193-4
719-8cd7-08b2f0d57a04"; the exception reported is: java.lang.
RuntimeException: failed to compile execlets of BPELProcess2_0

This error contained an exception thrown by the underlying deployment
module.
Verify the exception trace in the log (with logging level set to debug
mode).


        at com.collaxa.cube.engine.deployment.DeploymentManager.deployCom
ponent(DeploymentManager.java:200)
        at com.collaxa.cube.ejb.impl.CubeServerManagerBean._deployOrLoadC
omponent(CubeServerManagerBean.java:874)
        at com.collaxa.cube.ejb.impl.CubeServerManagerBean.deployComponen
t(CubeServerManagerBean.java:122)
        at com.collaxa.cube.ejb.impl.bpel.BPELServerManagerBean.deployCom
ponent(BPELServerManagerBean.java:87)
        at sun.reflect.GeneratedMethodAccessor4365.invoke(Unknown Source)
        Truncated. see log file for complete stacktrace
>
<7.4.2013 14:24:57 CEST> <Error> <oracle.integration.platform.blocks.
deploy.servlet> <SOA-21537> <Sending back error message: There was
an error deploying the composite on AdminServer: Error occurred
during deployment of component: BPELProcess2_0 to service engine:
implementation.bpel, for composite: LibsAndClasses: OR
ABPEL-05250

Error deploying BPEL suitcase.
error while attempting to deploy the BPEL component file "C:\Programs\
Oracle\Middleware\user_projects\domains\SOA_Dev\servers\AdminServer\dc\
soa_8606ace0-2193-4
719-8cd7-08b2f0d57a04"; the exception reported is: java.lang.
RuntimeException: failed to compile execlets of BPELProcess2_0

This error contained an exception thrown by the underlying deployment
module.
```

```
Verify the exception trace in the log (with logging level set to debug
mode).
..>
```

The following is the code in the BPEL process:

```
<extensionActivity>
  <bpelx:exec name="Java_Embedding1" xml:id="id_12" language="java">
    <![CDATA[XMLElement input = (XMLElement) getVariableData(
      "inputVariable", "payload",
      "/client:process/client:input");
String name = input.getTextContent();
addAuditTrailEntry("before "+ name);
String hash= DigestUtils.md5Hexa( name );
addAuditTrailEntry("after "+ hash);
setVariableData("outputVariable", "payload",
  "/client:processResponse/client:result", hash);]]>
  </bpelx:exec>
</extensionActivity>
```

In the preceding code, the `<bpelx:exec>` tag is embedded into the `<extensionActivity>` tag. We can also spot that `addAuditTrail()`, `getVariableData()`, and `setVariableData()` do not need any imports since they are a part of a standard set in the `<bpelx:exec>` package.

The code described in this recipe is valid for BPEL 2.0 processes. We will address the `<bpelx:exec>` tag in BPEL 1.1 processes in the next recipe.

Invoking third-party libraries from BPEL 1.1 process

This recipe explains how to include the code for invoking third-party libraries via the `<bpelx:exec>` tag in the source view.

Getting ready

We will amend the JDeveloper project from the *Adding third-party libraries to JDeveloper projects* recipe. We create an empty BPEL 1.1 process and leave the request and response messages unchanged.

How to do it...

To invoke a third-party library from the <bpelx:exec> tag, perform the following steps:

1. Open the empty BPEL 1.1 process. Since the output variable is not initialized yet, add the assign activity first. The following is the code for the assign activity:

```
<assign name="Assign1" xml:id="id_11">
  <copy xml:id="id_12">
    <from expression="string('')" xml:id="id_13"/>
    <to variable="outputVariable" part="payload" query="/
client:processResponse/client:result" xml:id="id_14"/>
  </copy>
</assign>
```

2. Simply initialize the output part with an empty string.
3. Further, add the <bpelx:exec> tag. Inside the <bpelx:exec> tag place the following Java code:

```
<bpelx:exec name="Java_Embedding1" xml:id="id_10" version="1.5"
language="java">
  <![CDATA[ <!—Java code --> ]]>
</bpelx:exec>
```

4. Read the content of the input variable and print the output on the audit trail as follows:

```
XMLElement input = (XMLElement) getVariableData("inputVariable",
"payload", "/client:process/client:input");
String name = input.getTextContent();
addAuditTrailEntry("before "+ name);
```

5. Then, call the class to convert the plain text to MD5 hash content and print the result to the audit trail as shown in the following code:

```
String hash= DigestUtils.md5Hex( name );
addAuditTrailEntry("after "+ hash);
```

6. Finally, set the result content to the output variable of the BPEL process as shown in the following code:

```
setVariableData("outputVariable", "payload", "/
client:processResponse/client:result", hash);
```

7. Now that we have all the code in place, we still need to add the imports to the BPEL process. Immediately after the <process> tag, put the following lines:

```
<bpelx:exec import="oracle.xml.parser.v2.XMLElement"/>
<bpelx:exec import="org.apache.commons.codec.digest.DigestUtils"/>
```

8. Now we are ready to deploy the BPEL process to the Oracle SOA Suite server.

How it works...

The Java code is embedded in `<bpelx:exec>` of the BPEL process. The same code gets deployed to the Oracle SOA Suite server.

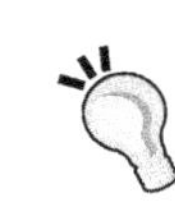

JDeveloper will not warn us if we make mistakes in the code. Again, it is advisable to test the deployment of the BPEL process in the integrated SOA server of JDeveloper prior to deploying it to the real Oracle SOA Suite server.

After we deploy the BPEL process, we can test it in the Oracle SOA Suite Enterprise Manager console. Go to the console and select our process (**LibsAndClasses**) from the SOA (**soa-infra**) tree. A window opens with the information about the BPEL process. Select the **Test** drop-down menu and then select **bpelprocess1_1_client_ep** as shown in the following screenshot:

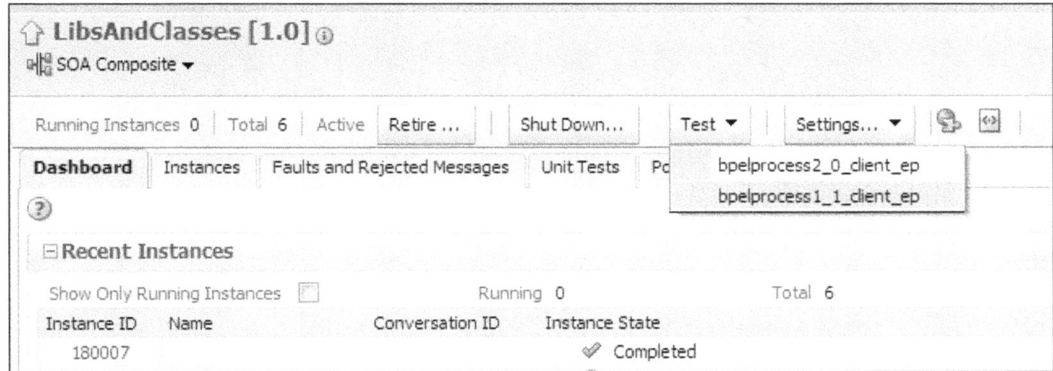

The **Test Web Service** window opens, and in **Input Arguments**, insert some data as input, for example, `jurij`. At the top-right corner, we click on the **Test Web Service** button. We receive an output as shown in the following screenshot:

Click on the **Launch Flow Trace** button. Then, in the **Flow Trace** window, click on the **BPELProcess1_1** link as shown in the following screenshot:

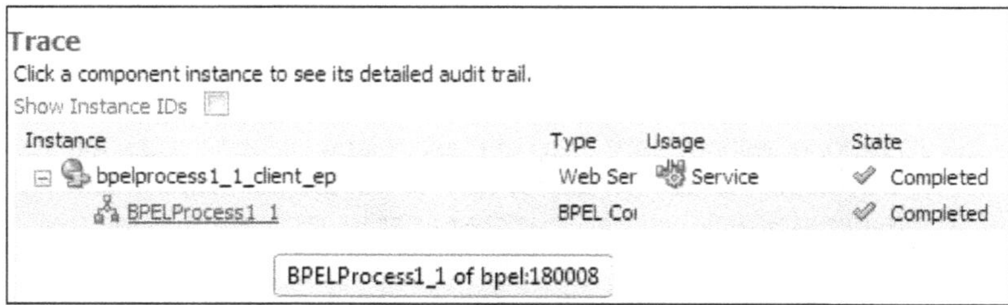
Trace
Click a component instance to see its detailed audit trail.
Show Instance IDs
Instance
Type
Usage
State
bpelprocess1_1_client_ep
Web Ser
Service
Completed
BPELProcess1_1
BPEL Co
Completed
BPELProcess1_1 of bpel:180008

In the **Audit Trail** tab, we can see that the conversion was between the input and output content as shown in the following screenshot:

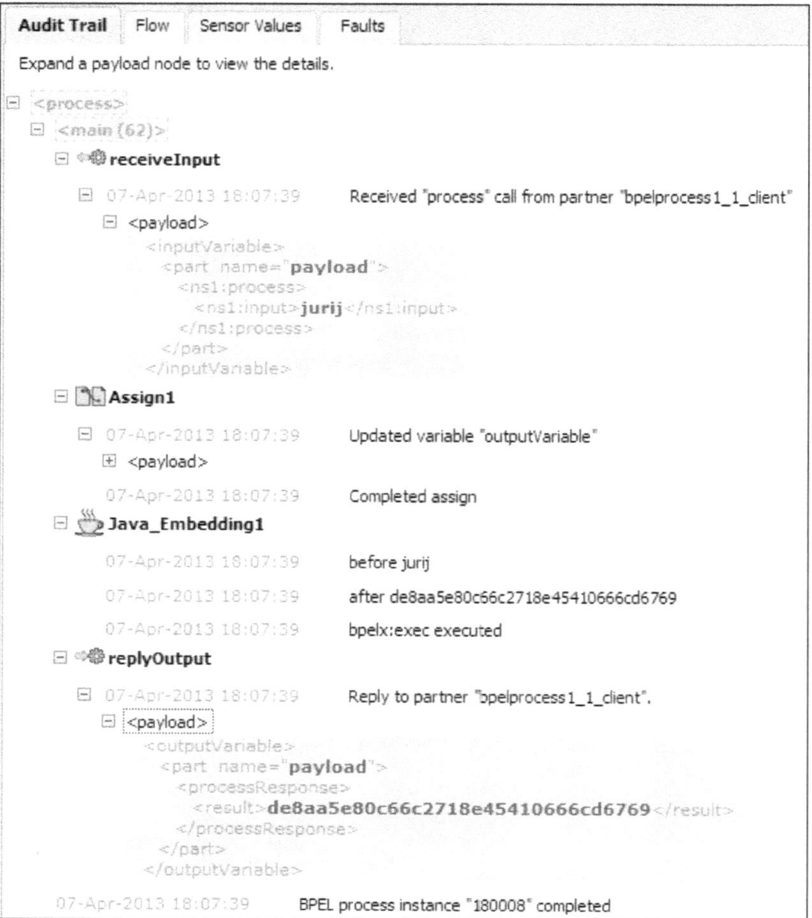
Audit Trail
Flow
Sensor Values
Faults
Expand a payload node to view the details.
<process>
<main (62)>
receiveInput
07-Apr-2013 18:07:39
Received "process" call from partner "bpelprocess1_1_client"
<payload>
<inputVariable>
<part name="payload">
<ns1:process>
<ns1:input>jurij</ns1:input>
</ns1:process>
</part>
</inputVariable>
Assign1
07-Apr-2013 18:07:39
Updated variable "outputVariable"
<payload>
07-Apr-2013 18:07:39
Completed assign
Java_Embedding1
07-Apr-2013 18:07:39
before jurij
07-Apr-2013 18:07:39
after de8aa5e80c66c2718e45410666cd6769
07-Apr-2013 18:07:39
bpelx:exec executed
replyOutput
07-Apr-2013 18:07:39
Reply to partner "bpelprocess1_1_client".
<payload>
<outputVariable>
<part name="payload">
<processResponse>
<result>de8aa5e80c66c2718e45410666cd6769</result>
</processResponse>
</part>
</outputVariable>
07-Apr-2013 18:07:39
BPEL process instance "180008" completed

There's more...

In this recipe, we put the Java code into the Java Embedding activity. Along with that, we need to insert import statements into the BPEL process.

To avoid inserting the import statements into the BPEL process, we can also use the fully qualified names of the classes. From our example, the following changed code will need to be placed where we read the content of the input variable:

```
oracle.xml.parser.v2.XMLElement input = (oracle.xml.parser.
v2.XMLElement) getVariableData("inputVariable", "payload", "/
client:process/client:input");
```

Another code change is needed where we convert the content:

```
String hash= org.apache.commons.codec.digest.DigestUtils.md5Hex( name
);
```

7
Accessing and Updating the Variables

In this chapter we will cover the following recipes:

- Defining global variables in a BPEL process
- Defining local variables in a BPEL process
- Initializing a variable with an XML literal
- Initializing a variable with an inline from-spec
- Copying content between the variables
- Accessing the fields within Element-based variables
- Accessing the fields within Message Type-based variables
- Assigning numerical values to the variables
- Applying mathematical calculations on data in the variables
- Assigning Boolean values to the variables
- Assigning date or time to the variables
- Updating the variables using the BPELX extensions
- Dynamic indexing of the variables

Introduction

The main role of a BPEL process is to orchestrate web services. Web services are presented in the BPEL processes as partner links. The orchestration is performed through the exchange of messages from one partner link to another. The variables hold the messages received from the partner links or from the message that is to be sent to the partner links. Of course, a variable can hold both types of messages at once. It is also possible that a variable can hold information that does not correspond to either the receiving or sending message.

A variable is described by the type of information it holds. The types of variable can be as follows:

- A WSDL message type
- An XML schema element
- An XML schema simple type

The variables belonging to the outermost scope (defined inside the `<scope>` element) are called global variables. They can be accessed from anywhere within a BPEL process. Alternatively, we define a local variable that is accessible only within the enclosing scope. We define the global variables when information needs to be accessible across a whole BPEL process. On the contrary, the local variables are defined when we need information only in some limited part of a BPEL process, usually inside the `<scope>` activity. We can actually draw a parallel with the Java programming language. In Java, the global variables are defined at the class level, while the local variables are defined inside the code block or methods.

The variables are tightly related to the scope definition, so the name of the variable must be unique within the scope definition. The variables are resolved against the nearest enclosing scope. If a global and local variable have the same name, the local variable takes precedence over the global when resolving the content of the variable.

Giving the same name to a global and local variable is bad practice, as the names can be ambiguous to the designer as well as to the developer of the BPEL process.

A variable is defined with the `<variable>` tag in a BPEL process. The type of the variable is defined through three exclusive attributes as follows:

- `messageType`: This refers to the WSDL message type variable
- `element`: This refers to the XML schema element variable
- `type`: This refers to the XML simple type variable

The variables can be used in different BPEL process activities as shown in the following table:

Activity	Description
invoke	With the `<invoke>` activity, we can define two variables (with attributes), input and output, depending on the type of partner link (one-way or two-way) we call.
receive	The `<receive>` activity definition contains the variable attribute where we define the name of the variable to hold the content of the request.
reply	The `<reply>` activity contains the variable attribute where we define the name of the variable that holds information to be sent back to the client calling the BPEL process.
catch	In the `<catch>` activity, the variable is defined through the `faultVariable` attribute. When a fault occurs in the BPEL process, the specific fault is assigned to the fault variable.

Generally, the global and local variables are uninitialized at the beginning of a BPEL process. To initialize the variables, we have a number of possibilities. One is at the instantiation of the BPEL process. At that time, the variable for the `<receive>` activity is initialized with the content of the request message. Another possibility is to assign some content to a variable within the BPEL process. This can be achieved through the `<assign>` activity or via the XSLT transformation. It is desirable to completely initialize the variable. However, when we don't have the complete information, we can also partially initialize the variable with the amount of data we currently have.

Defining global variables in a BPEL process

This recipe describes how to define a global variable inside a BPEL process in Oracle SOA Suite.

Getting ready

There are no special preparations required for this recipe. We create a project in JDeveloper with an empty synchronous BPEL process.

How to do it...

In the following steps, we will show you how to add a global variable to a BPEL process in JDeveloper:

1. We start by opening the BPEL process in JDeveloper. We then select the scope of the BPEL process. Note that it will be highlighted blue. We then select the variables icon in the BPEL process toolbar as shown in the following screenshot:

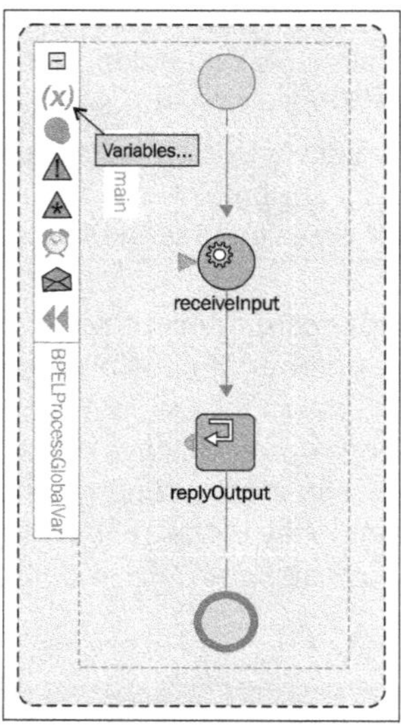

2. The dialog opens with the variables listed for the specified scope. We click on the plus (**+**) sign in the dialog as shown in the following screenshot:

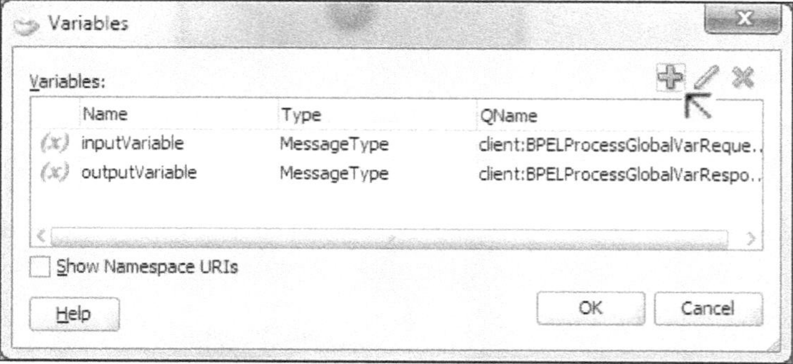

When BPEL is created through the BPEL process wizard in JDeveloper, we notice that it already has two global variables defined, one holding the request message and another one holding the response message.

3. The **Create Variable** dialog opens which is divided into three sections. We enter the variable name, select the variable type, and click on **OK**.

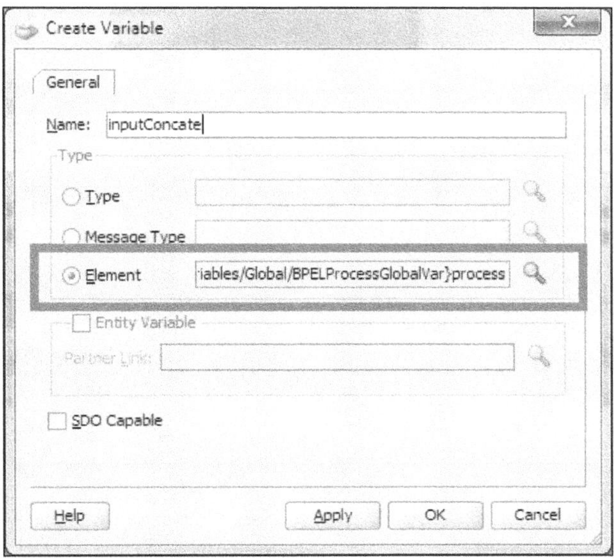

4. The newly defined variable is listed in the variables dialog and we click on the **OK** button. Now the global variable is defined in the BPEL process.

How it works...

Remember that the global variables belong to the outermost scope. After the definition of the global variable, we check the source of the BPEL process. We see that the new variable was defined in the section of the `<variables>` tag within the `<process>` tag and immediately after the `<partnerLinks>` tag as follows:

```
<variables>
  <!-- Reference to the message passed as input during
    initiation -->
  <variable name = "inputVariable"
    messageType = "client:BPELProcessGlobalVarRequestMessage"/>

  <!-- Reference to the message that will be returned to
    the requester-->
  <variable name = "outputVariable"
    messageType = "client:BPELProcessGlobalVarResponseMessage"/>
  <variable name = "inputConcate" element = "client:process"/>
</variables>
```

There's more...

Another way of defining a global variable is to insert the preceding code manually into the BPEL source code. We can also define a global variable from the BPEL process toolbar.

We select the icon from the BPEL process toolbar as shown in the following screenshot:

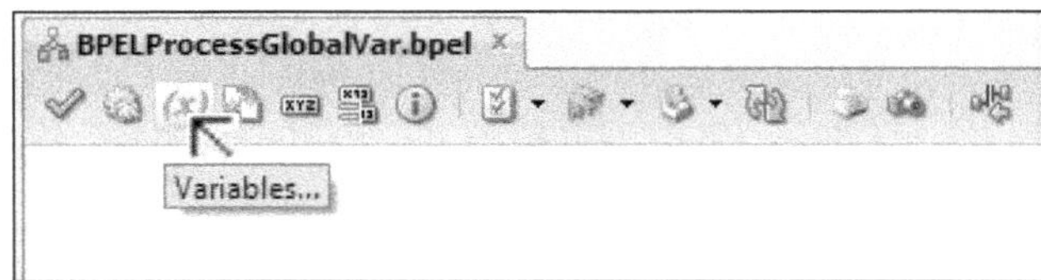

A slightly different dialog opens containing the variables defined in the BPEL process. We define the variable the same way as in the *How to do it...* section of this recipe by clicking on the plus (**+**) sign.

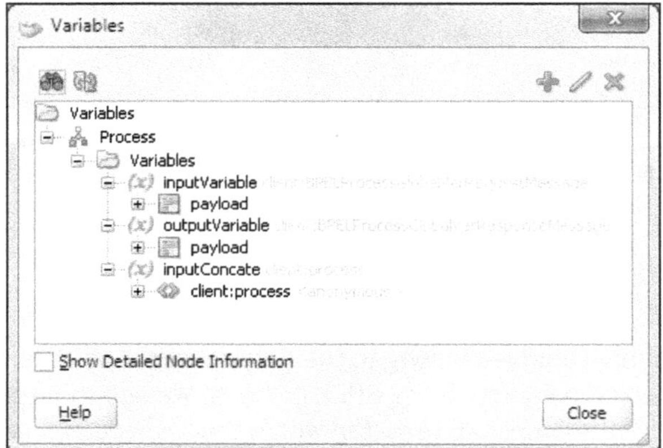

Creating the variable dialog

The dialog opens whenever we click on the plus (**+**) sign. It is divided into three sections as shown in the following screenshot:

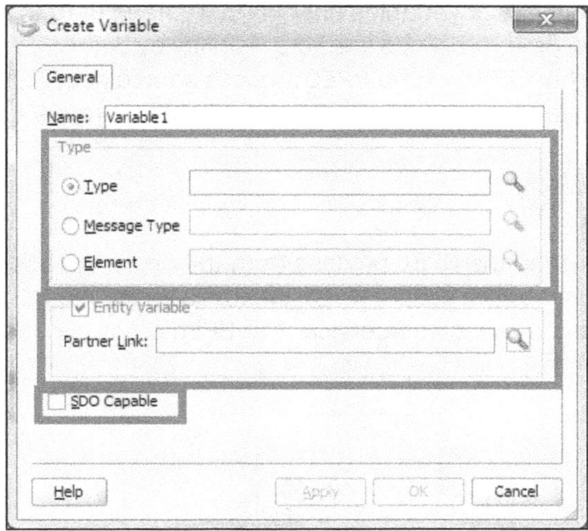

The topmost section is used to define the variable type. Remember that it can be either simple **Type**, the **Element** type, or **Message Type**. The middle section is used in case we want to define **Entity Variable**, which has its origin in **Partner Link:**. The bottom part presents the checkbox **SDO Capable**, which identifies **Service Data Object** (**SDO**) capable of utilizing the content from different sources through the **Data Access Service** (**DAS**), which enables access to data without knowing their real underlying implementation. The difference between the SDO variable and the standard DOM variable is in their underlying presentation. Hence, the different features are available to both types of variables.

More information on the SDO capability and DAS can be found at the following URL:

`http://docs.oracle.com/cd/E23943_01/dev.1111/e10224/bp_manipdoc.htm#SOASE85027`

See also

- To define local variables in a BPEL process, refer to the next recipe

Defining local variables in a BPEL process

Too many global variables can cause a lot of confusion and can also consume a lot of memory. Hence, we define global variables only when we need data to be available all the time. For that reason, we omit the scope variable visibility by defining them locally. By doing this, we also achieve higher clarity of the BPEL process source code. This recipe will explain the difference between global and local variables in the BPEL processes.

Getting ready

For this recipe, we will extend the BPEL process from the previous recipe. Note that the variables are tightly related to the scope, which encloses them. We will add a scope to our BPEL process and reuse the same web service. The BPEL process outlook is as shown in the following screenshot:

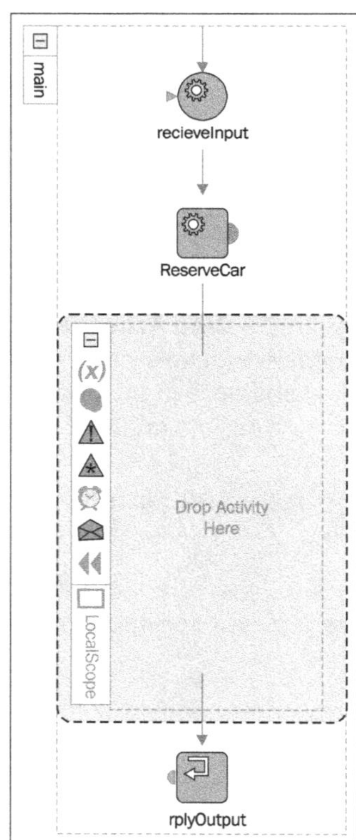

How to do it...

To define a local variable in a BPEL process, we perform the following steps:

1. We define a local variable by pressing the (**X**) icon in the left-side toolbar of the scope. The dialog for defining the variable opens and is the same regardless of the variable type (global or local). However, this time there are no variables in the dialog. This is reasonable, since there are no local variables defined yet.
2. We click on the plus (**+**) icon and create the variable as shown in the following screenshot:

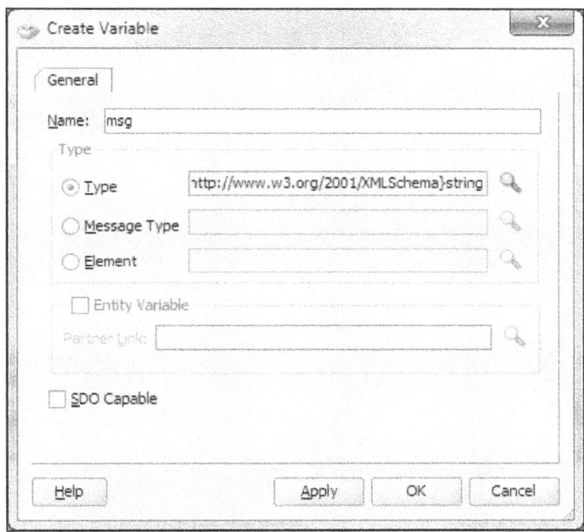

3. Click on the **OK** button. Notice how the new variable definition appeared in the **Variables** dialog. Again, click on the **OK** button. Now we have the new local variable defined in the `LocalScope` scope of the BPEL process.

How it works...

The easiest way to check the local variable definition is to examine the source code of the BPEL process. We search for the `msg` variable in the following code:

```
<scope name = "LocalScope" variableAccessSerializable = "no">
  <variables>
    <variable name = "msg" type = "xsd:string"/>
  </variables>
</scope>
```

The local variable is defined inside the scope definition. So, the variable is accessible as soon as we enter the scope. Consequently, we lose access to the variable as soon as we leave the scope enclosing the local variable definition.

There's more...

Similar to the global variable definition, we can also define the variable from the toolbar of the BPEL process. This time, we already have one local variable listed as shown in the following screenshot:

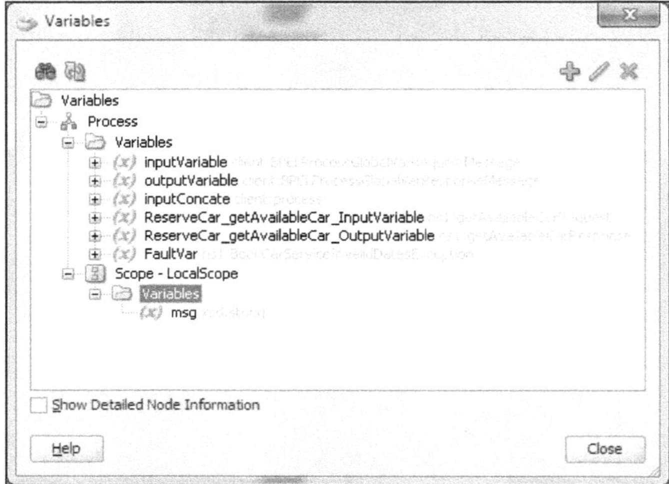

To define a global variable, we select the `Variables` folder under the **Process** node. However, to define a local variable, we need to select the `Variables` folder under the **Scope – LocalScope** node.

When creating the `<receive>`, `<reply>`, `<invoke>`, and `<catch>` activities, we have the possibility to create a global or local variable. This option is presented through the **Create Variable** dialog as shown in the following screenshot:

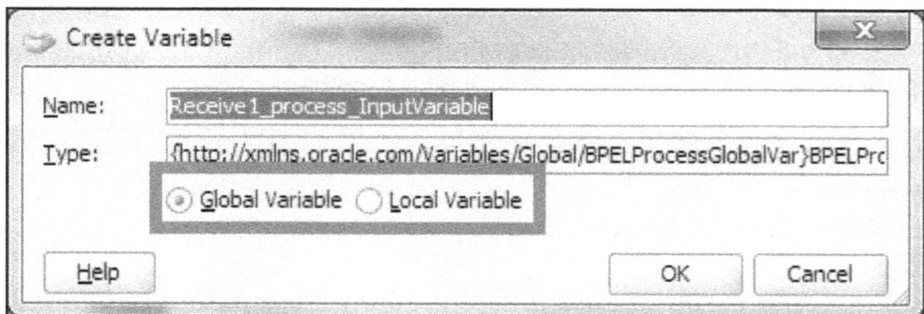

See also

- In this recipe we defined a variable. The variable itself does not contain any value. To set values to the variables, refer to the *Initializing a variable with an XML literal* and *Initializing a variable with an inline from-spec* recipes.

Initializing a variable with an XML literal

During the initialization phase, the variable receives its initial XML content. This content can be subject to various manipulations during the BPEL process flow. We are able to instantly assign the content of the variable if the source of the data already exists. This recipe explains how to initialize a variable with the XML content.

Getting ready

We create a new synchronous BPEL process (`VarInit.bpel`). We modify the request and response messages. The request message has the following schema:

```
<element name = "process">
  <complexType>
    <sequence>
      <element name = "name" type = "string"/>
      <element name = "birthYear" type = "int"/>
    </sequence>
  </complexType>
</element>
```

We need to provide the name and year of birth when starting the BPEL process instance. Similarly, we change the response message schema as follows:

```
<element name = "processResponse">
  <complexType>
    <sequence>
      <element name = "firstName" type = "string"/>
      <element name = "age" type = "string"/>
      <element name = "responseTime" type = "dateTime"/>
    </sequence>
  </complexType>
</element>
```

As a result of the BPEL process execution, we receive a name of the person, his/her age, and at what time the response from the BPEL process was sent.

How to do it...

The following steps show you how to initialize a variable with the XML literal content:

1. We will initiate the variable by using the assign activity. Open the BPEL process and add the assign activity into it.
2. Double-click on the added activity and select the icon for adding XML literals in the shape of a puzzle piece.

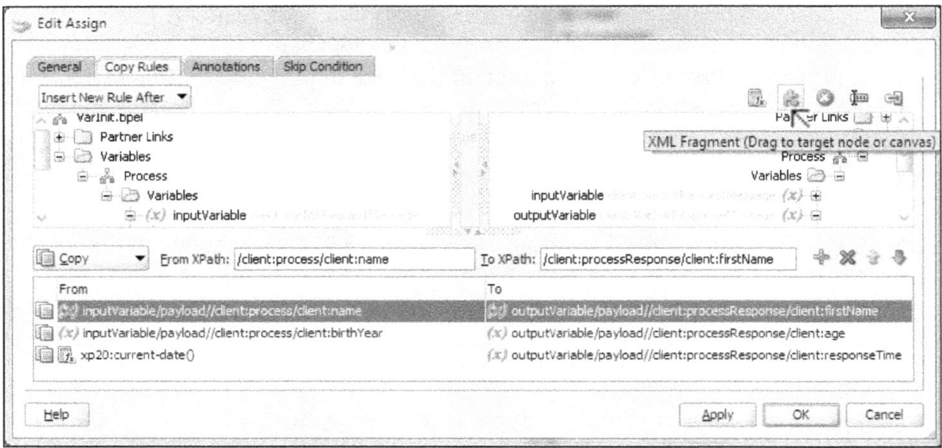

3. A dialog opens which enables us to enter the code for XML. We insert the code for initiating the variable; in our case, the output variable is as shown in the following screenshot:

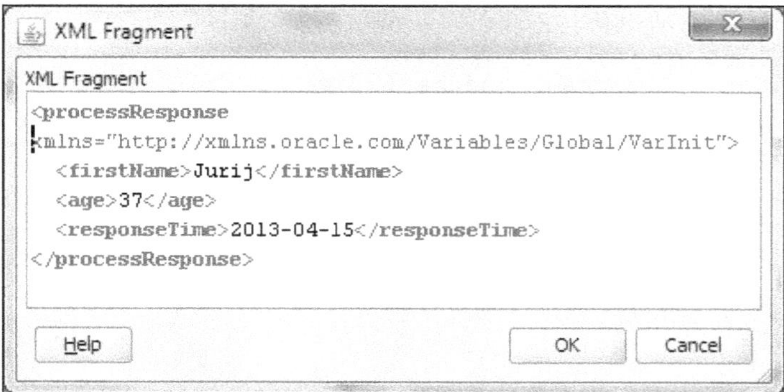

The XML literal must match the XML element definition in the XSD schema, so we must take care of that namespace as well as the tag names matching its definition.

4. Deploy the BPEL process and test it using the **Oracle Enterprise Manager Console**. We can inspect the initiated value of the variable in the **Audit Trail** as shown in the following screenshot:

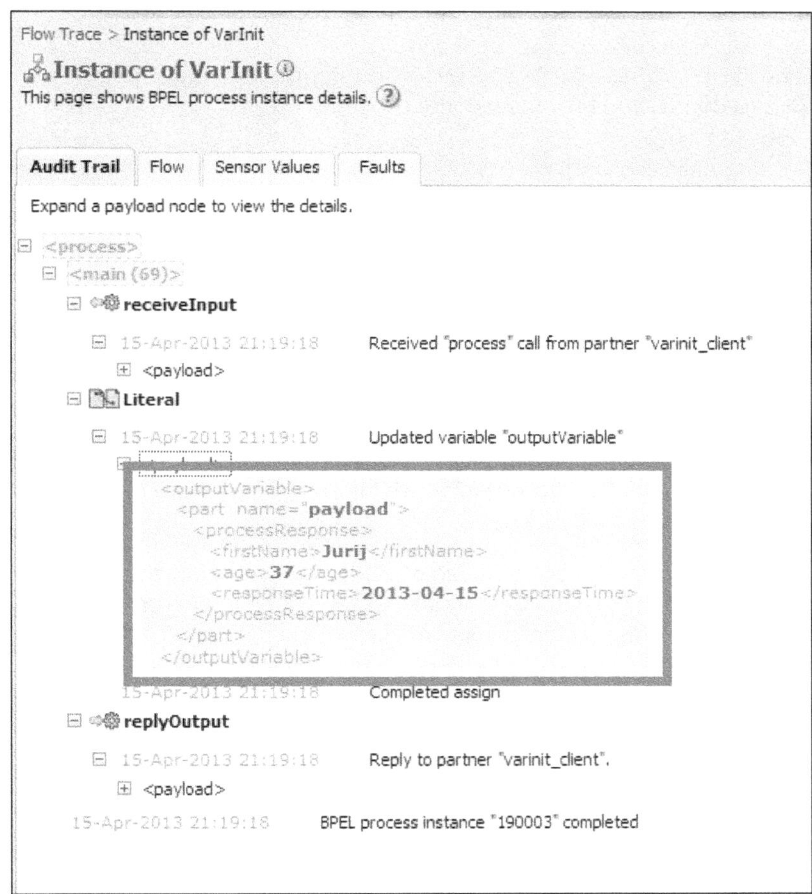

How it works...

All data in BPEL is represented in the XML format and so are all the variables. The types of variables are defined through the XML schema. The content of data in the variables is also presented in the XML data. So, whenever we perform an operation over a variable, we also perform an operation over the XML structure. By assigning an XML literal to a variable, we assign the XML content to the XML presentation of the variable.

In the BPEL process, where we assigned the XML literal to the variable, the following code appears:

```
<assign name = "Literal">
  <copy>
    <from><processResponse xmlns =
      "http://xmlns.oracle.com/Variables/Global/VarInit">
      <firstName>Jurij</firstName>
      <age>37</age>
      <responseTime>2013-04-15</responseTime>
    </processResponse></from>
    <to variable = "outputVariable" part = "payload"
      query = "/client:processResponse"/>
  </copy>
</assign>
```

There's more...

Another possibility is to partially initialize the variable. At some point during the BPEL process execution, we decide to initialize the variable with information we have and amend it later.

We modify the BPEL process by adding an additional assign activity. Now we have two assign activities in the BPEL process for the purpose of clarity. Let us modify the XML literal code in the `Literal` assign activity to initialize only part of the variable. We only fill the `firstName` element. The rest of the message consists of empty nodes as follows:

```
<copy>
  <from>
    <processResponse xmlns =
      "http://xmlns.oracle.com/Variables/Global/VarInit">
      <firstName>Hello</firstName>
      <age/>
      <responseTime/>
    </processResponse>
  </from>
  <to variable = "outputVariable" part = "payload"
    query = "/client:processResponse"/>
</copy>
```

The rest of the information can be filled in later with the assign activity.

See also

- For additional techniques regarding variable data manipulation, refer to the *Copying content between the variables* recipe

Initializing a variable with an inline from-spec

In the previous recipe, we explored how variables are initialized in a BPEL process. The recipe explained the initialization of variables using XML literals. This recipe explains the alternative way of initializing variables with an inline from-spec. The difference between the two mentioned recipes is that the initialization of a variable over an XML literal is performed from the assign activity, while initialization over an inline from-spec is performed at the variable definition.

The initialization of variables using an inline from-spec is only supported for BPEL 2.0 processes!

Getting ready

For this recipe, we will create an empty synchronous BPEL 2.0 process. We will reuse the request and response messages from the `VarInit.bpel` BPEL process we created in the previous recipe.

How to do it...

In the following steps, we will show you how to initialize a variable using an inline from-spec:

1. We open the BPEL process and click on the variables icon in the process toolbar.
2. We define a global variable with the name `FromSpecVar` as follows:

```
<variable name = "FromSpecVar"
  element = "client:processResponse"/>
```

3. In the **Variables** dialog, we select the `FromSpecVar` variable and click on the pencil icon to edit the variable configuration.

4. We select the **Initialize** tab in the **Edit Variable-FromSpecVar** dialog. From the **Type** drop-down selection, we choose the **Literal** option as shown in the following screenshot:

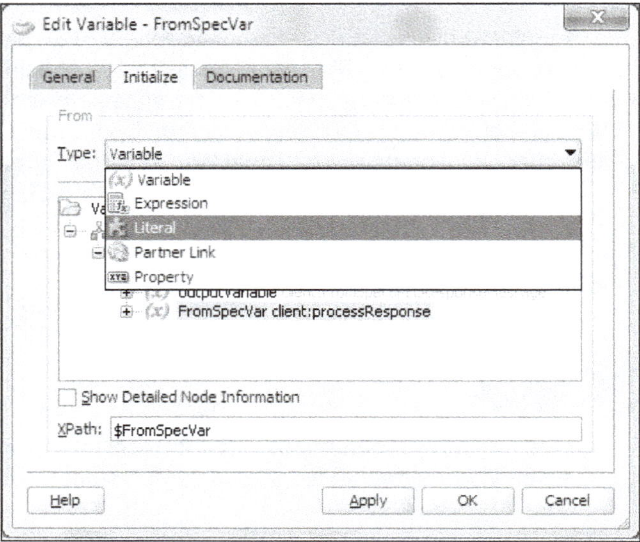

5. Enter the initialization XML code into the **Edit Variable** dialog and click on the **OK** button.

```
<client:processResponse xmlns:client =
  "http://xmlns.oracle.com/Variables/Global/FromSpecBPEL"
    xmlns = "http://docs.oasis-open.org/wsbpel/2.0
      /process/executable">
  <client:firstName>initName</client:firstName>
  <client:age>0</client:age>
  <client:responseTime>2013-04-16</client:responseTime>
</client:processResponse>
```

How it works...

The inline from-spec variable initiation functionality provides the ability to set up the values of a variable prior to making some dynamic changes to the variable. The initialization through literal is also useful when testing some part of a BPEL process for an unusual or unexpected situation.

> The initialization of variables using an inline from-spec is covered in BPEL Standard 2.0, Chapter 8.1, available at `http://docs.oasis-open.org/wsbpel/2.0/wsbpel-v2.0.html`.

The initialization of the variable with an inline from-spec creates the following structure in the BPEL source code:

```
<variables>
  <variable name = "FromSpecVar" element =
    "client:processResponse">
    <from>
      <literal>
        <client:processResponse xmlns:client =
          "http://xmlns.oracle.com/Variables/Global/FromSpecBPEL"
            xmlns = "http://docs.oasis-open.org/wsbpel
              /2.0/process/executable">
          <client:firstName>initName</client:firstName>
          <client:age>0</client:age>
          <client:responseTime>2013-04-16</client:responseTime>
        </client:processResponse>
      </literal>
    </from>
  </variable>
</variables>
```

The variable initialization starts with the `<from>` tag and continues with `<literal>` indicating that the variable will be initialized with literal. The definition continues with the variable content itself. The `<to>` tag is omitted since we already know the name and type of variable we want to initialize.

To test how the initialization works, we deploy the BPEL process to the Oracle SOA Suite server and run an instance of the BPEL process. Inspection of the **Audit Trail** shows that the initialization of the variable is executed before the BPEL process reads the request messages as shown in the following screenshot:

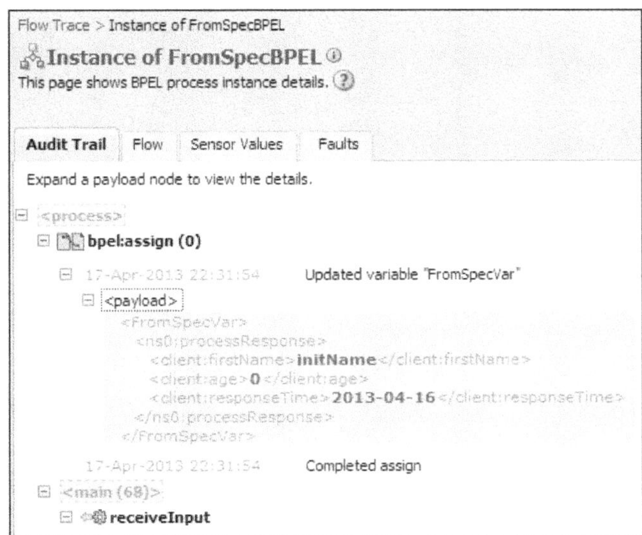

See also

- Another alternative for the variable initialization presents the transfer of the content using the assign activity. We address this topic in the *Copying content between the variables* recipe.

Copying content between the variables

One of the fundamental functionalities of a BPEL process is the manipulation of XML data from the request via various intermediate operations and transformations to the response. This recipe explains the principles of copying content between the variables.

Getting ready

For this recipe, we will clone the `FromSpecBPEL.bpel` process from the previous recipe and create two BPEL processes: `VarCopy1_1.bpel` (synchronous BPEL process, Version 1.1) and `VarCopy2_0.bpel` (synchronous BPEL process, Version 2.0).

How to do it...

The following steps explain how to copy content between variables in a BPEL process:

1. Open the `VarCopy1_1` BPEL process and add the assign (`AssignCopy`) activity.
2. Double-click on the assign activity. The **Edit Assign** dialog appears as shown in the following screenshot:

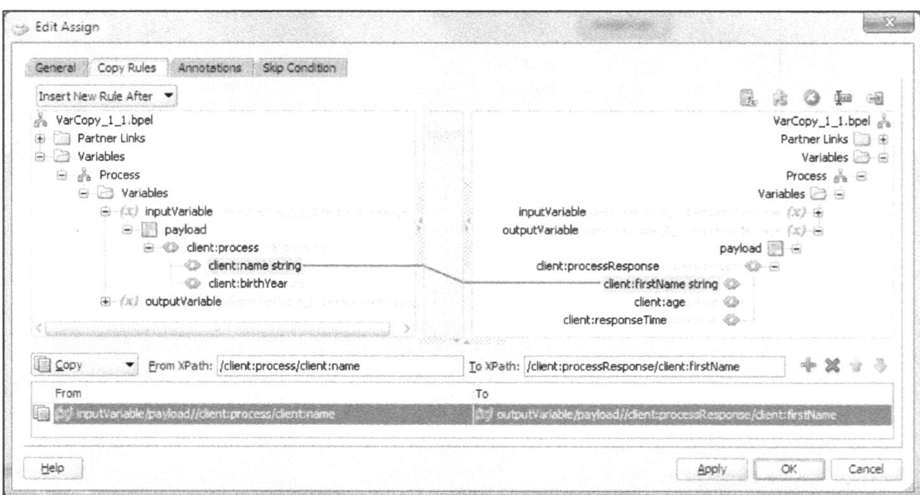

3. The top part of the **Copy Rules** tab is divided into three sections. We can consider the left side as the `from` part and the right side as the `to` part. The middle of the pane is reserved as a placeholder for various functions, such as functions, expressions, literals, and so on.
4. We copy the variable content by dragging the variable from the left part and dropping it on the variable on the right side. Upon completion, click on the **Apply** or **OK** button to confirm the copying rules.

How it works...

Behind the scenes, the visualization is transformed into the XML code. The copy between the variables is done directly, meaning there is no need to address the variables through the XPath queries.

It is also possible to copy more than just the variables. From-spec can also contain expressions, partner links, and literals.

There is also a difference in the version of specification that our BPEL process supports. Check the source code that we have now in the `VarCopy1_1` process as follows:

```
<copy>
  <from variable = "inputVariable" part = "payload"
    query = "/client:process/client:name"/>
  <to variable = "outputVariable" part = "payload"
    query = "/client:processResponse/client:firstName"/>
</copy>
// Perform the recipe on the VarCopy2_0 process. The source code
// we found there is as follows:
<copy>
  <from>$inputVariable.payload/client:name</from>
  <to>$outputVariable.payload/client:firstName</to>
</copy>
```

We can see the difference in the copy definitions of both the BPEL processes. However, the outcome of the copy operation is the same in both cases.

There's more...

One major difference between the BPEL 1.1 and BPEL 2.0 **Edit Assign** dialog is the visual presentation of the middle part of the dialog. The following screenshot is the middle part of the **Edit Assign** dialog from the BPEL 1.1 process:

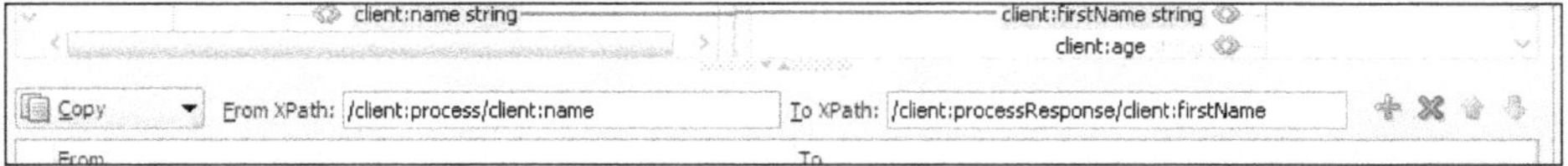

If we compare the same dialog in the BPEL 2.0 process, we find no such elements except for the icons on the right side. This functionality can now be found if we right-click on the from-to rule part of the **Edit Assign** dialog and select **Change rule type** as shown in the following screenshot:

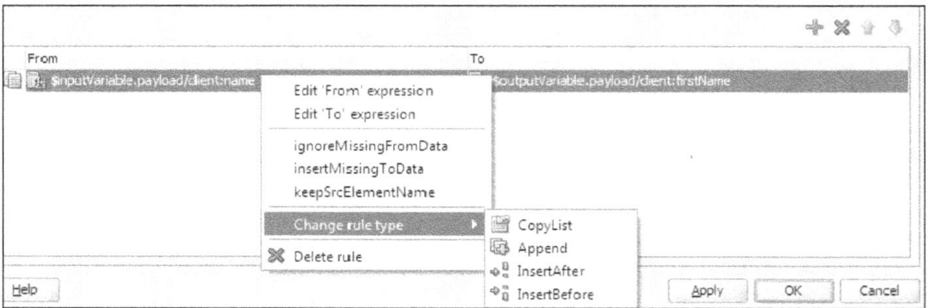

> The change between the versions was made mainly due to the improved data access mechanism in later BPEL processes. In Version 1.1, the variables were accessed through the XPath query. The newer version of the BPEL specification introduces different handling of the variable data access through the variable XPath binding or `$notation`. The variables as well as their part definitions can now be accessed via `$var.part/field`.

See also

- By changing the rule type, we influence the way in which new data is introduced into the variable. The choices in the **Edit Assign** dialog are presented as BPELX extensions. Refer to the *Updating the variables using the BPELX extensions* recipe to explore how to use the BPELX extensions in a BPEL process.

Accessing the fields within Element-based variables

This recipe explains the method for accessing Element-based variables. We will show you how to access the fields in variables that are Element-based.

Getting ready

We define two Versions (BPEL 1.1 and BPEL 2.0) of synchronous BPEL processes and name them `Manipulate1_1` and `Manipulate2_0`. In both the BPEL processes, we define the Element-based global variable `ResponseElement` as follows:

```
<variable name = "ResponseElement" element = "client:process"/>
```

The structure of the `process` element can be found in `Manipulate1_1.xsd` and `Manipulate2_0.xsd` as follows:

```
<element name = "process">
  <complexType>
    <sequence>
      <element name = "input" type = "string"/>
    </sequence>
  </complexType>
</element>
```

How to do it...

In the following steps, we will show you how to access the fields defined in the Element-based variables in a BPEL process:

1. Open the `Manipulate1_1` BPEL process and add the `AssignElement` assign activity.
2. The code for assigning the concatenated text and the content of the input field of the input variable to the `ResponseElement` global variable is as follows:

```
<copy>
  <from expression = "concat('Hello ', bpws:getVariableData
    ('inputVariable','payload',
      '/client:process/client:input'))"/>
  <to variable = "ResponseElement"
    query = "/client:process/client:input"/>
</copy>
```

Access to an Element-based variable is through the XPath query.

3. Assign the content of the Element-based variable to the Message Type-based variable as follows:

```
<copy>
  <from variable = "ResponseElement"
    query = "/client:process/client:input"/>
  <to variable = "outputVariable" part = "payload"
    query = "/client:processResponse/client:result"/>
</copy>
```

4. Click on the **OK** button to close the **Edit Assign** dialog.

How it works...

The recommended way of defining the Element-based variables is by using the XSD schema files. The Element-based variables then reference the XML schema complex types. The most common manipulation of an Element-based variable is achieved through the assign activity. For more complex manipulations, it is recommended to use the transformations that we covered in *Chapter 5, Transforming and Validating the BPEL Services*. To perform the activity, we must define the `from` and `to` clause inside the assign activity.

There's more...

In the BPEL 2.0 process, the notation in the source code is slightly different due to the improved variable accessibility mechanism:

1. Open the `Manipulate2_0` BPEL process and add the assign activity.
2. Assign the XML fragment content to the `ResponseElement` global variable.

```
<copy>
  <from>concat
    ('Hello ', $inputVariable.payload/client:input)</from>
  <to>$ResponseElement/client:input</to>
</copy>
```

3. Assign the content of the Element-based variable to the Message Type-based variable as follows:

```
<copy>
  <from>$ResponseElement/client:input</from>
  <to>$outputVariable.payload/client:result</to>
</copy>
```

4. Click on the **OK** button to close the **Edit Assign** dialog.

See also

- To learn how to work with the **Message Type** variables, refer to our next recipe, *Accessing the fields within the Message Type-based variables*

Accessing the fields within the Message Type-based variables

This recipe explains how to access fields within Message Type-based variables. We will reuse the two sample BPEL processes from the previous recipe since the request and response messages and their corresponding variables present Message Type-based variables.

Getting ready

This recipe builds on the two BPEL processes we created in the previous recipe named `Manipulate1_1` and `Manipulate2_0`.

How to do it...

This recipe will show you how to access fields in Message Type-based variables in a BPEL process:

1. Open the `Manipulate1_1` BPEL process and add the assign activity (`AssignMsgType`).
2. We assign the content from the request message to the content of the response message. We are actually performing the assignment between two Message Type-based variables as follows:

```
<copy>
  <from variable = "inputVariable" part = "payload"
    query = "/client:process/client:input"/>
  <to variable = "outputVariable" part = "payload"
    query = "/client:processResponse/client:result"/>
</copy>
```

Access to a Message Type-based variable is through the XPath query.

3. Assign the content of the Message Type-based variable to a simple Type-based variable as follows:

```
<copy>
  <from variable = "inputVariable" part = "payload"
    query = "/client:process/client:input"/>
  <to variable = "MyName"/>
</copy>
```

4. Click on the **OK** button to close the **Edit Assign** dialog.

How it works...

The definitions for the Message Type-based variables are mostly defined in the WSDL files and accessible through the XML schema complex types. The most common manipulation of an Element-based variable is achieved through the assign activity. To perform the activity, we define the `from` and `to` clause inside the assign activity.

There's more...

In the BPEL 2.0 process, the notation in the source code is slightly different due to the improved variable accessibility mechanism:

1. Open the `Manipulate2_0` BPEL process and add the assign activity.
2. We assign the content from the request message to the content of the response message. We are actually performing the assignment between two Message Type-based variables as follows:

```
<copy>
  <from>$inputVariable.payload/client:input</from>
  <to>$outputVariable.payload/client:result</to>
</copy>
```

3. Assign the content of the Element-based variable to the Message Type-based variable as follows:

```
<copy>
  <from>$inputVariable.payload/client:input</from>
  <to>$Myname</to>
</copy>
```

4. Click on the **OK** button to close the **Edit Assign** dialog.

Assigning numerical values to the variables

Assigning different numerical values to variables is not directly a BPEL or Java feature. However, BPEL variables are basically XML variables. The variable definitions are based on the XML schema where we define different numeric types for three variable elements.

Getting ready

This recipe builds on the two BPEL processes we created in the previous two recipes named `Manipulate1_1` and `Manipulate2_0`.

How to do it...

In the following steps, we define variables with various types in a BPEL process. All of the following variables can also be defined through the JDeveloper wizards the same way we defined the global and local variables:

1. Open the `Manipulate1_1` BPEL process and add the assign activity (`AssignNumerical`).

   We will define several variables for assigning the numerical values.

   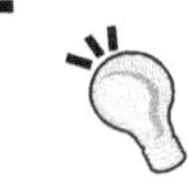

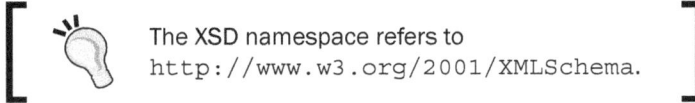

   The XSD namespace refers to `http://www.w3.org/2001/XMLSchema`.

2. Define the `xsd:int` variable as follows:

```
<variable name = "Var_int" type = "xsd:int"/>
```

3. Define the `xsd:long` variable as follows:

```
<variable name = "Var_long" type = "xsd:long"/>
```

4. Define the `xsd:short` variable as follows:

```
<variable name = "Var_short" type = "xsd:short"/>
```

5. Define the `xsd:decimal` variable as follows:

```
<variable name = "Var_decimal" type = "xsd:decimal"/>
```

6. Define the `xsd:float` variable as follows:

```
<variable name = "Var_float" type = "xsd:float"/>
```

7. Define the `xsd:double` variable as follows:

```
<variable name = "Var_double" type = "xsd:double"/>
```

Open the `AssignNumerical` assign activity to assign the numerical values to the variables. We define the following copy rules for the assign activity:

1. Assign the value `2013` to the `xsd:int` variable as follows:

```
<copy>
  <from expression = "2013"/>
  <to variable = "Var_int"/>
</copy>
```

2. Assign the value `9223372036854775807` to the `xsd:long` variable as follows:

```
<copy>
  <from expression = "9223372036854775807"/>
  <to variable = "Var_long"/>
</copy>
```

3. Assign the value `32767` to the `xsd:short` variable as follows:

```
<copy>
  <from expression = "32767"/>
  <to variable = "Var_short"/>
</copy>
```

4. Assign the value `1234.456` to the `xsd:decimal` variable as follows:

```
<copy>
  <from expression = "1234.456"/>
  <to variable = "Var_decimal"/>
</copy>
```

5. Assign the value `-1.2344e56` to the `xsd:float` variable as follows:

```
<copy>
  <from expression = "-1.2344e56"/>
  <to variable = "Var_float"/>
</copy>
```

6. Assign the value `-1.2344e56` to the `xsd:double` variable as follows:

```
<copy>
  <from expression = "-1.2344e56"/>
  <to variable = "Var_double"/>
</copy>
```

The numerical values are assigned to the variables through the XPath expressions. For example, in the **Expression Builder**, we can enter a number (`100`) to define the number value.

The XML schema types follow the value range conventions. However, BPEL ignores any checks against the value the variable is carrying. The validation of the values in the variables is left over to the developer of the BPEL process.

If, for example, we have the variable of the type `xsd:short` and we insert the value `32800` into the variable, even if the maximum allowed value is `32767`, BPEL will not report any errors.

There's more...

In BPEL 2.0, it is possible to initialize with the inline from-spec definition. For that purpose, we open the `Manipulate2_0` BPEL process and define the variables with the initialized values as follows:

```
<variable name = "Var_long" type = "xsd:long">
  <from>9223372036854775807</from>
</variable>
<variable name = "Var_short" type = "xsd:short">
  <from>32767</from>
</variable>
<variable name = "Var_decimal" type = "xsd:decimal">
  <from>1234.456</from>
</variable>
<variable name = "Var_float" type = "xsd:float">
  <from>1.2343444</from>
</variable>
<variable name = "Var_double" type = "xsd:double">
  <from>-1.23492111</from>
</variable>
```

You will notice that the code is simpler and cleaner compared to the BPEL 1.1 process.

See also

- We can use mathematical calculations with the numeric variables we defined in this recipe. Read the next recipe, *Applying mathematical calculations on data in the variables*, to explore the usage of mathematical calculations.

Applying mathematical calculations on data in the variables

JDeveloper provides the standard set of mathematical calculations that can be used in the BPEL processes. We will use the mathematical calculations on numerically defined variables.

Getting ready

This recipe continues the discussion of the BPEL process `Manipulate1_1` from the *Assigning numerical values to the variables* recipe.

We extend the request and response message structure in `Manipulate1_1.xsd`. The request message is extended with the `item` and `priceVAT` elements as follows:

```
<element name = "process">
  <complexType>
    <sequence>
      <element name = "input" type = "string"/>
      <element name = "item" type = "string"/>
      <element name = "priceVAT" type = "decimal"/>
      <element name = "child_no" type = "integer"/>
    </sequence>
  </complexType>
</element>
```

The response message is extended with the `priceNet` and `vat` elements as follows:

```
<element name = "processResponse">
  <complexType>
    <sequence>
      <element name = "result" type = "string"/>
      <element name = "priceNet" type = "decimal"/>
      <element name = "vat" type = "decimal"/>
      <element name = "child_selection" type = "string"/>
    </sequence>
  </complexType>
</element>
```

In this recipe, we will look at the calculation needed to insert the gross price of an item. In the BPEL process, we will calculate the net price of the item along with the VAT included in the gross price. We assume that the VAT included in the gross price is always 20 percent.

How to do it...

1. Open the BPEL process and add the assign activity (`MathCalc`).
2. We will now calculate the net price of the item. For that purpose, we use the divide, round, and multiply mathematical functions. Next, we calculate the VAT included in the gross price of the item.

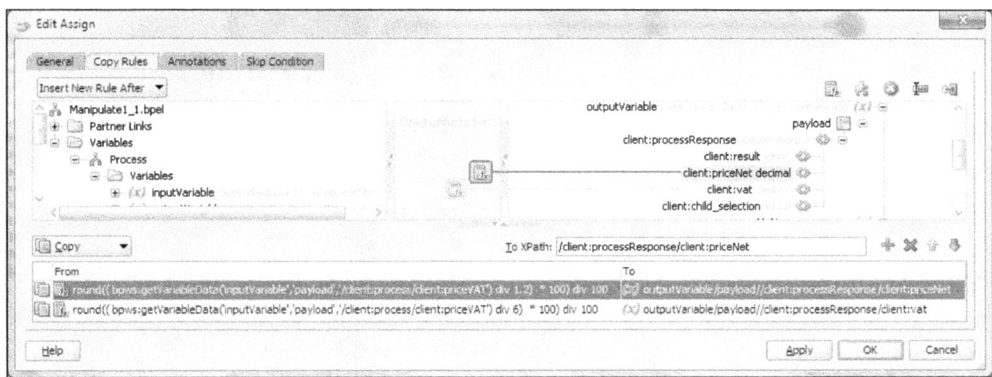

3. Deploy the BPEL process and run the instance of it on Oracle SOA Suite for the following input request:

```
<inputVariable>
  <part name = "payload" xmlns:xsi =
    "http://www.w3.org/2001/XMLSchema-instance">
    <ns1:process xmlns:ns1 =
      "http://xmlns.oracle.com/Variables/Global
        /Manipulate1_1">
      <ns1:input>Jurij</ns1:input>
      <ns1:item>PC</ns1:item>
   <ns1:priceVAT>100</ns1:priceVAT>
    </ns1:process>
  </part>
</inputVariable>
```

4. We receive the corresponding response from the BPEL process as follows:

```
<outputVariable>
  <part name = "payload" xmlns:xsi =
    "http://www.w3.org/2001/XMLSchema-instance">
    <processResponse xmlns =
      "http://xmlns.oracle.com/Variables/Global
        /Manipulate1_1">
```

```
        <result>Jurij</result>
      <priceNet>83.33</priceNet>
      <vat>16.67</vat>
       </processResponse>
     </part>
   </outputVariable>
```

How it works...

We can utilize the following most common mathematical functions from within the JDeveloper GUI:

Mathematical function	Source code signature	Function returns
abs	`xp20:abs()`	Absolute value.
add	`+`	Addition of two numbers.
ceiling	`ceiling()`	The smallest number that is not less than the argument and is of integer type.
count	`count()`	The number of nodes.
divide	`div`	The division of two numbers.
floor	`floor()`	The largest number that is not greater than the argument and is of integer type.
mod	`mod`	Reminder of the truncation division.
multiply	`*`	Multiplication of two arguments.
round	`round()`	Rounds the argument to the nearest integer number.
square-root	`oraext:square-root()`	Square root of the argument.
subtract	`-`	Subtraction of two numbers.
sum	`sum()`	Sum of all the arguments (nodes).
unary	`-()`	Invert the operation of the argument.

Assigning Boolean values to the variables

We can identify the logical conditions with a Boolean value. You will learn how to use Boolean values in the variables in this recipe.

Getting ready

This recipe continues the discussion of the BPEL process `Manipulate1_1` from the *Using mathematical calculations in the variables* recipe.

In the `Manipulate1_1` BPEL process, we define the Boolean variable as follows:

```
<variable name = "expensive_item" type = "xsd:boolean"/>
```

With this variable, we will check if the item is expensive or not.

How to do it...

The following steps explain how to assign and change a Boolean value of a variable:

1. Open the `Manipulate1_1` BPEL process.
2. Add the assign activity and name it `Boolean`.
3. We first initialize the variable to the `false` value as follows:

   ```
   <copy>
     <from expression = "false()"/>
     <to variable = "expensive_item"/>
   </copy>
   ```

4. We check if the item is expensive, by comparing the item price against the fixed amount criteria as follows:

   ```
   <copy>
     <from expression =
       "bpws:getVariableData('inputVariable', 'payload',
         '/client:process/client:priceVAT') > 1000"/>
     <to variable = "expensive_item"/>
   </copy>
   ```

5. Save the changes to the BPEL process and deploy it to Oracle SOA Server. We initiate an instance of the BPEL process with the following request message:

   ```
   <inputVariable>
     <part name = "payload" xmlns:xsi =
       "http://www.w3.org/2001/XMLSchema-instance">
   ```

```
        <ns1:process xmlns:ns1 =
          "http://xmlns.oracle.com/Variables/Global
            /Manipulate1_1">
          <ns1:input>Jurij</ns1:input>
          <ns1:item>454</ns1:item>
      <ns1:priceVAT>67755</ns1:priceVAT>
        </ns1:process>
      </part>
    </inputVariable>
```

Let's now check the **Audit Trail**. We search for the Boolean assign activity. The execution data shows that the variable `expensive_item` is initialized with the value `false`, and after the evaluation of the condition against the price and fixed amount criteria, it was set to `true` as follows:

```
<expensive_item xmlns:xsi =
  "http://www.w3.org/2001/XMLSchema-instance" xmlns:ns =
    "http://www.w3.org/2001/XMLSchema" xsi:type =
      "ns:boolean">false</expensive_item>
<expensive_item xmlns:xsi =
  "http://www.w3.org/2001/XMLSchema-instance" xmlns:ns =
    "http://www.w3.org/2001/XMLSchema" xsi:type =
      "ns:boolean">true</expensive_item>
```

Assigning date or time to the variables

BPEL enables many date and time operations. In this recipe, we explore how to manage date and time in BPEL processes.

Getting ready

We create an empty synchronous BPEL process (`DateTime.bpel`) and adjust the request message to accept date and time. In `DateTime.xsd`, we modify the process element as follows:

```
<element name = "process">
  <complexType>
    <sequence>
      <element name = "input" type="dateTime"/>
    </sequence>
  </complexType>
</element>
```

How to do it...

In the BPEL process, we define the variables that accept date and time as shown in the following screenshot:

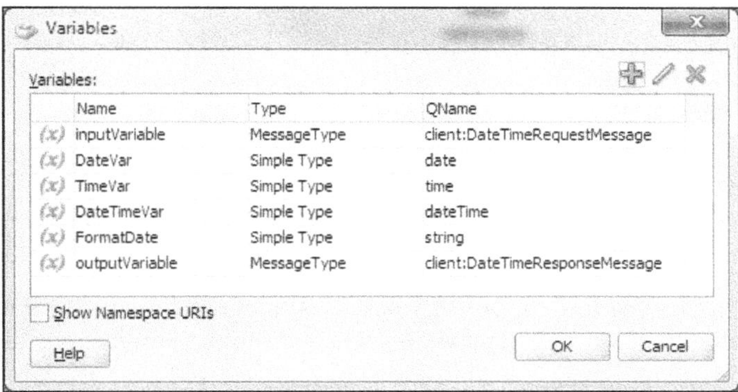

Next, add the assign activity, where we define the copy rules as follows:

1. With the `xp20:current-date()` function, we assign the current date to the `DateVar` variable.

   ```
   <copy>
     <from expression = "xp20:current-date()"/>
     <to variable = "DateVar"/>
   </copy>
   ```

2. With the `xp20:current-time()` function, we assign the current date to the `TimeVar` variable.

   ```
   <copy>
     <from expression = "xp20:current-time()"/>
     <to variable = "TimeVar"/>
   </copy>
   ```

3. With the `xp20:current-dateTime()` function, we assign the current date to the `DateTimeVar` variable.

   ```
   <copy>
     <from expression = "xp20:current-dateTime()"/>
     <to variable = "DateTimeVar"/>
   </copy>
   ```

4. With the `xp20:format-dateTime` function, we format the current date to the `FormatDate` variable and assign it to the response variable.

```
<copy>
  <from expression = "xp20:format-dateTime
    (bpws:getVariableData('FormatDate'),
      '[D01]/[M01]/[Y0001]')"/>
  <to variable = "FormatDate"/>
</copy>
<copy>
  <from variable = "FormatDate"/>
  <to variable = "outputVariable" part = "payload"
    query = "/client:processResponse/client:result"/>
</copy>
```

5. Now, we deploy the BPEL process, run an instance, and inspect the **Audit Trail** of the instance to see the various values assigned to the variables as shown in the following screenshot:

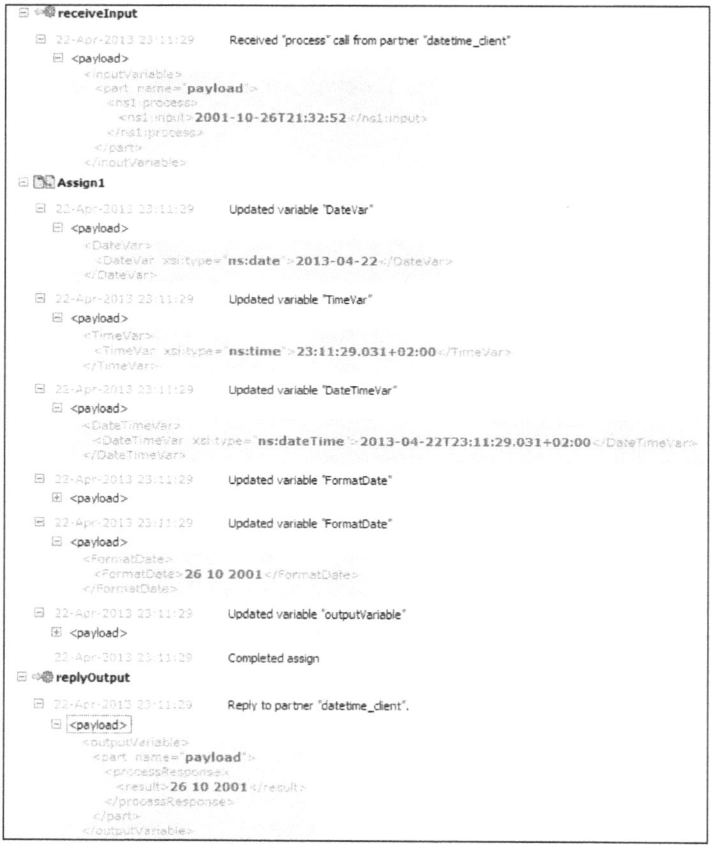

```
receiveInput
  22-Apr-2013 23:11:29    Received "process" call from partner "datetime_client"
    <payload>
      <inputVariable>
        <part name="payload">
          <ns1:process>
            <ns1:input>2001-10-26T21:32:52</ns1:input>
          </ns1:process>
        </part>
      </inputVariable>
Assign1
  22-Apr-2013 23:11:29    Updated variable "DateVar"
    <payload>
      <DateVar>
        <DateVar xsi:type="ns:date">2013-04-22</DateVar>
      </DateVar>
  22-Apr-2013 23:11:29    Updated variable "TimeVar"
    <payload>
      <TimeVar>
        <TimeVar xsi:type="ns:time">23:11:29.031+02:00</TimeVar>
      </TimeVar>
  22-Apr-2013 23:11:29    Updated variable "DateTimeVar"
    <payload>
      <DateTimeVar>
        <DateTimeVar xsi:type="ns:dateTime">2013-04-22T23:11:29.031+02:00</DateTimeVar>
      </DateTimeVar>
  22-Apr-2013 23:11:29    Updated variable "FormatDate"
    <payload>
  22-Apr-2013 23:11:29    Updated variable "FormatDate"
    <payload>
      <FormatDate>
        <FormatDate>26 10 2001</FormatDate>
      </FormatDate>
  22-Apr-2013 23:11:29    Updated variable "outputVariable"
    <payload>
  22-Apr-2013 23:11:29    Completed assign
replyOutput
  22-Apr-2013 23:11:29    Reply to partner "datetime_client".
    <payload>
      <outputVariable>
        <part name="payload">
          <processResponse>
            <result>26 10 2001</result>
          </processResponse>
        </part>
      </outputVariable>
```

Updating the variables using the BPELX extensions

This recipe explains how to utilize the BPELX extensions in order to manipulate content of the variables.

Getting ready

For this recipe, we will amend the BPEL processes from the *Copying content between the variables* recipe. Remember we designed two synchronous BPEL processes: one that supports BPEL 1.1 and one that supports BPEL 2.0. We will amend those two processes with a set of BPELX extensions.

For both the BPEL processes, we will extend the response message. We open the schema file (`VarCopy_1_1.xsd` and `VarCopy2_0.xsd`) and amend the content of the response schema element as follows:

```
<element name = "processResponse">
  <complexType>
    <sequence>
      <element name = "firstName" type="string"/>
      <element name = "age" type="int"/>
      <element name = "responseTime" type="dateTime"/>
      <element name = "child" type = "string" minOccurs =
        "1" maxOccurs = "unbounded"/>
    </sequence>
  </complexType>
</element>
```

The `child` element presents a list of string values.

How to do it...

The following steps show you how to update variables with various Oracle SOA Suite extension functions:

1. For this recipe, we will use the `CopyList` extension. Open the `VarCopy_1_1` BPEL process and add the assign activity.
2. Add the Element-type global variable `Var_CopyList` which is used as the manipulation variable for the XML data.

3. Add the assign activity into the BPEL process and add the following copy rules:
   - Initialize the global variable with a literal value.
   - Initialize the response message with the `firstName`, `age`, and `responseTime` information.
   - Copy the content of the `Var_CopyList` global variable to the `child` list of the response message by using the `copyList` operation. With this copy rule, change the operation to `CopyList`.

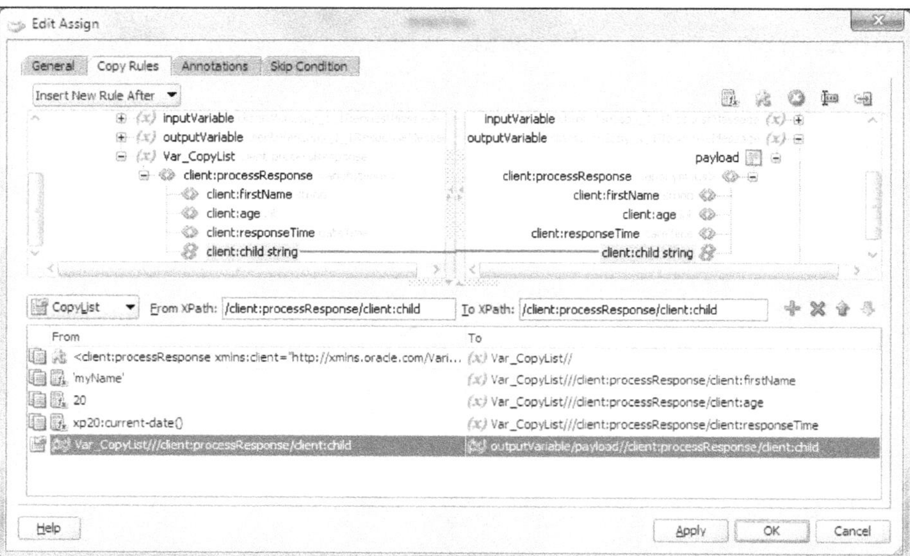

4. Click on **OK** to close the dialog.
5. Deploy the BPEL process to Oracle SOA Suite and execute it. In the **Audit Trail** of the BPEL process, we see that the global variable is initialized with a literal value as follows:

```
<Var_CopyList>
  <processResponse xmlns:client =
    "http://xmlns.oracle.com/Variables/Global/
      VarCopy_1_1" xmlns = "http://xmlns.oracle.com/
        Variables/Global/VarCopy_1_1">
    <client:firstName>initName</client:firstName>
    <client:age>0</client:age>
    <client:responseTime>2013-04-16</client:responseTime>
 <client:child>Ajda</client:child>
```

```
    <client:child>Urban</client:child>
  </processResponse>
</Var_CopyList>
```

6. After the global variable is updated and the `CopyList` rule has been executed, the response message is updated as follows:

```
<outputVariable>
  <part name = "payload" xmlns:xsi =
    "http://www.w3.org/2001/XMLSchema-instance">
    <processResponse xmlns =
      "http://xmlns.oracle.com/Variables/Global/
        VarCopy_1_1">
      <firstName>Jurij</firstName>
      <age>1975</age>
      <responseTime>2013-04-18</responseTime>
   <client:child xmlns:client =
     "http://xmlns.oracle.com/Variables/Global/VarCopy_1_1">
       Ajda</client:child>
   <client:child xmlns:client =
     "http://xmlns.oracle.com/Variables/Global/VarCopy_1_1">
       Urban</client:child>
    </processResponse>
  </part>
</outputVariable>
```

How it works...

The `CopyList` operation is especially useful in cases where we operate on a list of the same Element type. An alternative to using `CopyList` would be either to use the XSLT transformations or to create a set of copy rules where we would iterate through the list.

The source code in the BPEL 1.1 process for the `CopyList` operation is as follows:

```
<bpelx:copyList>
  <bpelx:from variable = "Var_CopyList" query =
    "/client:processResponse/client:child"/>
  <bpelx:to variable = "outputVariable" part = "payload"
    query = "/client:processResponse/client:child"/>
</bpelx:copyList>
```

The BPELX extension is seen as the namespace of the extension. The two additional elements that are used for the `CopyList` operation are `from` and `to`.

In BPEL 2.0, the same operation looks different due to the variable access simplification as follows:

```
<extensionAssignOperation>
  <bpelx:copyList>
    <bpelx:from>$Var_CopyList/client:child</bpelx:from>
    <bpelx:to>$outputVariable.payload/client:child</bpelx:to>
  </bpelx:copyList>
</extensionAssignOperation>
```

There's more...

We can also use the `bpelx:append` and `bpelx:InsertAfter` extensions for variable data manipulation.

In both the example BPEL processes, we add an additional assign activity for each BPELX extension for clarity. However, there is nothing to stop you from in using a different BPELX extension in a single assign activity.

bpelx:append

The `append` extension is used for adding additional information into already existing XML content. With the copy operation, the content might get deleted or overwritten; however, appending the extension ensures that the XML content is appended as expected. It is possible to append the content of a variable, expression, or XML fragment as follows:

1. In the BPEL process edit the assign activity.
2. Use the XML fragment to assign the content to the variable.
3. For the copy rule type, select **Append**.
4. Click on **OK** to close the dialog and confirm the assign configuration.

The code generated in `VarCopy_1_1` is as follows:

```
<bpelx:append>
  <bpelx:from>
    <client:child xmlns:client =
      "http://xmlns.oracle.com/Variables/Global/VarCopy_1_1">
        Bob</client:child>
  </bpelx:from>
  <bpelx:to variable = "outputVariable" part = "payload"
    query = "/client:processResponse"/>
</bpelx:append>
```

The code generated in `VarCopy2_0` is as follows:

```
<extensionAssignOperation>
  <bpelx:append>
    <bpelx:from>
      <bpelx:literal>
        <client:child xmlns:client =
          "http://xmlns.oracle.com/Variables/Global/VarCopy2_0">
            Bob</client:child>
      </bpelx:literal>
    </bpelx:from>
    <bpelx:to>$outputVariable.payload</bpelx:to>
  </bpelx:append>
</extensionAssignOperation>
```

bpelx:InsertAfter

The `InsertAfter` extension is also used for adding additional information into already existing XML content. It is possible to insert the content of a variable, expression, or XML fragment. The XML content is inserted immediately after the element defined by the `<to>` expression in the `InsertAfter` extension:

1. In the BPEL process edit the assign activity.
2. Use the XML fragment to assign the content to the variable.
3. For the copy rule type, select **InsertAfter**. We insert a new `<child>` element after first exiting the `<child>` element in the result variable.
4. Click on **OK** to close the dialog and confirm the assign configuration.

The code generated in `VarCopy_1_1` is as follows:

```
<bpelx:insertAfter>
  <bpelx:from>
    <client:child xmlns:client =
      "http://xmlns.oracle.com/Variables/Global/VarCopy_1_1">
        Hope</client:child>
  </bpelx:from>
  <bpelx:to variable = "outputVariable" part = "payload"
    query = "/client:processResponse/client:child[1]"/>
</bpelx:insertAfter>
```

The code generated in `VarCopy2_0` is as follows:

```
<extensionAssignOperation>
  <bpelx:insertAfter>
    <bpelx:from>
      <bpelx:literal>
        <client:child xmlns:client =
          "http://xmlns.oracle.com/Variables/Global/VarCopy2_0">
            Hope</client:child>
      </bpelx:literal>
    </bpelx:from>
    <bpelx:to>$outputVariable.payload/client:child[1]</bpelx:to>
  </bpelx:insertAfter>
</extensionAssignOperation>
```

Dynamic indexing of the variables

In situations where we have information in a list of the same elements, it is not possible to access a variable by name. Rather, we use indexing to access the variable data from a list.

Getting ready

We will examine dynamic indexing of the variables in the `Manipulate1_1` BPEL process from the *Assigning date or time to the variables* recipe.

First, let's extend the BPEL process by defining a new element in the `Manipulate1_1` schema file as follows:

```
<element name = "ChildrenElementType">
  <complexType>
    <sequence>
      <element name = "child" type = "string" minOccurs = "1"
        maxOccurs = "unbounded"/>
    </sequence>
  </complexType>
</element>
```

The Element-type variable is defined as an array of the `<child>` strings.

Also, we modify the request and response messages of the BPEL process. We amend the request message with the following element:

```
<element name = "child_no" type = "integer"/>
```

We will use this to input the element in the `child` list we want to query. We add the following element to the response message:

```
<element name = "child_selection" type = "string"/>
```

The Element-type variable will contain information about the selected child from the list.

How to do it...

In order to dynamically index the variable content, we perform the following steps:

1. We start by adding the assign scope (`DynamicScope`) and sequence activity (`DynamicSequence`) into our BPEL process.
2. Inside the scope, we define two local variables. The `ChildSelection` variable holds information about the list. We define `index` to perform the dynamic query in the list.

   ```
   <variables>
     <variable name = "ChildSelection"
       element = "client:ChildrenElementType"/>
     <variable name = "index" type = "xsd:integer"/>
   </variables>
   ```

3. We need to fill up the content into the input parameter variable. For that purpose, we add an assign activity (`InitChildren`) to initialize the list of information as follows:

   ```
   <assign name = "InitChildren">
     <copy>
       <from><client:ChildrenElementType xmlns:client =
         "http://xmlns.oracle.com/Variables/Global/
           Manipulate1_1">
         <client:child>Ajda</client:child>
         <client:child>Urban</client:child>
         </client:ChildrenElementType></from>
       <to variable = "ChildSelection"/>
     </copy>
   </assign>
   ```

4. Next, we build up the logic for the input variable validation. The building blocks consist of the `switch` activity with two decision branches. The positive branch checks if the `child_no` element is set in the request message and in the specified range.

```
<case condition = "bpws:getVariableData
  ('inputVariable','payload',
    '/client:process/client:child_no') &lt; 3 and
      bpws:getVariableData('inputVariable','payload',
        '/client:process/client:child_no') > 0">
```

5. If true, we retrieve the queried child element as follows:

```
<assign name = "GetDynamic">
  <copy>
    <from variable = "inputVariable" part = "payload"
      query = "/client:process/client:child_no"/>
    <to variable = "index"/>
  </copy>
  <copy>
    <from expression = "bpws:getVariableData
      ('ChildSelection','/client:ChildrenElementType')
        /client:child[bpws:getVariableData('index')]"/>
    <to variable = "outputVariable" part = "payload" query
      = "/client:processResponse/client:child_selection"/>
  </copy>
</assign>
```

6. Otherwise, we gracefully return the message to the caller as follows:

```
<assign name = "AssignNoAction">
  <copy>
    <from expression = "'No value for selection or
      selection out of bounds'"/>
    <to variable = "outputVariable" part = "payload"
       query =
         "/client:processResponse/client:child_selection"/>
  </copy>
</assign>
```

7. Deploy the BPEL process to Oracle SOA Suite and run an instance of it. As an input, insert the following data:

```
<inputVariable>
  <part name = "payload" xmlns:xsi =
    "http://www.w3.org/2001/XMLSchema-instance">
```

```
      <ns1:process xmlns:ns1 =
        "http://xmlns.oracle.com/Variables/Global/
          Manipulate1_1">
        <ns1:input>Jurij</ns1:input>
        <ns1:item>PC</ns1:item>
        <ns1:priceVAT>1234</ns1:priceVAT>
        <ns1:child_no>2</ns1:child_no>
      </ns1:process>
    </part>
  </inputVariable>
```

8. We receive the following response from the BPEL process:

```
<outputVariable>
  <part name = "payload" xmlns:xsi =
    "http://www.w3.org/2001/XMLSchema-instance">
    <processResponse xmlns =
      "http://xmlns.oracle.com/Variables/Global/
        Manipulate1_1">
      <result>Jurij</result>
      <priceNet>1028.33</priceNet>
      <vat>205.67</vat>
      <child_selection>Urban</child_selection>
    </processResponse>
  </part>
</outputVariable>
```

8
Exposing Java Code as a SOAP Service

This chapter contains the following recipes:

- Defining the service interface
- Preparing the service implementation
- Annotating Java code for web service creation
- Creating a document transport web service
- Creating a RPC transport web service
- Creating literal and encoded web services
- Using attachment types with web services
- Defining a web service returning no value
- Defining a web service returning a value
- Publishing a web service
- Testing a web service

Introduction

We already know that BPEL presents the orchestration technology in the **service-oriented architecture** (**SOA**). We have already learned quite a few functionalities of BPEL, but now it's time to learn more about the fundamental building blocks that are consumed by the BPEL processes. We are talking about the web services.

In this chapter, we will focus on the lifecycle of web services through the JAX-WS specification. Throughout the recipes, we will learn the bottom-up approach of developing a web service. Usually, we can find a piece of code suitable for exposure as a web service. Through the bottom-up approach, we achieve this goal.

We can also use the top-down approach for web service development, where the starting point of the development is a WSDL document. From the web service definition, we continue the implementation of the web service methods. This approach is preferred in scenarios where we need to implement a web service from the start and no code exists.

The JAX-WS web services conform to the JSR 224 specification, which in combination with the JSR 181 specification, defines a set of annotations with which we can decorate the Java code and convert it to the web service. The mentioned specifications are a part of the Java Standard Edition, Version 6.

Remember that web services can be seen as building blocks of larger applications. One of the main advantages of web services is their reusability in various business processes which saves time and money. We will explore several aspects of web services development from design, annotation, and different configuration possibilities. We will also discuss publishing and testing web services.

Throughout this chapter, we will work on a sample of a very simplified book library. The sample consists of two data classes: `BookRecord` and `Member`. The `BookRecord` class holds information about books and what books are reserved and borrowed. The `Member` class holds the information about the members of the library. The `Main` class is the `BookLibrary` class, which consists of the business logic of the library with operations such as adding member, add book, and reserve a book.

Defining the service interface

Through the service interface, a web service exposes functionality to the outer world. The interface methods can be simple, such as setting properties to more complex operations such as performing calculations or updating records in a database. We have described the WSDL interface in the introduction of *Chapter 2, Calling Services from BPEL*, however, in this recipe, we will work on the Java interface. We use the Java interface when the Java code itself will define the web service and the WSDL document of deployed web services is generated from the Java code.

Getting ready

We described in the *Introduction* section that the core of the sample is the `BookLibrary` class. However, the sample is not yet implemented. To set up a proper service interface, we define an exception in the project (`BookAlreadyBorrowed`). This exception will be thrown when any member of the library tries to borrow an already borrowed book. The exception extends the Java standard `Exception` class and overrides the constructors as shown in the following code:

```
public class BookAlreadyBorrowed extends Exception {
```

We will not describe specifically the `BookRecord` (holds information about books) and `Member` (holds information about members of the library) classes, because they present simple data access objects and are as such of no relevance to this recipe.

How to do it...

Following are the steps we need to perform to define the web service interface. We start by defining the Java interface class:

1. At the root of the JDeveloper project, right-click and select the **New...** option. In the **New Gallery** window, select the **Java Interface** artifact as shown in the following screenshot:

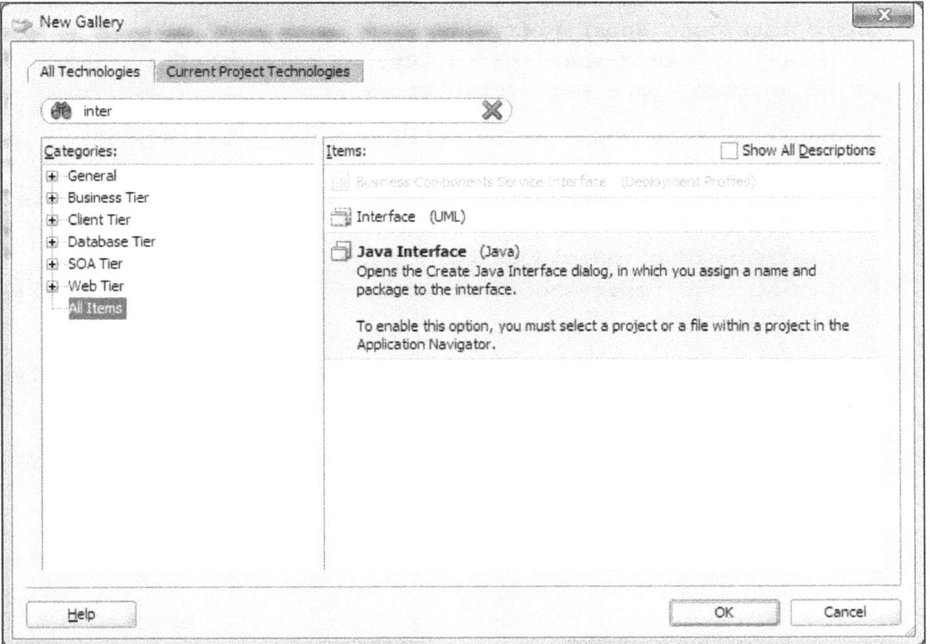

2. Click on the **OK** button. The **Create Java Interface** window opens. Enter the **Name** and **Package** fields and click on the **OK** button as shown in the following screenshot:

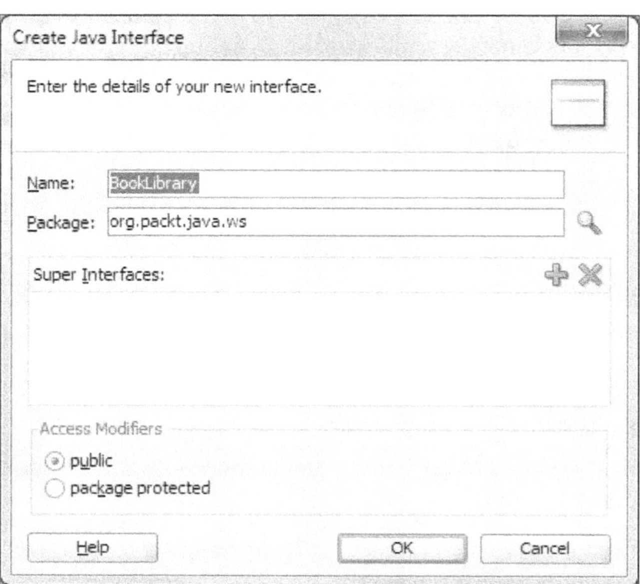

3. Now define the following methods that we will use for the library operations:

```
public interface BookLibrary {
    public int addMember(int id, String name, String surname,
String address, Date membershipExpiry);

    public int addBook(int id, String Author, String Title, int
Year);
    public void borrowBook(int member_id, int book_id) throws
BookAlreadyBorrowed;
    public void giveBackBook(int book_id);
    public void reserveBook(int member_id, int book_id) throws
BookAlreadyBorrowed;

    public Hashtable listMemberStat();
    public Hashtable listBookStat();
}
```

How it works...

In the Java interface, we defined the methods that perform the operations of the book library. The following table will define their description and behavior:

Interface method	Description
`addMember`	This method opens and adds new members to the book library.
`addBook`	This method adds new books to the book library and members can borrow it.
`borrowBook`	This method lets a member borrow the book from the library and the book is no longer available for borrowing. This method also checks if the book has already been borrowed.
`giveBackBook`	Using this method, a member returns the book to the library and the book is again available to be borrowed.
`reserveBook`	A member of the library can reserve the book (either by web, phone, SMS, and so on) and can come later to borrow it. This method also checks if the book has already been borrowed, since no reservation is possible for an already borrowed book.
`listMemberStat`	This is a convenient method that returns a list of all members.
`listBookStat`	This is a convenient method that returns a list of all the books and who borrowed each book.

See also

In this recipe, we defined the interface of the book library as a **Plain Old Java Object** (**POJO**). To expose the interface as a web service, we need to decorate the interface with annotations. Refer to the *Annotating Java code for web service creation* recipe to learn more about annotating an interface.

Preparing the service implementation

The service implementation is the next logical step after defining the service interface. With the implementation part, the code gets its business logic that enables it to perform successful operations. This recipe explains how to prepare a service implementation out of a service interface. By completing this implementation, we will be ready to define a web service.

Getting ready

In this recipe, we will add the `implementation` class to the JDeveloper project based on the interface defined in the *Defining the service interface* recipe.

How to do it...

Following are the steps involved in preparing a service implementation:

1. At the root of the JDeveloper project, right-click and select the **New...** option. In the **New Gallery** window, select the **Java Class** artifact as shown in the following screenshot:

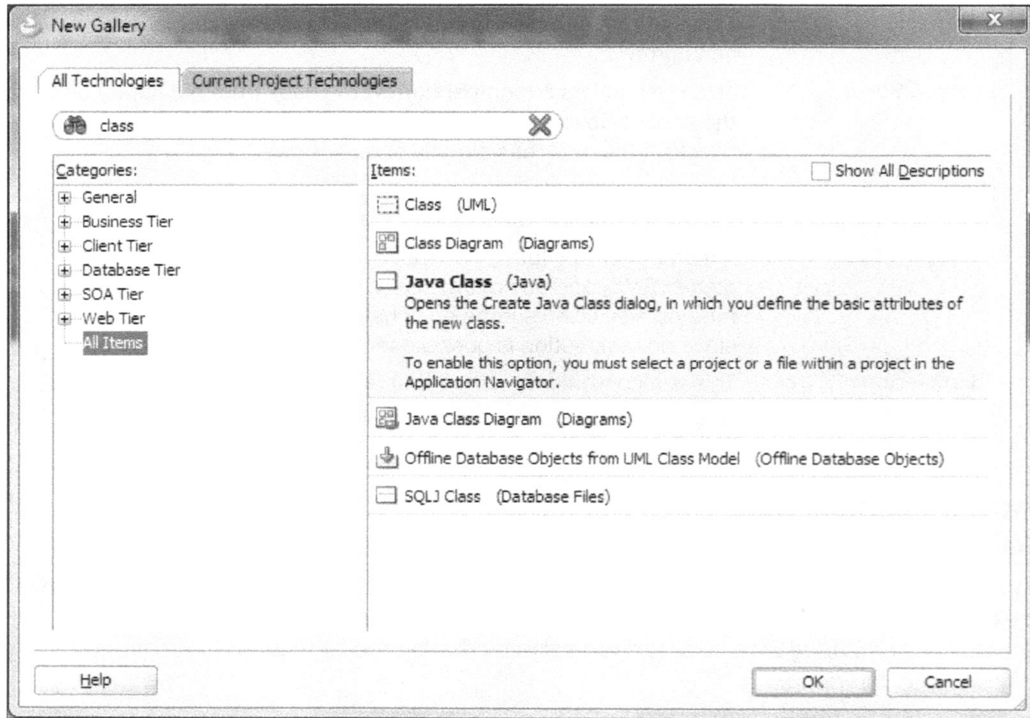

2. Click on the **OK** button. The **Create Java Class** window opens. Enter the **Name** and **Package** fields and add the `BookLibrary` interface under the **Implements** section. Then, click on the **OK** button as shown in the following screenshot:

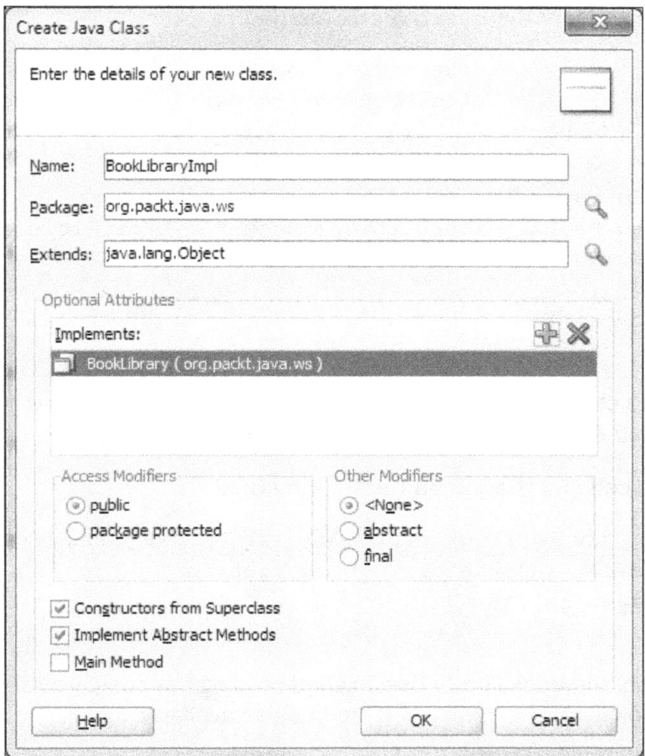

In the JDeveloper project, the `BookLibraryImpl` class is created with an empty constructor and methods. It is our task now to implement the methods. Since most of the methods are trivial, we will describe only three methods that carry out the operation of reservation, borrowing, and returning a book as follows:

The `reserveBook` method is shown as follows:

```
public void reserveBook(int member_id,
                        int book_id) {
  Member m= (Member)m_members.get(member_id);
  BookRecord b=  (BookRecord)m_books.get(book_id);
  b.setReserved(true);
}
```

The input parameters are taken and as a result the book gets reserved.

The following is the code for the borrowBook method:

```
public void borrowBook(int member_id,
                        int book_id) throws BookAlreadyBorrowed {
  Member m= (Member)m_members.get(member_id);
  BookRecord b=  (BookRecord)m_books.get(book_id);
  if (b.getBorrower() != null) {
    throw new BookAlreadyBorrowed("Book " + b.getTitle() + " was
already borrowed.");
  }
  b.setBorrower(m);
}
```

We first get the data structure of both input parameters, and if the book is not yet borrowed, we give the book to the member and mark the book as borrowed.

The following is the code for the giveBackBook method:

```
 public void giveBackBook( int book_id) throws BookAlreadyBorrowed {
  BookRecord b=  (BookRecord)m_books.get(book_id);
  b.setBorrower(null);
}
```

When the member of the book library has finished reading the book, we receive the book back. When the book is received, we mark the book as available again.

Now that we have the implementation ready, it is time to expose the functionality as a web service.

See also

In this recipe, we defined the concrete implementation of a book library as a POJO. To expose the implementation as a web service, we need to decorate the interface with annotations. Refer to our next recipe, *Annotating Java code for web service creation*, to learn more about annotating Java class implementation.

Annotating Java code for web service creation

When we identify the piece of Java code to become exposed as a web service, the decoration part needs to take place. This recipe will explain how to annotate the Java code in order to become as useful as a web service.

Getting ready

This recipe will be based on the code we created in the *Defining the service interface* and *Preparing the service implementation* recipes.

How to do it...

The following are the steps required to annotate Java code for web service creation:

1. In the JDeveloper project, select the class (`BookLibraryImpl.java`) and right-click on it. Choose the **Create Web Service...** option. The **Create Java Web Service** wizard appears where we enter the **Web Service Name** and **Port Name** and then click on **Next** as shown in the following screenshot:

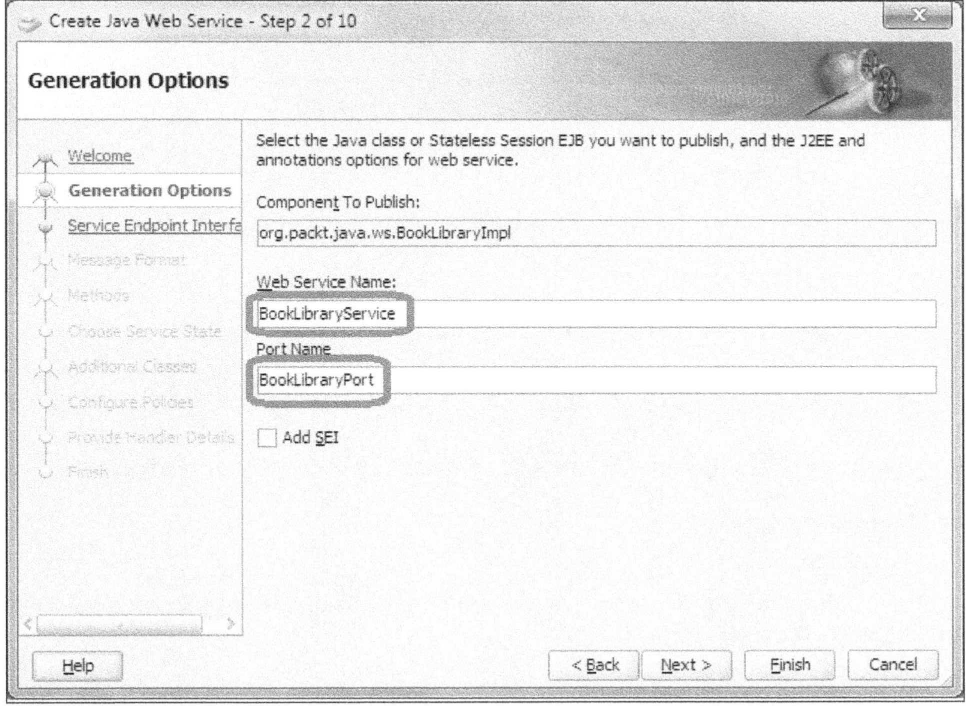

2. Accept the default options for the message format and click on **Next**. In the **Methods** step, select the methods that are candidates for the web service operations as shown in the following screenshot:

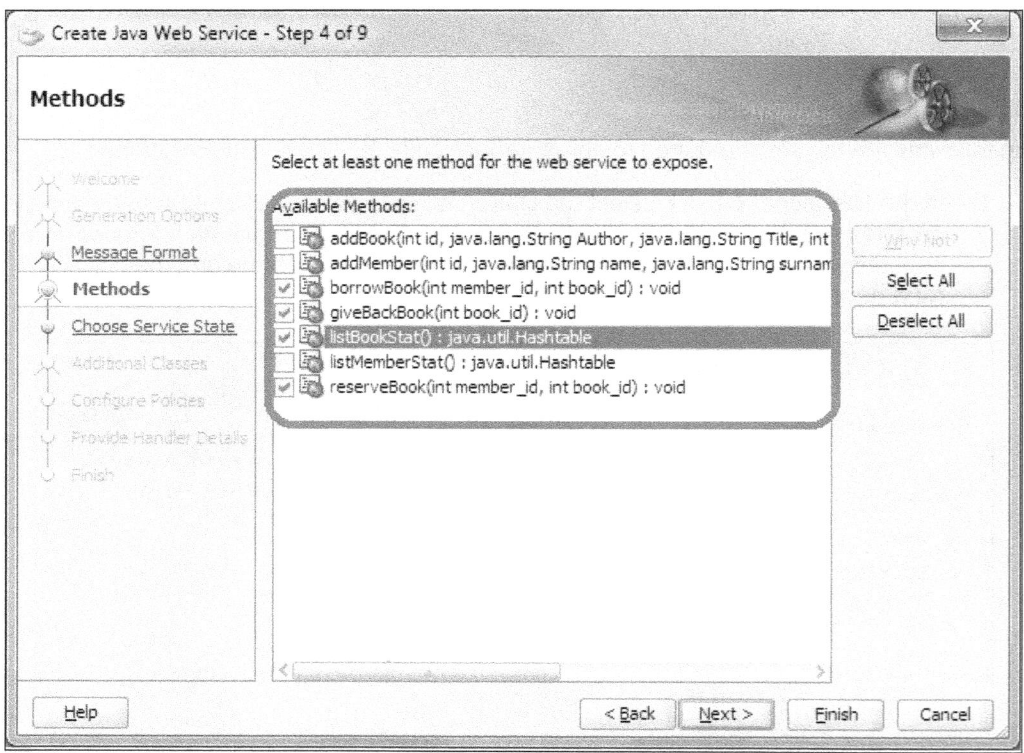

3. The rest of the steps are not relevant right now, so click on the **Finish** button.

How it works...

As a result of using the JDeveloper wizard to create the web service, we receive the annotated version of the POJO object.

During the process, annotations are added to the web service implementation class. Also note that the web service interface will not get annotated and requires a manual annotation step.

Let's inspect the web service implementation class (`BookLibraryImpl`). First, the class definition itself is annotated with the web service definition as shown in the following code:

```
@WebService(name = "BookLibrary", serviceName = "BookLibraryService",
portName = "BookLibraryPort")
public class BookLibraryImpl implements BookLibrary {
```

This definition contains the name of the web service, the service name of the web service, and the name of the port type.

> The service name defines the name of the web service, while the port type defines a set of operations exposed for integration.

We also see annotations on top of the methods that should not be exposed as web service operations, for example, the `listMemberStat` method:

```
@WebMethod(exclude = true)
public Hashtable listMemberStat() {
```

There's more...

The manual step of web service creation is the annotation of the web service interface. We open the `BookLibrary.java` interface class:

1. Annotate the interface with the `@WebService` annotation as shown in the following code:

   ```
   @WebService
   public interface BookLibrary {
   ```

2. Further, annotate each method that will carry out an operation with the `@WebMethod` annotation as shown in the following code:

   ```
     @WebMethod public void borrowBook(int member_id, int book_id)
   throws BookAlreadyBorrowed;
     @WebMethod public void giveBackBook(int book_id) throws
   BookAlreadyBorrowed;
     @WebMethod public void reserveBook(int member_id, int book_id)
   throws BookAlreadyBorrowed;
   ```

The project hierarchy in JDeveloper is also changed. A new folder was generated during web service creation. We can see the `Web Content` folder inside the `WEB-INF` folder where the `web.xml` file resides as follows:

```
<?xml version = '1.0' encoding = 'windows-1250'?>
<web-app xmlns:xsi="http://www.w3.org/2001/XMLSchema-instance"
         xsi:schemaLocation="http://java.sun.com/xml/ns/javaee http://
java.sun.com/xml/ns/javaee/web-app_2_5.xsd"
         version="2.5" xmlns="http://java.sun.com/xml/ns/javaee">
  <servlet>
    <servlet-name>BookLibraryPort</servlet-name>
    <servlet-class>org.packt.java.ws.BookLibraryImpl</servlet-class>
    <load-on-startup>1</load-on-startup>
```

```
    </servlet>
    <servlet-mapping>
      <servlet-name>BookLibraryPort</servlet-name>
      <url-pattern>/BookLibraryPort</url-pattern>
    </servlet-mapping>
</web-app>
```

The `web.xml` file shows that the web service created with JDeveloper and deployed to the Oracle WebLogic server will be exposed to the clients as a servlet.

See also

The web service defined in this recipe is now ready to be deployed and tested. Refer to the *Publishing a web service* recipe to learn how to deploy a web service. Also, refer to the *Testing a web service* recipe which explains what are the possibilities for testing a web service.

Creating a document transport web service

This recipe explains how to define a document transport for a web service. We divide transportation mechanisms into two parts. One is the **Remote Procedure Call** (**RPC**) transport and the second one is the document transport. Actually, these two transports define styles which we use for transferring messages and their values. In the document transport, we indicate that SOAP messages are using XML instances, meaning each part of a SOAP message is referring to the XML schema definition. This type is also the default transport type for JAX-WS.

Getting ready

In this recipe, we will amend the book library example.

How to do it...

The following are the steps we need to take in order to create the document transport style for our web service:

1. Open the `BookLibraryImpl.java` class file in JDeveloper.
2. To define the document transport for the web service, add the highlighted annotation to the web service code as follows:

   ```
   @WebService(name = "BookLibrary", serviceName =
   "BookLibraryService", portName = "BookLibraryPort")
   @SOAPBinding(style = SOAPBinding.Style.DOCUMENT)
   public class BookLibraryImpl implements BookLibrary {
   ```

How it works...

In a nutshell, document transport or document style (according to the `style` attribute) means that the whole interaction between clients and the web service is performed through the XML documents. The XML documents are based on the schemas behind, and present the whole entity such as `Member`, `Book`, `Order`, and `Payment`. The XML document enables high interoperability because the content is self-explanatory, based on the schemas, and there is no need to perform any additional validation rules. Also, XML is technology-neutral, and we can process the XML content on any platform or programming language.

As we talk about interoperability, the important aspect of web service lifecycle presents maintenance period. When a change in the data occurs, only a change in the schema needs to be performed and no other change is needed. When using document transport, the information from the client comes to the web service in a structured way. It is easy for a web service to transform such data and perform various validation rules on top of incoming data.

Now look at the result of the `new @SOAPBinding` annotation in our code. In JDeveloper, right-click on the `BookLibraryImpl.java` class and select **Show WSDL for Web Service Annotations**. In the generated WSDL that shows up in JDeveloper, search for the `<soap:binding>` tag as follows:

```
<soap:binding style="document" transport="http://schemas.xmlsoap.org/
soap/http"/>
```

We can see that for our service, we will use the document binding style over SOAP/HTTP transport.

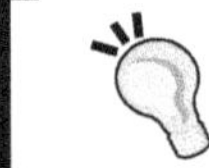

To use the document transport for a web service, there is no need to use the `@SOAPBinding` annotation since document transport defines default transport by the JAX-WS specification.

See also

To define a different transport type, refer to the *Creating a RPC transport web service* recipe.

Creating a RPC transport web service

This recipe explains how to annotate a web service in order to support the **Remote Procedure Call** (**RPC**) transport style. Using the RPC style, the body part of the SOAP message may contain only one element that is named after the operation. All parameters are represented as child elements of this element. The name of the child element must match the name of the parameter and the type of the element must match the type of the parameter.

Getting ready

For this recipe, we will use the example from the *Creating a document transport web service* recipe.

How to do it...

In the JDeveloper project, open the `BookLibraryImpl.java` file. Search for the `@SOAPBinding` annotation.

Now change the `style` attribute to `SOAPBinding.style.RPC` as shown in the following code:

```
@WebService(name = "BookLibrary", serviceName = "BookLibraryService",
portName = "BookLibraryPort")
//@SOAPBinding(style = SOAPBinding.Style.DOCUMENT)
@SOAPBinding(style = SOAPBinding.Style.RPC)
```

How it works...

The RPC transport style presents an alternative way for transferring data from the client towards the web service. The main difference from the document transport style is how parameters are formatted. Remember, with the document transport style, the parameters are defined through the schema which enables greater flexibility in case the web service methods are changed. On the other hand, the RPC transport style maps the input and output parameters according to the method definitions. The web service is presented as an application where a client delivers the parameters and not the content as is the case with the document transport style.

Let's examine the difference between the document and RPC transport styles. First, let's look at the document transport style for the `reserveBook` operation. The request and response message definitions are as follows:

```
<wsdl:message name="reserveBookInput">
    <wsdl:part name="parameters" element="tns:reserveBook"/>
</wsdl:message>
<wsdl:message name="reserveBookOutput">
    <wsdl:part name="parameters" element="tns:reserveBookResponse"/>
</wsdl:message>
```

The elements `tns:reserveBook` and `tns:reserveBookResponse` are defined in the corresponding schema:

```
<xsd:complexType name="reserveBook">
  <xsd:sequence>
```

```
      <xsd:element name="arg0" type="xsd:int"/>
      <xsd:element name="arg1" type="xsd:int"/>
    </xsd:sequence>
  </xsd:complexType>
  <xsd:element name="reserveBook" type="tns:reserveBook"/>
  <xsd:complexType name="reserveBookResponse">
    <xsd:sequence/>
  </xsd:complexType>
  <xsd:element name="reserveBookResponse" type="tns:reserveBookRespon
  se"/>
```

If we now check the definitions for the RPC transport style of the same operation, we will see the following definitions for the request and response messages:

```
<wsdl:message name="reserveBookInput">
  <wsdl:part name="arg0" type="xsd:int"/>
  <wsdl:part name="arg1" type="xsd:int"/>
</wsdl:message>
<wsdl:message name="reserveBookOutput"/>
<wsdl:message name="borrowBookInput">
  <wsdl:part name="arg0" type="xsd:int"/>
  <wsdl:part name="arg1" type="xsd:int"/>
</wsdl:message>
```

There is no further schema definition because input parameters are directly mapped to the messages. So, instead of communication via content as we do with the document transport style, we communicate through direct mapping of operations parameters.

Creating literal and encoded web services

With the previous two recipes, *Creating a document transport web service* and *Creating a RPC transport web service*, we addressed the transport style aspect of web service definition. This recipe will further address the usage of the SOAP binding. With the transport style, we get four combinations of possible usage as shown in the following table:

Transport style	Use
Document	Literal
Document	Encoded
RPC	Literal
RPC	Encoded

This recipe will give an explanation of all four combinations.

Getting ready...

In this recipe, we will amend the example from the previous recipe.

How to do it...

Open the `BookLibraryImpl.java` class in JDeveloper. Depending on the transport style and use, we modify the `@SOAPBinding` annotation in one of the following ways:

- **Document** transport style with **literal** use attribute:

  ```
  @SOAPBinding(style = SOAPBinding.Style.DOCUMENT, use =
  SOAPBinding.Use.LITERAL)
  ```

- **Document** transport style with **encoded** use attribute:

  ```
  @SOAPBinding(style = SOAPBinding.Style.DOCUMENT, use =
  SOAPBinding.Use.ENCODED)
  ```

- **RPC** transport style with **literal** use attribute:

  ```
  @SOAPBinding(style = SOAPBinding.Style.RPC, use = SOAPBinding.Use.
  LITERAL)
  ```

- **RPC** transport style with **encoded** use attribute:

  ```
  @SOAPBinding(style = SOAPBinding.Style.RPC, use = SOAPBinding.Use.
  ENCODED)
  ```

That's it. Choosing any of these combinations defined results in a one-liner combination of attributes inside the `@SOAPBinding` annotation.

How it works...

We will now explain what each of the transport style definitions and use attributes contribute to the resulting WSDL definition and how the definition is reflected within the SOAP request messages. We will explore the `reserveBook` operation.

Using the document transport style with the literal use attribute

The WSDL definition of the SOAP binding tag is defined as follows:

```
<soap:binding style="document" transport="http://schemas.xmlsoap.org/
soap/http"/>
```

The `reserveBook` operation is defined in WSDL with the following code:

```
<wsdl:operation name="reserveBook">
            <soap:operation soapAction=""/>
            <wsdl:input>
                <soap:body use="literal"/>
            </wsdl:input>
            <wsdl:output>
                <soap:body use="literal"/>
            </wsdl:output>
            <wsdl:fault name="BookAlreadyBorrowed">
                <soap:fault name="BookAlreadyBorrowed" use="literal"/>
            </wsdl:fault>
</wsdl:operation>
```

We identified the document transport style as well as the literal use of SOAP body formatting.

A sample of the SOAP request message is shown in the following code:

```
<env:Envelope xmlns:env="http://schemas.xmlsoap.org/soap/envelope/">
  <env:Header />
    <env:Body>
    <reserveBook xmlns="http://ws.java.packt.org/">
      <arg0 xmlns="">1</arg0>
      <arg1 xmlns="">1</arg1>
    </reserveBook>
  </env:Body>
  </env:Envelope>
```

The SOAP request message does not contain any type encoding info (they are empty). Also, it is possible to validate the content of the SOAP body element against the XML validator tool because all the elements are defined by the XSD schema.

Using the document transport style with the encoded use attribute

The document transport style with the encoded use attribute is not supported by the JAX-WS annotations. Actually, no implementation follows this combination, since it lacks conformance to the web service interoperability specification.

The interoperability of web services is defined in the WS-I Basic Profile specification at `http://ws-i.org/Profiles/BasicProfile-1.2-2010-11-09.html`.

Using the RPC transport style with the literal use attribute

The WSDL definition of the SOAP binding tag is defined as shown in the following code:

```
<soap:binding style="rpc" transport="http://schemas.xmlsoap.org/soap/
http"/>
```

The `reserveBook` operation is defined in WSDL as shown in the following code:

```
<wsdl:operation name="reserveBook">
    <soap:operation soapAction=""/>
    <wsdl:input>
        <soap:body use="literal" namespace="http://ws.java.packt.org/"
parts="arg0 arg1"/>
    </wsdl:input>
    <wsdl:output>
        <soap:body use="literal" namespace="http://ws.java.packt.
org/"/>
    </wsdl:output>
    <wsdl:fault name="BookAlreadyBorrowed">
        <soap:fault name="BookAlreadyBorrowed" use="literal"/>
    </wsdl:fault>
</wsdl:operation>
```

We identified the RPC transport style as well as the literal use of SOAP body formatting.

A sample of the SOAP request message is shown in the following code:

```
<env:Envelope xmlns:env="http://schemas.xmlsoap.org/soap/envelope/">
  <env:Header />
  <env:Body>
    <target:reserveBook xmlns:target="http://ws.java.packt.org/">
      <arg0>1</arg0>
      <arg1>1</arg1>
    </target:reserveBook>
  </env:Body>
</env:Envelope>
```

We can see a similar structure of SOAP request message as with the document/literal combination. Also, the SOAP request message does not contain any type encoding info (they are empty). In both cases, we see that the name of the operation is present in the SOAP message body. The distinction between the two concepts is in their ability to validate the body content of the SOAP request message. With the RPC/literal combination, we have trouble validating the content of the body because every element is defined inside the WSDL document and is not part of the schema.

Using the RPC transport style with the encoded use attribute

Similar to the document/encoded combination, the RPC/encoded combination is not supported by the latest versions of JAX-WS releases. The reason lies in the fact that the afore mentioned two combinations lack the compliance to the WS-I Basic Profile specification.

There's more...

Remember we said that the document/literal binding style is not fully compliant with WS-I Basic Profile. For that purpose, an additional transport and use combination is available; that is the document or literal-wrapped combination, which is fully compliant with WS-I Basic Profile and also uses the preferred binding style.

To use the document/literal-wrapped combination web service, we need to use the third parameter in the `@SOAPBinding` annotation as shown in the following code:

```
@SOAPBinding(style = SOAPBinding.Style.DOCUMENT, use = SOAPBinding.
Use.LITERAL, parameterStyle = SOAPBinding.ParameterStyle.WRAPPED)
```

The `javax.jws.soap.SOAPBinding.ParameterStyle` enables two constants: `BARE` and `WRAPPED`. If we don't specify anything, the default value is `BARE`.

Let's compare the WSDL and SOAP message request between the document/literal and document/literal-wrapped styles.

The `reserveBook` operation is defined in WSDL as shown in the following code:

```
<wsdl:operation name="reserveBook">
  <wsdl:input message="tns:reserveBookInput" xmlns:ns1="http://www.
w3.org/2006/05/addressing/wsdl"
    ns1:Action=""/>
  <wsdl:output message="tns:reserveBookOutput" xmlns:ns1="http://www.
w3.org/2006/05/addressing/wsdl"
    ns1:Action=""/>
  <wsdl:fault name="BookAlreadyBorrowed" message="tns:BookAlreadyBorr
owed"/>
</wsdl:operation>
```

Note that there is no literal use attribute defined in the WSDL document. Also, the SOAP request message remains the same when the client calls a web service.

Using attachment types with web services

In use case scenarios, we may need to transfer documents, media, and other files with web services. These kinds of elements are defined with **Multipurpose Internet Mail Extensions** (**MIME**) types. The JAX-WS specification enables the **Message Transmission Optimization Mechanism** (**MTOM**) feature which enables efficient transfer of binary content via SOAP messages. This recipe explains how to use the MIME types with web services.

Getting ready

We will amend the example from the *Creating literal and encoded web services* recipe in order to complete this recipe.

How to do it...

To show the usage of MIME types in a web service, we will implement an additional method that enables the upload of an eBook to the `book` library:

1. Open the `BookLibrary` interface and add the following code:

```
@WebMethod public void uploadBook(String bookName, DataHandler
data);
```

2. Open `BookLibraryImpl` and amend the code with the following lines. We first need to decorate the class with the `@MTOM` annotation as shown in the following code:

```
@MTOM
@WebService(name = "BookLibrary", serviceName =
"BookLibraryService", portName = "BookLibraryPort")
@SOAPBinding(style = SOAPBinding.Style.DOCUMENT, use =
SOAPBinding.Use.LITERAL, parameterStyle = SOAPBinding.
ParameterStyle.WRAPPED)
public class BookLibraryImpl implements BookLibrary {
```

3. We still need to implement the new method:

```
public void uploadBook(String bookName, @XmlMimeType("application/
pdf") DataHandler data) {
      try {
        File file = new File("C:\\temp\\books\\" + bookName +
".pdf");

        OutputStream output = new BufferedOutputStream(new
FileOutputStream(file));
        data.writeTo(output);
```

```
            output.close();
        } catch (Exception e) {
            throw new WebServiceException(e);
        }
    }
```

Initially, the name of the book file is generated. Then, the content is read from the data handler to the output stream. At the end, we close the output stream.

How it works...

Let us inspect the WSDL document, especially the SOAP binding tag definition as shown in the following code:

```
<binding name="BookLibraryPortBinding" type="tns:BookLibrary">
  <wsp:PolicyReference URI="#Mtom.xml"/>
  <soap:binding transport="http://schemas.xmlsoap.org/soap/http"
style="document"/>
<binding>
```

Beside the binding information, we can also see a `PolicyReference` tag which enables MTOM on the web service. The request message of the `uploadBook` operation has the following code in the schema:

```
<xs:complexType name="uploadBook">
  <xs:sequence>
    <xs:element name="arg0" type="xs:string" minOccurs="0"/>
    <xs:element xmlns:ns1="http://www.w3.org/2005/05/xmlmime"
name="arg1" ns1:expectedContentTypes="application/pdf"
type="xs:base64Binary" minOccurs="0"/>
  </xs:sequence>
</xs:complexType>
```

The content of the file is transferred through `arg1`. The type of `arg1` is `base64Binary`, which means that binary content is transferred. A particularly interesting attribute is `expectedContentTypes`. Remember we annotate the `data` parameter of the `uploadBook` method with the `@XmlMimeType("application/pdf")` annotation. This is translated into the `expectedContentTypes="application/pdf«` attribute.

A sample of the SOAP request message is shown in the following code:

```
<soapenv:Envelope xmlns:soapenv="http://schemas.xmlsoap.org/soap/
envelope/" xmlns:ws="http://ws.java.packt.org/">
  <soapenv:Header/>
  <soapenv:Body>
    <ws:uploadBook>
      <arg0>packt_book</arg0>
```

```
        <arg1>
          <inc:Include href="cid:SampleBook.pdf" xmlns:inc="http://www.
w3.org/2004/08/xop/include"/>
        </arg1>
      </ws:uploadBook>
    </soapenv:Body>
</soapenv:Envelope>
```

We enter `packt_book` as `arg0`. Now look at the argument `arg1`. This argument holds the information about the book we want to upload. Actually, it holds the reference to the book. We can see the MTOM in action here. The `arg1` argument holds the reference to the other part of the message (`cid:SampleBook.pdf`) where we can see the content of the book. We have omitted the complete request message as it is too long and would go through several pages. According to the web service operation implementation, we would expect to find the PDF book document at the `C:\temp\books\packt_book.pdf` location. Indeed, the file is there, and if we open it with our favorite PDF reader, we will see the content as shown in the following screenshot:

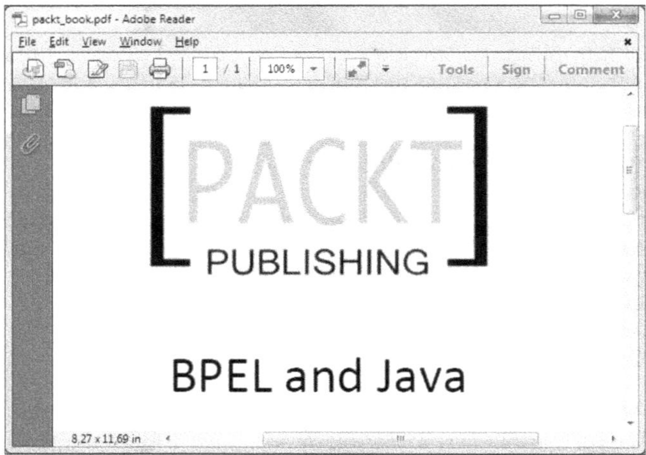

Defining a web service returning no value

This recipe explains how to define a web service that will return no value. We distinguish between two types of web service operations that return no value. The first one is synchronous and is where a client waits for a web service operation to finish; however, no content result is expected. This is also called one-way. The second one is a web service operation that is performed in an asynchronous way, where a client does not wait for the response. The content result is either not expected or is handled in a different part of the client code. This type of communication is called asynchronous pooling or callback. The JAX-WS also supports request-response communication as **message exchange protocol** (**MEP**). However, this type of communication is used for the methods that return a value.

Getting ready

In this recipe, we will amend the example from the *Creating literal and encoded web services* recipe.

How to do it...

We will prepare one method (`reserveBook`) that can be used in asynchronous communication with the client where a book is reserved but the client does not expect the response or checks the status of the book in a different part of the code.

Open the `BookLibraryImpl` class and browse to the `reserveBook` method. Annotate the method with the `@Oneway` annotation as shown in the following code:

```
@Oneway
@WebMethod
public void reserveBook(int member_id,
                        int book_id) throws BookAlreadyBorrowed {
```

How it works...

We already have methods in the code that return no value, such as `borrowBook` and `giveBackBook`.

For the `borrowBook` method, let's inspect the WSDL document. The operation is defined as follows:

```
<operation name="borrowBook">
  <input message="tns:borrowBook"/>
  <output message="tns:borrowBookResponse"/>
  <fault message="tns:BookAlreadyBorrowed"
name="BookAlreadyBorrowed"/>
</operation>
```

The operation has a definition for the input message, output message, and fault message. The definition for the output message is as shown in the following code:

```
<xs:complexType name="borrowBookResponse">
  <xs:sequence/>
</xs:complexType>
```

The output message is empty, meaning that we will receive no data from the web service operation on the response. The `borrowBook` method is already prepared for synchronous communication where a client will wait for the web service call to finish; however, no response data is expected. We can use such a design for the scenarios, where the web service finishes quickly and to also check that the web service was executed successfully.

Let us now inspect the `reserveBook` web service operation. The WSDL definition of the operations is as shown in the following code:

```
<operation name="reserveBook">
  <input message="tns:reserveBook"/>

</operation>
```

In this case, only the input is defined and no output messages. This web service operation is prepared for asynchronous communication where the client will not wait for a web service operation to finish or the response is handled elsewhere in the code. In any case, the client does not expect any data from the web service operation.

See also

To learn more about cases where data from a web service operation call is utilized, refer to our next recipe.

Defining a web service returning a value

This recipe explains how to define a web service with operations that return a value to the client. The methods that are returning values are used in synchronous and asynchronous communication. The best practice when using multiple parameters in web service methods is to define the complex elements and their corresponding complex objects. This also applies to the returning types.

However, we don't always have the ability to define by the best practice. Indeed, when integrating existing applications, we usually bump into legacy methods which we are not able to change.

Getting ready

We will use the book library example that we have used throughout the chapter and enable one of the non-exposed class methods to become a web service operation that returns a value to the client.

How to do it...

The steps involved in defining a web service methods that return values are as follows:

1. In JDeveloper, open the `BookLibrary.java` interface class. In front of the `addBook` method, add the `@WebMethod` annotation and save the file.

   ```
   @WebMethod public int addBook(int id, String Author, String Title,
   int Year);
   ```

2. Now open the `BookLibraryImpl.java` implementation class. Remove the annotation from the `addBook` method as shown in the following code:

   ```
   @WebMethod(exclude = true)
   public int addBook(int id, String Author, String Title, int Year)
   {
   ```

3. Now we have a method that returns a value (`book id`) to the client.

How it works...

Let's examine the WSDL document that describes the newly defined operation. The operation consists of an input and output message. No fault message is defined. The following is the code:

```
<operation name="addBook">
  <input message="tns:addBook"/>
  <output message="tns:addBookResponse"/>
</operation>
```

The input message consists of four parameters defining the book as shown in the following code:

```
<xs:complexType name="addBook">
  <xs:sequence>
    <xs:element name="arg0" type="xs:int"/>
    <xs:element name="arg1" type="xs:string" minOccurs="0"/>
    <xs:element name="arg2" type="xs:string" minOccurs="0"/>
    <xs:element name="arg3" type="xs:int"/>
  </xs:sequence>
</xs:complexType>
```

The output (response) message is more interesting. This message consists of one parameter defining the ID of the added book as shown in the following code:

```
<xs:complexType name="addBookResponse">
  <xs:sequence>
    <xs:element name="return" type="xs:int"/>
  </xs:sequence>
</xs:complexType>
```

Note that the web service operation now returns the value of type integer and holds the ID of the added book.

See also

To learn how to publish and test a web service, refer to the two upcoming recipes.

Publishing a web service

This recipe explains how to prepare a web service for publishing. The publishing of a web service represents the step in the lifecycle where the implementation gets exposed and is available for integration. In this recipe, we will show you how to deploy a web service from JDeveloper to the WebLogic server.

Getting ready

We will use the example that we have amended throughout this chapter to complete this recipe.

How to do it...

Following are the steps required to publish a web service from JDeveloper to the WebLogic server:

1. In JDeveloper, at the project root node, right-click and select the **Deploy** | **WebServices...** option as shown in the following screenshot:

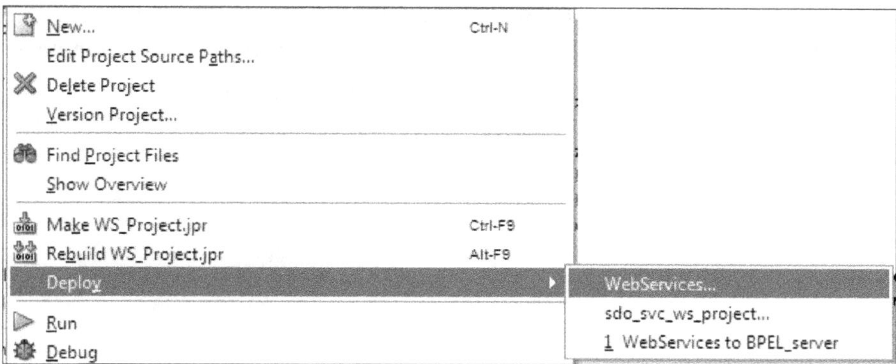

2. The **Deploy WebServices** wizard opens. Select the **Deploy to Application Server** option and click on **Next**.
3. The next page opens the server list where we select our BPEL server and click on **Next** as shown in the following screenshot:

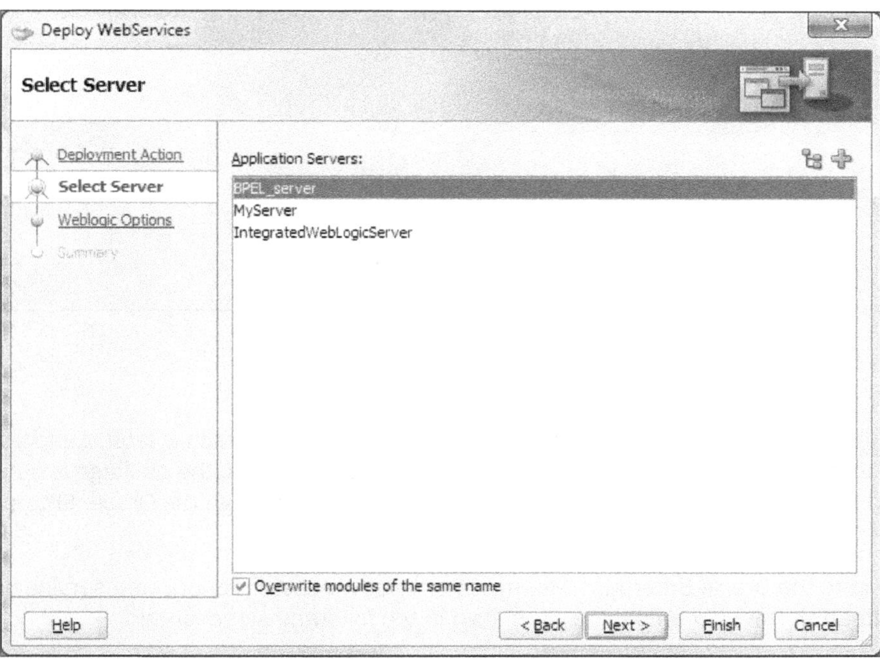

4. The next page shows the **Weblogic Options** that can be configured. We won't change anything right now, so simply confirm the given options and click on **Summary**.
5. The **Summary** page shows the deployment summary, and we can check if the configuration is as expected. Click on the **Finish** button; we are satisfied with the deployment configuration. The deployment will now start.

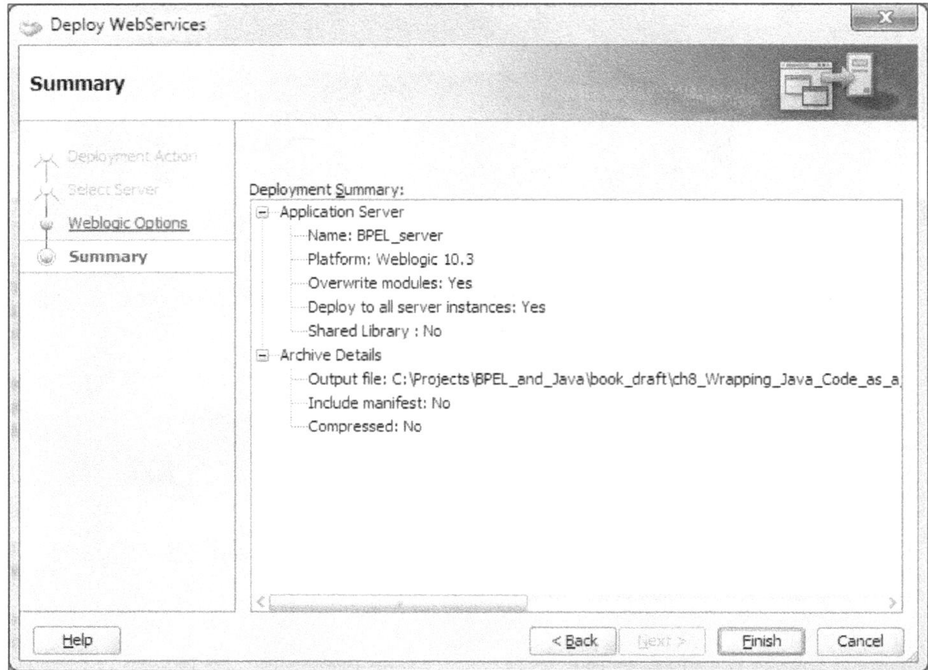

How it works...

As a result of the deployment process, a WAR archive is created which is later deployed to the application server. Although we select to deploy to the BPEL server, the package is actually deployed to the Weblogic application server and propagated through the Oracle Enterprise Manager Console.

Let's log in to the Oracle Enterprise Manager Console. We search for our web service under the **Application Deployments** folder as shown in the following screenshot:

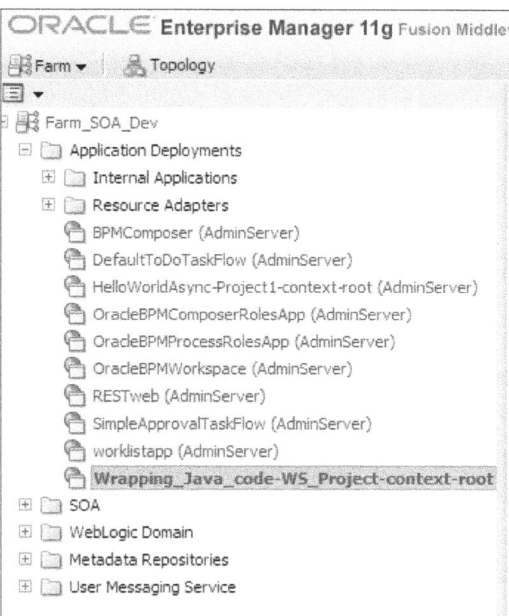

When we click on our web service, the application deployment window opens on the right side of the pane with a number of options and statistics.

See also

Now that we have deployed the web service, it is time to test how well our web service is performing. Refer to the next recipe to learn the ways of testing a web service.

Testing a web service

This recipe explains one of the most important aspects of the web service lifecycle; that is, testing. We will show you how web service testing can be performed through the Oracle Enterprise Manager Console and Oracle Weblogic Server Administration Console. We can also efficiently test web services using other professional tools, such as SoapUi, TestMaker, and WebInject.

These tools can be downloaded at the following URLs:

- **SoapUi**: This tool can be downloaded at `http://www.soapui.org/`
- **TestMaker**: This tool can be downloaded at `http://www.pushtotest.com/products.html`
- **WebInject**: This tool can be downloaded at `http://webinject.org/`

Getting ready

For this recipe, we will use the web service that was defined at the start of the chapter and amended throughout the recipes in this book; that is, the book library web service.

How to do it...

The following are the steps involved into testing of web service in the Oracle Enterprise Manager Console:

1. First, we will describe how to test a web service through the Oracle Enterprise Manager Console. Thus, we first log in to the console. Remember, we mentioned that web services can be found below the **Application Deployment** node.
2. Then, expand the **Application Deployment** node and select our web service.
3. On the right side, the web service management window opens as shown in the following screenshot:

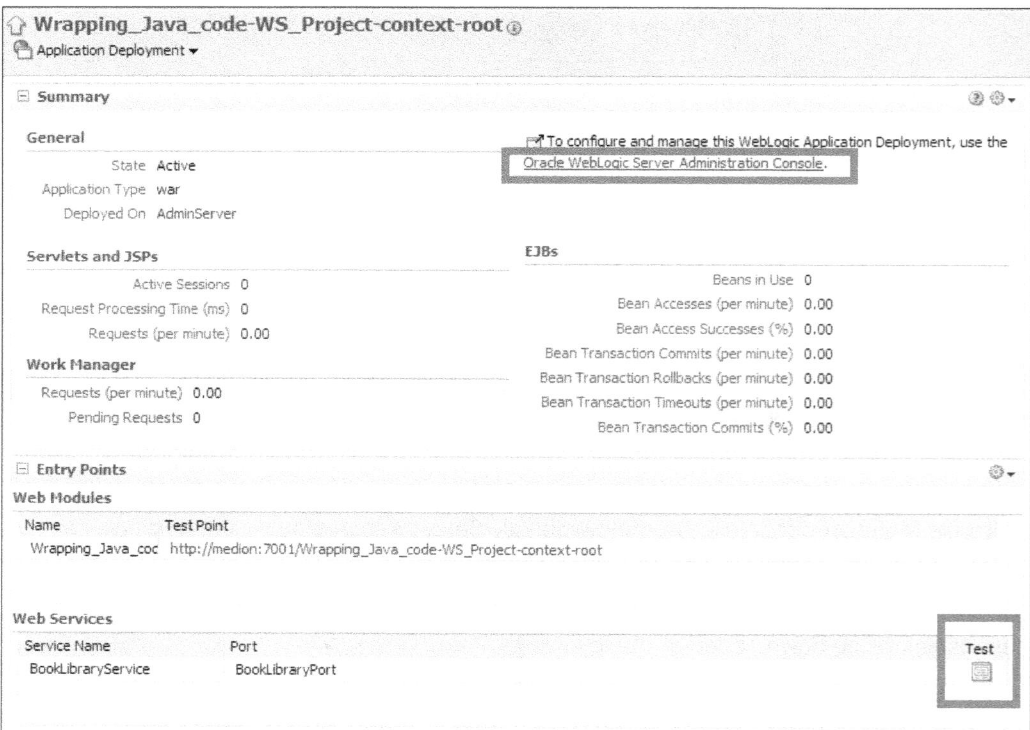

4. Under the **Summary** section, we have the option to manage the deployment and testing of a web service through the Oracle Weblogic Server Administration Console with a link. Under the **Web Services** section, we have a **Test** option to test a web service in the Oracle Enterprise Manager Console. We click on the icon and the familiar window for the tests opens as shown in the following screenshot:

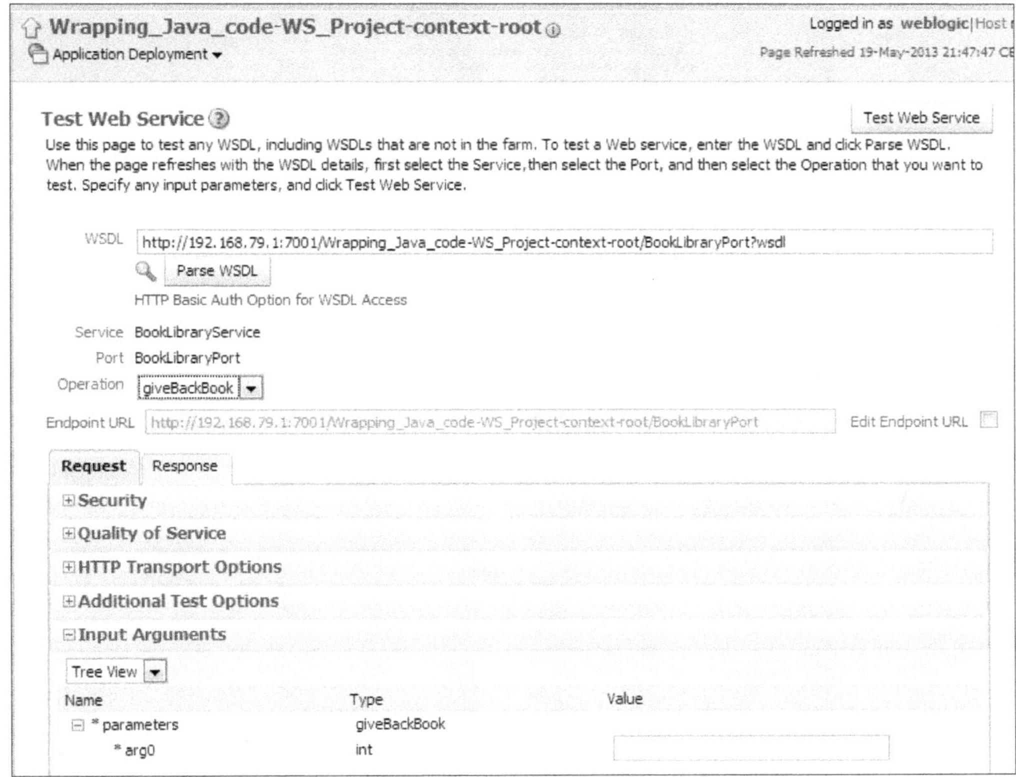

5. Select the operation, enter the input parameters, and click on the **Test Web Service** button. Under the **Request** tab, we see the input data, and after the web service operation is performed, we will see the results under the **Response** tab.

There's more...

In step 3, we see that under the **Summary** section, we have the option to manage the deployment and testing through the Oracle Weblogic Server Administration Console with a link. By clicking on the link, we are transferred to the Oracle Weblogic Server Administration Console.

Under the **Domain Structure**, select the **Deployments** option.

Under the **Summary of Deployments**, we select our web service and expand the **Web Service** node. Click on the web service link as shown in the following screenshot:

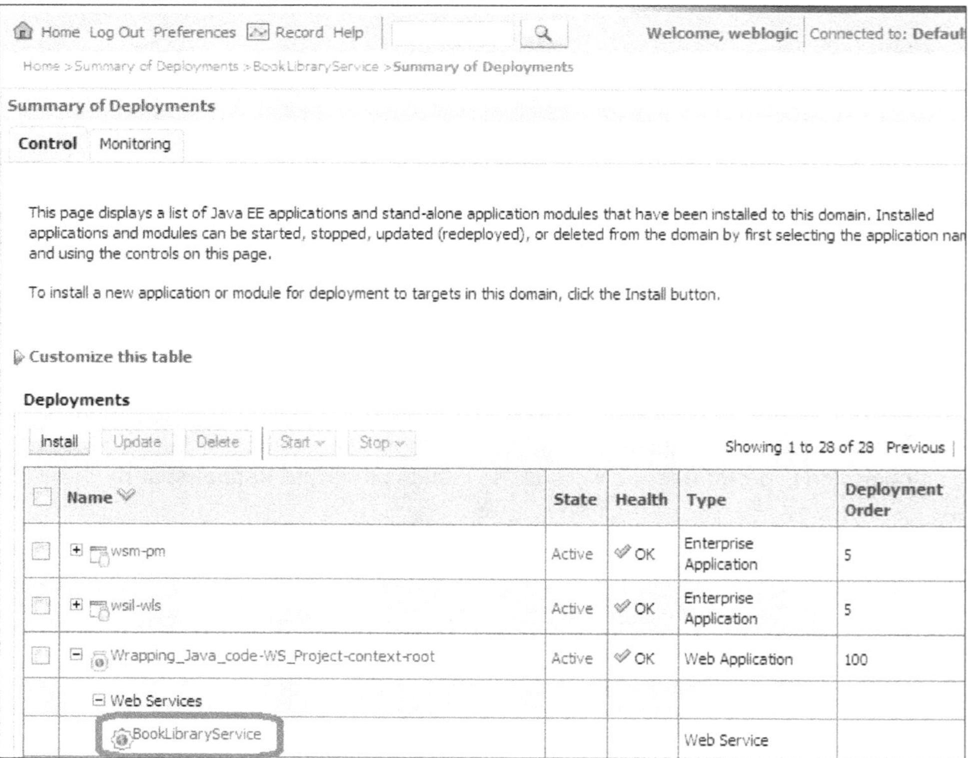

The **Settings** window for our web service opens. Select the **Testing** tab and again expand the web service node. We will get two links. One link leads to the WSDL document and the second link brings up the test client as shown in the following screenshot:

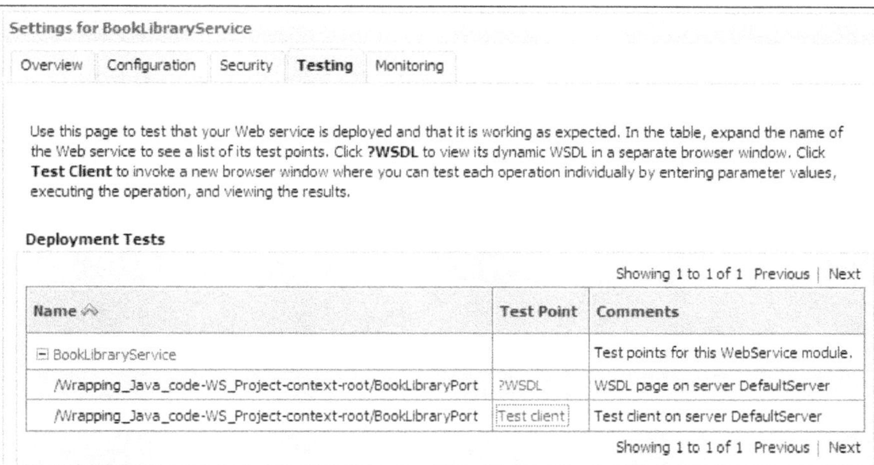

Settings for BookLibraryService
Overview
Configuration
Security
Testing
Monitoring
Use this page to test that your Web service is deployed and that it is working as expected. In the table, expand the name of the Web service to see a list of its test points. Click ?WSDL to view its dynamic WSDL in a separate browser window. Click Test Client to invoke a new browser window where you can test each operation individually by entering parameter values, executing the operation, and viewing the results.
Deployment Tests
Showing 1 to 1 of 1 Previous | Next
Name
Test Point
Comments
BookLibraryService
Test points for this WebService module.
/Wrapping_Java_code-WS_Project-context-root/BookLibraryPort
?WSDL
WSDL page on server DefaultServer
/Wrapping_Java_code-WS_Project-context-root/BookLibraryPort
Test client
Test client on server DefaultServer
Showing 1 to 1 of 1 Previous | Next

9
Embedding Java Code Snippets

This chapter contains the following recipes:

- Preparing the development sandbox for Java Embedding activity code in JDeveloper using the Java code placeholder in the BPEL process
- Invoking Java code from the BPEL process
- Reading the BPEL process variables
- Setting the BPEL process variables
- Invoking `SessionBean` from the BPEL process
- Exploring the use of the utility functionality
- Adding a log to the BPEL **Audit Trail**
- Reading the process instance data
- Getting the BPEL process status data

Introduction

The BPEL specification defines a finite set of activities. One of the options is to define our own functional activity via the Java Embedding activity. With the Java Embedding activity we can define any behavior in Java programming language. The Java Embedding activity can be used when we have some Java code that performs some small scale task, while we don't want to develop the complete solution as the Java application.

> Note that Java Embedding is not defined by the BPEL specification. Rather, it is defined as the Oracle BPEL extension. Use this precaution when migrating the BPEL processes between different BPEL servers, as it may lead to incompatibility issues.

Inside the Java Embedding activity, we can use standard Java classes, methods exposed by the BPEL environment, and user defined extension classes. We will see this in this chapter. We can call it a session EJB3 bean.

From inside the Java Embedding activity we can access BPEL process variables. With an appropriate method, we can read variable content and set it as well. The activity provides us with methods to put a query in the BPEL process information.

In general, we use the Java Embedding activity to execute a small piece of the code. It is not intended to be used for business logic implementation. When we need to implement large business logic, it is recommended to develop the web service and then utilize it from the BPEL process.

Preparing the development sandbox for the Java Embedding activity code in JDeveloper

The disadvantage of the Java Embedding activity is a rigid editor for entering the Java code. When preparing Java code for the Java Embedding activity, it is advisable to use more advanced tools (IDE's), which provide at least an auto-complete option. However, with developing the code outside of BPEL environment comes another difficulty, and that is the lack of the Java Embedding activity method support.

This recipe explains how to develop Java code outside of the rigid Java Embedding activity editor and retain the comfort of the BPEL development environment.

How to do it...

Here are the steps we need to take to prepare the development sandbox for the Java Embedding activity code in JDeveloper:

1. We start by creating an application workspace in JDeveloper. Inside the application workspace, create a new Java project (`JavaEmbeddDevel`).
2. Add the library that contains the BPEL runtime execution classes. Right-click on the project node and select the **Project Properties...** option. The **Project Properties** dialog opens.

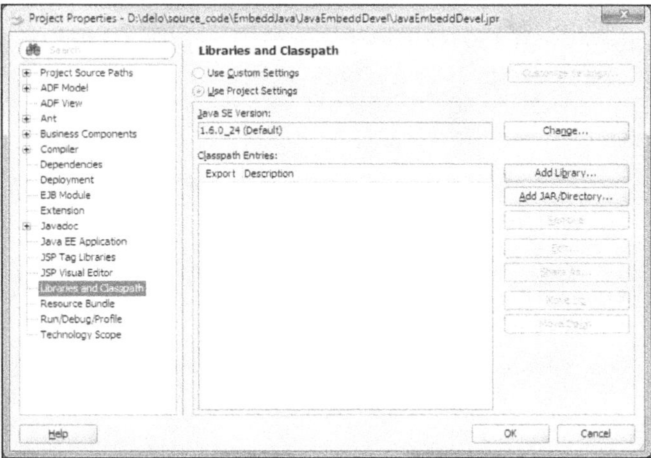

3. Select **Libraries and Classpath** from the options tree. Click on the **AddLibrary...** button to add libraries to the project. The **Add Library** dialog opens where we can find a number of libraries under the **Extension** node.

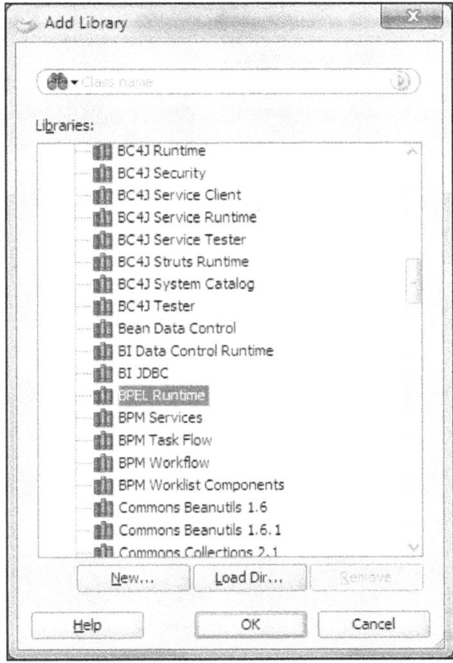

4. From the list we select the **BPEL Runtime** library and click on the **OK** button to close all the dialogs.

5. Create the Java class to be used for the development in the Java project. We name the class (`MyExecLet`), enter the package name (`org.packt.execlet`), and enter the class that we need to extend in order to implement the Java Embedding activity (`com.collaxa.cube.engine.ext.bpel.v1.nodes.BPELXExecLet`). Click on the **OK** button to create the class.

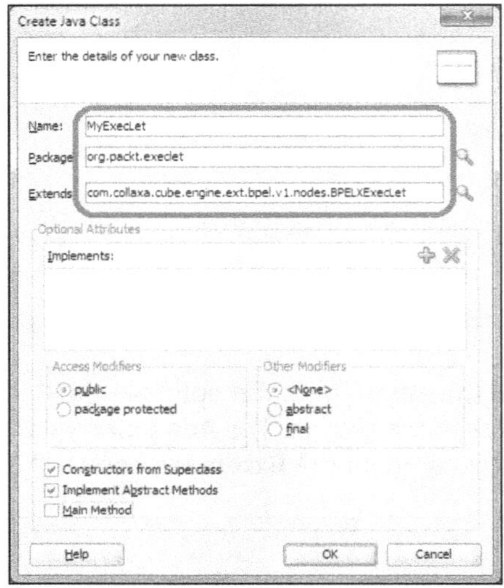

Open the newly generated class, right-click on the editor pane, and select the **Source and Override methods...** option. The **Override Methods** dialog opens where we select the **execute** method from the list and click on the **OK** button.

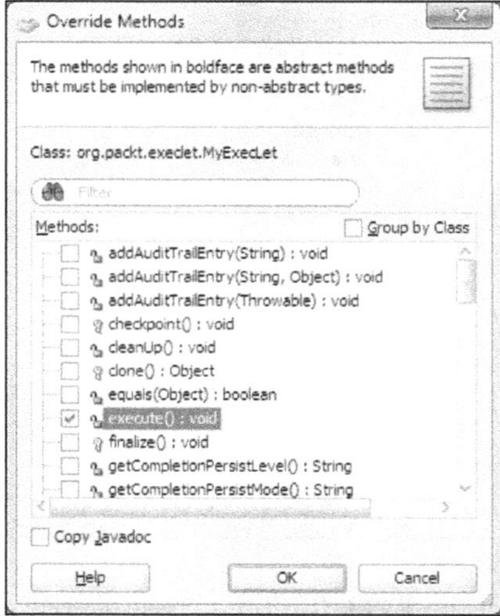

How it works...

When the BPEL process contains the Java Embedding activity, the Java code is executed inside the `BPELXExecLet` class. More precisely, the code is inserted into its `execute()` method.

In the recipe, we have added the BPEL Runtime library into the JDeveloper project libraries. By inspecting the content of the BPEL Runtime library more closely, we see that it consists of just one JAR file (`orabpel.jar`). Inside the JAR file, there is the `BPELXExecLet` class, which we extend in our project. With `BPELXExecLet`, we also receive access to all the methods we are able to access from within the Java Embedding activity.

Through the recipe we prepared the development environment, where we are able to prepare syntactically correct code for the Java Embedding activity.

Note that we are not able to run the code, since there is no BPEL runtime environment present. To really test the code in runtime, we have to copy the code into the Java Embedding activity inside the BPEL process and run it.

See also

When we have code ready to be used in the BPEL process, it is time to move into the real BPEL process. In the upcoming two recipes (*Using the Java code placeholder in BPEL process* and *Invoking Java code from the BPEL process*), we address the use of Java code inside the BPEL process.

Using the Java code placeholder in the BPEL process

When using Java code inside the BPEL process we use the Java Embedding activity. At the moment both versions of BPEL processes (1.1 and 2.0) are widely used. Consequently, we will address the use of the Java code placeholder in both types of BPEL processes.

Getting ready

To complete this recipe, we need nothing special. We just create an empty composite with two empty synchronous BPEL processes. We name them `BPEL_and_Java_1_1` and `BPEL_and_Java_2_0`, each addressing its BPEL version respectively.

How to do it...

The steps involved in using the Java code placeholder in the BPEL process are as follows:

1. Open the **BPEL_and_Java_1_1** process.
2. From the **Component Palette**, select **Oracle Extensions**.
3. Pick the **Java Embedding** component and drop it into the BPEL process. We can see the BPEL process with the Java Embedding activity inside it.

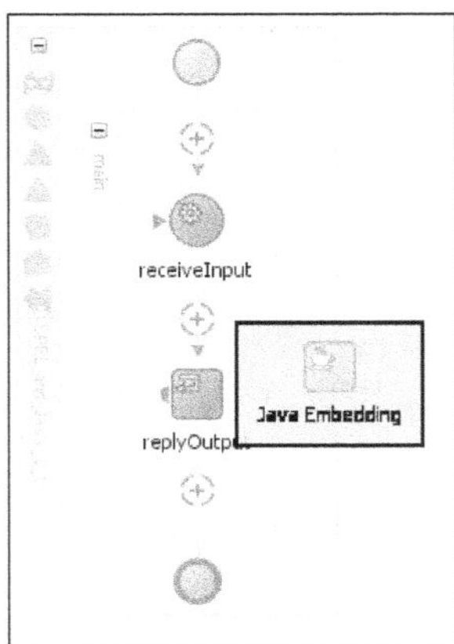

4. Now open the **BPEL_and_Java_2_0** process.
5. Again in the **Component Palette** select **Oracle Extensions**.
6. Pick the **Java Embedding** component and drop it into the BPEL process. We have created the BPEL 2.0 process with the Java Embedding activity inside it.

How it works...

Placing the Java Embedding activity into the BPEL process enables us to use the Java code in the BPEL process. Let us now compare both versions of BPEL processes.

The Java Embedding activity definition in the `BPEL_and_Java_1_1` process is as follows:

```
<bpelx:exec name="Java_Embedding1"/>
```

The definition in the `BPEL_and_Java_2_0` process is as follows:

```
<extensionActivity>
  <bpelx:exec name="Java_Embedding1"/>
</extensionActivity>
```

We see that in BPEL version 2.0, the process has the *Java Embedding* activity surrounded by the `<extensionActivity>` tag.

If we compare the Java Embedding configuration dialog, we can see that there is almost no difference between the BPEL versions.

See also

To learn how to include the code into the Java Embedding activity, refer to the *Invoking Java code from the BPEL process* recipe.

Invoking Java code from the BPEL process

This recipe explains how to use Java code in the BPEL process from within the Java Embedding activity.

Getting ready

For this recipe to complete, we will update the sample from the previous recipe. We will utilize the `BPEL_and_Java_2_0` process in order to show how to invoke Java code from the Java Embedding activity. In this recipe, we will read the input date variable and with the help of the Java Embedding activity set the result to the output variable. The output variable will take the input date and calculate which day in week the date presents.

We also need to open the BPEL process schema (`BPEL_and_Java_2_0.xsd`). Inside the schema we modify the input and output message definition:

```
<element name="process">
  <complexType>
    <sequence>
      <element name="input_date" type="date"/>
    </sequence>
  </complexType>
</element>

<element name="processResponse">
  <complexType>
    <sequence>
      <element name="day_of_date" type="string"/>
    </sequence>
  </complexType>
</element>
```

How to do it...

Open the `BPEL_and_Java_2_0` process in JDeveloper.

Double-click on the `Java_Embedding1` activity. The edit dialogs opens, where we enter the Java code inside the `Code Snippet` field. We enter the code that will read the content of the input date variable and as an output we return what day is presented by the date:

1. Read the content of the input variable:

   ```
   String input_date= ((oracle.xml.parser.v2.XMLElement)getVariab
   leData("inputVariable","payload","/client:process/client:input_
   date")).getTextContent();
   ```

2. The content is returned as a string, so we have to parse it to to parse it to the `java.util.Date` object:

   ```
   java.text.SimpleDateFormat sdf_input = new java.text.
   SimpleDateFormat("yyyyy-mm-dd hh:mm:ss");
   java.util.Date dt= new java.util.Date();

   try {
     dt= sdf_input.parse(input_date);
   } catch (java.text.ParseException e) {
     e.printStackTrace();
   }
   ```

   The parsing part must be enclosed with a try/catch block, as it may throw an error on parsing problems.

3. We create a simple formatter that takes only a day out of the whole date:

   ```
   java.text.SimpleDateFormat sdf = new java.text.
   SimpleDateFormat("E");
   String dateStr = sdf.format(dt);
   ```

4. Finally, we set the value of the formatter date to the output variable:

   ```
   setVariableData("outputVariable", "payload", "/
   client:processResponse/client:day_of_date", dateStr);
   ```

How it works...

The code snippet is included in the Java Embedding activity in the BPEL process. When deploying the BPEL process, the BPEL engine tries to compile the code snippet and if that succeeds, the BPEL process gets deployed. We notice that two methods are called out of the context: `getVariableData` and `setVariableData`. Those two methods present convenient methods to get value out of the BPEL process variable and to set the value of the BPEL process variables respectively.

When we run the instance of our BPEL process, there is not much information in the **Audit Trail**:

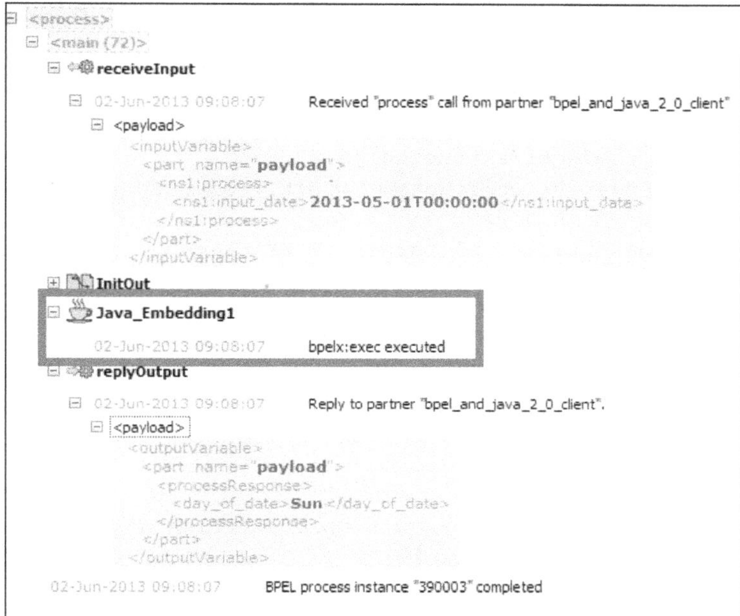
<process>
<main (72)>
receiveInput
02-Jun-2013 09:08:07
Received "process" call from partner "bpel_and_java_2_0_client"
<payload>
<inputVariable>
<part name="payload">
<ns1:process>
<ns1:input_date>2013-05-01T00:00:00</ns1:input_date>
</ns1:process>
</part>
</inputVariable>
InitOut
Java_Embedding1
02-Jun-2013 09:08:07
bpelx:exec executed
replyOutput
02-Jun-2013 09:08:07
Reply to partner "bpel_and_java_2_0_client".
<payload>
<outputVariable>
<part name="payload">
<processResponse>
<day_of_date>Sun</day_of_date>
</processResponse>
</part>
</outputVariable>
02-Jun-2013 09:08:07
BPEL process instance "390003" completed

We can see that the Java Embedding activity presents a black box, which simply states it was executed. Namely, the **Audit Trail** does not capture the intermediate status of the Java Embedding activity execution.

Note that if we also want to get some intermediate information about Java Embedding activity execution, then we should use the `addAuditTrailEntry` method.

There's more...

One of the deficiencies of the Java Embedding activity is the restriction of using the import statement inside code snippets. We used fully qualified names in the code. However, the problem in more complex code with in-depth class hierarchies is that code gets hard to read and maintain. Remember, when code is getting more complex, it is time we think of moving the code out of the BPEL process and create an independent web service or EJB. Then, we call the web service or EJB from the BPEL process.

To overcome this obstacle, we can use import statements in the BPEL process definition. Immediately after the `<process>` tag, we state the Java classes we wanted to import. That way we no longer need to use fully qualified names inside the Java Embedding activity. Let us try now to rewrite our code and import needed classes first. We need to import the following four classes:

```
<import location="java.text.ParseException" importType="http://
schemas.oracle.com/bpel/extension/java"/>
<import location="java.text.SimpleDateFormat" importType="http://
schemas.oracle.com/bpel/extension/java"/>
<import location="java.util.Date" importType="http://schemas.oracle.
com/bpel/extension/java"/>
<import location="oracle.xml.parser.v2.XMLElement" importType="http://
schemas.oracle.com/bpel/extension/java"/>
```

If we now examine the code itself, it is much cleaner and more understandable:

```
//get request data
String input_date= ((XMLElement)getVariableData("inputVariable","paylo
ad","/client:process/client:input_date")).getTextContent();

//parse it to the date
SimpleDateFormat sdf_input = new SimpleDateFormat("yyyy-mm-dd
hh:mm:ss", Locale.ENGLISH);
Date dt= new Date();

try {
  dt= sdf_input.parse(input_date);
} catch (ParseException e) {
  e.printStackTrace();
}

//now format it to the new date
SimpleDateFormat sdf = new SimpleDateFormat("E", Locale.ENGLISH);
String dateStr = sdf.format(dt);

//assign it to response variable
setVariableData("outputVariable", "payload", "/client:processResponse/
client:day_of_date", dateStr);
```

See also

The `getVariableData` method is described in more detail in the *Reading the BPEL process variables* recipe in this chapter. To learn more about the `setVariableData` method, refer to the *Setting the BPEL process variables* recipe in this chapter as well. We examine the `addAuditTrailEntry` method in the *Adding a log to the BPEL Audit Trail* recipe in this chapter.

Reading the BPEL process variables

When using the Java Embedding activity, we need to read data from the BPEL process in order to perform the designed operation. This recipe explains how to read data from the BPEL variables.

How to do it...

Open the `BPEL_and_Java_1_1` process and add the Java Embedding activity (`ReadVar`) into the BPEL process.

1. To read data from BPEL process input variable, we utilize the `getVariableData` function in the `ReadVar` code snippet:

   ```
   oracle.xml.parser.v2.XMLElement input_var= (oracle.xml.parser.
   v2.XMLElement)getVariableData("inputVariable","payload","/
   client:process/client:input");
   ```

2. The `getVariableData` returns the `Object` type, and in our case it is `XMLElement` to which we also cast the result. The `XMLElement` class contains convenient methods to access the content:

   ```
   String input_var_txt= input_var.getTextContent();
   ```

How it works...

The Java Embedding activity provides three types of `getVariableData` methods:

- `Object getVariableData(String name) throws BPELFault`
- `Object getVariableData(String name, String partOrQuery) throws BPELFault`
- `Object getVariableData(String name, String part, String query)`

Depending on our needs, we choose the proper method. All three methods return the content of the variable depending on the parameters we provide.

There's more...

A more convenient way of reading the BPEL process variables is through the use of intermediate variables inside the BPEL process.

In the BPEL process we define a variable. For our example, the BPEL definition of the variable would be as follows:

```
<variable name="Input_Txt_Var" type="xsd:string"/>
```

We also add the assign activity (`ReadInput`), which copies the content of the input BPEL variable to the `Input_Txt_Var` variable:

```
<assign name="ReadInput">
  <copy>
    <from variable="inputVariable" part="payload"
       query="/client:process/client:input"/>
    <to variable="Input_Txt_Var"/>
  </copy>
</assign>
```

Let us now amend the `ReadVar` activity in order to read data from the BPEL variable:

```
String input_txt_from_var= (String)getVariableData("Input_Txt_Var");
```

The code is now much simpler and easier to understand.

See also

We have just completed the recipe for reading data from the BPEL process variable. As soon as we perform the operation on the data, we wish to send the result back to the BPEL process variable. To learn how to send data to the BPEL process variable refer to our next recipe, *Setting the BPEL process variables*.

Setting the BPEL process variables

This recipe explains how to send the data to the BPEL process variable.

Getting ready

In order to complete the recipe, we will update the `BPEL_and_Java_1_1` process schema (`BPEL_and_Java_1_1.xsd`). The new element in the response message is `clientResponseMsg`:

```
<element name="processResponse">
  <complexType>
     <sequence>
      <element name="resultFmtBPEL" type="string"/>
      <element name="resultFmtJava" type="string"/>
      <element name="clientResponseMsg" type="string"/>
    </sequence>
  </complexType>
</element>
```

The newly defined element will be used to return the changed input message to the client.

How to do it...

Open the `BPEL_and_Java_1_1` process and insert the Java Embedding activity (`SetVar`).

Double-click on the `SetVar` activity to insert a code snippet.

1. First we read the input data:

   ```
   String input_txt_from_var= (String)getVariableData("Input_Txt_
   Var");
   ```

2. In the next step we will reverse the input text:

   ```
   StringBuilder sb = new StringBuilder();
   for (int i = input_txt_from_var.length() - 1; i >= 0; i--)
     sb.append(input_txt_from_var.charAt(i));
   ```

3. Finally, we assign the result to the `clientResponseMsg` element of the BPEL process output variable:

   ```
   setVariableData("outputVariable","payload","/
   client:processResponse/client:clientResponseMsg", sb.toString());
   ```

How it works...

The Java Embedding activity provides three types of `setVariableData` methods:

- `void setVariableData(String name, Object value)`
- `void setVariableData(String name, String part, Object value)`
- `void setVariableData(String name, String part, String query, Object value)`

Depending on our needs, we choose the appropriate method. The methods have similar signatures to `getVariableData`, with the difference they don't return any values and contain an additional attribute, `value`, that is used to set the content of the variable.

Invoking Session bean from the BPEL process

Session beans are defined by the Java Enterprise Edition specification. They are divided into stateless and stateful beans. A stateless session bean operates on the operation level. This means that after the operation is executed, the state of the session bean is not preserved. On the contrary, stateful beans preserve state across a multi-operation level.

This recipe will explain how to call a session bean operation from the Java Embedding activity from the BPEL process.

Getting ready

To complete the recipe, we will create a project in JDeveloper and a session bean that will act as exchange money operation on ATM. The session bean will calculate how much money the customer will get, based on the amount of money inserted into ATM, exchange rate of the currency, and deduced fee.

1. We start by creating a generic project in JDeveloper and naming it `ExchangeATM`. Right-click on the project node and select the **New...** option. Select the **Session Bean (EJB)** option from the **New Gallery** window.

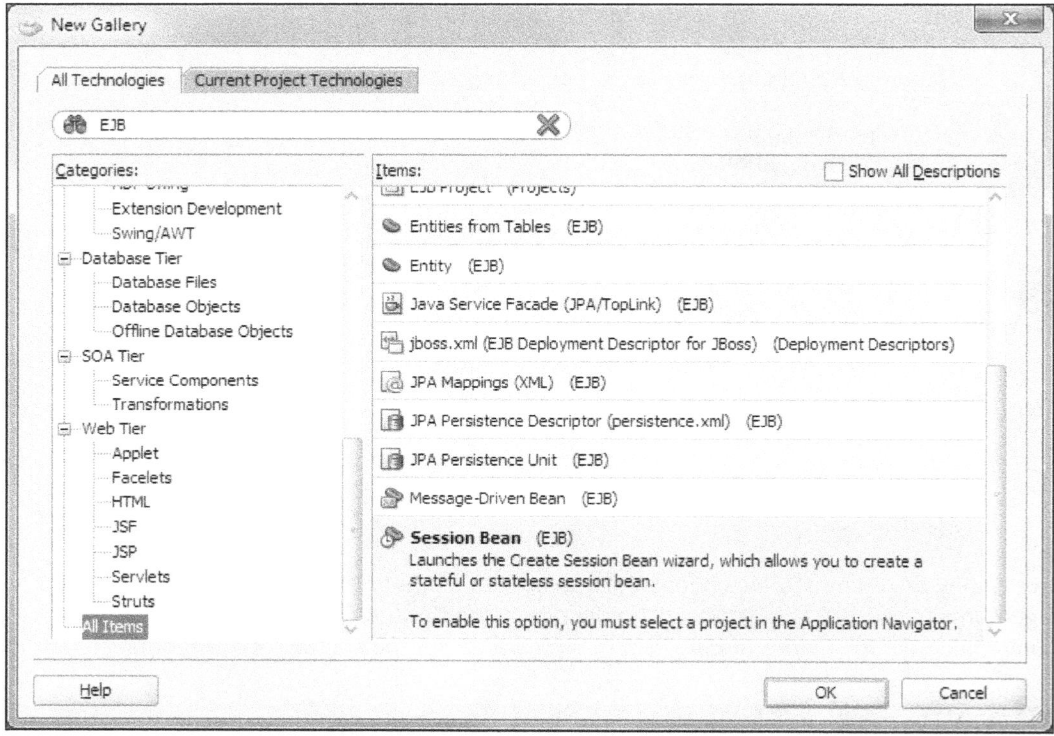

2. In the **Create Session Bean** wizard select the **Enterprise JavaBeans 3.0** option and continue to the next step.

3. We change the **EJB Name** and **Mapped Name** fields in the **EJB Name and Options** step of the wizard.

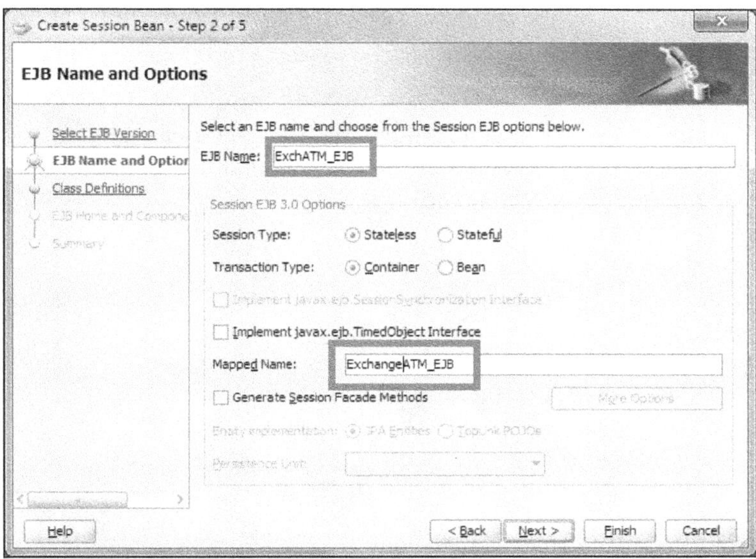

4. We name the session bean in the next step of the wizard `org.packt.ejb.atm.ExchATM_EJB`.
5. In the last step we name the local and remote interfaces and finish the wizard.

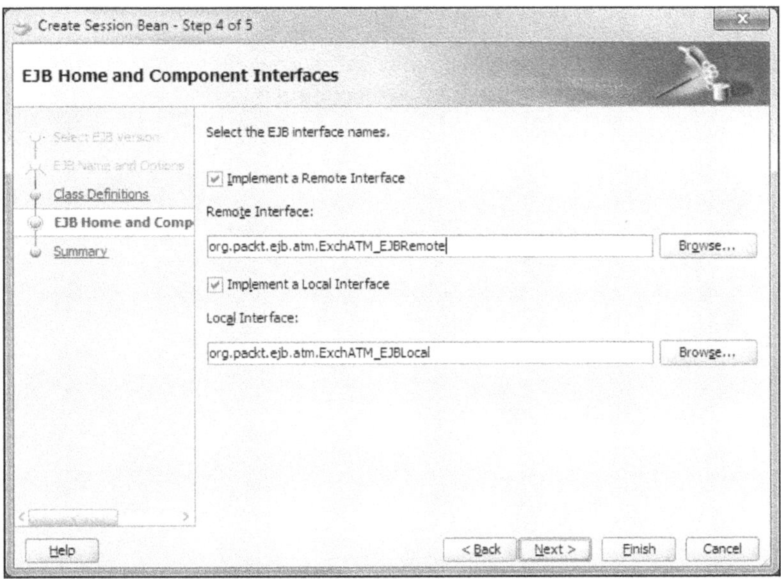

Now we have the session bean created in the JDeveloper project. We have to add the code to perform the calculation and deploy it to the WebLogic server.

1. We add the following method to all the interfaces and implementation:

   ```
   public double exchangeMoney(double originalAmount, String
   currency);
   ```

2. The implementation looks rather simple. We read the exchange rate and calculate the exchange amount. Based on the exchange amount, we deduce the fee.

   ```
   public double exchangeMoney(double originalAmount, String
   currency) {
     double fee= 0.95; //5 %
     double rate= ((Double)rates.get(currency)).doubleValue();

     double excMoneyNoFee= originalAmount * rate;
     double excMoneyWFee= excMoneyNoFee * fee;

     return excMoneyWFee;
   }
   ```

3. We deploy the session bean by configuring the deployment descriptor. We won't describe the deployment process in detail, as it is rather trivial and does not require any special configuration steps.

How to do it...

The following steps will explain how to achieve this:

1. First we will extend the schema of input and output messages to support the ATM operation. The expanded input message schema is as follows:

   ```
   <element name="process">
     <complexType>
       <sequence>
         <element name="input_date" type="date"/>
         <element name="atm_amount" type="double"/>
         <element name="atm_curr" type="string"/>
       </sequence>
     </complexType>
   </element>
   ```

2. The output schema has the following structure after modification:

```
<element name="processResponse">
  <complexType>
    <sequence>
      <element name="day_of_date" type="string"/>
      <element name="exchangeMsg" type="string"/>
    </sequence>
  </complexType>
</element>
```

3. Open the `BPEL_and_Java_2_0` process. Insert another Java Embedded activity and name it `Java_ATM`.
4. Insert the code into Java Embedding activity code snippet. Initially, we read the input parameters as follows:

```
String input_amt= ((oracle.xml.parser.v2.XMLElement)getVariableDat
a("inputVariable","payload","/client:process/client:atm_amount")).
getTextContent();
String input_curr= ((oracle.xml.parser.v2.XMLElement)getVariableDa
ta("inputVariable","payload","/client:process/client:atm_curr")).
getTextContent();
```

5. Cast the input amount to the input variable type of the EJB bean:

```
double dbl_amt= Double.parseDouble(input_amt);
```

6. We enclose the rest of the code into the try/catch block that handles the exceptions with the Java naming service. Prepare the environment for the Java naming service and create the initial context:

```
  java.util.Hashtable env = new java.util.Hashtable();
  // WebLogic Server 10.x connection details
  env.put( javax.naming.Context.INITIAL_CONTEXT_FACTORY,
"weblogic.jndi.WLInitialContextFactory" );
  env.put(javax.naming.Context.PROVIDER_URL, "t3://
localhost:7001");
  javax.naming.Context context = new javax.naming.InitialContext(
env );
```

7. Initiate the lookup for the EJB session bean:

```
  Object obj= context.lookup("ExchangeATM_EJB#org.packt.ejb.atm.
ExchATM_EJBRemote");
```

8. We perform the operation on the EJB session bean if we receive the reference to it and set the text to the output message:

```
   if (obj != null)
  {
   org.packt.ejb.atm.ExchATM_EJBRemote atmBean= (org.packt.ejb.
atm.ExchATM_EJBRemote)obj;

   double exchMoney=atmBean.exchangeMoney(dbl_amt, input_curr);

   setVariableData("outputVariable", "payload", "/
client:processResponse/client:exchangeMsg", "ATM gives back " +
exchMoney + " EUR.");

  }
```

How it works...

We lookup EJBs (Enterprise JavaBeans) through **Java Naming and Directory Interface** (**JNDI**). We have access to the JNDI from the Java Embedding activity. Unfortunately, the JNDI of the BPEL process is connected to the BPEL cube instance and EJBs are registered into the Oracle WebLogic server. That is why we have to set up the JNDI environment manually and address EJBs through our own JNDI context.

To learn more on JNDI and RMI, the following resources are available:

- `http://www.oracle.com/technetwork/java/jndi/docs/index.html`
- `http://docs.oracle.com/javase/6/docs/technotes/guides/rmi/`

Through the JNDI we receive a link to the remote interface of the EJB. Based on the interface definition, we are able to call the methods on the EJB.

Another possibility to call EJBs is through SOAP messages. The implementation of EJB as a web service is rather simple, as it merely contains the usage of JAX-WS annotations, for example.

There is also another possibility for calling the EJB from the BPEL process and that is through a Spring component. We can develop the Spring component that calls the EJB. In the SCA composite we than add the Spring component and link it with the BPEL process.

Using the utility functionality

Oracle SOA Suite defines a set of utility functions to perform various operations. However, there is no unified place where we find the utility functions. In this recipe, we will learn how to format a message with the `ora:format` utility function and then implement the same functionality inside the Java Embedding activity.

Getting ready

To start, we will use the `BPEL_and_Java_1_1` process. We change the schema definition of the response message. Open the `BPEL_and_Java_1_1.xsd` file and change the response part of the element:

```
<element name="processResponse">
  <complexType>
    <sequence>
      <element name="resultFmtBPEL" type="string"/>
     <element name="resultFmtJava" type="string"/>
    </sequence>
  </complexType>
</element>
```

Open the `BPEL_and_Java_1_1` process and place a new assign activity (`FormatBPEL`) into it. The code for the assign activity is as follows:

```
<assign name="FormatBPEL">
 <copy>
  <from expression="ora:format('At {0} on {1} the BPEL was
initiated with the following input parameter: {2}.',xp20:current-
time(),xp20:current-date(),bpws:getVariableData('inputVariable','paylo
ad','/client:process/client:input') )"/>
  <to variable="outputVariable" part="payload"
    query="/client:processResponse/client:resultFmtBPEL"/>
 </copy>
</assign>
```

With the code, we formatted a message that contains the date and input message information. We assign the result to the output part of the variable (`resultFmtBPEL`).

How to do it...

We will now format the same message with the help of the Java Embedding activity. Start by adding the Java Embedding activity (`FormatJava`) into the `BPEL_and_Java_1_1` process. The code snippet for the `FormatJava` activity is as follows:

1. We start by reading the content of the input variable:

   ```
   String input_txt= ((oracle.xml.parser.v2.XMLElement)getVariableD
   ata("inputVariable","payload","/client:process/client:input")).
   getTextContent();
   ```

2. Instantiate the `MessageFormat` class for the formatting:

   ```
   java.text.MessageFormat mfmt= new java.text.MessageFormat("At {0,
   time} on {0,date} the BPEL was intatiated with the following input
   parameter: {1}.");
   ```

3. Fill the variable of the object to be formatted:

   ```
   Object[] objs = {new java.util.Date(), input_txt};
   ```

4. Perform the actual formatting and send the results of the formatting to the output variable part (`resultFmtJava`):

   ```
   String result= mfmt.format(objs);
   setVariableData("outputVariable", "payload", "/
   client:processResponse/client:resultFmtJava", result);
   ```

How it works...

Both the methods described in this recipe use the same principle of formatting the messages. Actually, the BPEL method `ora:format` uses the same Java class that we used in this recipe (`java.text.MessageFormat`).

Oracle defines a set of utility functions to be utilized, summarized by the section in which we can find them in JDeveloper Expression Builder.

Advanced functions

Function name	**What function does**
`ora:format`	Formats the message based on the Java message formatting expression.
`ora:genEmptyElem`	Generates the specified number of empty elements specified by QName parameter.
`ora:getChildElement`	Returns the child element (index) of the given element.

Mathematical functions

Function name	What the function does
oraext:max-value-among-nodeset	Returns the maximum integer value from the list of given nodes. The nodes must be presented as text nodes.
oraext:min-value-among-nodeset	Returns the minimum integer value from the list of given nodes. The nodes must be presented as text nodes.
oraext:square-root	Returns the square root of the input number

Adding a log to the BPEL Audit Trail

Throughout the recipes in this chapter we saw quite a few lines of auditing (addAuditTrailEntry). We did not explore them in any of the recipes, as this recipe is dedicated to exploring the possibilities of auditing in the Java Embedding activity.

How to do it...

Open the BPEL_and_Java_1_1 process and insert the Java Embedding activity (Auditing).

We insert the code into a snippet as follows:

1. Initially, we read the content of the input data. Note that we added the auditing method that outputs the input variable content:

```
Object input_obj= getVariableData("Input_Txt_Var");
addAuditTrailEntry("Input data", input_obj);
```

2. In the try/catch block, we convert the content of the input variable to a double number. If the type of input variable content presents a number, we audit the converted number, otherwise we report the exception that occurred during the transformation:

```
try {
  Double whatNumber = Double.parseDouble((String)input_obj);
  addAuditTrailEntry("Number is:", whatNumber);
} catch (NumberFormatException nfe) {
  addAuditTrailEntry("Not a number ?");
  addAuditTrailEntry(nfe);
}
```

How it works...

The Java Embedding activity offers three `addAuditTrailEntry` method signatures for auditing information:

- `void addAuditTrailEntry(String message)`
- `void addAuditTrailEntry(String message, Object detail)`
- `void addAuditTrailEntry(Throwable t)`

We are able to audit a simple string `message`. If we want to output information about the objects, we can use the auditing method with two parameters: a string `message` and an object `detail`. In cases of handling exceptions, we utilize the auditing method that accepts the `throwable` parameter.

Let us now instantiate the BPEL process and enter a number as an input parameter. Inspect the **Audit Trail** to see the auditing information:

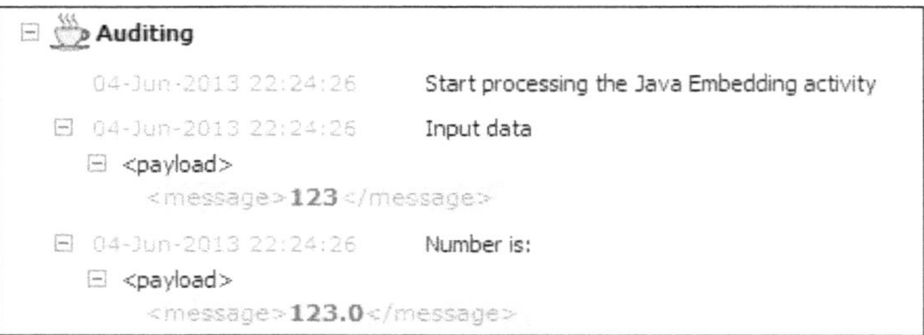
Auditing
04-Jun-2013 22:24:26
Start processing the Java Embedding activity
04-Jun-2013 22:24:26
Input data
<payload>
<message>123</message>
04-Jun-2013 22:24:26
Number is:
<payload>
<message>123.0</message>

Additionally, run another instance of the BPEL process and enter the content of the parameter that is not a number (for example, abc). Check the **Audit Trail** now and check the auditing information of the exception:

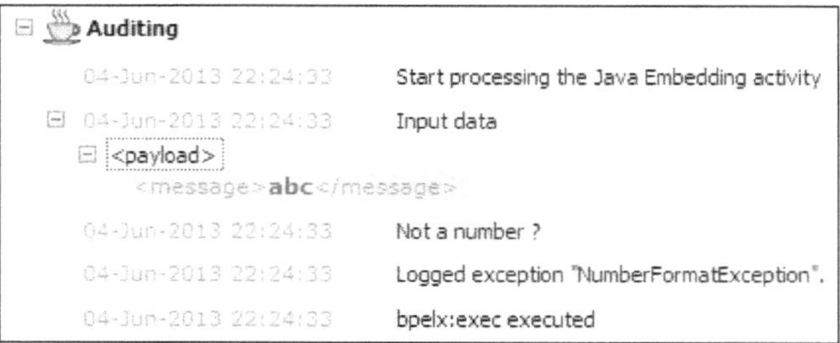
Auditing
04-Jun-2013 22:24:33
Start processing the Java Embedding activity
04-Jun-2013 22:24:33
Input data
<payload>
<message>abc</message>
04-Jun-2013 22:24:33
Not a number ?
04-Jun-2013 22:24:33
Logged exception "NumberFormatException".
04-Jun-2013 22:24:33
bpelx:exec executed

Reading the process instance data

The Java Embedding environment as well as the BPEL functions support the functionality that retrieves information about the running BPEL process instance, such as the process instance ID, process name, composite name, process instance title, and so on. The information can then be used for logging purposes, notification purposes, and error handling.

This recipe explains how to utilize the process instance data inside the Java Embedding activity.

Getting ready

To complete the recipe, we extend the response message schema (`BPEL_and_Java_2_0.xsd`) in the `BPEL_and_Java_2_0` process with additional fields, as follows:

```
<element name="processResponse">
 <complexType>
  <sequence>
   <element name="day_of_date" type="string"/>
   <element name="exchangeMsg" type="string"/>
   <element name="prc_inst_id" type="long"/>
   <element name="prc_inst_title" type="string"/>
   <element name="prc_inst_creator" type="string"/>
  </sequence>
 </complexType>
</element>
```

How to do it...

Open the `BPEL_and_Java_2_0` process and add the Java Embedding activity (`Java_Process_Data`).

We double click on the `Java_Process_Data` activity and put the code from the following steps into the Java Embedding activity code snippet:

1. Read the BPEL process instance ID with the following:

   ```
   long prc_id= getInstanceId();
   ```

2. Read the BPEL process title with the following:

   ```
   String prc_title= getTitle();
   ```

3. Read the creator name with the following:

   ```
   String prc_creator= getCreator();
   ```

   Note that creator always returns an empty result for an unknown reason.

4. Finally, we set the values to the output variable elements:

```
if (prc_id > 0)
  setVariableData("outputVariable", "payload", "/
client:processResponse/client:prc_inst_id", prc_id);
if (prc_title != null)
  setVariableData("outputVariable", "payload", "/
client:processResponse/client:prc_inst_title", prc_title);
if (prc_creator != null)
  setVariableData("outputVariable", "payload", "/
client:processResponse/client:prc_inst_creator", prc_creator);
```

It is recommended to use an if statement guard, since the BPEL engine throws `RuntimeException` in case of null values.

Let us now deploy and instantiate the BPEL process. In **Audit Trail** we can observe the output variable filed with data about running the BPEL process:

```
replyOutput
  04-Jun-2013 22:51:13    Reply to partner "bpel_and_java_2_0_client".
    <payload>
      <outputVariable>
        <part name="payload">
          <processResponse>
            <day_of_date>Tor</day_of_date>
            <exchangeMsg>ATM gives back 327.10134 EUR.</exchangeMsg>
            <prc_inst_id>400025</prc_inst_id>
            <prc_inst_title>Instance #400025 of BPEL_and_Java_2_0</prc_inst_title>
            <prc_inst_creator/>
          </processResponse>
        </part>
      </outputVariable>
```

There's more...

The information about the BPEL process can also be retrieved from the BPEL process without Java Embedding.

Insert the assign activity (`BPEL_Process_Data`) into the `BPEL_and_Java_2_0` process.

Double-click on the `BPEL_Process_Data` and configure the following expressions for the retrieval of BPEL process information:

```
<assign name="BPEL_Process_Data">
  <copy>
```

```
      <from>ora:getInstanceId()</from>
      <to>$outputVariable.payload/client:prc_inst_id</to>
    </copy>
    <copy>
      <from>ora:getCompositeName()</from>
      <to>$outputVariable.payload/client:prc_inst_title</to>
    </copy>
    <copy>
      <from>concat(ora:getCreator(), '')</from>
      <to>$outputVariable.payload/client:prc_inst_creator</to>
    </copy>
  </assign>
```

If we re-deploy the BPEL process and instantiate it again, we will see the BPEL process information filled into the output variable element directly, without the use of Java Embedding functionality:

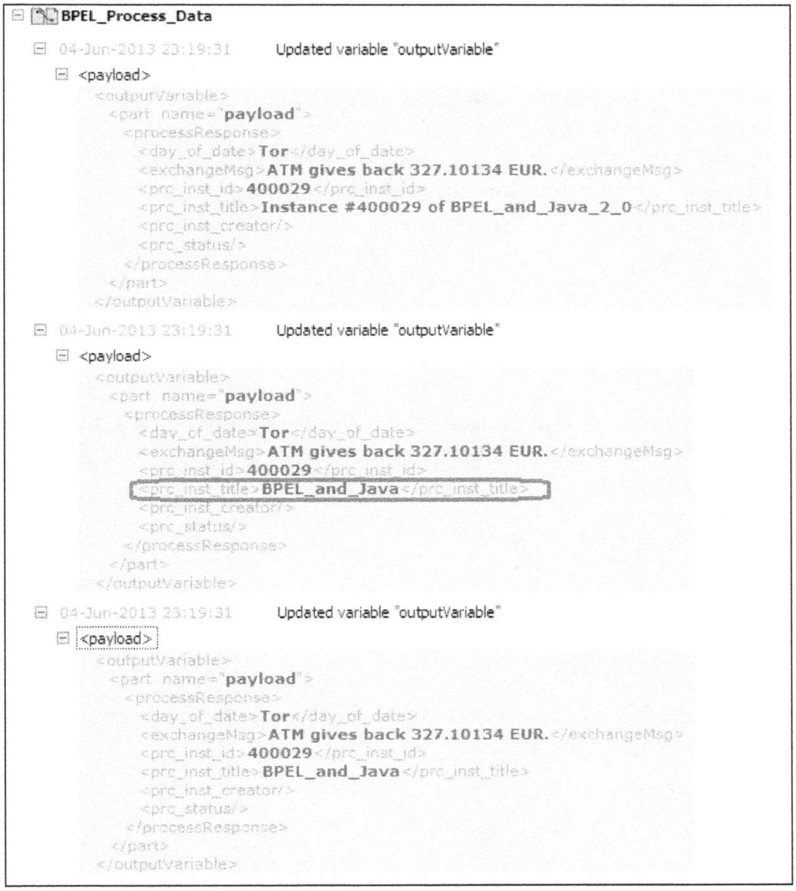

```
BPEL_Process_Data
  04-Jun-2013 23:19:31    Updated variable "outputVariable"
    <payload>
      <outputVariable>
        <part name="payload">
          <processResponse>
            <day_of_date>Tor</day_of_date>
            <exchangeMsg>ATM gives back 327.10134 EUR.</exchangeMsg>
            <prc_inst_id>400029</prc_inst_id>
            <prc_inst_title>Instance #400029 of BPEL_and_Java_2_0</prc_inst_title>
            <prc_inst_creator/>
            <prc_status/>
          </processResponse>
        </part>
      </outputVariable>
  04-Jun-2013 23:19:31    Updated variable "outputVariable"
    <payload>
      <outputVariable>
        <part name="payload">
          <processResponse>
            <day_of_date>Tor</day_of_date>
            <exchangeMsg>ATM gives back 327.10134 EUR.</exchangeMsg>
            <prc_inst_id>400029</prc_inst_id>
            <prc_inst_title>BPEL_and_Java</prc_inst_title>
            <prc_inst_creator/>
            <prc_status/>
          </processResponse>
        </part>
      </outputVariable>
  04-Jun-2013 23:19:31    Updated variable "outputVariable"
    <payload>
      <outputVariable>
        <part name="payload">
          <processResponse>
            <day_of_date>Tor</day_of_date>
            <exchangeMsg>ATM gives back 327.10134 EUR.</exchangeMsg>
            <prc_inst_id>400029</prc_inst_id>
            <prc_inst_title>BPEL_and_Java</prc_inst_title>
            <prc_inst_creator/>
            <prc_status/>
          </processResponse>
        </part>
      </outputVariable>
```

We can see that the difference exists with `<prc_inst_title>`, because there is no exact function in the BPEL environment.

Getting the BPEL process status data

This recipe explains how to retrieve the current status of the BPEL process.

Getting ready

In order to complete this recipe, we will extend the output variable of the BPEL process. Thus, we open the `BPEL_and_Java_2_0.xsd` schema file and add an additional element to retrieve the BPEL process status data:

```
<element name="processResponse">
  <complexType>
    <sequence>
      <element name="day_of_date" type="string"/>
      <element name="exchangeMsg" type="string"/>
      <element name="prc_inst_id" type="long"/>
      <element name="prc_inst_title" type="string"/>
      <element name="prc_inst_creator" type="string"/>
      <element name="prc_status" type="string"/>
    </sequence>
  </complexType>
</element>
```

How to do it...

Open the `BPEL_and_Java_2_0` process and add the Java Embedding activity (`Java_Process_Status`). Double-click on the `Java_Process_Status` activity and put in the code snippet:

```
String prc_status= getStatus();

if (prc_status != null)
  setVariableData("outputVariable", "payload", "/
client:processResponse/client:prc_status", prc_status);
```

The code retrieves the BPEL process status and sets its value to the BPEL process output variable element `<prc_status>`.

Let us now deploy and instantiate the BPEL process. In **Audit Trail** we can observe the output variable filed with data about running the BPEL process:

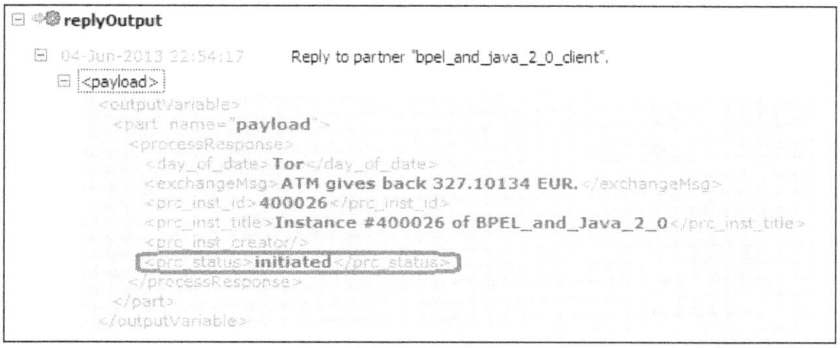

```
replyOutput
  04-Jun-2013 22:54:17    Reply to partner "bpel_and_java_2_0_client".
    <payload>
      <outputVariable>
        <part name="payload">
          <processResponse>
            <day_of_date>Tor</day_of_date>
            <exchangeMsg>ATM gives back 327.10134 EUR.</exchangeMsg>
            <prc_inst_id>400026</prc_inst_id>
            <prc_inst_title>Instance #400026 of BPEL_and_Java_2_0</prc_inst_title>
            <prc_inst_creator/>
            <prc_status>initiated</prc_status>
          </processResponse>
        </part>
      </outputVariable>
```


How it works...

The BPEL processes that run in Oracle SOA Suite have a number of states in which the BPEL process can reside:

State	BPEL process
0	Initiated (`STATE_INITIATED`)
1	Open and running (`STATE_OPEN_RUNNING`)
2	Open and suspended (`STATE_OPEN_SUSPENDED`)
3	Open and faulted (`STATE_OPEN_FAULTED`)
4	Closed and pending cancelled (`STATE_CLOSED_ PENDING_CANCEL`)
5	Closed and completed (`STATE_CLOSED_COMPLETED`)
6	Closed and faulted (`STATE_CLOSED_FAULTED`)
7	Closed and canceled (`STATE_CLOSED_CANCELLED`)
8	Closed and aborted (`STATE_CLOSED_ABORTED`)
9	Closed and stale (`STATE_CLOSED_STALE`)

For example, if we run the following SQL statement on the Oracle database (assuming we have Oracle XE database):

```
SELECT
CIKEY,
c.status,
CASE state
WHEN 0 THEN 'initiated'
```

```
WHEN 1 THEN 'open.running'
WHEN 2 THEN 'open.suspended'
WHEN 3 THEN 'open.faulted'
WHEN 4 THEN 'closed.pending_cancel'
WHEN 5 THEN 'closed.completed'
WHEN 6 THEN 'closed.faulted'
WHEN 7 THEN 'closed.cancelled'
WHEN 8 THEN 'closed.aborted'
WHEN 9 THEN 'closed.stale'
ELSE 'unknown'
END state_text
FROM dev_soainfra.cube_instance c
ORDER BY c.CIKEY;
```

We can see the same information as the `getStatus()` method in the Java Embedding activity will report to us.

10
Using XML Facade for DOM

In this chapter, we will cover the following recipes:

- Setting up an XML facade project
- Generating XML facade using ANT
- Creating XML facade from XSD
- Creating XML facade from WSDL
- Packaging XML facade into JAR
- Generating Java documents for XML facade
- Invoking XML facade from BPEL processes
- Accessing complex types through XML facade
- Accessing simple types through XML facade

Introduction

The **Business Process Execution Language** (**BPEL**) is based on XML, which means that all the internal variables and data are presented in XML. In this book, we cover both BPEL and Java. As both the technologies are complementary, we seek ways to ease the integration of the technologies. In order to handle the XML content from BPEL variables in Java resources (classes), we have a couple of possibilities:

- Use DOM (Document Object Model) API for Java, where we handle the XML content directly through API calls. An example of such a call would be reading from the input variable:

```
oracle.xml.parser.v2.XMLElement input_cf= (oracle.xml.parser.
v2.XMLElement)getVariableData("inputVariable","payload","/
client:Cashflows");
```

We receive the `XMLElement` class, which we need to handle further, either be assignment, reading of content, iteration, or something else.

- As an alternative, we can use XML facade though **Java Architecture for XML Binding** (**JAXB**). JAXB provides a convenient way of transforming XML to Java or vice-versa. The creation of XML facade is supported through the `xjc` utility and of course via the JDeveloper IDE. The example code for accessing XML through XML facade is:

```
java.util.List<org.packt.cashflow.facade.PrincipalExchange>
princEx= cf.getPrincipalExchange();
```

We can see that there is neither XML content nor DOM API anymore. Furthermore, we have to access the whole XML structure represented by Java classes.

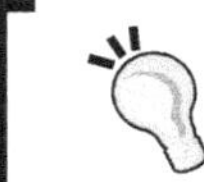

> The latest specification of JAXB at the time of writing is 2.2.7, and its specification can be found at the following location: `https://jaxb.java.net/`.

The purpose of an XML facade operation is the marshalling and un-marshalling of Java classes. When the originated content is presented in XML, we use un-marshalling methods in order to generate the correspondent Java classes. In cases where we have content stored in Java classes and we want to present the content in XML, we use the marshalling methods.

JAXB provides the ability to create XML facade from an XML schema definition or from the WSDL (Web Service Definition/Description Language). The latter method provides a useful approach as we, in most cases, orchestrate web services whose operations are defined in WSDL documents.

Throughout this chapter, we will work on a sample from the banking world. On top of this sample, we will show how to build the XML facade. The sample contains the simple XML types, complex types, elements, and cardinality, so we cover all the essential elements of functionality in XML facade.

Setting up an XML facade project

We start generating XML facade by setting up a project in a JDeveloper environment which provides convenient tools for building XML facades. This recipe will describe how to set up a JDeveloper project in order to build XML facade.

Getting ready

To complete the recipe, we need the XML schema of the BPEL process variables based on which we build XML facade. Explore the XML schema of our banking BPEL process. We are interested in the structure of the BPEL request message:

```
<xsd:complexType name="PrincipalExchange">
  <xsd:sequence>
    <xsd:element minOccurs="0"
      name="unadjustedPrincipalExchangeDate" type="xsd:date"/>
    <xsd:element minOccurs="0"
      name="adjustedPrincipalExchangeDate" type="xsd:date"/>
    <xsd:element minOccurs="0" name="principalExchangeAmount"
      type="xsd:decimal"/>
    <xsd:element minOccurs="0" name="discountFactor"
      type="xsd:decimal"/>
  </xsd:sequence>
<xsd:attribute name="id" type="xsd:int"/>
</xsd:complexType>

<xsd:complexType name="CashflowsType">
  <xsd:sequence>
    <xsd:element maxOccurs="unbounded" minOccurs="0"
      name="principalExchange" type="prc:PrincipalExchange"/>
  </xsd:sequence>
</xsd:complexType>

<xsd:element name="Cashflows" type="prc:CashflowsType"/>
```

The request message structure presents just a small fragment of cash flows modeled in the banks. The concrete definition of a cash flow is much more complex. However, our definition contains all the right elements so that we can show the advantages of using XML facade in a BPEL process.

How to do it...

The steps involved in setting up a JDeveloper project for XML façade are as follows:

1. We start by opening a new **Java Project** in JDeveloper and naming it **CashflowFacade**. Click on **Next**.

2. In the next window of the **Create Java Project** wizard, we select the default package name `org.packt.cashflow.facade`. Click on **Finish**. We now have the following project structure in JDeveloper:

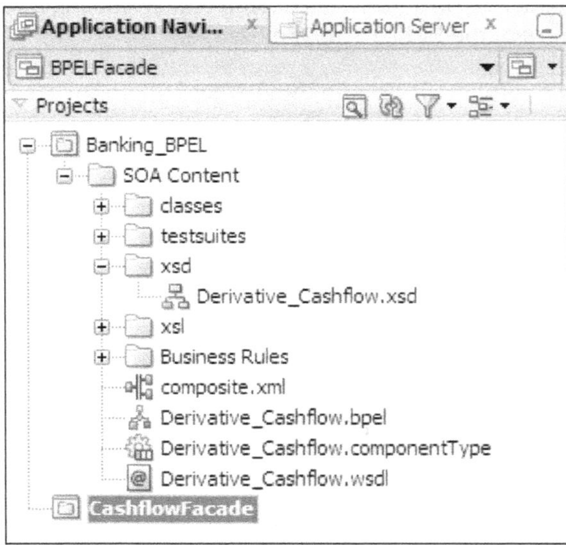

3. We have created a project that is ready for XML facade creation.

How it works...

After the wizard has finished, we can see the project structure created in JDeveloper. Also, the corresponding file structure is created in the filesystem.

See also

To learn how to generate XML facade via the ANT utility, refer to our next recipe, *Generating XML facade using ANT*.

Generating XML facade using ANT

This recipe explains how to generate XML facade with the use of the Apache ANT utility. We use the ANT scripts when we want to build or rebuild the XML facade in many iterations, for example, every time during nightly builds. Using ANT to build XML façade is very useful when XML definition changes are constantly in phases of development. With ANT, we can ensure continuous synchronization between XML and generated Java code.

The official ANT homepage along with detailed information on how to use it can be found at the following URL: `http://ant.apache.org/`.

Getting ready

By completing our previous recipe, we built up a JDeveloper project ready to create XML facade out of XML schema. To complete this recipe, we need to add ANT project technology to the project. We achieve this through the **Project Properties** dialog:

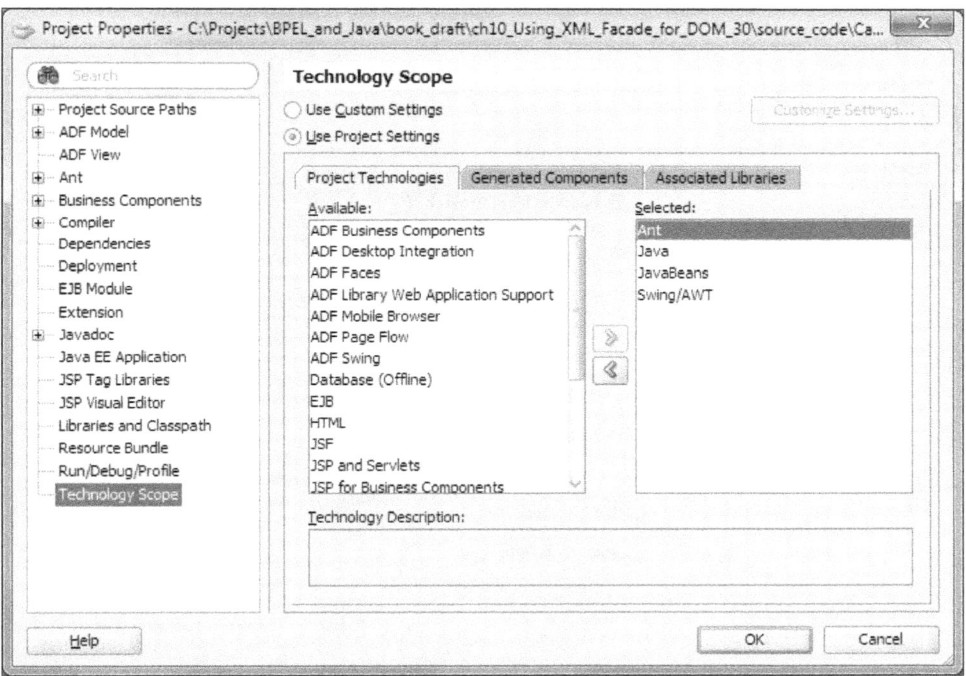

How to do it...

Here are the steps we need to take to create a project in JDeveloper for building XML façade with ANT:

1. Create a new ANT build file by right-clicking on the **CashflowFacade** project node, select **New**, and choose **Buildfile from Project (Ant)**:

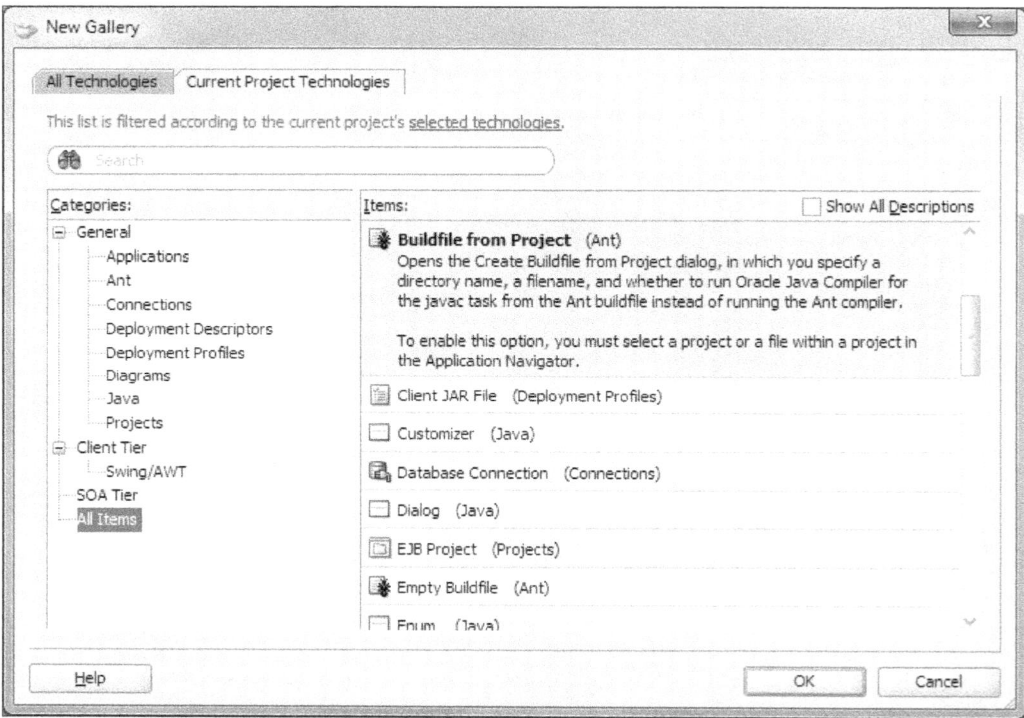

2. The ANT build file is generated and added into the project under the **Resources** folder. Now we need to amend the `build.xml` file with the code to build XML facade.
3. We will first define the properties for our XML facade:

```
<property name="schema_file" location="../Banking_BPEL/xsd/
Derivative_Cashflow.xsd"/>
<property name="dest_dir" location="./src"/>
<property name="package" value="org.packt.cashflow.facade"/>
```

4. We define the location of the source XML schema (it is located in the BPEL process). Next, we define the destination of the generated Java files and the name of the package.

5. Now, we define the ANT target in order to build XML facade classes. The ANT target presents one closed unit of ANT work. We define the build task for the XML façade as follows:

```
<target name="xjc">
  <delete dir="src"/>
  <mkdir dir="src"/>
  <echo message="Compiling the schema..." />
  <exec executable="xjc">
    <arg value="-xmlschema"/>
    <arg value="${schema_file}"/>
    <arg value="-d"/>
    <arg value="${dest_dir}"/>
    <arg value="-p"/>
    <arg value="${package}"/>
  </exec>
</target>
```

6. Now we have XML facade packaged and ready to be used in BPEL processes.

How it works...

ANT is used as a build tool and performs various tasks. As such, we can easily use it to build XML facade. Java Architecture for XML Binding provides the `xjc` utility, which can help us in building XML facade.

We have provided the following parameters to the `xjc` utility:

- `Xmlschema`: This is the threat input schema as XML schema
- `d`: This specifies the destination directory of the generated classes
- `p`: This specifies the package name of the generated classes

There are a number of other parameters, however we will not go into detail about them here. Based on the parameters we provided to the `xjc` utility, the Java representation of the XML schema is generated. If we examine the generated classes, we can see that there exists a Java class for every type defined in the XML schema. Also, we can see that the `ObjectFactory` class is generated, which eases the generation of Java class instances.

There's more...

There is a difference in creating XML facade between Versions 10g and 11g of Oracle SOA Suite. In Oracle SOA Suite 10g, there was a convenient utility named schema, which is used for building XML facade. However, in Oracle SOA Suite 11g, the schema utility is not available anymore.

To provide a similar solution, we create a template class, which is later copied to a real code package when needed to provide functionality for XML facade. We create a new class `Facade` in the called `facade` package. The only method in the class is static and serves as a creation point of `facade`:

```
public static Object createFacade(String context, XMLElement doc)
throws Exception {

  JAXBContext jaxbContext;
  Object zz= null;

  try {
    jaxbContext = JAXBContext.newInstance(context);

    Unmarshaller unmarshaller = jaxbContext.createUnmarshaller();
    zz = unmarshaller.unmarshal(doc);

    return zz;
  } catch (JAXBException e) {
    throw new Exception("Cannot create facade from the XML content. "
+ e.getMessage());
  }
}
```

The class code implementation is simple and consists of creating the JAXB context. Further, we un-marshall the context and return the resulting class to the client. In case of problems, we either throw an exception or return a null object.

Now the calling code is trivial. For example, to create XML facade for the XML content, we call as follows:

```
Object zz = facade.Facade.createFacade("org.packt.cashflow.facade",
document.getSrcRoot());
```

See also

To learn how to create facade using JDeveloper from XSD (XML Schema Definition Language), refer to the next recipe–*Creating XML facade from XSD.*

Creating XML facade from XSD

This recipe describes how to create XML facade classes from XSD. Usually, the necessity to access XML content out of Java classes comes from already defined XML schemas in BPEL processes.

How to do it...

We have already defined the BPEL process and the XML schema (`Derivative_Cashflow.xsd`) in the project. The following steps will show you how to create the XML facade from the XML schema:

1. Select the **CashflowFacade** project, right-click on it, and select **New**. Select **JAXB 2.0 Content Model from XML Schema**.

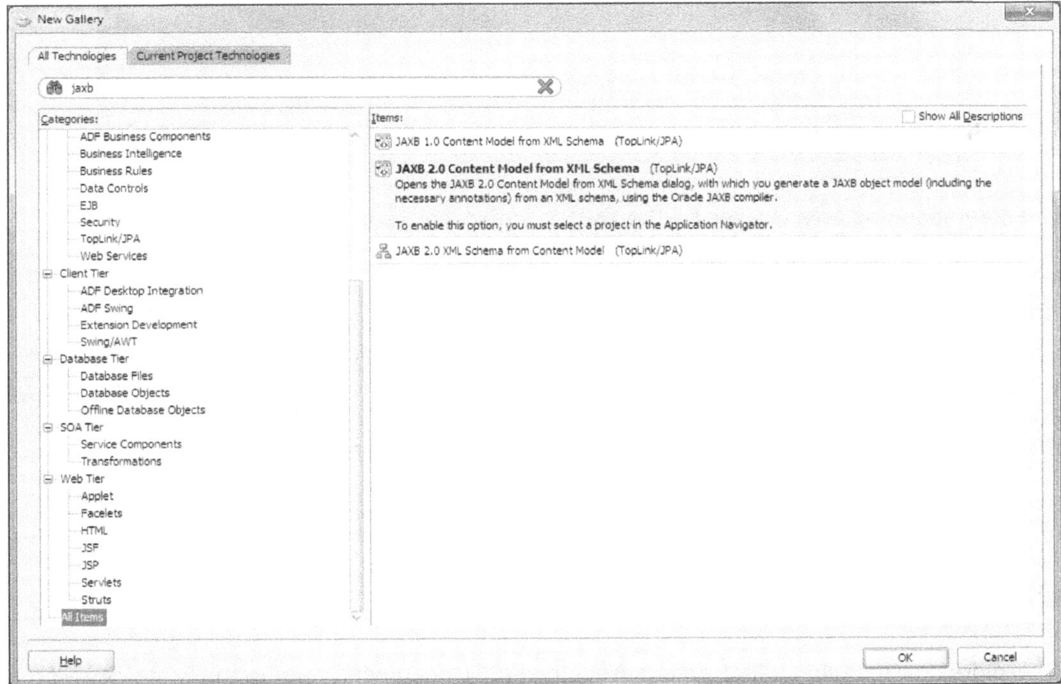

2. Select the schema file from the **Banking_BPEL** project. Select the **Package Name for Generated Classes** checkbox and click on the **OK** button.

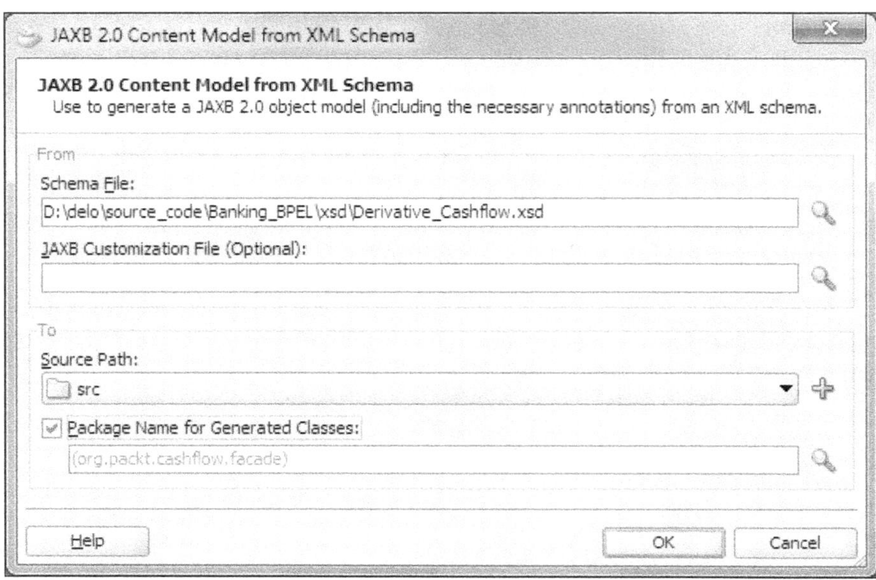

The corresponding Java classes for the XML schema were generated.

How it works...

Now compare the classes generated via the ANT utility in the *Generating XML facade using ANT* recipe with this one. In essence, the generated files are the same. However, we see the additional file `jaxb.properties`, which holds the configuration of the JAXB factory used for the generation of Java classes.

It is recommended to create the same access class (`Facade.java`) in order to simplify further access to XML facade.

See also

To explore how to build up XML facade from the WSDL document, refer to the *Creating XML facade from WSDL* recipe.

Creating XML facade from WSDL

It is possible to include the definitions of schema elements into WSDL. To overcome the extraction of XML schema content from the WSDL document, we would rather take the WSDL document and create XML facade for it. This recipe explains how to create XML facade out of the WSDL document.

Getting ready

To complete the recipe, we need the WSDL document with the XML schema definition. Luckily, we already have one automatically generated WSDL document, which we received during the **Banking_BPEL** project creation.

We will amend the already created project, so it is recommended to complete the *Generating XML facade using ANT* recipe before continuing with this recipe.

How to do it...

Here are the steps involved in creating XML façade from WSDL:

1. Open the ANT configuration file (`build.xml`) in JDeveloper.
2. We first define the property which identifies the location of the WSDL document:

```
<property name="wsdl_file" location="../Banking_BPEL/Derivative_
Cashflow.wsdl"/>
```

3. Continue with the definition of a new target inside the ANT configuration file in order to generate Java classes from the WSDL document:

```
<target name="xjc_wsdl">
  <delete dir="src/org"/>
  <mkdir dir="src/org"/>
  <echo message="Compiling the schema..." />
  <exec executable="xjc">
    <arg value="-wsdl"/>
    <arg value="${schema_file}"/>
    <arg value="-d"/>
    <arg value="${dest_dir}"/>
    <arg value="-p"/>
    <arg value="${package}"/>
  </exec>
</target>
```

4. From the configuration point of view, this step completes the recipe.
5. To run the newly defined ANT task, we select the `build.xml` file in the **Projects** pane. Then, we select the **xjc_wsdl** task in the **Structure** pane of JDeveloper, right-click on it, and select **Run Target "xjc_wsdl"**:

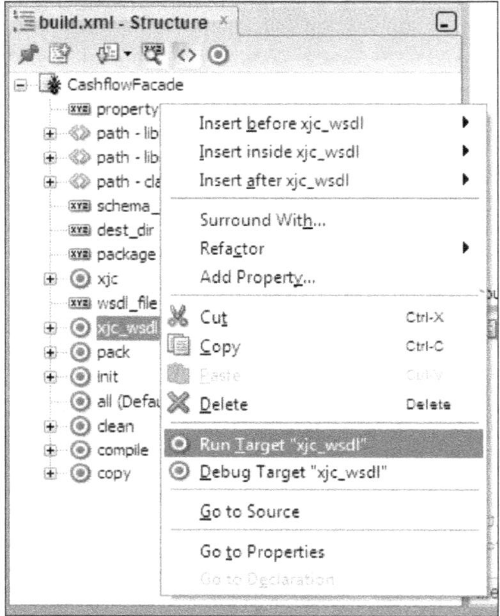

How it works...

The generation of Java representation classes from WSDL content works similar to the generation of Java classes from XSD content. Only the source of the XML input content is different from the `xjc` utility.

In case we execute the ANT task with the wrong XML or WSDL content, we receive a kind notification from the `xjc` utility. For example, if we run the utility `xjc` with the parameter `-xmlschema` over the WSDL document, we get a warning that we should use different parameters for generating XML façade from WSDL.

Note that generation of Java classes from the WSDL document via JAXB is only available through ANT task definition or the `xjc` utility. If we try the same procedure with JDeveloper, an error is reported.

See also

Now that the Java presentation of XML content is created, it is time to create a JAR (Java Archive) package for the BPEL process and provide documentation for our XML facade. The mentioned two tasks are covered in the following two corresponding recipes: *Packaging XML facade into JAR* and *Generating Java documents for XML facade*.

Packaging XML facade into JAR

This recipe explains how to prepare a package containing XML facade to be used in BPEL processes and in Java applications in general.

Getting ready

To complete this recipe, we need the XML facade created out of the XML schema. Also, the generated Java classes need to be compiled.

How to do it...

The steps involved for packaging XML façade into JAR are as follows:

1. We open the **Project Properties** by right-clicking on the **CashflowFacade** root node.
2. From the left-hand side tree, select **Deployment** and click on the **New** button. The **Create Deployment Profile** window opens where we set the name of the archive.

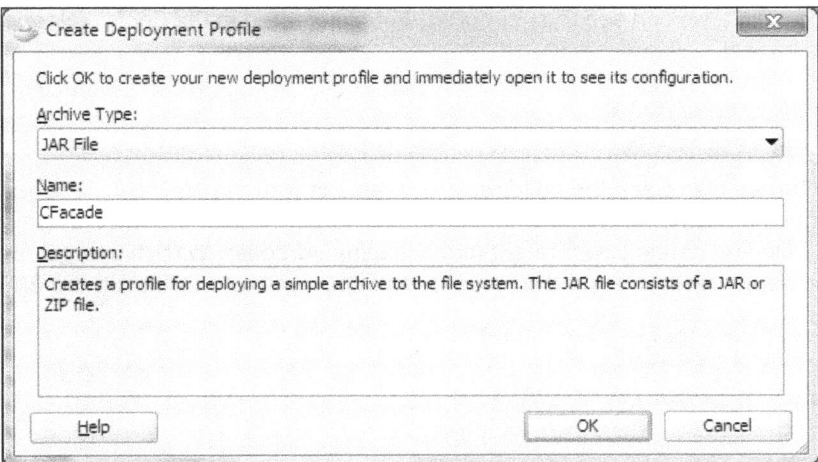

3. Click on the **OK** button. The **Edit JAR Deployment Profile Properties** dialog opens where you can configure what is going into the JAR archive. We confirm the dialog and deployment profile as we don't need any special configuration.
4. Now, we right-click on the project root node (**CashflowFacade**), then select **Deploy** and **CFacade**. The window requesting the deployment action appears. We simply confirm it by pressing the **Finish** button:

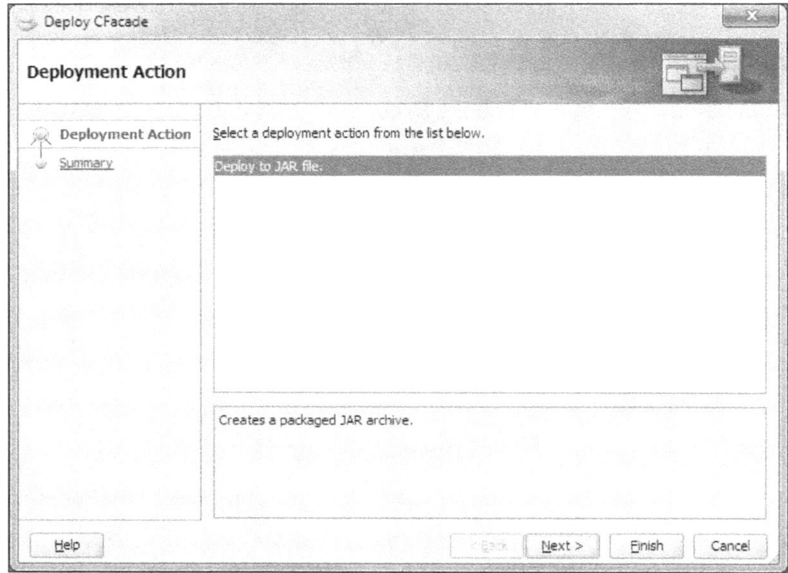

5. As a result, we can see the generated JAR file created in the deploy folder of the project.

There's more...

In this chapter, we also cover the building of XML facade with the ANT tool. To support an automatic build process, we can also define an ANT target to build the JAR file. We open the `build.xml` file and define a new target for packaging purposes. With this target, we first recreate the deploy directory and then prepare the package to be utilized in the BPEL process:

```
<target name="pack" depends="compile">
  <delete dir="deploy"/>
  <mkdir dir="deploy"/>
  <jar destfile="deploy/CFacade.jar"
     basedir="./classes"
     excludes="**/*data*"
  />
</target>
```

To automate the process even further, we define the target to copy generated JAR files to the location of the BPEL process. Usually, this means copying the JAR files to the SCA-INF/lib directory:

```
<target name="copyLib" depends="pack">
  <copy file="deploy/CFacade.jar" todir="../Banking_BPEL/SCA-
    INF/lib"/>
</target>
```

The task depends on the successful creation of a JAR package, and when the JAR package is created, it is copied over to the BPEL process library folder.

See also

Besides the generation, implementation, and packaging of XML facade, it is also a good habit to provide the documentation. This is especially helpful, when the designers of XML facade and the BPEL process are two different developers. To learn how to prepare the Java documents for XML facade, refer to the next recipe—*Generating Java documents for XML facade*.

Generating Java documents for XML facade

Well prepared documentation presents important aspect of further XML facade integration. Suppose we only receive the JAR package containing XML facade. It is virtually impossible to use XML facade if we don't know what the purpose of each data type is and how we can utilize it. With documentation, we receive a well-defined XML facade capable of integrating XML and Java worlds together. This recipe explains how to document the XML facade generated Java classes.

Getting ready

To complete this recipe, we only need the XML schema defined. We already have the XML schema in the **Banking_BPEL** project (Derivative_Cashflow.xsd).

How to do it...

Here are the steps we need to take in order to generate Java documents for XML facade:

1. We open the Derivative_Cashflow.xsd XML schema file.
2. Initially, we need to add an additional schema definition to the XML schema file:

```
<xsd:schema attributeFormDefault="unqualified"
  elementFormDefault="qualified"
  targetNamespace="http://xmlns.oracle.com/BPELFacade/Banking_
BPEL/Derivative_Cashflow"
```

```
        xmlns:xsd="http://www.w3.org/2001/XMLSchema"
    xmlns:prc="http://xmlns.oracle.com/BPELFacade/Banking_BPEL/
Derivative_Cashflow"
    xmlns:jxb="http://java.sun.com/xml/ns/jaxb" jxb:version="2.1">
</xsd:schema>
```

3. In order to put documentation at the package level, we put the following code immediately after the `<xsd:schema>` tag in the XML schema file:

```
<xsd:annotation>
  <xsd:appinfo>
    <jxb:schemaBindings>
      <jxb:package name="org.packt.cashflow.facade">
      <jxb:javadoc>This package represents the XML facade
       of the cashflows in the financial derivatives
       structure.</jxb:javadoc>
   </jxb:package>
  </jxb:schemaBindings>
 </xsd:appinfo>
</xsd:annotation>
```

4. In order to add documentation at the `complexType` level, we need to put the following lines into the XML schema file. The code goes immediately after the `complexType` definition:

```
<xsd:annotation>
  <xsd:appinfo>
    <jxb:class>
      <jxb:javadoc>This class defines the data for the
      events, when principal exchange occurs.</jxb:javadoc>
    </jxb:class>
  </xsd:appinfo>
</xsd:annotation>
```

5. The elements of the `complexType` definition are annotated in a similar way. We put the annotation data immediately after the element definition in the XML schema file:

```
<xsd:annotation>
  <xsd:appinfo>
    <jxb:property>
      <jxb:javadoc>Raw principal exchange
      date.</jxb:javadoc>
    </jxb:property>
  </xsd:appinfo>
</xsd:annotation>
```

6. In JDeveloper, we are now ready to build the `javadoc` documentation. So, select the project **CashflowFacade** root node. Then, from the main menu, select the **Build and Javadoc CashflowFacade.jpr** option. The `javadoc` content will be built in the `javadoc` directory of the project.

How it works...

During the conversion from XML schema to Java classes, JAXB is also processing possible annotations inside the XML schema file. When the conversion utility (`xjc` or execution through JDeveloper) finds the annotation in the XML schema file, it decorates the generated Java classes according to the specification.

The XML schema file must contain the following declarations. In the `<xsd:schema>` element, the following declaration of the JAXB schema namespace must exist:

```
xmlns:jxb="http://java.sun.com/xml/ns/jaxb" jxb:version="2.1"
```

Note that the `xjb:version` attribute is where the Version of the JAXB specification is defined. The most common Version declarations are 1.0, 2.0, and 2.1.

The actual definition of `javadoc` resides within the `<xsd:annotation>` and `<xsd:appinfo>` blocks. To annotate at package level, we use the following:

```
<jxb:schemaBindings>
<jxb:package name="PKG_NAME">
  <jxb:javadoc>TEXT</jxb:javadoc>
</jxb:package>
</jxb:schemaBindings>
```

We define the package name to annotate and a `javadoc` text containing the documentation for the package level.

The annotation of `javadoc` at class or attribute level is similar to the following:

```
<jxb:class|property>
 <jxb:javadoc>TEXT</jxb:javadoc>
</jxb:class|property>
```

If we want to annotate the XML schema at `complexType` level, we use the `<jaxb:class>` element. To annotate the XML schema at element level, we use the `<jaxb:property>` element.

There's more...

In many cases, we need to annotate the XML schema file directly for various reasons. The XML schema defined by different vendors is automatically generated. In such cases, we would need to annotate the XML schema each time we want to generate Java classes out of it. This would require additional work just for annotation decoration tasks.

In such situations, we can separate the annotation part of the XML schema to a separate file. With such an approach, we separate the annotating part from the XML schema content itself, over which we usually don't have control. For that purpose, we create a binding file in our **CashflowFacade** project and name it `extBinding.xjb`. We put the annotation documentation into this file and remove it from the original XML schema. We start by defining the binding file header declaration:

```
<jxb:bindings version="1.0"
        xmlns:jxb="http://java.sun.com/xml/ns/jaxb"
        xmlns:xs="http://www.w3.org/2001/XMLSchema">
  <jxb:bindings schemaLocation="file:/D:/delo/source_code/Banking_
BPEL/xsd/Derivative_Cashflow.xsd" node="/xs:schema">
```

We need to specify the name of the schema file location and the root node of the XML schema which corresponds to our mapping. We continue by declaring the package level annotation:

```
        <jxb:schemaBindings>
        <jxb:package name="org.packt.cashflow.facade">
          <jxb:javadoc><![CDATA[<body>This package represents
           the XML facade of the cashflows in the financial
           derivatives structure.</body>]]>
          </jxb:javadoc>
        </jxb:package>
        <jxb:nameXmlTransform>
          <jxb:elementName suffix="Element"/>
        </jxb:nameXmlTransform>
      </jxb:schemaBindings>
```

We notice that the structure of the package level annotation is identical to those in the inline XML schema annotation. To annotate the class and its attribute, we use the following declaration:

```
  <jxb:bindings node="//xs:complexType[@name='CashflowsType']">
   <jxb:class>
    <jxb:javadoc>
  <![CDATA[This class defines the data for the events, when
  principal exchange occurs.]]>
    </jxb:javadoc>
   </jxb:class>
     <jxb:bindings
     node=".//xs:element[@name='principalExchange']">
```

```
        <jxb:property>
         <jxb:javadoc>TEST prop</jxb:javadoc>
        </jxb:property>
      </jxb:bindings>
   </jxb:bindings>
```

Notice the indent annotation of attributes inside the class annotation that naturally correlates to the object programming paradigm.

Now that we have the external binding file, we can regenerate the XML facade.

> Note that external binding files are not used only for the creation of `javadoc`. Inside the external binding file, we can include various rules to be followed during conversion. One such rule is aimed at data type mapping; that is, which Java data type will match the XML data type.

In JDeveloper, if we are building XML facade for the first time, we follow either the *Creating XML facade from XSD* or the *Creating XML facade from WSDL* recipe. To rebuild XML facade, we use the following procedure:

1. Select the XML schema file (`Cashflow_Facade.xsd`) in the **CashflowFacade** project. Right-click on it and select the **Generate JAXB 2.0 Content Model** option.

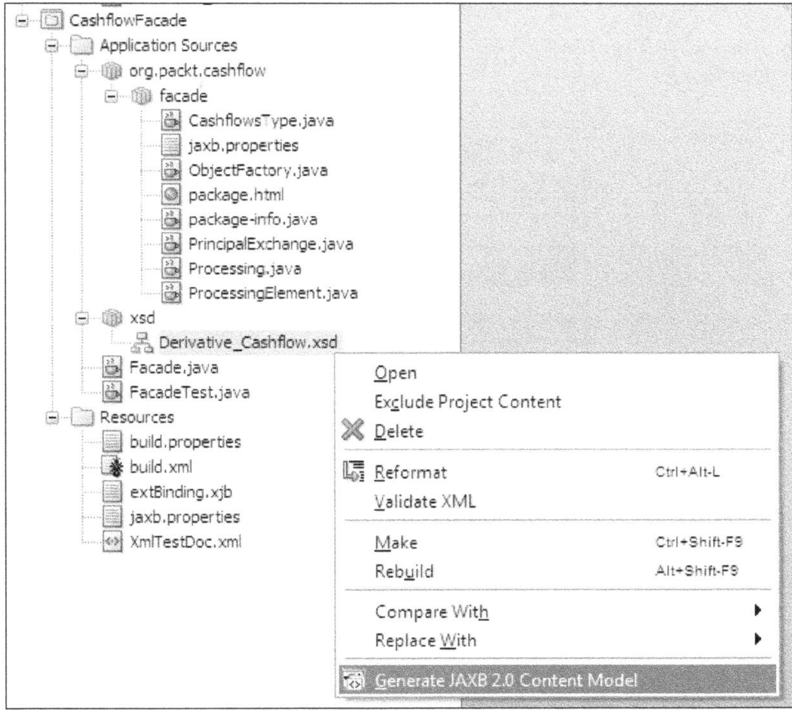

2. The configuration dialog opens with some already pre-filled fields. We enter the location of the **JAXB Customization File** (in our case, the location of the `extBinding.xjb` file) and click on the **OK** button.

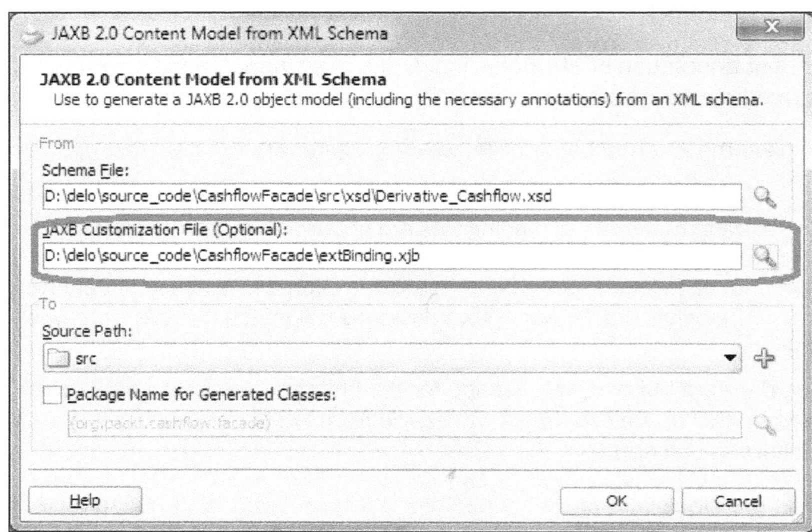

3. Next, we build the `javadoc` part to get the documentation. Now, if we open the generated documentation in the web browser, we can see our documentation lines inside.

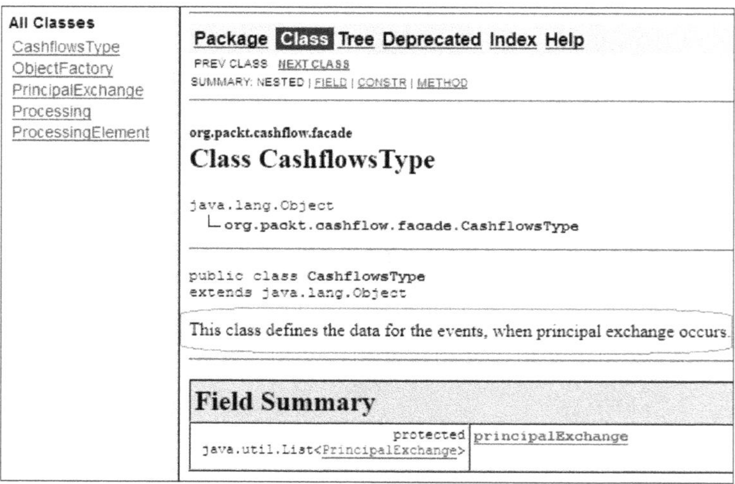

See also

Now that we have built the XML facade and prepared the `javadoc` documentation, it is time to use the XML facade in a BPEL process. We will deal with the use of XML facade in our next recipe.

Invoking XML facade from BPEL processes

This recipe explains how to use XML facade inside BPEL processes. We can use XML façade to simplify access of XML content from Java code. When using XML façade, the XML content is exposed over Java code.

Getting ready

To complete the recipe, there are no special prerequisites. Remember that in the *Packaging XML facade into JAR* recipe, we defined the ANT task to copy XML facade to the BPEL process library directory. This task basically presents all the prerequisites for XML facade utilization.

How to do it...

Open a BPEL process (`Derivative_Cashflow.bpel`) in JDeveloper and insert the Java Embedding activity into it:

1. We first insert a code snippet. The whole code snippet is enclosed by a try catch block:

   ```
   try {
   ```

2. Read the input cashflow variable data:

   ```
   oracle.xml.parser.v2.XMLElement input_cf= (oracle.xml.parser.
   v2.XMLElement)getVariableData("inputVariable","payload","/
   client:Cashflows");
   ```

3. Un-marshall the XML content through the XML facade:

   ```
     Object obj_cf = facade.Facade.createFacade("org.packt.cashflow.
   facade", input_cf);
   ```

4. We must cast the serialized object to the XML facade class:

   ```
   javax.xml.bind.JAXBElement<org.packt.cashflow.facade.
   CashflowsType> cfs = (javax.xml.bind.JAXBElement<org.packt.
   cashflow.facade.CashflowsType>)obj_cf;
   ```

5. Retrieve the Java class out of the `JAXBElement` content class:

```
org.packt.cashflow.facade.CashflowsType cf= cfs.getValue();
```

6. Finally, we close the try block and handle any exceptions that may occur during processing:

```
} catch (Exception e) {
  e.printStackTrace();
  addAuditTrailEntry("Error in XML facade occurred: " +
e.getMessage());
}
```

7. We close the **Java Embedding** activity dialog. Now, we are ready to deploy the BPEL process and test the XML facade.

Actually, the execution of the BPEL process will not produce any output, since we have no output lines defined. In case some exception occurs, we will receive information about the exception in the audit trail as well as the BPEL server console.

How it works...

We add the XML facade JAR file to the BPEL process library directory (`<BPEL_process_home>\SCA-INF\lib`). Before we are able to access the XML facade classes, we need to extract the XML content from the BPEL process. To create the Java representation classes, we transform the XML content through the JAXB context. As a result, we receive an un-marshalled Java class ready to be used further in Java code.

See also

To learn how to access various variables inside an un-marshalled Java class, refer to the following two recipes: *Accessing simple types through XML facade* and *Accessing complex types through XML facade*.

Accessing complex types through XML facade

The advantage of using XML facade is to provide the ability to access the XML content via Java classes and methods. This recipe explains how to access the complex types through XML facade.

Getting ready

To complete the recipe, we will amend the example BPEL process from the *Invoking XML facade from BPEL processes* recipe.

How to do it...

The steps involved in accessing the complex types through XML façade are as follows:

1. Open the `Banking_BPEL` process and double-click on the `XML_facade_node` Java Embedding activity.
2. We amend the code snippet with the following code to access the complex type:

   ```
   java.util.List<org.packt.cashflow.facade.PrincipalExchange>
   princEx= cf.getPrincipalExchange();
   ```

3. We receive a list of principal exchange cash flows that contain various data.

How it works...

In the previous example, we receive a list of cash flows. The corresponding XML content definition states:

```
<xsd:complexType name="PrincipalExchange">
  <xsd:sequence>
  </xsd:sequence>
  <xsd:attribute name="id" type="xsd:int"/>
</xsd:complexType>
```

We can conclude that each of the principle exchange cash flows is modeled as an individual Java class.

Depending on the hierarchy level of the complex type, it is modeled either as a Java class or as a Java class member. Complex types are organized in the Java object hierarchy according to the XML schema definition. Mostly, complex types can be modeled as a Java class and at the same time as a member of an other Java class.

See also

We can now access XML complex types through XML facade. To learn how to access simple types over XML facade, refer to our next recipe, *Accessing simple types through XML facade*.

Accessing simple types through XML facade

This recipe explains how to access simple types through XML facade.

Getting ready

To complete the recipe, we will amend the example BPEL process from our previous recipe, *Accessing complex types through XML facade*.

How to do it...

1. Open the **Banking_BPEL** process and double-click on the **XML_facade_node** Java Embedding activity.
2. We amend the code snippet with the code to access the XML simple types:

```
for (org.packt.cashflowfacade.PrincipalExchange pe: princEx) {
  addAuditTrailEntry("Received cashflow with id: " + pe.getId() +
"\n" +
            "  Unadj. Principal Exch. Date ...: " + pe.getUnadjust
edPrincipalExchangeDate() + "\n" +
            "  Adj. Principal Exch. Date .....: " + pe.getAdjusted
PrincipalExchangeDate() + "\n" +
            "  Discount factor ...............: " +
pe.getDiscountFactor() + "\n" +
            "  Principal Exch. Amount ........: " +
pe.getPrincipalExchangeAmount() + "\n"
            );
}
```

3. With the preceding code, we output all Java class members to the audit trail. Now if we run the BPEL process, we can see the following part of output in the BPEL flow trace:

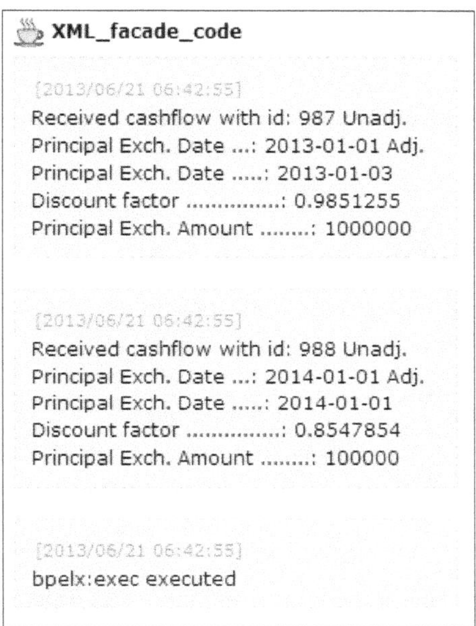

XML_facade_code
[2013/06/21 06:42:55]
Received cashflow with id: 987 Unadj.
Principal Exch. Date ...: 2013-01-01 Adj.
Principal Exch. Date .....: 2013-01-03
Discount factor ....: 0.9851255
Principal Exch. Amount ....: 1000000
[2013/06/21 06:42:55]
Received cashflow with id: 988 Unadj.
Principal Exch. Date ...: 2014-01-01 Adj.
Principal Exch. Date .....: 2014-01-01
Discount factor ....: 0.8547854
Principal Exch. Amount ....: 100000
[2013/06/21 06:42:55]
bpelx:exec executed

How it works...

The XML schema simple types are mapped to Java classes as members. If we check our example, we have three simple types in the XML schema:

```
<xsd:complexType name="PrincipalExchange">
  <xsd:sequence>
   <xsd:element minOccurs="0" name="unadjustedPrincipalExchangeDate" 
type="xsd:date"/>
   <xsd:element minOccurs="0" name="adjustedPrincipalExchangeDate" 
type="xsd:date"/>
   <xsd:element minOccurs="0" name="principalExchangeAmount" 
type="xsd:decimal"/>
   <xsd:element minOccurs="0" name="discountFactor" 
type="xsd:decimal"/>
  </xsd:sequence>
  <xsd:attribute name="id" type="xsd:int"/>
</xsd:complexType>
```

The simple types defined in the XML schema are `<xsd:date>`, `<xsd:decimal>`, and `<xsd:int>`. Let us find the corresponding Java class member definitions. Open the `PrincipalExchange.java` file. The definition of members we can see is as follows:

```
@XmlSchemaType(name = "date")
protected XMLGregorianCalendar unadjustedPrincipalExchangeDate;
@XmlSchemaType(name = "date")
protected XMLGregorianCalendar adjustedPrincipalExchangeDate;
protected BigDecimal principalExchangeAmount;
protected BigDecimal discountFactor;
@XmlAttribute
protected Integer id;
```

We can see that the mapping between the XML content and the Java classes was performed as shown in the following table:

XML schema simple type	Java class member
`<xsd:date>`	`javax.xml.datatype.XMLGregorianCalendar`
`<xsd:decimal>`	`java.math.BigDecimal`
`<xsd:int>`	`java.lang.Integer`

Also, we can identify that the XML simple type definitions as well as the XML attributes are always mapped as members in corresponding Java class representations.

11
Exposing Java Code as a Web Service

This chapter contains the following recipes:

- Creating a service endpoint interface
- Using non-exposable methods of service interface
- Annotating the service endpoint interface with `@WebService`
- Annotating the service endpoint interface with `@SOAPBinding`
- Wrapping exceptions into faults
- Defining a request wrapper for a web service
- Defining a response wrapper for a web service
- Defining a one or two way web service
- Defining the direction of the parameters
- Publishing a web service without an application server

Introduction

Real production environments still operate on many legacy applications that are written in a variety of programming languages. As the adaptation of the applications for integration presents a big work effort and costs a lot of money, a better approach is to expose the application functionality through API and web services. Other mechanisms for integration are also mentioned in this book, such as REST, JMS, EJB, and so on. This way, however, it is easier to integrate other applications with legacy application, as we can integrate different applications in a technology-neutral manner. Also, we can take advantage of other web service features such as interoperability and reusability.

As this book addresses Java and BPEL, we cover the aspects of how to expose the already existing Java code as a web service. To some extent, we already covered this in *Chapter 8, Exposing Java Code as a SOAP Service*. We start by defining the service interface which presents the entry point for other applications to integrate. The rest of the recipes cover usage of annotations for web service decoration. The last recipe shows you how to publish a web service without using an application server. In the early stages, such publishing might present a much better alternative as opposed to using an application server.

Throughout this chapter, we will work on the sample application we have prepared. The sample presents a simplified version of a credit card gateway for processing purchases, refunding, and voiding operations. The application consists of the following two components:

- A credit card operations module (`CreditCardGateway.java`): Operators are able to perform various operations. We omit the user interface design for simplicity.
- A backend operations module (`BackEndSystem.java`): Presents the core of the credit card operations.

Throughout the recipes, we will explore the ways in which to expose functionality of the sample application as a web service in order to enable credit card operations by other parties automatically without human intervention.

Creating a service endpoint interface

This recipe explains how to create a service endpoint interface. A **Service Endpoint Interface** (**SEI**) is used in Java for exposing JavaBeans as web services, or more accurately, SEI defines the methods of Java code to be exposed as web services. The interface class must extend the `java.rmi.Remote` interface and all methods of the interface must throw `java.rmi.RemoteException`.

How to do it...

In our example application, the most appropriate part of the application to expose is the credit card operations module. It already contains all the relevant methods that we want to expose:

1. We right-click on `CreditCardGateway.java` in JDeveloper.
2. Select **Create Web Service...**. The **Create Web Service** wizard opens at Step 2:

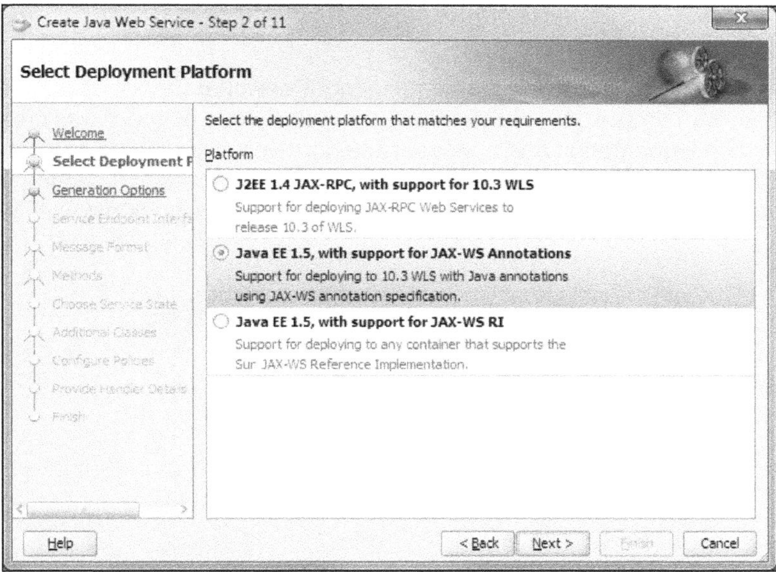

3. Select **Next**, and on the next page, select **Add SEI**. Then, click on **Finish**.

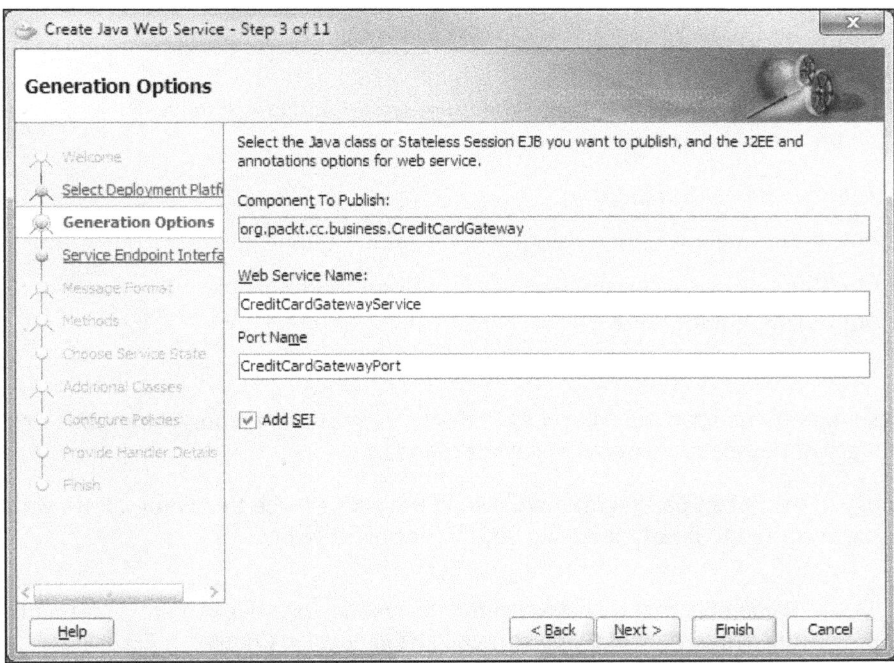

4. We have now generated a web service ready to be deployed.

How it works...

Let us first start by checking the new elements in the JDeveloper project as a result of web service creation. We can see a new node where the web service element was created. There is a web service implementation and a web service port type class. We can also inspect the WSDL of the web service by right-clicking on the web service class and selecting **Show WSDL for Web Service Annotations** in JDeveloper. Another element presents the web content with a `web.xml` file, which indicates that we deploy our web service as an application.

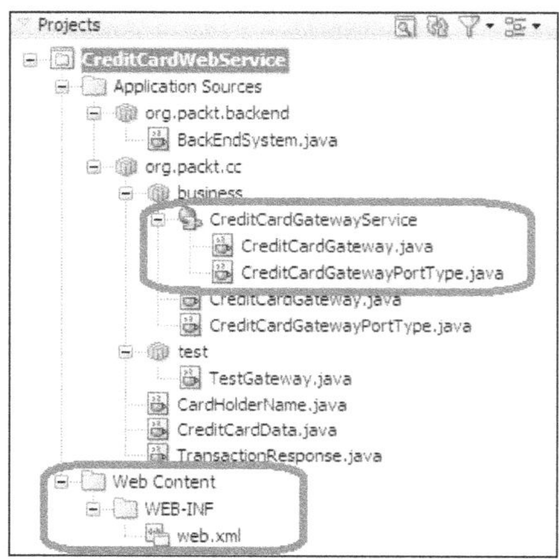

If we deploy a web service to the Oracle SOA Suite server and check its WSDL document, we can see the following operations exposed:

- `AuthoriseCreditCard`
- `Purchase`
- `Refund`
- `OutputTransactions`
- `Void`

All of these operations have public access in the `JavaBean` definition. All methods marked as private are not exposed as web service operations.

The analogy to the object paradigm exists also in the web service technology. If we want the method in `JavaBean` to be exposed, we have to declare it public.

Remember that we have covered the creation of a deployment profile and the deployment of a web service itself in detail in *Chapter 8, Exposing Java Code as a SOAP Service* in the *Publishing a web service* recipe.

Using non-exposable methods of service interface

This recipe explains the usage of methods that are not exposed through a web service interface. These methods are private to the web service implementation and cannot be used for integration through the web service mechanism. In the Java code, such methods have `private` access as well.

How to do it...

In the `CreditCardGateway` class, , we implement the `Void` credit card operation which checks whether the credit card data is authorized and if a possibility of fraud exists. If the transaction is accepted, then we forward the request of the backend system.

```
public TransactionResponse Void(String token, BigDecimal amount) {
  if ( isAuthorised(token) && isFraud(token) ) {
    BackEndSystem.getInstance().voidOp(UUID.fromString(token), 
amount);
    return new TransactionResponse("Success.", 20002, token);
  } else {
    return new TransactionResponse("Authorization invalid or fraud 
suspect.", 9997, null);
  }
}
```

As a result of the transaction, we send the operation data back to the client.

How it works...

We can see the following two methods in the previous code snippet:

- `isAuthorised`
- `isFraud`

These two methods have a private scope in the `CreditCardGateway` class and likewise are not exposed as a web service operation.

Furthermore, the `BackEndSystem.getInstance().voidOp` call implements the a to the public method of a backend system, which is not exposed as a web service operation either.

We can see that with `JavaBean`, we can freely decide what public methods will become available and are exposed as web service operations.

Annotating the service endpoint interface with @WebService

This recipe explains the possibilities of annotating a service endpoint interface with the `@WebService` annotation. In the *Annotating Java code for web service creation* recipe in *Chapter 8, Exposing Java Code as a SOAP Service*, we covered a similar topic. Here, we provide a more in-depth view of the `@WebService` annotation and explore the parameters we can set for the `@WebService` annotation.

Getting ready

In this recipe, we will continue the development of the web service from the *Creating a service endpoint interface* recipe in this chapter.

How to do it...

Here are the steps we need to perform to annotate the SEI with the `@WebService` annotation:

1. Right-click on the web service class (`org.packt.cc.business.CCGateSvc`) and select the **Properties...** option in JDeveloper. The **Java Web Service Editor** opens where you can configure the web service creation process.

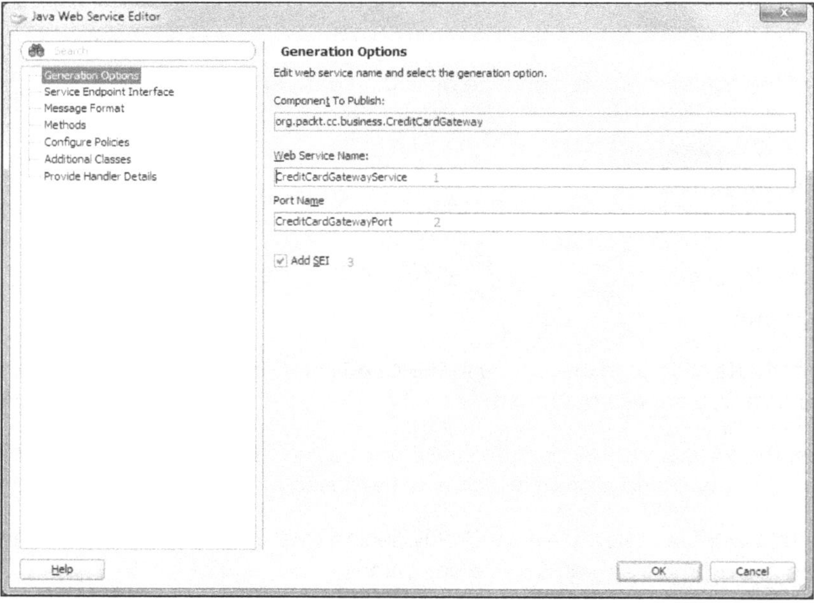

2. Enter `CCGateSvc` as the service name and `CCGateSvcPort` as the service port name.
3. In the **General Options** section, we can configure the web service name, its port name, and check the service endpoint interface.
4. Furthermore, in the **Service Endpoint Interface** dialog box, we configure the SEI parameters.

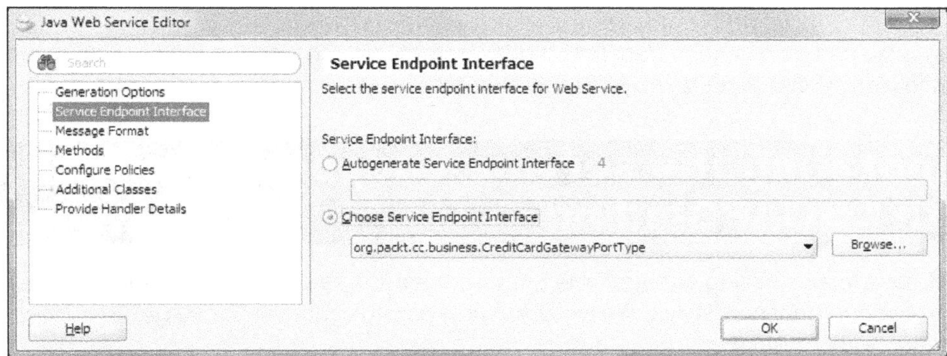

5. Select the **Autogenerate Service Endpoint Interface** option and enter `org.packt.cc.business.CCGatePortType`.

How it works...

Remember before we started changing the web service, the definition of the web service in `CreditCardGateway.java` was:

```
@WebService(endpointInterface = "org.packt.cc.business.
CreditCardGatewayPortType")
```

The new definition of the web service is given here:

```
@WebService(serviceName = "CCGateSvc", portName = "CCGateSvcPort",
endpointInterface = "org.packt.cc.business.CCGatePortType")
```

By changing the service name (1) in the **Java Web Service Editor**, we set the **serviceName** attribute in the `@WebService` annotation. When we change the port name (2) in the **Java Web Service Editor**, we set the **portName** attribute in the `@WebService` annotation. By checking the **Add SEI** checkbox (3), we add the SEI into the JDeveloper project. Finally, autogenerate SEI name (4) in the **Java Web Service Editor** affects the `endpointInterface` attribute in the `@WebService` annotation.

The `@WebService` annotation also has the ability to set the `name` (holding information about the web service name), `targetNamespace` (identifies the namespace of the web service), and `wsdlLocation` (when we have WSDL already defined, we set this attribute to point to it). It is not possible to set attributes in JDeveloper, however we can set them manually.

See also

To learn how to define various transport modes, refer to the *Annotating the service endpoint interface with @SOAPBinding* recipe in this chapter.

Annotating the service endpoint interface with @SOAPBinding

This recipe explains how to annotate the SEI with the `@SOAPBinding` annotation in order to support various transport styles. We will also show how to configure the `@SOAPBinding` annotation with JDeveloper.

Getting ready

In this recipe, we will configure the web service from the *Annotating the service endpoint interface with @WebService* recipe in this chapter.

How to do it...

The steps involved in annotating a web service with `@SOAPBinding` from JDeveloper are as follows:

1. Right-click on the web service class (`org.packt.cc.business.CCGateSvc`) and select the **Properties...** option in JDeveloper to open the **Java Web Service Editor**.

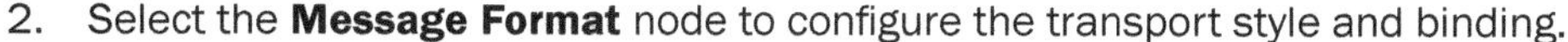

2. Select the **Message Format** node to configure the transport style and binding.

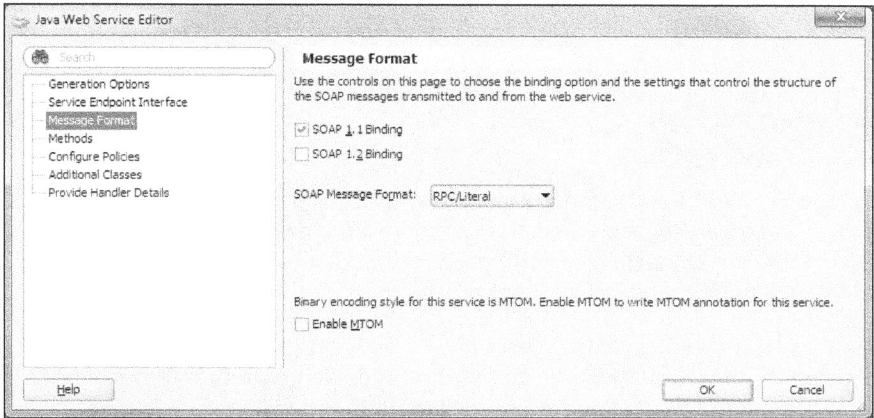

3. Select the **RPC/Literal** option and click on the **OK** button.

How it works...

The default SOAP message binding and style combination is document/wrapped, and as such it does not need the `@SOAPBinding` annotation for the web service.

When setting other binding and style combinations for the web service, we get the web service with the `@SOAPBinding` annotation. For `RPC/literal` binding style, we get the following annotation generated in `CCGatePortType.java`:

```
@SOAPBinding(style = SOAPBinding.Style.RPC)
```

[We have described the `@SOAPBinding` annotation in detail in the *Creating LITERAL and ENCODED web services* recipe in *Chapter 8, Exposing Java Code as a SOAP Service.*]

Wrapping exceptions into faults

This recipe explains the definition of faults in web services. Faults are one of the fundamental concepts of handling errors in web services. Usually, web services throw an exception as a result of an unsuccessful operation. This recipe will explain how to define faults for an operation in case of a date format mismatch.

Getting ready

In this recipe, we will amend the implementation of our web service example from the *Annotating the service endpoint interface with @SOAPBinding* recipe.

How to do it...

We will change the source code of our example so that it will throw an exception in case there is a problem with processing a credit card operation. Now, if we run the example, even if the authorization fails, the processing is performed further. A more correct approach would be to handle faults and stop processing if a fault occurs.

We open the `CreditCardGateway.java` file in JDeveloper and search for the `AuthoriseCreditCard` method. We change the code so that it throws the exception if the expiry date cannot be recognized. An excerpt of the modified code is next:

```
public TransactionResponse AuthoriseCreditCard(CreditCardData ccd,
BigDecimal amount) throws Exception {

  try {
    .
    Date today = new Date();
    Date date = new SimpleDateFormat("MM/yy", Locale.ENGLISH).
parse(expiry);
    .
  } catch (ParseException e) {
    throw new Exception("Unable to parse date.");
  }

  return new TransactionResponse("Success.", 10000, UUID.randomUUID().
toString());
}
```

Right-click on the web service node in JDeveloper and select **Regenerate Web Service from Source**. As a result, we get newly annotated Java code.

How it works...

We identify no change regarding the annotations in the code and also WSDL remains the same. However, deploying and running the web service now captures the fault in case of problems with parsing the expiry date.

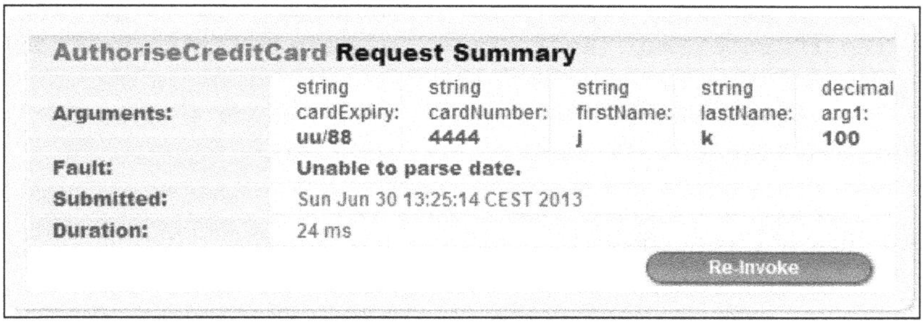

AuthoriseCreditCard Request Summary

Arguments:	string cardExpiry: **uu/88**	string cardNumber: **4444**	string firstName: **j**	string lastName: **k**	decimal arg1: **100**
Fault:	**Unable to parse date.**				
Submitted:	Sun Jun 30 13:25:14 CEST 2013				
Duration:	24 ms				

Re-Invoke

There's more...

We used the `Exception` class in order to throw the exceptions. Usually, it is recommended to use a named exception as they bring more expressiveness to the integration plus the additional possibility for the BPEL process to use the `<catch>` activity which captures name exceptions/faults. We will create a named exception and use it for the same purpose; that is, parsing dates.

We create a new class in JDeveloper and name it `ExpiryDateException`. We override the default constructors of the `Exception` class.

Now, we change the `AuthoriseCreditCard` method signature of the `CreditCardGateway` class, as shown in the following code snippet:

```
public TransactionResponse AuthoriseCreditCard(CreditCardData ccd,
BigDecimal amount) throws ExpiryDateException {
and change the catch part of the exception handling:
  } catch (ParseException e) {
    throw new ExpiryDateException("Unable to parse date.");
    //e.printStackTrace();
    //return new TransactionResponse("Expiry date invalid.",
        1002, null);
}
```

Originally, the fault thrown from the web service was as follows:

```
<detail>
  <ns2:exception xmlns:ns2="http://jax-ws.dev.java.net/" class="java.
lang.Exception">
    <message>Unable to parse date.</message>
    <ns2:stackTrace>
```

```
        <ns2:frame class="org.packt.cc.business.CreditCardGateway"
file="CreditCardGateway.java" line="54" method="AuthoriseCreditCard"
/>
      </ns2:stackTrace>
    </ns2:exception>
  </detail>
```

With the newly defined exception, the fault information gets slightly different and more informative:

```
<detail>
  <ns2:exception xmlns:ns2="http://jax-ws.dev.java.net/" class="org.
packt.cc.exception.ExpiryDateException">
    <message>Unable to parse date.</message>
    <ns2:stackTrace>
      <ns2:frame class="org.packt.cc.business.CreditCardGateway"
file="CreditCardGateway.java" line="53" method="AuthoriseCreditCard"
/>
    </ns2:stackTrace>
  </ns2:exception>
</detail>
```

Defining a request wrapper for a web service

This recipe describes a method of defining a request wrapper for a web service that is built from Java code. A request wrapper is used by the marshalling process and specifies the bean that is used at runtime. This approach is used in most scenarios when we start developing a web service out of WSDL and want to provide a different Java implementation code.

Getting ready

In this recipe, we will build upon the example from the *Wrapping exceptions into faults* recipe.

How to do it...

We create a new wrapper class in JDeveloper and name it `AuthoriseRequest`. The content of the class is trivial; it contains two members and its getter/setter methods. The annotations of the class are more interesting:

```
@XmlAccessorType(XmlAccessType.FIELD)
@XmlType(name = "auth", propOrder = {
  "ccd",
```

```
    "amount"
})
public class AuthoriseRequest {
```

With these annotations, we define the XML complex type `auth` with two members: `ccd` and `amount`.

Now we open the `CCGatePortType` class because we need to annotate the `AuthoriseCreditCard` method. We first annotate the parameters of the operation with the `@WebParam` annotation. We continue by annotating the method with the `@RequestWrapper` annotation:

```
@RequestWrapper(localName = "auth", className = "org.packt.
cc.business.AuthoriseRequest", targetNamespace = "http://www.
mastercard.com/proc/")
@WebMethod
public TransactionResponse AuthoriseCreditCard(
  @WebParam(name = "ccd") CreditCardData ccd,
  @WebParam(name = "amount") BigDecimal amount) throws
RemoteException;
```

That is it. The request wrapper is defined and we can now use the modified WSDL definition when calling the web service.

How it works...

Usually, the request wrapper is used when the web service is generated from the WSDL document. However, this does not stop us from using a similar approach when building a web service from Java code.

Now, compare the WSDL definition of the `AuthoriseCreditCard` operation messages before using the request wrapper and after the change. Before the code change, the definition of the request message was as follows:

```
<xs:element name="AuthoriseCreditCard" type="tns:AuthoriseCreditCa
rd"/>
<xs:complexType name="AuthoriseCreditCard">
  <xs:sequence>
    <xs:element name="ccd" type="tns:creditCardData" minOccurs="0"/>
    <xs:element name="amount" type="xs:decimal" minOccurs="0"/>
  </xs:sequence>
</xs:complexType>
```

After the change, we can see a difference in the request message definition:

```
<xs:schema xmlns:ns1="http://business.cc.packt.org/" xmlns:xs="http://
www.w3.org/2001/XMLSchema" version="1.0" targetNamespace="http://www.
mastercard.com/proc/">
 <xs:import namespace="http://business.cc.packt.org/"
schemaLocation="http://localhost:7101/CreditCardGateway-
CreditCardWebService-context-root/CCGateSvcPort?xsd=2"/>
 <xs:element name="auth" nillable="true" type="ns1:auth"/>
</xs:schema>

<xs:complexType name="auth">
 <xs:sequence>
  <xs:element name="ccd" type="tns:creditCardData" minOccurs="0"/>
  <xs:element name="amount" type="xs:decimal" minOccurs="0"/>
 </xs:sequence>
</xs:complexType>
```

We can see that the name of the request message was changed. The names of the parameters remain the same because we did not change them. Since we defined a namespace in the `@RequestWrapper` annotation, a new schema definition was created in order to support the new element.

See also

To learn how to define a response wrapper, refer to our next recipe—*Defining a response wrapper for a web service*.

Defining a response wrapper for a web service

This recipe explains how to define a response wrapper for a web service. Similar to the request wrapper, we can also define a response wrapper for a web service operation. As with the request wrapper, the response wrapper is used by the marshalling process to provide proper conversion between Java code and XML content at runtime.

Getting ready

In this recipe, we will amend the example from the *Defining a request wrapper for a web service* recipe.

How to do it...

We start this recipe in a similar way to how we started the *Defining a request wrapper for a web service* recipe. Create a new class named `AuthoriseResponse` in JDeveloper. We omit the getter and setter methods, so the final code of the class is as follows:

```
@XmlAccessorType(XmlAccessType.FIELD)
@XmlType(name = "AuthoriseResponse", propOrder = {
    "response"
})
public class AuthoriseResponse {

  @XmlElement(name = "return")
  private TransactionResponse response;

    public AuthoriseResponse() {
  }
}
```

We annotate the class to define the XML structure of the response message. We also annotate the private member `response` to become a return XML element.

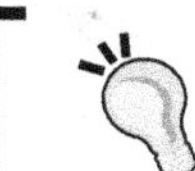

> Note that a prerequisite for the member of a response wrapper name is `return`. As `return` is a reserved word in Java language, we must annotate the member variable with the `@XmlElement` annotation.

In cases where we don't specify the return XML element, we receive the following error at deployment time:

```
javax.xml.bind.JAXBException: return is not a valid property on class
org.packt.cc.business.AuthoriseResponse
```

How it works...

As with the request wrapper, we notify the changes in the WSDL document in the response wrapper.

Without the `@ResponseWrapper` annotation, the response for our operation in WSDL looks like the following snippet:

```
<xs:element name="AuthoriseCreditCardResponse" type="tns:AuthoriseCred
itCardResponse"/>

<xs:complexType name="AuthoriseCreditCardResponse">
 <xs:sequence>
```

```
    <xs:element name="return" type="tns:transactionResponse"
minOccurs="0"/>
  </xs:sequence>
</xs:complexType>
```

The response message consists of an XML element that holds the response information. With the annotated source code, the WSDL document is modified to the following:

```
<xs:element name="authResponse" nillable="true"
type="ns1:AuthoriseResponse"/>

<xs:complexType name="AuthoriseResponse">
  <xs:sequence>
    <xs:element name="return" type="tns:transactionResponse"
minOccurs="0"/>
  </xs:sequence>
</xs:complexType>
```

The response element is created in a separate XML schema, as we defined the namespace to be different from the web service. Also, the name of the XML type that holds the response information has changed from `AuthoriseCreditCardResponse` to `AuthoriseResponse`.

Defining a one or two way web service

This recipe explains how to define a one or two way web service. You might think that the title is misguided since all methods are by default exposed as two way web services. With that in mind, we will focus more on defining a one way web service.

How to do it...

We will define the `OutputTransactions` method as a one way operation of a web service. Open the `CCGatePortType` class in JDeveloper. Put the `@OneWay` annotation next to the `OutputTransaction` method:

```
@WebMethod
@Oneway
public void OutputTransactions() throws RemoteException;
```

That is it. With this annotation, the web service operation will become a one way operation, meaning the client will not wait for the response.

How it works...

The best way to see how the one way annotation works is through the WSDL document web service using expose operations. If we have default behavior (that is, two way web service operations), there is the following signature of operation in the WSDL document:

```
<operation name="OutputTransactions">
  <input message="tns:OutputTransactions"/>
  <output message="tns:OutputTransactionsResponse"/>
</operation>
```

We see that in both request and response message definitions, even the method itself does not return anything, as in two-way mode, the client waits for a web service response. We modified the code of the `OutputTransactions` method so that it sleeps for 5 seconds before printing the transaction. This is for testing purposes so that we can show how one way invocation works. Let us invoke the `OutputTransaction` operation and observe the web server console window. The client window is seen as follows:

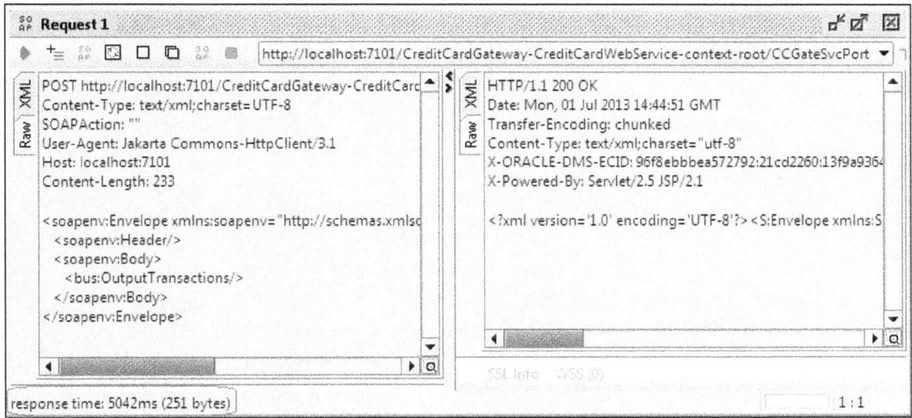

The output from the server console shows:

```
-----------------------------
Performed transactions:  Mon Jul 01 16:44:56 CEST 2013
-----------------------------
```

We can see that the response time took 5042 ms, which means that the client waited the while whole time the web service was processing a request.

Now let us try the same with the `@OneWay` annotated web service. The execution of the `OutputTransaction` operation shows:

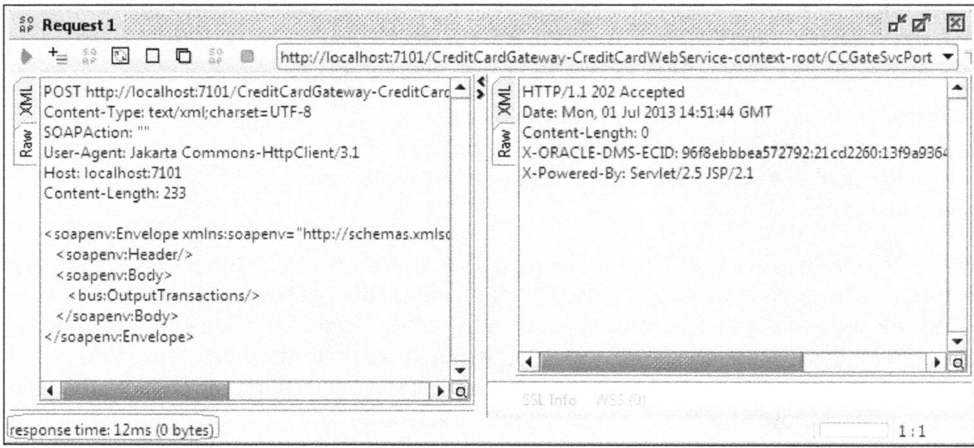

The server console output now shows the following:

```
-----------------------------
Performed transactions:  Mon Jul 01 16:51:49 CEST 2013
-----------------------------
```

The client request now lasts 12 ms and the processing of the client is continued.

> Note that the `@OneWay` annotation should not be mixed with the asynchronous operation of a web service. Clients calling `@OneWay` annotated web service operations do not expect any response. On the other hand, clients calling asynchronous web service operations do expect a response in some part of the code. The request is either queued or somehow stored for later reference. This usually happens with long-running calls and on systems with heavy loads.

Defining the direction of the parameters

This recipe explains how to set different direction annotation attributes for the web service operation parameters. With the direction of the parameters, we define the flow of the values between web service and client. To receive more than one value from a web service, we have several possibilities. We can define a Java class that is returned by the method. We can also return values through return parameters as well as over method input parameters (value by reference). When using the last scenario, the annotation for defining parameter direction comes in handy.

Getting ready

In this recipe, we will amend the example from the *Defining a one or two way web service* recipe.

How to do it...

The direction of parameters is defined through the port type. We first open the `CCGatePortType` class. We will add annotations to the `Refund` method:

```
@WebMethod
@WebResult(name = "RefundResponse")
public TransactionResponse Refund(@WebParam(name = "token", mode =
WebParam.Mode.IN) String token,
                    @WebParam(name = "amount", mode = WebParam.Mode.
INOUT) Holder<BigDecimal> amount) throws RemoteException;
```

We changed the `Refund` method code as well so that it deduces the fee from the amount to be refunded, which is omitted due to no relevance to the current recipe.

How it works...

In this recipe, we used the `@WebParam` annotation. For the direction of the parameters, we set the `mode` attribute. The meaning of the `mode` attribute is as follows:

- `WebParam.Mode.IN`: The direction of the parameters is strictly input, meaning we expect no value changes to the input variable.
- `WebParam.Mode.OUT`: The direction of the parameters is strictly transferring results to the output. This means there is no real expected input value, however an output value is expected.
- `WebParam.Mode.INOUT`: The direction of parameters is input and output. We set the value to the parameter at the input and we also expect a value at its output.

When applying the `WebParam.Mode.OUT` or `WebParam.Mode.INOUT` mode, we need to use the `Handler` class instead of regular method variable declarations. The `Handler` class takes care of transferring values from and to the operation parameter.

By comparing the WSDL document of the deployed web service before and after the code change, it shows the difference in the `RefundResponse` complex type definition:

```
<xs:complexType name="RefundResponse">
 <xs:sequence>
  <xs:element name="amount" type="xs:decimal" minOccurs="0"/>
```

```
    <xs:element name="RefundResponse" type="tns:transactionResponse"
minOccurs="0"/>
   </xs:sequence>
  </xs:complexType>
```

We can see that a new `element` amount is present in the response message definition. The cause lies in the fact that the `amount` parameter is defined as an input and output parameter in Java code.

Publishing a web service without an application server

This recipe explains the method of exposing a web service to clients without deploying it to the application server.

How to do it...

In Java code, we create the web service publisher class and name it as `PublisherCCGateway`.

Do not forget to check the **Main Method** option in the **Create Java Class** wizard in JDeveloper.

We enter the following Java code into the newly created class:

```
public class PublisherCCGateway {

  public static void main(String[] args) {
    Endpoint.publish("http://localhost:9999/cc/gateway", new
CreditCardGateway());
  }
}
```

We can now run the web service publisher as a normal Java application.

How it works...

The `javax.xml.ws.Endpoint` class is part of Java SE 6. With the help of this class, we are able to publish the web service without the use of an application server. The web service is packed and published in the JVM HTTP server built in Java SE 6. With the help of the `publish()` method, we define the web service endpoint along with the port and provide the web service implementation class. More information about the Endpoint class can be accessed at the following URLs:

- `http://docs.oracle.com/javase/6/docs/api/javax/xml/ws/Endpoint.html`
- The web service is published via the JAX-WS mechanism to the following address: `http://localhost:9999/cc/gateway`
- We can access the WSDL document at the well-known extension to the main address: `http://localhost:9999/cc/gateway?wsdl`

Index

X

Thank you for buying
BPEL and Java Cookbook

About Packt Publishing

Packt, pronounced 'packed', published its first book "*Mastering phpMyAdmin for Effective MySQL Management*" in April 2004 and subsequently continued to specialize in publishing highly focused books on specific technologies and solutions.

Our books and publications share the experiences of your fellow IT professionals in adapting and customizing today's systems, applications, and frameworks. Our solution-based books give you the knowledge and power to customize the software and technologies you're using to get the job done. Packt books are more specific and less general than the IT books you have seen in the past. Our unique business model allows us to bring you more focused information, giving you more of what you need to know, and less of what you don't.

Packt is a modern, yet unique publishing company, which focuses on producing quality, cutting-edge books for communities of developers, administrators, and newbies alike. For more information, please visit our website: `www.PacktPub.com`.

About Packt Enterprise

In 2010, Packt launched two new brands, Packt Enterprise and Packt Open Source, in order to continue its focus on specialization. This book is part of the Packt Enterprise brand, home to books published on enterprise software – software created by major vendors, including (but not limited to) IBM, Microsoft and Oracle, often for use in other corporations. Its titles will offer information relevant to a range of users of this software, including administrators, developers, architects, and end users.

Writing for Packt

We welcome all inquiries from people who are interested in authoring. Book proposals should be sent to `author@packtpub.com`. If your book idea is still at an early stage and you would like to discuss it first before writing a formal book proposal, contact us; one of our commissioning editors will get in touch with you.

We're not just looking for published authors; if you have strong technical skills but no writing experience, our experienced editors can help you develop a writing career, or simply get some additional reward for your expertise.

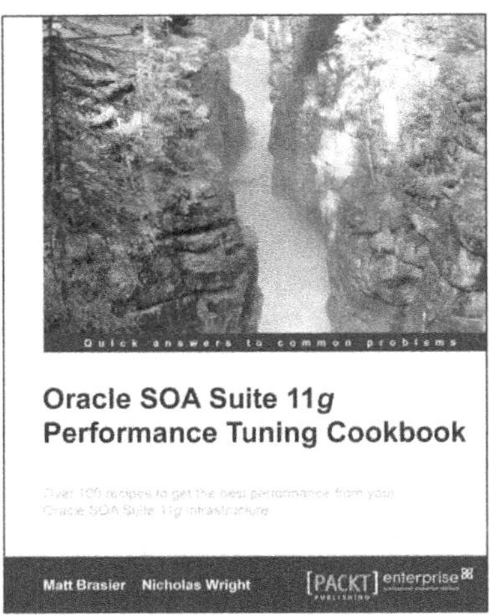

Oracle SOA Suite 11*g* Performance Tuning Cookbook

ISBN: 978-1-84968-884-0 Paperback: 328 pages

Over 100 recipes to get the best performance from your Oracle SOA Suite 11*g* unfrastructure

1. Tune the Java Virtual Machine to get the best out of the underlying platform
2. Learn how to monitor and profile your Oracle SOA Suite applications
3. Discover how to design and deploy your application for high-performance scenarios

---

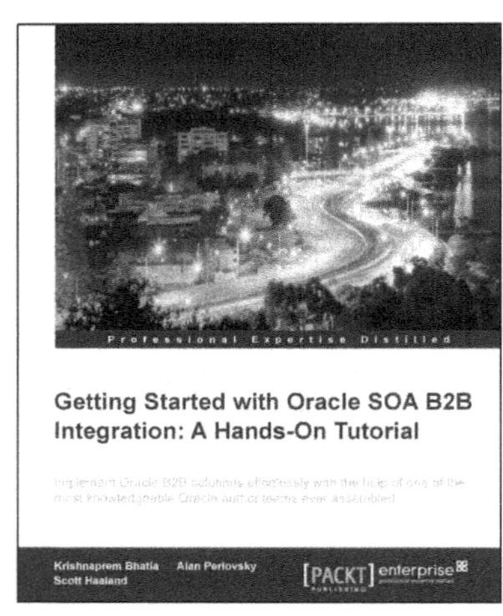

Getting Started with Oracle SOA B2B Integration: A Hands-On Tutorial

ISBN: 978-1-84968-886-4 Paperback: 332 pages

Implement Oracle B2B solutions effortlessly with the help of one of the most knowledgeable Oracle author teams ever assembled

1. Design, implement and monitor B2B transactions quickly using this clear, detailed and practical guide
2. Wide coverage and detailed discussion of Oracle B2B functionality and features for the new and advanced users
3. Full of practical examples, illustrations and product screenshots explained with clear, step-by-step instructions

Please check **www.PacktPub.com** for information on our titles

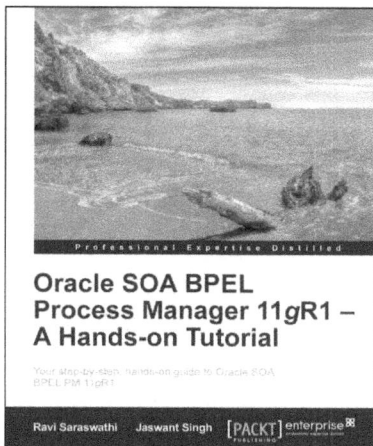

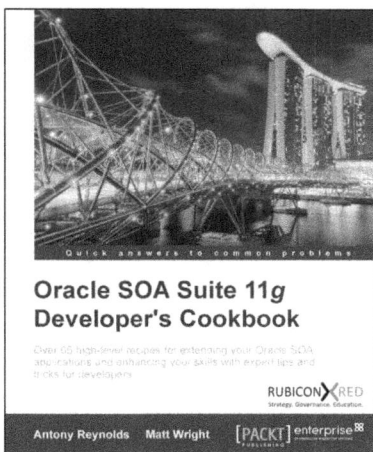

www.ingramcontent.com/pod-product-compliance
Lightning Source LLC
Chambersburg PA
CBHW082105220326
41598CB00066BA/5374

* 9 7 8 1 8 4 9 6 8 9 2 0 5 *